THE NEW DOGS OF WAR

THE NEW DOGS OF WAR

Nonstate Actor Violence in
International Politics

Ward Thomas

CORNELL UNIVERSITY PRESS   ITHACA AND LONDON

First published 2021 by Cornell University Press

Library of Congress Cataloging-in-Publication Data

Names: Thomas, Ward, 1963– author.
Title: The new dogs of war : nonstate actor violence in international politics / Ward Thomas.
Description: Ithaca [New York] : Cornell University Press, 2021. | Includes bibliographical references and index.
Identifiers: LCCN 2020057676 (print) | LCCN 2020057677 (ebook) | ISBN 9781501758898 (hardcover) | ISBN 9781501758911 (pdf) | ISBN 9781501758904 (epub)
Subjects: LCSH: Political violence. | Non-state actors (International relations) | Security, International.
Classification: LCC JC328.6 .T563 2021 (print) | LCC JC328.6 (ebook) | DDC 327.1/17—dc23
LC record available at https://lccn.loc.gov/2020057676
LC ebook record available at https://lccn.loc.gov/2020057677

To my parents

Contents

Acknowledgments

Over the far too many years I have worked on this project, I have been blessed with the support of a large number of people. Many provided helpful comments on papers and chapter drafts, including Deborah Avant, Lionel Beehner, Charli Carpenter, Martha Finnemore, John Gentry, Eugene Gholz, Stuart Kaufman, Elizabeth Kier, Travis LaCouter, Tony Lang, Jonathan Mercer, Sarah Percy, Arie Perliger, Ullrich Petersohn, Richard Price, Sarah Sewall, Brent Steele, Bonnie Weir, and participants in colloquia at the University of Pittsburgh, the University of Washington, and the University of Texas. Greg Burnep, Aws Shemmeri, and Justinas Sileikas provided outstanding research assistance and incisive thoughts that significantly improved the final product. Any errors of fact and interpretation that remain, of course, are my own.

It is a pleasure, too, to acknowledge the generous support of the Office of the Provost, the Committee on Fellowships, Research, and Publication, and the Department of Political Science at the College of the Holy Cross. I also thank staff members at Dinand Library at Holy Cross and Beaman Memorial Library in West Boylston, Massachusetts.

This is the second book I have published with Cornell University Press, and both times the experience has been wonderful. A common denominator was Roger Haydon, whose insight and support was as indispensable as it had been two decades before. Upon Roger's retirement Mahinder Kingra stepped into the role without missing a beat. Mary Kate Murphy and Karen Hwa significantly improved the manuscript with their careful editing and patiently answered innumerable questions. Finally, Don McKeon's copyediting was admirably detailed and nuanced.

I am extremely grateful to the friends and colleagues who provided encouragement, inspiration, and moral support, including Rosalind Briscoe, Diane Alleva Caceres, Tony Cashman, Loren Cass, Tom Corsi, Steven Kocs, Richard and Arvene Krushensky, Leslie Manning, Linda Mason Wilgis, Tracy Melton, Sally Phelps, Jane Powell, Herb Wilgis, Stephanie Yuhl, and members of the Poconos Writers' Workshop and the Low Country Writers' Cooperative.

My greatest debt of gratitude is to my family. Over the course of this project my sons Jack and Patrick have grown into young men, and I am tremendously proud of them both. My parents have been fonts of support and encouragement for literally longer than I can remember, and it is with profound appreciation that I dedicate this book to them. Finally, my wife Kari has been endlessly patient and boundlessly supportive. I owe her everything.

THE NEW DOGS OF WAR

THE FALL AND RISE OF NONSTATE VIOLENCE

State sovereignty is not what it used to be. Although states are not on the verge of extinction, the classical Westphalian model—unitary government with a monopoly on violence and dominion over its territory—is clearly on the wane. Observers of globalization have noted the increasing permeability of state borders and the prevalence of transnational economic and cultural forces.[1] Similarly, global governance scholars have highlighted the ways in which institutions other than states decisively shape many aspects of life in the twenty-first century.[2] Many have seen the declining power of the state as a positive development, celebrating the success of international activism, nongovernmental organizations (NGOs), and transnational civil society in changing state practices in the fields of human rights, arms control, and environmental protection, among others.[3] Moreover, scholars, activists, and even many states themselves have heralded the Responsibility to Protect (R2P) doctrine as a welcome refinement, if not a redefinition, of global norms about what sovereignty entails.[4]

Not all manifestations of the decline of sovereignty, however, are beneficial. One of the most significant, and potentially alarming, is the erosion of the state monopoly on transnational violence. To a greater degree than at any time in generations, actors other than states are using military force in ways that impact the international system. These actors fit varying descriptions, from the nefarious to the respectable. On one end of the spectrum are transnational terrorist networks, which have become a central subject of international concern since the attacks of September 11, 2001. Almost as menacing are nonstate militias and paramilitary groups, which have played a significant role in almost every conflict since the end of the Cold War, including in the Balkans, Afghanistan, Sudan, Libya, Iraq, and Syria. More respectable but still often problematic are private military and security companies (PMSCs), which provide military and military-related services to clients ranging from NGOs and corporations to states as large and capable as the United States (which has employed PMSCs extensively in Iraq and Afghanistan) and Russia (which has used them in a combat capacity in Ukraine and Syria).[5]

This book examines this dramatic growth in nonstate actor violence, focusing on the crucial role played in this trend by changes in international norms. The most commonly cited definition of the state is the one devised by Max Weber over a century ago: "the form of human community that (successfully) lays claim to the monopoly on legitimate physical violence."[6] Although many commentators overlook it, the word "legitimate" here is not an afterthought. When states consolidated their dominant institutional status by forging a monopoly on the means of transnational violence in the eighteenth and nineteenth centuries, they did so not simply through the exercise of material power but also through the construction of norms about what constituted the legitimate use of force.[7] These norms, indeed, were at the heart of the classical Westphalian model of state sovereignty and helped to anchor sovereign states in a privileged position as the central constitutive actors in the international system.[8] The recent prominence of nonstate militias, transnational terrorist networks, and the private military and security industry therefore represents a transformation that is both portentous and puzzling. While one would expect states to zealously defend the norms assuring their monopoly on legitimate violence, in some cases they seem complicit in contributing to its erosion. Not only do many states employ PMSCs, but a number have also aligned themselves with less reputable actors, including militias and terrorist organizations. While "terrorism" per se is still widely condemned, there is a sobering lack of global consensus about who is a terrorist and who is not, and methods long condemned as barbaric are sometimes defended as morally acceptable.[9] In contemporary international politics, the legitimacy or illegitimacy of any particular group increasingly hinges on its political goals, whereas in past generations the very use of force itself by a nonstate actor would be deemed illegitimate.

In the following chapters, I tackle this puzzle, trying to understand the rise of nonstate violence by bringing attention back to the word "legitimate" in Weber's definition. In doing so, I address the question of how to explain the relatively rapid decline of the norm against actors other than states using military force—a norm that once resided at the conceptual core of the sovereign states system.

Nonstate Violence Makes a Comeback

International politics was once rife with military entrepreneurs, private armies, and other forces unaffiliated with national governments. After the Westphalian revolution of the 1600s, however, newly powerful sovereign states eventually came to view such actors as threats to international order and by the early nineteenth century had largely driven them out of business.[10] What is not always appreciated is that this was accomplished not just through greater material resources and military power but also through the restructuring of norms.[11] What was important, in other words, was not simply that nonstate actors lacked the material means to use interstate violence (indeed, this was often not the case) but that there was a powerful international consensus that doing so would be illegitimate. Therefore, one of the most significant sources of state power was not material but ideational, resting on norms held throughout the international system. To be sure, as some scholars have noted, reality was frequently less tidy than the Westphalian model would suggest. States' control over their territories has rarely been absolute, and nonstate actor violence has never been entirely absent.[12] Nevertheless, there was more to the state's "monopoly on force" than merely wishful thinking. Large-scale institutional challengers did in fact recede nearly into irrelevance, and armed nonstate actors tended to be contained within domestic, or more often colonial, contexts.[13]

What has occurred in the past several decades constitutes a significant change in both the frequency with which nonstate actors use force and the scale on which they use it. One widely cited measure of this is that interstate war—the classic model of conflict that undergirds much international law, as well as most military doctrine—has become rare, while intrastate war is common.[14] Fifty-one of the sixty-nine armed conflicts active in 2018 were non-international, and almost all eighteen of the international conflicts involved nonstate actors to some degree.[15] Furthermore, armed nonstate groups are responsible for more "nonwar" violent deaths each year than violent deaths in interstate and intrastate war combined.[16] While most such groups are small, some number into the tens of thousands. Many, moreover, are shockingly well armed; as of 2014, over sixty reportedly possessed guided weapons capable of bringing down military aircraft or civilian airliners.[17] Armed nonstate groups pose significant threats not only to the security of governments but to human security as well, often systematically targeting civilians and committing a broad range of human rights abuses.[18] Another telling sign is that the most powerful countries in the world regard groups such as al-Qaeda and the Islamic State of Iraq and Syria (ISIS) as high-level security threats.[19] An expert roundtable convened by Harvard's Program on Humanitarian Policy and Conflict Research (PHPCR) concluded that "these actors, once viewed as merely prospective subjects of the criminal justice system, . . . have come to overwhelmingly fight the wars of the twenty-first century."[20] Beyond their number and scale, contemporary violent nonstate actors represent a departure from the past in the degree to which their existence has been accepted and sometimes even supported by other types of actors in the international system. As noted, many states have backed nongovernmental forces whose goals coincided with their own, and a growing number use private contractors to pursue their foreign policy interests. Some nonstate groups have had their right to use force endorsed by the United Nations, some have been deemed to possess the same rights under international law as uniformed militaries (and allowed to participate in making that law), and some have been granted observer status at the UN and other international bodies.[21] And while few defend terrorism as such, almost every group accused of terrorism by some states can find others willing to defend it against those accusations. In short, nonstate actor violence has acquired, in some forms and in some settings, considerable legitimacy.

Categorizing nonstate actor violence can be tricky. Distinctions among types of organization can be blurry and arbitrary, with overlaps among categories common. For example, Phil Williams identifies six types of violent nonstate actors: warlords, militias, paramilitary forces, insurgencies, terrorist organizations, and criminal organizations and youth gangs.[22] Although he differentiates among them using various criteria (including their motivation, whether they control territory, their relationship to the state, whether they are led by a charismatic individual, and whether they provide governance or social welfare services), Williams acknowledges that some organizations could be placed in more than one category or in different categories at different times.[23] Similar problems are evident throughout the literature on nonstate actors.[24] A related difficulty is that the categories themselves are often contested, especially those that carry moral connotations. This is notoriously the case when it comes to labeling an organization as "terrorist," for reasons I explain in chapter 4, but is also crucial in the PMSC case, as private purveyors of military and security services have tried to distance themselves from the stigma associated with "mercenaries." Indeed, the contestation of these categories is an important part of the story I tell in this book and helps to explain both the multiplicity of terms sometimes used to refer to violent nonstate actors and the stakes involved in this choice of terminology.

Examples abound of the challenges of labeling nonstate groups. Lebanon-based Hezbollah, for instance, is a nonstate organization that has many of the characteristics of a conventional military force—one that by some accounts is more powerful than the Lebanese army.[25] It is designated as a terrorist organization by most Western states and the Arab League, while many other countries regard it as a legitimate national resistance movement. It functions as a political party within Lebanon, holding over 10 percent of the seats in parliament and playing an influential role in the ruling coalition, but also carries out its own foreign policy, such as sending forces to fight for President Bashar al-Assad in Syria's civil war.[26] And while it claims no sovereign territory, it provides extensive social and public order services in southern Lebanon, running schools, hospitals, utilities, and construction projects. Similar in many ways is the Palestinian group Hamas, condemned as a terrorist organization by many Western states but which has served as the de facto governing authority in the territory of Gaza since 2006, when it won a majority on the Palestinian Legislative Council. A different sort of example of ambiguity in categorizing armed nonstate actors was the September 2012 militant attack on the US diplomatic post in Benghazi, Libya, which killed Ambassador Chris Stevens and three other Americans, including two private contractors working for the Central Intelligence Agency (CIA). There was a Libyan security detail assigned to protect the facility, of which half were contractors employed by a British PMSC and half were members of an organization called the February 17 Martyrs Brigade, an Islamist militia with close ties to the Libyan government.[27] If the Hezbollah and Hamas cases illustrate the elusiveness of a bright line between militias and terrorists, the role of the February 17 group in the Benghazi case shows that the line between private contractors and militias can also sometimes be muddled. All three cases, moreover, speak generally to the growing prevalence of nonstate actors in roles traditionally associated with states.

In this study, I consider militias and paramilitaries together in a somewhat generic category of armed nonstate groups. Some scholars use "militia" to refer only to progovernment groups, but there are limitations to this approach, as the degree of cooperation with the state is sometimes unclear and can change quickly.[28] I therefore do not distinguish among groups on this basis, whether they operate as de facto adjuncts of the state or are in open rebellion against it. In either case, it is hard to overstate the significance of these groups in contemporary international politics. They have been involved in every armed conflict in the twenty-first century, and some are stronger than the national armies in states where they operate. Such forces fought both alongside and against American troops in Afghanistan and in Iraq, where militias contributed to the horrific sectarian violence that followed the fall of Saddam Hussein but also assisted US and Iraqi government forces during the Anbar Awakening starting in 2006. In Libya they played a key role both in overthrowing Moammar Qaddafi in 2011 and in fomenting the chaos that has ensued there since.[29] In the form of the Kurdish Peshmerga and People's Protection Union (YPG), they were the United States' primary partner in ground operations against ISIS in Iraq and Syria. They have made their presence felt in Europe as well. Militias and paramilitary forces were key belligerents in the Balkan Wars of the 1990s, and the Kosovar Liberation Army (KLA) was pivotal in Kosovo gaining its independence from the Federal Republic of Yugoslavia—assisted by the 1999 air campaign of the North Atlantic Treaty Organization (NATO). They have fought on both sides of the conflict in eastern Ukraine since 2014 and have formed in other Eastern European states in response to the prospect of Russian aggression.[30]

Transnational terrorism is the type of nonstate actor violence that has gotten the most attention and provoked the most concern. The al-Qaeda attacks of September 11, 2001, immediately reconfigured US foreign policy, which has in turn reconfigured significant parts of the Middle East and Southwest Asia, as well as relations between the Islamic and Western worlds. Subsequent operations by al-Qaeda and its affiliates in Europe, Asia, and Africa further demonstrated the reach of the organization. The apotheosis of transnational terrorism in the twenty-first century, however, may have been the ascendance of ISIS, an offshoot of al-Qaeda that seized large areas of eastern Syria and western Iraq in which it declared a caliphate in 2014. Beyond this unprecedented territorial presence, the group carried out attacks in a dozen other countries, including the United Kingdom, France, Lebanon, Russia, Spain, and Turkey, and its regional affiliates have roiled already volatile situations in Afghanistan and Libya. Al-Qaeda and ISIS, however, are but two of the dozens of groups named as terrorist organizations by the US government, and for many of these the terrorist designation is more controversial.[31] Indeed, among the categories of nonstate violence, terrorism carries by far the strongest moral opprobrium and unsurprisingly is also the most vociferously contested. As I explain in chapter 4, for nearly a century the conventional basis for distinguishing between terrorism and other modes of political violence was whether the violence directly targeted noncombatants. That criterion itself, however, would become hotly contested and is now one among many contending factors, many of them overtly political, that determines who is labeled a terrorist. One implication of this is that the distinctions between terrorist organizations and other nonstate groups can be fluid and even arbitrary—a fact that is both an analytical problem and an illustration of the point that various types of nonstate violence should be examined together as different facets of an important dynamic in global politics.

The increasingly important role played by PMSCs has generated considerable scholarly and popular interest.[32] Private contractors have become a regular presence in war zones, and states are turning to them for a growing range of services, from rear-echelon support to direct involvement in combat. Since the end of the Cold War, they have monitored ceasefires in Bosnia, Kosovo, and East Timor, assisted in putting down rebellions in Sierra Leone, Angola, and Burundi, and trained national militaries in over a dozen countries.[33] They constituted a significant component of the American presence in Afghanistan and Iraq, at times outnumbering uniformed US forces. In these theaters, PMSC contractors guarded bases, convoys, and government officials, gathered and analyzed intelligence, interrogated prisoners, and in some cases accompanied CIA personnel on counterterrorism raids.[34] Moreover, it is not just states that are employing these firms. Multinational corporations retain them extensively to protect their interests throughout the world, and intergovernmental and NGOs use them to provide security in dangerous environments. Indeed, their ubiquity prompted Norwegian security experts Ase Ostensen and Tor Bukkvoll to write in 2018 that "over the past couple of decades, private military and security companies . . . have become instrumental to modern warfare."[35]

To be sure, by and large the PMSC industry is more reputable than the other types of nonstate actors I address in the book. Most contractors are well-trained professionals who adhere to standards of conduct endorsed by states and international organizations. Partly as a result, scholars rarely consider PMSCs alongside other actors as elements of the erosion of the state's monopoly on military force. Still, there are good reasons to include them in this study. As I argue in chapter 5, their ascendance was rooted in the same normative changes that contributed to the emergence of other modes of nonstate violence. Moreover, the industry raises some of the same questions about the implications for state sovereignty and control over violence in the international system—a point I discuss in chapter 6. Finally, there is no question that the use of PMSCs has often been controversial. Reckless behavior by contractors has provoked concerns about the industry and seriously harmed the interests of their state clients. The most notorious such incident was the killing of seventeen Iraqi civilians by Blackwater security guards in Nisour Square in Baghdad in September 2007, which caused a serious rift between the US and Iraqi governments and contributed to what some saw as a premature withdrawal of American troops from the country in 2011. Private contractors also were involved in abusive practices in the 2004 Abu Ghraib prison scandal in Iraq and even afterward continued to be used extensively by the United States as interpreters and interrogators at detention facilities.[36] Other cases prompted worries that PMSCs were able to operate independently, beyond the effective control of states. In 1997, the British PMSC Sandline International was caught importing arms into Papua New Guinea against the terms of a UN arms embargo and UK government policy, leading to a scandal and parliamentary investigation.[37] Also in the 1990s, South Africa–based Executive Outcomes came under criticism for various reasons, including its ties to commercial mining interests and its use of indiscriminate fuel-air explosives in Angola.[38] Moreover, some PMSCs have ventured beyond providing support services for national militaries to participating in combat themselves.[39] P. W. Singer observed in 2005 that "the private military industry now offers every function that was once limited to state militaries."[40] Today there are firms that can muster something akin to a fully equipped battalion-sized fighting unit, including the Wagner Group, which fights under contract to Russia in eastern Ukraine and Syria and which saw over a hundred of its employees killed in a heated battle against US troops in Syria in February 2018.[41] One Wagner contractor explained: "Wagner is no ordinary private military company. It is a miniature army. We had it all, mortars, howitzers, tanks, infantry fighting vehicles, and armored personnel carriers."[42]

This move toward what Singer calls "the tip of the spear" is a disquieting development. First, these potent capabilities and the shadowy nature of some of the PMSCs that wield them may allow client states such as Russia to evade full accountability for their actions, thus emboldening dangerously aggressive and adventurist foreign policies. Second, it again raises concerns about the dangers of the attenuation of control over the use of military force, especially if in the future PMSCs are able to operate independently of strict governmental control or use these capabilities for clients other than states. These questions are ultimately inseparable from larger questions about the fundamental nature of the international system, the actors it comprises, and the norms that constitute those actors and govern their behavior.

Understanding the Return of Nonstate Violence

The literature on nonstate violence is a house with many mansions. Most studies focus on one type of actor rather than the trend as a whole. Works on terrorism alone could fill a library. Other studies look at terrorist groups together with militias and other armed groups, but these authors almost invariably exclude PMSCs.[43] The burgeoning research on PMSCs, meanwhile, usually treats them as a phenomenon unto themselves. Nevertheless, there are similarities among these various bodies of work. Two variables in particular are consistently cited as critical to the emergence of nonstate actor violence. The first is the profusion of weak and failing states in the international system, which many studies cite as the single most important factor in the rise of violent nonstate groups.[44] Richard H.

Shultz, Douglas Farah, and Itamara V. Lochard argue that one critical manifestation of state weakness is the abundance of "lawless and ungoverned areas that are beyond the authority of government. This creates safe havens in which armed groups can establish secure bases for self-protection, training, planning, and launching operations against local, regional, and global targets."[45] Literature on the causes of terrorism, likewise, sees weak and failed states as a key contributing factor. One problem, of course, is that such governments typically lack the power to successfully clamp down on terrorist groups within their borders.[46] Another is that the dearth of social services in weak states creates not just geographical voids but also institutional ones, which nonstate organizations can step into by providing security, education, infrastructure, and other benefits, thus earning them support within the population and a growing pool of recruits.[47] State weakness is also at the heart of most analyses of the growth of PMSCs. As we shall see in chapter 5, research on PMSCs often explains their rise explicitly in terms of supply and demand, tracing both events that have contributed to an abundant supply of trained military personnel and those that have spurred demand for military and security services that could not be met by national armies. While weak states are not the only clients of PMSCs, their limited military capabilities create a critical part of the demand for contractors' services. The growing number of weak states, exacerbated by the withdrawal of support from their superpower sponsors after the end of the Cold War, created what Singer calls a "gap in the market of security" that PMSCs have been able to fill.[48] Zeev Maoz and Belgin San-Akca argue that state weakness contributes to nonstate violence in another way as well, as "states that are dissatisfied with the prevailing status quo but who are relatively weak tend to use NAGs [nonstate armed groups] as a tool for harassing their rivals."[49]

A second factor that appears in most explanations of the recent upsurge in armed nonstate groups is globalization. Globalization is a complex and multifaceted subject, which scholars describe as contributing to nonstate violence in various ways. For example, globalization gives nonstate actors access to previously unattainable resources.[50] One example that appears throughout the literatures on these different groups is the global arms trade, which makes even relatively large and sophisticated weapons available for purchase. Another is the radical advance in technology that allows information and capital to flow quickly across vast distances and to broad audiences. This has been especially important for terrorist organizations, facilitating funding and providing a transformative vehicle for recruitment and propaganda.[51] In general, globalization has accelerated change in ways that expose the limitations of national governments. In her seminal study on PMSCs, Deborah Avant observes, "In a globalizing world, market pressures, technology, and social change create new demands for goods that states have difficulty supplying."[52] Moreover, Avant notes, the scope of globalization has contributed to the "increasingly transnational character" of the market for private force.[53]

So, what is wrong with these explanations? As far as they go, not very much: they identify far-reaching dynamics that undoubtedly contribute to nonstate actor violence and make cogent arguments in support of their claims. However, even very good analyses can have blind spots that lead them to neglect important parts of the overall picture. I have mentioned that although much is written about militias, terrorist organizations, and PMSCs, they are rarely all considered together. This is surprising, given that they are all prominent examples of a seismic shift in one of the foundational norms in the international system: that states, and only states, may legitimately employ violence, both within and across national borders. In fact, this normative shift itself has received little attention; some authors mention it, but few explore it in depth. Most assume that the shift was a natural result of the rise of violent nonstate actors or, to put it another way, that the norm changed following the change in practice, without having much influence on how practice unfolded in the first place.[54] Indeed, when these accounts identify factors that precipitated the emergence of these actors and new patterns of behavior, they tend to cite material rather than normative variables. This reflects the influence of rationalist, or rational choice, assumptions in international relations scholarship. Because rationalist theory defines the structure of the international political system primarily in terms of the material capabilities of its constituent actors, it fosters a strongly materialist orientation. Starting from that foundation, rationalist political science essentially applies the theoretical assumptions of market economics to political calculations. In other words, it applies what James G. March and Johan P. Olsen refer to as the "logic of consequentiality," assuming that actors (whether individuals or collective entities like states) make choices so as to optimize their outcomes. This is done without concern for what may be seen as normatively good, right, or appropriate—a sort of inquiry March and Olsen say is governed by a different logic, the "logic of appropriateness."[55] Consequently, rationalist work tends to discount the significance of ideas, and certainly of normative judgments, in global politics.

To be clear, literature on violent nonstate actors does not entirely neglect ideational factors. For example, in discussing state weakness, some authors note that states lack not only the material capacity to perform the functions traditionally associated with sovereignty but also the sense of legitimacy that commands allegiance from their citizens.[56] Similarly, some describe the influence of globalization not only as expanding markets and accelerating global flows of resources and information but also breeding discontent and a sense of dislocation in developing countries.[57] Nevertheless, it is the material manifestations of these phenomena that receive the most emphasis. State weakness is seen as significant, then, because it creates voids into which nonstate actors can move, whether they be power vacuums, gaps in the security market, or ungoverned territories. Likewise, globalization facilitates nonstate actor violence not only by increasing the global arms trade but also by creating large numbers of "underemployed, urbanized young men."[58] Even more important, little attention is paid to the core normative question in Weber's definition: what types of actors may *legitimately* wield physical violence?[59] We must recall, however, that the state's monopoly on force rested not just on the "logic of consequentiality" but a healthy dose of the "logic of appropriateness" as well. Put another way, the proposition that political violence was the province of the state alone was a strongly prescriptive formulation as well as a description of empirical reality. Indeed, by most accounts, the norm that only states could legitimately use force in the international system was a widely held and powerful injunction.[60] As recently as 1994, Janice Thomson wrote that practices of nonstate violence were "not only prohibited but have become unthinkable. The institutionalized prohibitions against them are taken for granted."[61] Her timing was ironic, for even then such practices were building. Nevertheless, the fact that the state monopoly on force was at that time seen as robust and deeply institutionalized underscores the dramatic nature of this transformation.

There are good reasons to pay closer attention to the normative side of this story. A now extensive body of research shows that norms can and do exercise causal influence, not only constraining actors' choices but also shaping the very interests and identities that define the goals those choices seek to achieve.[62] This work is typically associated with the analytical strategy of constructivism, which asserts that ideas, as well as tangible material variables, are important aspects of the structure of the international system.[63] In this case a constructivist would be struck that a norm that provided states with a monopoly on legitimate interstate violence did not pose a more formidable obstacle to the rise (or, historically speaking, the return) of nonstate military actors. Even if the question is viewed in realist-friendly terms of power and interest, since the normative change involves nothing less than an erosion of the sovereign prerogatives of the most powerful actors on the world stage, it presents a puzzle that warrants a more serious investigation than it has gotten.

A constructivist approach to the rise of nonstate actor violence, first, would recognize that norms can be causal variables, capable of shaping actors' behavior by creating incentives that limit some choices and encourage others. A second premise, however, is that norms can be not only causes but also effects (or, in social science parlance, both independent and dependent variables).[64]

Therefore, it is important to understand not only the impact of ideas but also where they come from, how and why they change, and what leads actors to be more or less receptive to different ideas at different times. It is difficult to model normative change in the abstract, since norms are the products of a complex combination of historically contingent social, political, technological, and other conditions. Nevertheless, norms do not come out of nowhere, nor do well-established and highly valued norms yield easily to the emergent demands of foreign policy. Because they reflect structural aspects of the international system, changes in important norms—of which the state monopoly on force is certainly one—can be both barometers and portents of significant change in the system.[65] A well-known example is the renegotiation of the constitutive arrangements of the European international system in the seventeenth century, leading to the "Westphalian order." The norms that arose from the settlement of the Thirty Years War in 1648 were reflections of both material realities and changing ideas about power and legitimacy, and in turn they not only described but also shaped international relations for centuries thereafter.[66] In the cases under consideration here, therefore, we should be attentive to evidence that the return of nonstate actor violence is rooted not only in material and political developments but also in changes in ideas about the relationship between sovereign states and the use of force.

Indeed, violent nonstate actors did not appear from thin air. Several normative changes, some of them widely and justifiably celebrated, contributed to their emergence. One was the extension of sovereignty to formerly colonized territories and the associated changes in international norms surrounding decolonization in the 1950s through 1970s. Another was the UN Charter regime restricting the use of force, along with the post–Nuremburg trials principle that leaders can be held personally responsible for aggression and crimes against humanity. These changes (or, as I call them in chapter 2, "macronormative transformations") represented a dramatic reconfiguration of the classical model of state sovereignty and a significant circumscription of sovereign prerogatives. These developments in turn had far-reaching effects upon other international practices and norms, which were indispensable in setting the stage for the return of nonstate violence. This is not to suggest that these macronormative shifts were lamentable developments. Rather, it is to make a point about the importance of context for international norms. Ideas are not only powerful but also stubbornly resistant to incoherence. Just as the cognitive dissonance caused by holding logically contradictory beliefs can force individuals to reassess their assumptions, dissonance among international norms can be hard to sustain. When taken together with the many undeniable material and political changes in an age of nationalism and globalization, post-1945 efforts to limit some of the more pernicious aspects of state power contributed to the erosion of that power in other areas. This created what I call a "crisis of coherence" for the norm against nonstate violence that was exploited by those contesting the state monopoly on force. The result has been to invest armed nonstate groups with a measure of legitimacy, facilitating their emergence as important actors on the international stage.

The Value Added of a Norms-Based Approach

Readers accustomed to materialist explanations might ask what is gained by reaching back several decades to examine the influence of changes in international norms. All political phenomena, after all, are products of many causes, and to be useful explanations must simplify, focusing on those causes most important to comprehending what is going on. Norm-based explanations, some might argue, add layers of complexity without adding commensurately to understanding.

There are three reasons why examining the role of norms is important here. First, without it our understanding of the reemergence of nonstate violence is so incomplete as to be misleading. Without realizing that changing attitudes about state prerogatives were causes and not simply effects of the presence of armed nonstate groups, we cannot understand why nonstate force was relatively rare for generations or why it returned when it did. Second, examining the normative foundations for these changes, as well as their implications, allows us to see connections among trends that a materialist approach might miss. Once we understand the impact post–World War II macronormative changes had on international politics, we can identify common assumptions and ideas that contributed to the return of nonstate violence across a variety of circumstances. In other words, one can only fully understand these trends as aspects of an overarching transformation in the international system. This in turn helps to explain not only the significant overlap among the geographical areas in which different types of nonstate actors tend to operate but also the frequency with which these sectors intersect and collude. Finally, and perhaps most important, giving short shrift to normative variables makes it harder to appreciate what these changes may mean for future patterns of international relations. This is a persistent problem for rationalist explanations since they focus on short- or medium-term cost-benefit calculations. For reasons I discuss in the next chapter, even rational decisions can yield unintended outcomes—but these are often overlooked, especially if they are evident mainly in changing norms and ideas, which are no less important than material facts but can be harder to discern. Here, the fact that several different types of nonstate violence stem from common historical events and normative underpinnings tells us something about the future we might not otherwise know. In this case, it is the sobering prospect that these trends might well converge in unexpected and potentially unwelcome ways.

The Plan of the Book

This book, then, offers a complementary explanation of recent trends in non-state actor violence in international politics. Chapter 2 provides the theoretical framework for the project, examining an important but neglected cause of normative change. Literature on normative change usually describes it either as a result of the deliberate efforts of "norm entrepreneurs" or as a reaction to "shocks to the system" that transform norms in response to exogenous changes. There is, however, a different avenue of normative change, one characterized by the contestation of preexisting norms whose coherence has been undermined in unintended ways by changes in other norms to which they bear a logical or mutually constitutive relationship. This can be understood through what I call "the principle of normative coherence." Just as it can be difficult for an individual to hold mutually inconsistent beliefs at the same time, the existence of logically contradictory norms in the international system creates tensions that subject them to increased scrutiny. Because norms seldom exist in isolation, changes in some norms, especially significant constitutive norms that define actors' roles or relationships, can trigger crises of coherence for others. This creates opportunities for various stakeholders to contest norms that are newly vulnerable to reinterpretation, renegotiation, or outright repudiation.

This underappreciated and undertheorized dynamic of normative change calls attention to relationships and processes that help explain how a norm so important to state power has declined so startlingly. Indeed, the macronormative shifts I have mentioned—one granting independence to colonized peoples and the other greatly reducing states' discretion in choosing to use force—ultimately made it more difficult to sustain the vision of sovereignty that gives states a monopoly on force and set the stage for nonstate actors to contest that monopoly. This shows how prevailing materialist explanations for these trends are not only incomplete but also sometimes get causal relationships backwards, as changing ideas about the relationship between sovereign states and political violence often contributed to the rise of, and the demand for, nonstate military force rather than the other way around.

Chapter 3 is the case study on nonstate militias and paramilitary groups, which are major players in many of the world's most violent and intractable conflicts. The power and influence of these actors has grown dramatically, in large part due to changing norms governing the legitimate use of military force in the decades after World War II. Breaking the state's monopoly on violence entailed a huge departure from the normative status quo ante, in which armed nonstate groups were viewed as presumptively illegitimate because of the threat they posed to order. The normative imperative of decolonization put pressure on this assumption, however, and provided the impetus for national liberation movements and their allies to contest norms governing the use of force, the coherence of which had been undermined by the macronormative transformations in the post-1945 international system and by the actions of many colonial powers themselves. The ensuing triumph of the principle of national self-determination thus also produced what amounted to an endorsement by the international community, including most former imperial powers, of the right of liberation movements to use force to attain their goals (something several had been doing, to be sure, before the broad acceptance of their right to do so). Moreover, acknowledging the right of nonstate groups to fight for independence created pressure to accept the guerrilla tactics they employed in doing so, which entailed the contestation of longstanding norms governing the conduct of warfare. These processes proved influential, contributing to the destabilization of other norms and setting the stage for other types of nonstate actors (including terrorist organizations and PMSCs) to assert their own rights to wield force.

Chapter 4 explores the growth in transnational terrorist organizations and the global debate over terrorism against which it unfolded. While "terrorist" remains a strongly pejorative term, there is remarkably little agreement about who it should apply to or even what it means. Indeed, international negotiations on the subject often devolve into exercises in moral relativism captured by the axiom "One person's terrorist is another person's freedom fighter." Nevertheless, these positions are not merely self-serving "spin" but rather reflect a normative divergence that is a complex product of international political processes. The 1960s, 1970s, and 1980s saw terrorism go from a concept whose definition was uncontroversial to a heavily politicized epithet, with scant international consensus on what the term meant or who the "bad guys" were. Crucial to this was the legitimization of guerrilla warfare described in chapter 3, which opened the door to contesting some of the most fundamental norms about the use of force, including the prohibition of targeting civilians—norms that, again, had become unsettled and increasingly incoherent in the preceding decades. In these contentious debates, both proponents of radical change and conservative powers adopted definitions of "terrorism" that privileged their own priorities and continue to define competing perspectives on the subject. This unsettled normative context, in turn, enabled the emergence of an organizational and operational model that would spawn groups such as al-Qaeda and ISIS.

Chapter 5 examines the return of entrepreneurial violence to the international system in the form of PMSCs. Scholars have identified several important causes of the ascendance of PMSCs, including a global surplus of trained military personnel, increasing demand for military services (driven on one hand by weak states unable to sustain capable forces and on the other by increasingly sophisticated weapon systems), and the impetus in some Western democracies toward the privatization of government services. As I have noted, however, the literature curiously neglects the role played by changing norms about who may wield military force. In fact, the macronormative changes described in chapter 2 had far-reaching effects upon other international practices and understandings that were indispensable in clearing the way for the return of private purveyors of force. The ensuing crisis of coherence for the norm against private force created an opportunity for PMSCs and their allies to contest the status quo. These efforts have largely succeeded: the use of private contractors has grown exponentially, and PMSCs have disassociated themselves from the negative connotations of "mercenarism" and fended off calls to abolish the industry, instead swinging international consensus toward a permissive regime of light regulation and oversight.

Chapter 6 returns to the idea that the case studies of nonstate violence examined in the book are in fact parts of a single phenomenon—one with important implications for the international system. There are in fact growing connections among the three types of nonstate actors profiled in chapters 3 through 5, as well as between them and other manifestations of nonstate violence such as transnational organized crime. These connections raise important questions about the relationship between sovereignty and violence and possibly ominous portents for the future of international order. Because the question of who is empowered to use force is closely tied to the problem of the tractability of international violence, the stakes involved in the use of force by transnational nonstate actors are indeed high.

COHERENCE AND CONTESTATION

Explaining International Normative Change

To be useful, a theory should be able to explain the big stuff. This includes not just the fundamental dynamics that govern a system but also changes in those dynamics or in the identity of major players. Clearly, the erosion of states' monopoly on the use of military force is one of those game-changing transformations. It is striking, therefore, that none of the major theoretical approaches to international relations (IR) provides a clear explanation of this phenomenon.

Realism employs a state-centric approach that simply assumes that states are the predominant actors in the international system.[1] The idea that formerly marginal entities could wield international clout is beyond the theoretical premises of realism, and even if it were not, realists would struggle to explain why sovereign states would allow these entities to gain the ability to do so, thereby threatening states' privileged position. Realists would not find it useful to describe this transformation in terms of changes in the norms of state sovereignty since they ascribe no causal significance to norms, viewing them merely as epiphenomenal reflections of the interests of the most powerful actors in the system.[2] While neoliberal institutionalists do see norms as important, they are bound by some of the same limitations as realists, including their state-centric theoretical premises. Moreover, their view of norms as instrumental devices to allow states to pursue their interests by ameliorating collective action problems would leave them hard-pressed to explain changes in norms independent of changes in states' interests, especially when these normative changes seem to diminish state prerogatives.

Among the major theoretical schools, constructivism would be most likely to emphasize the role of norms in the rise of nonstate actor violence. Indeed, constructivists would see this as a major shift in international norms since it entails the modification of state sovereignty, one of the key norms that define the very nature of global politics. Such norms are called "constitutive norms" because they constitute the structure of the international system, the identities of actors within it, and the rights, responsibilities, and expectations that go along with those identities. The idea that only states should be allowed to use military force is not just a rule that forbids certain actors from doing certain things (what constructivists would call a "regulative norm")—it is a central feature of the institution of sovereign statehood itself. Constructivists might therefore see nonstate actor violence as evidence of a fundamental reordering of the international system.

While constructivist literature provides a useful framework for appreciating the significance of this transformation, however, it may be less effective in helping us to understand why it is happening. To be sure, constructivists have not neglected the problem of normative change. Indeed, the need to understand change was an important theme in early constructivist critiques of materialist theories, which were seen as too static.[3] A key premise of constructivism, as I mentioned in chapter 1, is that norms can be both independent and dependent variables, shaping behavior and institutions in the international system but also being shaped by them. Put another way, it is important to explain not only the causal significance of ideas (which has been a strength of constructivist scholarship) but also why certain ideas attain prescriptive status at certain times. As Martha Finnemore and Kathryn Sikkink put it, "norm shifts are to the ideational theorist what changes in the balance of power are to the realist."[4] Nevertheless, there are gaps in the constructivist literature on norm change that become apparent in trying to understand the rise of nonstate actor violence.

Constructivist accounts of normative change tend to fall within two general explanations. The most common category of explanation focuses on the spread of new ideas by processes of argument and persuasion, often through the efforts of "norm entrepreneurs" who push states to adopt norms to which they are ethically committed.[5] These norm entrepreneurs are typically NGOs or aggregations of activists or technical experts who advocate change in particular issue areas. If their efforts succeed, national decision-makers adopt the new norms, which may eventually become embedded in the structures of political and social institutions. Constructivist studies have shown how norm entrepreneurs have been instrumental in reducing human rights violations, curbing environmental degradation, advancing law of war and arms control treaties, enhancing the prospects of women in various countries, and ending the Cold War.[6] In this model, normative change is neither random nor accidental: it occurs through the direct and intentional actions of agents working toward that end—a process Finnemore and Sikkink refer to as "strategic social construction," "in which actors strategize rationally to reconfigure preferences, identities, or social context."[7] Such efforts, they argue, help explain momentous normative transformations such as European integration, decolonization, and the rise of human rights regimes. Indeed, the most optimistic accounts of the shift in power from states to transnational actors are those that focus on norm entrepreneurs.

A second category of explanation for normative change points to shake-ups in societal norms caused by major traumatic events such as wars, depressions, and revolutions. Because of their radically disjunctive nature, such exogenous "shocks to the system" can cause leaders, societies, and even entire systems to discard old ideas and to be unusually receptive to new ones.[8] So, for example, constructivists have traced the move from mercenary to citizen armies in Europe to the shock of the Napoleonic conquests, to the rise of pacifism in Germany and Japan to the disastrous defeat those countries suffered in World War II, and to changes in the form of state sovereignty in response to "major systemic crises such as world wars or widespread political upheavals."[9] This type of explanation is especially prominent in accounts of changes in important constitutive norms. By their very nature, constitutive norms do not change often, and when they do, that change is often linked to a cataclysmic upheaval in the system as a whole. It should be noted that while the "norm entrepreneur" explanation emphasizes the role of agency and the "exogenous shock" explanation emphasizes the role of structure, they are not mutually exclusive. Most shock-based accounts of norm change at least implicitly acknowledge that even within a radically transformed structure, agency remains important. In other words, traumatic events do not simply realign norms automatically; they can motivate the efforts of norm entrepreneurs and make political elites and societies more likely to be persuaded by their entreaties.

While useful in explaining a range of cases, constructivist accounts of normative change remain incomplete. One problem is the consistently optimistic perspective on norms found in this work. Indeed, an implicit assumption in the vast majority of constructivist literature is that when norms change, they change for the better.[10] This tendency is particularly common in work on norm entrepreneurs, where cases typically focus on morally committed activists seeking to spread liberal principles, but even scholars who emphasize exogenous shocks usually examine cases in which a society embraces new ideas that are better than the old ones.[11] This progressivist bias creates both empirical and theoretical blind spots in constructivism. Empirically, it makes it difficult to explain changes that produce norms with potentially troubling implications—such as the rise of nonstate actor violence, which threatens the diffusion of conflict throughout the international system in ways largely beyond the control of states and international institutions. Theoretically, it tends to obscure certain questions that are important in understanding how norms work. Two such questions are particularly significant to this study.

First, constructivism pays far more attention to how norms rise than how they decline. This is perhaps to be expected in literature that emphasizes success stories, where what is important is how liberal norms spread, moving from small communities of the ethically committed to broad societal acceptance. Finnemore and Sikkink's influential description of the "life cycle" of a norm, for example, ends at maturity, with the norm at its most powerful.[12] As anyone who has reached middle age can attest, this tells only part of the story of any life cycle. History is replete with examples of norms that once commanded unquestioning acceptance but are now extinct or even forgotten. In the relatively scant constructivist work that does address the decline and death of norms, the norm in question is almost always a "bad norm" that deserves to die. So, constructivists have recounted the decline of such practices as slavery, dueling, foot binding, and extraterritorial jurisdiction as the result of norm entrepreneurs' efforts to abolish them as inconsistent with liberal principles.[13] While the state monopoly on military force is complex in its moral implications, it clearly does not fit into this rogues' gallery.

A second important issue neglected by constructivism is the problem of unintended consequences. This is by no means a new or obscure problem; scholars have long noted that policies and actions can produce results that are unplanned and even unanticipated, making the effects of particular decisions difficult to predict.[14] Although the failure to accurately foresee consequences can result from miscalculation or ignorance of relevant facts, the problem is also endemic in an environment of considerable complexity, where many variables, including the future behavior of numerous other actors, will shape how events unfold.[15] The more complex the system and the longer the time frame, the more pronounced these difficulties become. As Robert Jervis notes, although this does not make policymaking impossible, it sometimes frustrates the intentions of the policymakers: "In a system, actions have unintended effects on the actor, others, and the system as a whole, which means that one cannot infer results from desires and expectations and vice versa."[16] Given the complex and intersubjective nature of norms, it is especially difficult to predict how particular choices will translate into a particular set of beliefs over the long term. Consequently, normative change can sometimes follow unanticipated paths. This means that the constructivist literature's emphasis on purposive agency does not tell the whole story and that there can be consequences that frustrate the "strategic social construction" efforts that Finnemore and Sikkink refer to or that at least create unforeseen—and perhaps undesirable—side effects.

It is important to note, however, that constructivist scholars' neglect of these factors is the product of their case selection rather than any fundamental flaw in their theoretical premises. There is no reason why constructivism cannot also help explain morally dubious outcomes, such as when societies embrace "bad norms" (racism, sexism, or xenophobia, for example) or reject "good" ones. It is possible to imagine, for example, a constructivist explanation of Germany's descent into fascism in the 1930s, highlighting how the shocks of the defeat in World War I and the global depression disposed some members of an increasingly desperate population to turn toward the Nazi Party. While the Nazis were not the sort of "norm entrepreneurs" we are accustomed to thinking about, there can be little doubt that they did play that role. Similarly, there is no reason why constructivism cannot explain not only how norms are born and grow but also how, and why, they decline and die. There is a considerable literature on which attributes and conditions are most propitious for a norm to attain prescriptive status; examining normative decline may require applying these insights in reverse.[17] By the same token, constructivism also provides the theoretical and methodological tools (such as process tracing) to take fuller account of the unintended consequences problem. This is an important task because it allows us to better understand not only how norms shape behavior but also the relationships among them and how these relationships shape the processes by which norms change over time. My goal in this chapter, therefore, is not to propose a comprehensive theory of norm change nor to overhaul the constructivist theoretical framework. Rather, I wish to highlight an understudied and overlooked dynamic by which norms change, often with significant results.

The Principle of Normative Coherence

Sometimes, existing norms that are not directly challenged nevertheless find their influence diminished by changes in other norms. To understand this, it is helpful to consider what I will call "the principle of normative coherence." This principle has two main premises. The first is that specific norms seldom stand alone but instead rest on an ideational foundation of other norms, institutions, and understandings. Ann Florini explains: "No norm exists in a vacuum. The social relationships in which states are enmeshed depend on a web of shared normative understandings about what behavior is acceptable. Any new norm must fit coherently with other existing norms."[18] The second premise is that it is difficult to hold mutually inconsistent beliefs at the same time. Psychologists refer to this as cognitive dissonance, which can lead individuals to experience stress until they are able to reassess their beliefs and resolve the contradiction.[19] Similarly, the existence of logically contradictory norms in the international system creates tensions that are hard to sustain. Robert Jackson refers to this as "an institutional logic of human societies: that if an institution is operative among one set of people, then an alternative institution that contradicts it cannot also be operative among them at the same time."[20]

Taken together, these premises mean that changes in norms seldom occur in isolation. Their ripple effects can be significant and can disturb previously settled understandings and beliefs. In fact, Neta Crawford points to this as an obstacle to getting actors to accept new norms "if doing so requires rethinking an entire complex of related normative, scientific, practical, and identity beliefs which an individual has become convinced are good and see no other reason to challenge."[21] The effect can be especially profound when there are changes in overarching constitutive norms that define actors' roles or relationships across a broad range of circumstances. Again, the most prominent example is state sovereignty, which is actually not a single norm but a bundle of many interrelated norms, rights, and attributes.[22] Moreover, the interrelatedness of the norms constituting sovereignty means that the effects of changes are not necessarily felt only from the top down: modifications of ancillary norms can create pressure on other norms within the bundle and sometimes even the constitutive norm itself. International legal scholar Michael J. Glennon describes this in terms of legal "regimes" and "subregimes": "Sovereignty is the ordering principle of the root regime, and, thus, of every subregime. An erosion of sovereignty within the use-of-force subregime could portend the erosion of sovereignty within other subregimes as well—perhaps even within the root regime."[23]

In some cases, of course, the major implications of normative change will be clear in advance, as when the rise of one norm obviously entails the commensurate decline of another. Slavery in the United States and abolitionism, for example, are antithetical opposites: by definition, slavery was dead the moment abolitionism triumphed. The tension between norms is not always so clear-cut, however. In some cases contradictions between norms may be subtle or conditional, manifesting themselves only after some time. Indeed, they may be unintended, unforeseen, and even unwelcome.

There are many examples of the power of normative coherence in international politics. One of the more familiar (and one that is important in the rise of nonstate violence) is the role of norms of self-determination and racial equality in bringing an end to colonialism in the decades after World War II. Despite the League of Nations' earlier endorsement of self-determination, international commitment to the principle was tepid and conditional until it cohered with emerging civil rights norms after 1945. As Jackson observes, "in an age of equality it was difficult to justify a practice grounded in hierarchy—even if it was benevolent or the people it affected were as yet not sufficiently equipped or prepared to operate a modern state."[24] Therefore, once these norms gained wide support in and among states in the international system, it became impossible to sustain colonialism, even if the foci of the civil rights movements were initially almost exclusively domestic.[25] Normative coherence also played a critical role in the fall of the Soviet Union. Mikhail Gorbachev intended for the policy of *glasnost* (openness) to serve the relatively narrow purpose of facilitating the restructuring of the hidebound Soviet bureaucracy, but the free speech and criticism it spawned proved impossible to contain within that context. Once in the open, popular discontent with the government proliferated until the regime's position became untenable. Crawford notes in her account of decolonization: "Piecemeal reforms may alter the system, and the capabilities of actors within it, in ways that either normatively or pragmatically motivated reformers do not anticipate and perhaps never intended. . . . Thus, relatively small changes may avalanche into large, unanticipated openings for reform, further argument, and institutionalization."[26]

By the same logic, it is difficult to apply a broad norm selectively or to carve out exceptions to a norm for specific circumstances without undermining the coherence of the norm across the board. When in 1999 NATO intervened in Serbia on behalf of Kosovo without UN Security Council approval, NATO secretary-general Javier Solana denied setting a significant precedent, describing the action as "the exception from the rule [against intervention in states' domestic affairs], not an attempt to create new international law."[27] Nevertheless, the episode entirely reframed the debate over the justifiability of intervention, giving birth to the R2P doctrine and being cited as a precedent for the Security Council–backed intervention in Libya in 2011 and the US near-intervention in Syria in 2013.[28] Similarly, the international community has at various times tried to limit the application of the principle of national self-determination only to those peoples seeking independence from colonial rule, out of concern that it might otherwise lead to a destabilizing spiral of separatist claims.[29] Despite this, a broad range of subnational groups have taken up the mantle of self-determination, with important implications, as we shall see in chapters 3 and 4. The problem is that it has proved difficult to circumscribe the principle in a way that does not seem arbitrary and incoherent.

One way of describing this is that the logic inherent in strong norms can "spill over," exercising influence beyond the sorts of cases or circumstances to which the norm most directly applies. This is often apparent in the differences between international norms and international law. Although norms and law are interrelated, they are not one and the same. In fact, there is often considerable divergence between norm-driven behavior and behavior required by law. When there is such a divergence, it is usually the norm that matters more. This is partly a matter of definition: because the concept of norms (understood as "collective understandings of the proper behavior of actors") captures both a sense of what actors *ought* to do and what they *usually* do, they better reflect widely prevailing practice than law, which sometimes sets standards not yet commonly met in practice.[30] The "spillover" effects of a norm can stigmatize actions that might be legally permissible or, by the same token, compel or justify actions that might violate the law.[31] In other words, what is lawful is less important than what is viewed as legitimate. Here again the principle of normative coherence comes into play. The resolution of tensions between norms and laws, or between different norms, can be shaped by many factors, but the relative coherence of the rules at issue is a significant determinant. If a rule is based on rejected beliefs or logic (whether ethical or causal) that no longer hangs together, it will be difficult to sustain. Indeed, this dynamic of normative spillover played an important part in the rise of militias, terrorist organizations, and PMSCs, as we shall see in the next three chapters.

Crisis and Contestation

Sometimes, then, existing norms are plunged into crisis by changes in other norms to which they bear some logical connection. They are, in effect, collateral damage—the indirect and unintended casualties of actions aimed at a different target. Still, norms suffering what I will refer to as a "crisis of coherence" do not simply disappear. In any system there will be actors who are invested in certain norms and who will resist attempts to change or discard them. Consequently, even damaged norms seldom go down without a fight. They are, however, far more vulnerable to challenge, leading to a process of contestation in which stakeholders argue the merits of their respective positions, try to reinterpret the specifics or application of the norm, or question or defend the coherence of the norm. Contestation is an important part of how norms change and a reminder that however important structure might be in shaping norms and behavior, human agency plays an indispensable role. As Finnemore says, "social institutions are continually being contested, albeit to varying degrees at different times.... These contestation processes are political. In fact, normative contestation is in large part what politics is all about: competing values and understandings of what is good, desirable, and appropriate in our collective, communal life."[32]

I have argued elsewhere that people and groups may follow norms because they are morally committed to them, because they see it as in their interests to do so, or some combination of the two.[33] The same reasons explain why people and groups might choose to contest existing norms. Although norms typically become influential when they serve the interests of a large number of society's members, there are almost always some within a society who believe certain norms do not reflect their beliefs or work against their interests. James G. March and Johan P. Olsen note that actors integrated into a political system will generally "see what they like" and "like what they see," but for those alienated from the system, the opposite is true.[34] While at any time there may therefore be some contestation of even the strongest and most widely held norms, as long as a norm remains healthy and coherent this contestation is unlikely to be effective. When the norm suffers a crisis of coherence, however, not only may its opponents feel emboldened to step up their efforts to contest it, these efforts are also more likely to gain traction among others in society, some of whom may themselves become mobilized to oppose the norm. Likewise, the moral commitment to norm change that animates many norm entrepreneurs is more apt to arise when a norm becomes incoherent, perhaps by the juxtaposition of the old norm with newer norms that increasingly define society's expectations about legitimate behavior. Moreover, the changes that contributed to the declining coherence of the norm may actually create new types of actors who might be negatively disposed to the existing norm from the start. I argue in chapter 3, for example, that the state monopoly on military force was undermined by the importance of partisan resistance groups in World War II, some of which later used the growing international acceptance of their armed status to legitimize their fight for national liberation. And as we shall see in chapter 5, companies providing military and security services emerged only after cracks began to appear in the norm against the private use of force, but once on the scene they became energetic and effective participants in the continuing contestation of that norm.

Actors contesting international norms employ a variety of means commonly used by social movements: they will attempt to raise awareness, build coalitions with like-minded groups, seek organizational partners and platforms for their efforts, and sometimes champion legislation.[35] At the core of contestation, however, is the use of rhetoric and argumentation to try to educate and persuade others. At the core of these rhetorical efforts, in turn, is often the principle of normative coherence. In his study of international norm change, Wayne Sandholtz notes that "there is a powerful inclination for participants in normative systems to seek consistency; without consistency, rules do not fulfill their function of providing for stable expectations."[36] This need for consistency, Sandholtz argues, places a premium on analogical reasoning and appeals to precedent.

A party involved in a dispute over norms "must offer the most convincing arguments possible that her position in the current dispute best fits what the rules require and best conforms to the ways in which previous disputes were resolved (precedent)."[37] Analogical reasoning is formalized in many legal systems in the decisive role played by precedent and *stare decisis*, but it is a crucial component of any system of norms or rules.[38] Analogical reasoning, of course, directly reflects the principle of normative coherence, which can both undermine old norms and help establish new ones. Paradoxically, then, even those attempting to overturn old norms make their arguments within an established (if fluid) normative context and will usually construct those arguments by reference to principles within that context that are widely accepted.

Indeed, almost all of the rhetorical strategies scholars have associated with norm entrepreneurs are grounded in the power of analogy and normative coherence. Several studies, for example, highlight the importance of "framing," which is "using language that names, interprets, and dramatizes" events and normative imperatives in ways that allow them to "resonate with broader public understandings and [be] adopted as new ways of talking about and understanding issues."[39] Similarly, Richard Price notes that activists pushing for an international ban on antipersonnel land mines (APLs) succeeded by "grafting a new norm onto existing norms." In that case, ban proponents drew an analogy between APLs and chemical weapons, which were widely condemned as indiscriminate devices that cause unnecessary suffering.[40] More recently, gay rights activists in the United States compared the push for the legalization of gay marriage to the civil rights movements of the 1950s and 1960s that ended institutionalized discrimination against racial minorities.[41] Elements of both "framing" and "grafting" are evident in the strategy popularly known as "rebranding," a term borrowed from the business world, by which something (in commerce, a company or product but in other settings perhaps a practice, idea, or group) is given a new name in order to evoke positive associations or avoid negative ones. Especially in a sociopolitical context, rebranding typically relies on analogical reasoning, either in the positive sense of associating the phenomenon in question with practices and institutions that are viewed favorably or in the negative sense of avoiding association with those viewed unfavorably—a sort of "grafting" in reverse. When the George W. Bush administration wished to disassociate waterboarding and certain other interrogation methods from "torture," it used the term "enhanced interrogation techniques"—a branding that was necessary because international law bans torture per se. In chapters 4 and 5, I discuss similar attempts to disassociate certain practices from terms that still elicit viscerally negative responses: "terrorism" and "mercenarism."

While framing, grafting, and rebranding are most useful in educating and persuading others to embrace a new norm, norm advocates also draw on normative coherence and precedent to outmaneuver actors who remain opposed to such change. Because even strong actors wish to avoid appearing hypocritical or arbitrary in their commitment to norms, it is sometimes possible to use their prior actions or statements as leverage to compel them to accept, or at least accede to, a new norm. One example is what Loren Cass calls "'norm entrapment'—the inability to pursue a preferred policy that violates a norm because of prior rhetorical affirmation of that norm."[42] Cass argues that European Union states' previous insistence on state-by-state domestic greenhouse gas reductions in the late 1990s "trapped" them into opposing a viable emissions trading regime that most of them wanted. Price argues that a similar strategy succeeded in getting many states to sign the 1997 Ottawa Convention banning APLs, even against their strategic interests. In that case, Price claims, "social pressures of international reputation" were important in inducing states to acknowledge that refusing to sign the ban was inconsistent with their professed commitment to humanitarian principles.[43]

A related strategy used against actors resisting normative change is to call attention to instances in which they violated the very norm they now seek to defend. As we shall see in chapters 3 and 4, for example, the actions of the Western powers in World War II undermined their later opposition to guerrilla warfare as well as their insistence on the inviolability of noncombatant immunity.[44] With this strategy, those contesting norms in effect kill two birds with one stone: they identify a precedent for the position they espouse, and they tar their opponents with the brush of hypocrisy, thereby diminishing their credibility and standing to make normative claims. While actors may try to justify their prior behavior by construing the norm narrowly or citing extenuating circumstances, these claims are difficult to defend, as I have argued, and usually end up diminishing the norm in question.

Sometimes an embattled norm survives this process of contestation. For example, the economic norms of liberal internationalism embodied in the Bretton Woods institutions have to date weathered challenges from the New International Economic Order movement in the 1970s and dependency theorists' call for developing countries to reject participation in global markets. In other cases, an impasse results that ultimately is resolved only through armed struggle—as in the bloody victory of the norm against slavery in the American Civil War. There, even a norm with an overwhelmingly compelling ethical basis was strongly resisted because it threatened a practice that was deeply embedded in the identity and interests of certain powerful actors. Indeed, it is important to recognize that international norms operate in a world in which stark considerations of power and interest play an important role. Viewed in this light, the demise of the norm against nonstate actor violence presents a striking puzzle. Here, a constitutive norm that defines and supports the prerogatives of major actors has declined sharply without a significant struggle—a historical rarity.

In this case, I argue, the state monopoly on military force was the collateral damage of campaigns against other key norms. Indeed, the decline of the norm was precipitated and undergirded by two of the most ambitious and significant macronormative transformations in history, both of which are widely and justifiably viewed as salutary in their own right.[45] While both these transformations resulted from purposive efforts—the type of "strategic social construction" Finnemore and Sikkink refer to—a secondary effect of each was to change norms in such a way that made it harder to sustain the vision of sovereignty that gives states exclusive control over international violence. This damaged norm was, in turn, aggressively contested by those with a stake in allowing different types of nonstate actors the right to use force, laying the groundwork for the trends explored in the case studies.

The Retreat from *Raison d'État* in the Use of Force

One of the two macronormative changes that facilitated the return of private violence was, ironically, a groundbreaking measure intended to curb violence: the dramatic post–World War II revision of the international legal regime governing when states are permitted to use military force. For centuries previously, war had been seen as a legitimate tool of statecraft, in both theory and practice. While the tenets of just war doctrine had been a constraint (if only a marginally effective one) through the Middle Ages and Renaissance, the Westphalian revolution of the seventeenth century ushered in the age of autonomous states, giving rulers nearly unfettered discretion. With the new institutional form of state sovereignty came the ideology of *raison d'état*, an ethos of state interest that relieved rulers of the need to answer to the Roman Catholic Church or any other authority. Indeed, the right to make war in the national interest was deemed one of the core prerogatives that defined the institution of sovereignty.[46] From the Thirty Years War to the middle of the twentieth century, therefore, there had been few meaningful legal or normative limits on states' rights to use force.

The cataclysms of the world wars, however, revealed the danger inherent in this discretion. Although the Covenant of the League of Nations and interwar agreements such as the Kellogg-Briand Pact of 1928 included some restrictions, these proved ineffectual. It was the carnage of World War II that shocked the international community into drastically rethinking the status quo. In Martin van Creveld's words, "states, having discovered the forces of nationalism as first proclaimed by the likes of Moser and Herder, transformed themselves from instruments for imposing law and order into secular gods; and . . . having increased their strength out of all proportion by invading their citizens' minds and systematically picking their pockets, they used that strength to fight each other (1914–45) on such a scale, and with such murderous intensity, as almost to put an end to themselves."[47] This trauma led "norm entrepreneurs" of various types, including citizens and their governments alike, to seek a new legal and normative order that would significantly limit states' freedom of action, not as a secondary effect but as a moral and practical imperative. This was a classic case of strategic social construction set in motion by a major shock to the system. The machinery of warfare had become too destructive, it was reasoned, for the logic of raison d'état to prevail any longer.

Within a year of the war's conclusion, there were two significant manifestations of this new thinking. One was the trial of Nazi leaders for war crimes at Nuremberg, which established principles that signaled a clean break from raison d'état, including the idea that individuals could be held personally responsible for criminal deeds committed in their service to the state. This exploded the long-standing conceit that national policies, however odious, were to be imputed only to the nation itself and not to the individuals who shaped and enacted them. Another innovation at Nuremberg was the charge of "waging a war of aggression"—an action that for the previous three hundred years had been part of a leader's job description. The implication of this charge was clear: not all wars were legitimate, and leaders could be held to account for pursuing illegitimate ones.[48] Within weeks, the UN General Assembly unanimously endorsed the "Nuremberg Principles" as binding international law.[49]

The second manifestation of the new thinking was the UN Charter itself, whose central principle was that the use or threat of force against other states was impermissible. Although it carved out exceptions to that principle, these were carefully circumscribed: states could use force in self-defense against an armed attack or when authorized to do so by a vote of the Security Council.[50] So, in the space of a few traumatic years, the use of military force went from a sovereign right to an action that is illegal in all but certain narrowly defined circumstances. As K. J. Holsti notes, absent those circumstances, "war has been de-legitimized as an instrument of policy."[51] To be sure, as a practical constraint, the UN Charter regime is far from airtight; violations remain frequent. Nevertheless, it forms the core of the contemporary law of *jus ad bellum* and enjoys the privileged status of *jus cogens*, a peremptory legal obligation binding on all states.[52] Perhaps more to the point, the charter has shaped the terms of debate in the international community about the legitimacy of the use of force, as demonstrated by the controversies that now invariably ensue when military action is taken unilaterally. Compared to the days of raison d'état, there is no doubt that the norm has changed.

This has rightly been praised as a significant step forward for the international community. As I have argued, however, just as beneficial policies can have unintended consequences, so too can beneficial norms have effects that unsettle consensus on other questions. Those pressing for the new rules did not seek to undermine states' monopoly on violence, only to limit when that monopoly could be used. Nevertheless, the rules exerted pressure on that monopoly in at least two important ways.

The Withdrawal of Deference to State Discretion

The institutional and symbolic power of sovereign statehood reached its zenith in the early twentieth century. By this time, states had taken on significance far greater than the sum of the functions and governmental bodies that constituted them. Van Creveld refers to the period from 1789 to 1945 as the era of "the state as an ideal" and argues that by harnessing the power of nationalism, states had become "secular gods."[53] As noted, the post-1945 regime created significant constraints on states where few had existed. Besides simply limiting their freedom of action, however, the new restrictions on the use of force and the Nuremberg precedent of holding leaders individually responsible for state crimes both reflected and contributed to the decline of the status of states as all-powerful masters of the international system. The new rules sent the message that states were not ends in themselves but had responsibilities both to their citizens and to others in the international system. Moreover, they marked an end to the unquestioning assumption that state governments spoke for, and acted in the best interests of, their citizens, and that their actions were therefore entitled to the deference they had long received. This withdrawal of deference on questions of war and peace would eventually be echoed by a more thoroughgoing skepticism about the prudence and beneficence of national governments.[54] As Van Creveld notes, "while states continue to carry out some important functions, two centuries after the French Revolution first enlisted modern mass nationalism, many of them seem to have run out of people who believe in them, let alone are willing to act as cannon fodder on their behalf."[55] The diminished status of state governments can today be seen in matters as mundane as the declining profitability of national postal services in the face of private competition and as momentous as the rise of human rights as a central issue in IR, under the auspices of which the

R2P doctrine seeks to redefine the strictures of the principle of state sovereignty altogether.[56] A critical first step, however, was the revocation of the states' carte blanche on questions of jus ad bellum. French prime minister Georges Clemenceau had complained during World War I that "war is too serious a matter to be left to generals"; the clear verdict after World War II was that it was in fact too serious to be left entirely to governments themselves. In the face of this dramatic repudiation of state prerogatives, which states themselves recognized as necessary, it would prove difficult to sustain the classical vision of sovereignty that had flourished not long before. One casualty was the close and powerful association between the state and war, two traditional components of which were the state's monopoly on the discretion to make war and its monopoly on the means of doing so. Over the long term, the revocation of the first of these monopolies could not help but weaken the second.

The Contextualization of the Right to Use Force

Another significant effect of the post–World War II transformation in norms governing the use of force was to reorder the relative importance of the traditional jus ad bellum criteria in international legal and moral calculus. The new regime effectively shifted the central question from *who* was using force to *why* force was being used. In the Westphalian paradigm, after all, as long as a government was sovereign, its decision to go to war was beyond moral or legal scrutiny. After 1945, however, it was not enough for a state to act with "proper authority" (to borrow the terminology of the just war tradition)—it was required to have "just cause" as well.

The new regime thus replaced a categorical judgment (that sovereign states are justified in making war) with a conditional judgment (that sovereign states can justifiably make war only under certain circumstances). Categorical norms are considerably more powerful than conditional norms, largely because they operate peremptorily, as decisive factors in decision-making. Categorical prohibitions, for example, shape behavior not by taking certain options off the table but by preventing them from even becoming "options" that actors are conscious of in the first place. They are therefore much more likely to be internalized by actors and embedded in policymaking assumptions and institutions.[57] In the Westphalian model, the categorical permission for states to use force settled the legal and ethical matter, precluding further argumentation about the specific merits of the case. Theoretically, the post-1945 regime retained the criterion of state status as proper authority to use force but only as a threshold condition to then make substantive claims about justifiability, which were now the crux of the matter. The heightened focus on these case-by-case details—the particulars of the grievances, the competing claims of justice, and so on—in turn tended to overshadow the threshold condition of sovereign statehood itself. So, while the drafters of the UN Charter neither intended nor envisioned that nonstate actors would have equal standing to use force, one effect of this change was to devalue the institutional status of the actor using force and prioritize more contextual questions.

The tension this has generated with the state monopoly on force has been more than simply theoretical. The most important illustration of this is the international community's support for the use of force by nonstate groups on behalf of peoples seeking self-determination and political independence, which I examine in chapter 3. The tension has been evident in other contexts as well, however, including the debate over the justifiability of the US-led war against Iraq that began in 2003. At that time, many (including former US president Jimmy Carter) suggested that because the primary requirement for force to be legitimate under the charter was approval by the UN Security Council, the Security Council itself, rather than the sovereign state, was the only institution that could satisfy the jus ad bellum criterion of "proper authority."[58] In effect, the essence of the argument was that post-1945 norms, particularly the requirement of just cause as determined by the Security Council, superseded the criterion of statehood as a threshold requirement for using force. Therefore, in contextualizing the right of states to use force, the post–World War II retreat from the logic of raison d'état helped shift the focus of the jus ad bellum judgment onto the ends for which force was being used. As I will argue, this would have further significance when combined with the ascendance of consequentialist normative reasoning in the same period.

Decolonization

The second macronormative transformation that created pressure upon the norm against nonstate violence was the wave of decolonization that transformed the international system in the decades after World War II. This was a profound change that completely reversed centuries of practice, during which the possession of colonial territories by strong states was a ubiquitous and, by widespread consensus, natural and inevitable feature of the international system. Starting with the independence of a few colonies soon after 1945, the trend grew in the 1950s. In 1960, a year that witnessed the creation of seventeen new sovereign states, the UN General Assembly passed the Declaration on the Granting of Independence to Colonial Countries and Peoples without a dissenting vote.[59] From 1955 to 1965, membership in the UN increased from 60 to 117 states, the majority of new members being former colonies in Africa.[60]

As Robert Jackson and Neta Crawford have shown, this transformation was primarily the result not of material changes, such as the redistribution of power within the system, but rather of changes in international norms.[61] In the course of a generation, attitudes about colonialism changed from matter-of-fact acceptance to strong and categorical condemnation. As noted earlier, Jackson largely attributes this to the ascendance of norms such as racial equality and self-determination and the unsustainability of the contradictions between these principles, which Western societies were embracing domestically, and colonial practices. Again, normative coherence and contestation played vital roles in this process; the yearning for independence may have arisen indigenously within the colonies, but it became irresistible only once it was expressed in terms the colonizers recognized as their own. In 1964, a British historian identified the key to decolonization as "the assimilation by Asians and Africans of western ideas, techniques and institutions, which could be turned against the occupying powers—a process in which they proved far more adept than most Europeans had anticipated."[62] In the end, the victory over colonialism was resounding; self-determination for former colonies became a nonnegotiable point.

Decolonization unquestionably qualifies as a "macronormative" shift in international norms: it redefined relationships among political entities of various types, established new expectations and standards of legitimate behavior, and changed even the institution of sovereignty itself. Given the principle of normative coherence, we should therefore not be surprised that decolonization and the ideas that went along with it forced a reshuffling of other international norms and institutions. Two such changes are especially relevant to this study.

The Reassessment of Core Sovereign Functions

Decolonization not only reflected a major normative transformation in judgments about who deserves to be sovereign states—it also entailed a simultaneous normative transformation in the conception of what it *means* to be a sovereign state. Jackson describes this as the move from "positive" sovereignty, which emphasized the capabilities of a government to provide goods to its citizens and defend the state against aggression, to "negative" or "juridical" sovereignty, which instead emphasized the legal autonomy of states and their right to be free from external intervention. This redefinition of sovereignty, Jackson argues, was a necessary adjunct to decolonization not only because its emphasis on nonintervention fit well with the decolonization ethos but also because the political entities created by the process lacked the very capabilities "positive" sovereignty assumed. Not only did "negative" sovereignty protect new states from the predations of great powers—it delegitimized the practice of delaying their independence on the grounds that they were unprepared to effectively protect or govern themselves.[63]

Because decolonization required defining state sovereignty in "negative" terms of legal rights and prohibitions rather than "positive" terms of empirical capabilities, it created a logical tension with the traditional conception of what it meant to be a sovereign state. What previously defined statehood were the inalienable core functions that states—and only states—could perform.[64] Of these, none was more important than the security function: keeping order within the state and defending it against armed attack.[65] With few exceptions, however, the states created by decolonization were unable to effectively perform this function. Part of the problem was that many new states were simply too poor to sustain effective militaries, but this lack of material resources was often exacerbated by other factors, including low literacy rates and authoritarian forms of government.[66] Even more important was the low level of societal cohesion in these states. Ironically, although nationalist movements were important in many states' drives for independence, as Jackson writes, the new states were "not usually based on nationalities either ethnic or historical. Ethnonations only rarely coincided with colonial jurisdictions and most colonies never developed into authentic political nationalities."[67] Consequently, as Steven David explains, typically in such countries "groups owe allegiance to and act for interests other than the national interest. Instead of identifying with the state, individuals identify with ethnic, religious, or regional groupings. . . . Rather than transcending the differences among these different groups, the state is often simply the representative of the group that holds power in the capital."[68] In his landmark study of the effect of domestic social structures on military effectiveness, Stephen Rosen argues that such divisions are likely to produce weak military organizations, either because the societal fissures will be replicated within the military or because they will prompt the state to isolate the military from society, which will generate distrust and possibly internal discord.[69]

One practical implication of the military weakness of postcolonial states has been chronic insecurity: it is no coincidence that a disproportionately large number of these states have been plagued by interstate and intrastate war.[70] It has also, however, placed significant pressure on the state monopoly on military force. First, of course, it has contributed to material conditions that have led both governments and substate groups to turn to nonstate actors (such as militias and private firms) for security. But there was also an important normative implication, rooted in the considerable disconnect between the traditional understanding of sovereign statehood and a reality to which it bore little resemblance. This was to disassociate the institution of sovereign statehood from the core functions that had once defined it, including the military function. In this regard, Weber's definition of sovereignty as "the monopoly on the legitimate use of physical force" stands in stark contrast to Van Creveld's observation that the developing world "is characterized by nothing so much as the fact that the state never succeeded in establishing an effective monopoly over violence."[71] In short, if effectively wielding force is no longer something that many governments do, then it is hard to argue that it remains something that, by definition, *only* governments *can* do.

The Normative "Revolt against the West"

A second aspect of decolonization's effect on the norm against nonstate violence stems from what has been called "the revolt against the West": the rejection by non-Western states and societies of the institutions of their former colonial masters.[72] The first goal of this "revolt," and its most obvious material manifestation, was decolonization itself. The indispensable normative component of that struggle, however, had implications beyond colonialism and would reconfigure the international landscape in ways that continue to shape relations between the postcolonial and Western worlds.

At the heart of this challenge was a denial of the presumption that existing international institutions embodied objective or universally valid principles. New states and their allies pointed out that despite the pretense of objectivity, almost all extant international law and norms originated in the Westphalian European system, which became global largely through conquest and economic coercion. These institutions were therefore attacked not only because they reflected cultural judgments that might be invalid in non-Western settings but also because they were seen as tools used to exercise hegemony over the non-Western world.[73] As Hedley Bull succinctly put it, "the international legal rules . . . were not only made by the European or Western powers, they were also in substantial measure made *for* them."[74] Moreover, because the structures of power that undergirded Western dominance were not simply military or political, mere formal independence was not enough to overcome them. Thus, empowered by their growing numbers and growing sense of solidarity, newly independent or simply newly assertive non-Western states continued to press not only for reforms to the system but also for the redress of injustices it created. One dimension of this was what Bull calls "the struggle for economic justice," which emerged from the 1964 UN Conference on Trade, Aid, and Development, and reached a high-water mark with the 1974 UN General Assembly declaration endorsing a "New International Economic Order."[75] This proposal, which sought to replace the liberal internationalist Bretton Woods regime with a system featuring favorable terms of trade for developing states, ultimately failed, but the idea that developing states are entitled to preferential terms in international economic dealings would gain some measure of acceptance in certain contexts.[76] More broadly, however, the "revolt" eventually transcended any particular issue area to become the central normative paradigm through which much of the developing world viewed its relations with the West. Drawing on what Ramesh Thakur calls "narratives of grievance," the ethos of resistance that had emerged naturally in the cause of liberation grew into what was in some cases an almost reflexive stance of generalized anti-Westernism.[77] The "revolt against the West" has thus provided an ideological template for a broad range of actors, states and nonstates alike, for whom the rejection of Western norms has provided a valuable political stance and in some cases a raison d'être itself.

This development has had considerable impact upon many norms relating to the prerogatives of sovereign states. Indeed, Jackson portrays the entire decolonization project as primarily a renegotiation of the structure of state sovereignty itself, initiated by non-Western actors who skillfully exploited contradictions among Western norms.[78] However, as non-Western states grew in number and influence and the norms that marginalized them became less coherent, it became less important, Bull notes, for "the moral appeal [of non-Western arguments] to be cast in the terms that would have most resonance within Western societies. . . . [Non-Westerners] have become freer to adopt a different rhetoric that sets Western values aside, or at all events places different interpretations upon them."[79] This freedom would only intensify the pressure that decolonization was already creating on the state monopoly on military force. Within the context of decolonization itself, of course, the tension was fairly obvious: the prohibition of nonstate violence was a norm born of the Western state-building experience and was wielded against peoples colonized by Western states.[80] The same was true, moreover, of the opprobrium on guerrilla tactics, which would come to be closely associated with national liberation movements struggling against colonialism. Even the fundamental *jus in bello* rule of noncombatant immunity, which purportedly embodied universal humanitarian principles, would be scrutinized for the way in which it reflected cultural and political assumptions of a provenance that was not only Western but explicitly Christian. These tensions would play important roles in the changes in international norms discussed in the case studies.

Ancillary Normative Changes

Even beyond the ways I have just described, the twin macronormative transformations of the retreat from raison d'état and decolonization contributed to ancillary changes in other norms that further eroded the state monopoly on armed force.

The Demilitarization of Society

Historically, military force was central to the development of the state, both in the rise of the institution of sovereignty and in defining the state's relationship to its citizens.[81] Indeed, the growing power of state governments shaped the very notion of citizenship. As Anthony Giddens explains, peoples are more likely to consciously regard themselves as "citizens" "the more the administrative scope of the state begins to penetrate the day-to-day activities of its subjects. . . . The expansion of state sovereignty means that those subject to it are in some sense—initially vague, but growing more and more definite and precise—aware of their membership in a political community and of the rights and obligations such membership confers."[82] Nowhere were these rights and obligations more salient than in war. If the state's ultimate duty to its citizens was to protect them from the predations of outsiders, citizens' ultimate duty to the state was to provide it with the manpower necessary to accomplish this task. War thus inevitably came to occupy a central place in the legendry of states and in the hearts and minds of their citizens. One need only wander the streets of a European or American capital to see an abundance of monuments and landmarks that attest to this fact.

By 1945, however, romantic notions of warfare as the embodiment of patriotic glory were in tatters in many societies.[83] The ensuing rejection of raison d'état as sufficient justification to go to war heightened the growing ideational disjuncture with traditional ideas of citizenship. Van Creveld argues that changing attitudes toward war have deprived states of a crucial "emotionally unifying factor": "States can develop a strong appeal to the emotions only so long as they prepare for, and wage, war. If, for any reason, they should cease to do so, then there will be no point in people remaining loyal to them any more than, for example, General Motors or IBM, which is tantamount to saying that much of their *raison d'être* will have been lost."[84] Martin Shaw contends that modern industrial societies, especially in Europe, have become "post-military," in that war and the preparation for war no longer "dominated all social relations and cultural forms."[85] This transformation has been noted not only by commentators from the ideological left such as Shaw but also by conservatives such as Robert Kagan.[86] Kagan argues that contemporary European states have internalized a worldview in which military force is presumptively illegitimate, international problems are best addressed through multilateral cooperation, and the threat of major interstate war is less prevalent than in the past. This European skepticism of force, he argues, "represents a conscious rejection of the European past."[87] Kagan quotes former German foreign minister Joschka Fischer as expressing the new ethos: "The core of the concept of Europe after 1945 was and still is a rejection of the European balance-of-power principle and the hegemonic ambitions of individual states that had emerged following the Peace of Westphalia in 1648."[88] This concept, of course, is the very one inherent in the UN Charter regime itself.

The nexus between the state and the military is even weaker in postcolonial societies, largely because in most of them it was never very strong to begin with.

In the colonial experience, the relationship of the regular military to the population was often one perceived of as oppressor and oppressed, which remains true in all too many postcolonial states. As noted above, few new states developed strong military institutions, and even in countries that gained their independence through armed opposition, this history has rarely translated into a strong bond between the nationalist ethos and the national army. And although some postcolonial societies have strong and deep-seated warrior cultures, the warrior ethos often manifests in ways that undermine rather than support state cohesion, such as warlordism and the prevalence of strong militias.

This ideational change has had significant political ramifications. European states, as well as some other major powers such as Japan, which has explicitly embraced postmilitarism, spend less on defense, put greater stock in international law, and are less inclined to commit their forces overseas than in the past.[89] To be sure, not all states are equally committed to this vision.[90] Nevertheless, even among powers less reticent about using force, the relationship among the state, the military, and society at large has changed considerably since 1945. The United States, along with Britain, was among the first of several of the world's leading military powers to abandon conscription in favor of all-volunteer forces.[91] Moreover, many commentators have observed that Western powers are increasingly casualty-averse, making them less willing to send their troops into intense or prolonged combat situations.[92] Even such an advanced military as that of the United States found its resources severely strained by the low-intensity counterinsurgency campaign in Afghanistan. These factors have to some degree contributed to the material demand for nonstate force in the form of private military and security contractors, as discussed in chapter 5. More fundamentally, however, they are part and parcel of a shift in norms regarding the relationship between war and society. Of course, states have not stopped making war any more than they have stopped printing currency or propagating arcane regulations. The point, instead, is that war is no longer regarded as the quintessential purpose of the state, and when it occurs, it is the business not of society as a whole but, as with currency and regulatory bureaucracy, only a specialized professional subset of it. To this extent, it has become increasingly anachronistic to view the military function as a defining, much less a heroic, characteristic of state sovereignty itself.

The Ascendance of Consequentialist Normative Reasoning

Another change in international norms after 1945 has been in the nature of normative reasoning itself. To appreciate this, one must understand the distinction between two common approaches to assessing the morality of actions or policies. One is "deontological ethics," which judges the morality of an action or policy by whether it conforms to a rule or rules that embody a priori moral principles. (For this reason, the deontological position is sometimes referred to as "rule-based" ethics.) The other is "consequentialism," which holds that the moral quality of an action or policy is defined by the consequences it brings about.[93] Deontological rules are categorical, applying equally to all actors and all situations, while consequentialism envisions that some actions may be wrong under some circumstances but right under others. Thus, a consequentialist's take on a deontological command such as "Thou shalt not kill" might be "Thou shalt not kill *unless* by doing so one can avoid a greater evil, or achieve a greater good." Historically, most norms governing state behavior in the international system have taken the form of deontological rules. In fact, what we commonly think of as "norms," especially regulative norms that prescribe or prohibit certain behaviors, are by definition deontological devices. So, for example, the system has rules specifying how foreign emissaries are to be treated, when it is acceptable or unacceptable to resolve disputes using military force, who may be targeted in battle, and so on. Ethical or "good" behavior is that which conforms to these rules, while those violating the rules are subject to condemnation. A consequentialist perspective, on the other hand, focuses less on the rules themselves and more on whether the action in question leads to a desirable outcome.

Conditions since 1945 have made the international system more amenable to consequentialism, while making it more difficult to sustain a system of deontological norm-based standards. One significant reason for this was the enormous pressure put on international norms by World War II itself. By the end of the war, even those fighting against the genocidal horrors of Nazism were themselves indiscriminately bombing Axis cities and embracing guerrilla tactics that flouted the traditional laws of armed conflict. These practices so clearly violated preexisting norms, and often had such appalling effects, that they could be justified only by consequentialist logic.[94] To be sure, given the supremely high stakes involved in the war, this logic may have been compelling, but there is little doubt that these choices did lasting damage to the norms that had been cast aside. The same was true of many central features of the Cold War era, none more strikingly than nuclear deterrence, which rested on the inescapably consequentialist logic of preventing the ultimate evil of nuclear war by being prepared to wipe out tens of millions of enemy civilians at a moment's notice.[95]

As I have suggested, frequent violations will significantly weaken a norm, even if those violating it claim to have done so only because extraordinary circumstances demanded it. The precedent set by these actions, however, undermines not only the specific norms in question but also the entire system of deontological rules of which those norms were a part. Normative exceptionalism is hard to contain. The idea that actors are permitted to violate norms if they believe the outcome justifies it is logically at odds with the idea that norms, even strong ones, are ethically obligatory. Widespread normative exceptionalism therefore tends to make consequentialist reasoning more powerful, while consequentialism in turn carves out more space for actors to claim special circumstances in demurring from norms or contextualizing them to limit their scope.

The cogency of consequentialism in the post-1945 international system, therefore, allowed those contesting the state monopoly on force to appeal to the legitimacy of the *ends* they were pursuing, regardless of the possibly troubling or problematic implications of the *means* through which they were pursuing them. The twin macronormative transformations I have discussed contributed to consequentialism in some ways (for example, the emphasis on contextual factors in the new jus ad bellum regime), but more important was that they provided overarching, morally compelling ends to which the international community was strongly committed. So, for example, while the principles behind decolonization were deontological, the desire to achieve it as completely and expeditiously as possible became the desirable consequence that justified violating, or at least reinterpreting, other important norms. As we shall see in the case studies, this sort of reasoning, this balancing of means and ends, would become a common contestation strategy for nonstate actors seeking the right to use force, bolstering the armed struggle against colonial domination, justifying the use of tactics that put civilians at increasing risk, and helping PMSCs in their efforts to legitimize the market for private force by accentuating contextual "just cause" arguments regarding the nature of the contracts they accept and the prospect of alleviating humanitarian crises.

One result of the ascendance of consequentialism has been the decline of some norms that proved incompatible with the new macronorms. In other cases, however, norms have not necessarily declined but have come to be applied asymmetrically, so that different actors are effectively held to different standards. This "normative asymmetry" would be out of place in a deontological normative scheme, in which rules are typically categorical, applying equally to all actors regardless of their identity or circumstances. Of course, there has frequently been a de facto asymmetry in terms of compliance with or enforcement of international norms, as the anarchical structure of the international system has often allowed great powers to break the rules with some measure of impunity. While this remains true in all too many cases, since 1945 a kind of asymmetry has arisen that differs in two ways. First, it typically goes to the substantive content of norms rather than their enforcement; that is, the norms explicitly endorse different rules for different actors. Second, its beneficiaries are some of the weakest actors in the international system rather than the strongest. This normative asymmetry, for example, is inherent in programs providing developing states with preferential rights under trade regimes, environmental regimes, and debt relief. Broadly, it is evident in efforts intended to redress past injustices or systemic disadvantages, which in effect selectively suspend, moderate, or reinterpret rules of *procedural* fairness in order to achieve *substantive* fairness. Jackson refers to this as "global affirmative action," claiming that the changes in the norms of sovereign state-hood required to accommodate the states created by decolonization resulted in what amounts to a separate system altogether. Postcolonial "quasi-states," Jackson writes, "are not simply less skilled and successful at playing the same sovereignty game, they are in fact playing a somewhat different game than first and second division states with novel rules adapted to their special circumstances. The new rules provide them with constitutional advantages—like handicaps given to poor golfers."[96]

For the purposes of this book, the most relevant examples of normative asymmetry involve asymmetrical rules for military force, in both the jus ad bellum and jus in bello realms. In the former, the UN authorized the use of force by nonstate liberation movements that did not meet the UN Charter criteria, and in the latter, Protocol I of 1977 approved the use of guerrilla tactics by opposition groups but not for government troops—in both cases to advance the goals of decolonization. Moreover, as I argue in chapters 3 and 4, because of the principle of normative coherence, the effective bifurcation of the law of armed conflict under Protocol I contributed directly to an unauthorized but clear de facto asymmetry in the application of the norm of noncombatant immunity that continues to decisively shape the use of force, in both warfare and terrorism.[97]

The Enhanced Normative Authority of New Actors

Finally, the post–World War II macronormative changes shifted the global distribution of power not just in material terms but also in terms of the ability to shape international norms. The material shift, of course, was marked by the rise of the Cold War superpowers and the end of the dominance of longstanding powers such as Britain, France, and Germany. The normative shift, which received far less attention, increased the influence both of otherwise weak states that in earlier times would have had almost no sway in international politics and of new types of actors whose very existence arose from the changing norms that made this shift possible.

This was more than the usual reshuffling of great powers that often follows large systemic wars. Throughout history, and certainly in the Westphalian era, great powers were almost infinitely more influential and capable of achieving the outcomes they desired than states with weak militaries and few material resources. Indeed, this fact is central to realist theory and goes a long way toward explaining why realists dismiss the power of nonmaterial factors such as norms. While there is plenty of evidence that norms have always been more influential than realists assume, it is nevertheless true that great powers have been able to exert disproportionate influence in shaping those norms, in terms of both their content and their enforcement.[98] Since World War II, however, this has less often been the case, as small, weak states have sometimes been able to achieve their goals through normative means. Again, decolonization provides the most obvious example. While on the question of decolonization itself the weak states were, to be sure, supported by both the United States and the Soviet Union, this was not true of some of the normative changes that followed in its wake, including the legitimization of nonstate violence and guerrilla warfare detailed in chapters 3 and 4.

To some extent, the newfound influence of these states was a function of strength in numbers. There were simply more states in the system than at any other time in the Westphalian era (a fact that itself reflected the macronormative transformations I have discussed), and new states shared many of the same concerns, allowing them to form a cohesive bloc on many issues. More important, however, was that the postwar international system featured not just a redistribution of power but also a change in the currency of power itself. The retreat from raison d'état devalued appeals to national interest and enhanced the value of appeals to normative principles. This in turn increased the importance of principled arguments in the process of norm construction, opening space for contestation by actors who in an earlier time would never have been heard. As Louis Henkin notes in explaining the newfound power of minor states, "with an ideology and rhetoric of justice and equality, concentrated in multilateral forums, widely and effectively disseminated, . . . the counters of influence in the international system are changed, and political weapons loom larger than in the past."[99] In short, after World War II, norms themselves became more important, which made certain states more important and created opportunities for even further normative change.

Indeed, it may not be going too far to say that international politics took a "principled turn" after World War II. Of course, it is important not to overstate this point. There is no question that great powers still wield enormous influence, including in norm-making, or that all states remain committed above all else to their own interests. Nevertheless, norms now play an obvious role in how states define those interests. I have written elsewhere about the importance of the norm of noncombatant immunity in modern wars; since that time, it has shaped the conduct of the wars in Afghanistan and Iraq, as well as events in Libya and Egypt during and after the 2011 uprisings.[100] In 2013, the taboo against chemical weapons nearly drove the United States to intervene in the Syrian crisis, even when almost every other consideration pointed toward continuing American noninvolvement. To be sure, states also often use norms cynically, following them selectively or citing them to justify policies grounded on less noble motives. Even then, however, it is worth remembering that in earlier eras it was rarely necessary for states to adopt any such pretense. For most of history, either states proceeded with unabashed honesty about their efforts at aggrandizement (as would be entirely appropriate, after all, when raison d'état is the guiding principle), or their interests aligned more conveniently with the principles that purportedly inspired them, whether taking up the "civilizing mission" of imperialism, saving the souls of indigenous peoples, or stamping out heresy.

This revaluation of the currency of power benefited not only weaker states but also intergovernmental and NGOs. Thomas Risse observes: "Debates in the international public sphere differ from diplomatic negotiations in bi- or multilateral settings in various respects. First, they are more open in terms of access, since public spheres are usually not confined to state actors. Nonstate actors such as nongovernmental organizations (NGOs) or advocacy networks participate regularly in international public discourses. . . . The more an issue is subject to public scrutiny, the more likely it becomes that materially less privileged actors have access to the discourse and that their arguments carry the day and convince an audience. . . . The moral power and authority of many NGOs seems to be directly related to this feature of public discourses."[101] While Risse focuses on NGOs, his argument explains the growing influence of "less privileged actors" of all descriptions. One example is the UN, which, as Inis Claude wrote in the mid-1960s, "has come to be regarded, and used, as a dispenser of politically significant approval and disapproval of the claims, policies, and actions of states. . . . While the voice of the United Nations may not be the authentic voice of mankind, it is clearly the best available facsimile thereof."[102] The UN General Assembly, in particular, assumed a role in norm-making far out of proportion to the limited institutional powers granted it by the UN Charter. Indeed, legal scholar Richard Falk argued that the General Assembly had become so important in defining the content of customary international law on some matters that it was performing a "quasi-legislative role" in international politics.[103] This trend, moreover, further reinforced the growing influence of postcolonial states, which because of decolonization came to make up a majority in the General Assembly and thus were increasingly influential within a body that was itself increasingly influential. Finally, as Risse suggests, NGOs also benefited from the rising power of normative legitimacy, becoming increasingly important in setting the agenda for IGOs such as the UN and in some cases playing the central role in creating treaty regimes, such as the 1992 Rio Treaty on environmental issues and the 1997 Ottawa Convention banning APLs.[104]

The enhanced normative authority of these new actors would become very important in the contestation of norms that privileged sovereign states, especially traditional great powers from the West. Bull described it as nothing less than "the dismantling of the old order," which he said had been "assisted by a transformation of the legal and moral climate of international relations which the Third World states themselves . . . have played the principal role in bringing about. Commanding majorities of votes as they do in the political organs of the UN and able to call upon the prestige of numbers, not merely of states but of persons accruing to the states claiming to represent a majority of the world's population, they have overturned the old structure of international law and organization that once served to sanctify their subject status."[105] The increasing efficacy of normative argumentation thus empowered new actors in the contestation process and made new strategies available to them.

Conclusion

In this chapter, I have suggested that big changes in practice typically do not happen without big changes in ideas. Therefore, when we see previously minor actors having a major impact in international politics, it is worth asking what role changes in norms that define roles and prescribe behaviors in the system may have played in this shift. I have also identified two large-scale macronormative transformations, and several related or ancillary changes, that had potentially unsettling ramifications for the state monopoly on the legitimate means of force. I hope that by doing this I have made it plausible to imagine that this monopoly could suffer a crisis of coherence that would render it vulnerable to contestation by those seeking to challenge the existing normative order. What I have not done to this point is provide empirical evidence that such a "crisis" in fact existed, that such contestation occurred or that this process contributed to the changed landscape we see today. That is the task I undertake in the next three chapters.

PARTISANS, LIBERATORS, AND MILITIAS

Normative Change and the Legitimization of Nonstate Violence

The civil war raging in Syria since 2011 is one of the twenty-first century's most tragic and consequential conflicts, claiming almost half a million lives and forcing twelve million people from their homes.[1] The flow of refugees escaping the conflict has itself had tremendous implications, destabilizing other states in the Levant and contributing to the rise of nationalist movements throughout Europe and the Brexit movement in Britain.[2] The war has also altered the geopolitical landscape, empowering states such as Iran and Russia while blunting US influence, and perhaps ambitions, in the Middle East. While by definition any civil war involves nonstate forces, Syria's has been exceptional for the number, variety, and impact of nonstate actors involved. Fighting against the Assad regime have been over a thousand militias (including about twenty numbering several thousand fighters each), ranging from secular forces seeking democracy to radical jihadists intent on establishing a fundamentalist caliphate.[3] Also important has been the US-supported Kurdish YPG, which controls Kurdish-majority areas in Syria and has played a key role in anti-ISIS ground operations after 2014.[4] The Assad regime itself, moreover, has relied heavily on nonstate forces, including the Lebanese militia Hezbollah, Iranian-backed Shi'ite militias, Russian paramilitary units, and Syrian militias that backed Assad but occasionally battled government forces, and that may threaten the postwar stability of Syria.[5] Indeed, the Syrian conflict illustrates what is likely to be a common model for twenty-first-century "proxy war," with rival states clashing not through client states but rather through their support of various nonstate belligerent groups.[6] While Syria is an especially salient case, militias are important, and volatile, aspects of the politics of many countries around the world, including Afghanistan, Brazil, Colombia, India, Iraq, Libya, Mali, Myanmar, Somalia, and Yemen, to name just a few.[7]

Before examining how these groups became so prevalent, a couple of points of clarification may be helpful. First, as I noted in chapter 1, I use the term "militias" to refer to armed nonstate groups in a fairly general sense, regardless of whether they are aligned with the national government. While many scholars limit the use of the term to progovernment forces, the practice is by no means universal.[8] As I have argued, purportedly precise taxonomies of violent non-state actors often break down in practice, but more to the point, they obscure the similarities among these groups, which tend to be more fundamental than the differences. For example, if one compares the Irish Republican Army and other republican paramilitary groups to the Ulster Volunteer Force, the Ulster Defense Association, and various other unionist militias in Northern Ireland, one is struck by the similarities among them, in organization, propaganda, and (sadly) tactics.[9] In some cases, furthermore, groups have fought both for and against the national government at different times, as was the case with various Iraqi Sunni militias. I am therefore unconvinced that there are always analyti-cally meaningful distinctions to be made among militias, paramilitaries, forces led by "warlords," and so on, especially for my purposes here. Another reason I include antigovernment forces in my discussion of militias is that the nor-mative changes I discuss in this chapter empowered armed groups of various descriptions, whether aligned with the government or not. In fact, the most important normative shift in this regard was the legitimization of armed resis-tance to colonial governments, which transformed what had previously been regarded as criminal rebellion into an expression of self-determination that was endorsed by international society.

A second clarification is to acknowledge that, in practice, violent nonstate actors were never as rare as the norms of Westphalian sovereignty would sug-gest. Certainly, armed rebellion has existed in every age. This does not mean, however, that there were not strong norms against rebellion, any more than the occurrence of murder means there is not a strong norm against unlawful killing. Indeed, throughout the Westphalian era, substate violence was both outlawed and stigmatized, and consequences for engaging in it were typically severe. It is worth noting, too, that in this era much nonstate violence occurred in colo-nial settings (in terms of both colonized peoples opposing the government and the government using local armed groups to squelch resistance to its author-ity), whose model of extraterritorial rule does not fit easily into the Westphalian notion of sovereignty. In any case, in the decades since World War II, armed non-state groups have become more numerous and influential, are more frequently supported by foreign governments, and have attained a degree of legitimacy their predecessors did not enjoy.[10]

In this chapter, I argue that these developments were strongly influenced by changes in international norms. I develop this argument in four sections. First, I briefly describe how states in the Westphalian period worked to establish monopolies over the use of force, by both physical coercion and the construction of norms justifying their authority and delegitimizing alternative sources of power. While this process played out internationally in the eighteenth and nineteenth centuries, the suppression of domestic nonstate violence happened earlier in the Westphalian period and was indeed a central element in the process of state-building that was to define sovereignty in the Westphalian system. The result was a normative framework that strongly condemned organized substate violence well into the twentieth century. The second section recounts how this normative framework was challenged in the twentieth century, and especially in the years following World War II, by the principle of national self-determination. This principle, nominally endorsed by the Allied side in both world wars, challenged the long-standing practice of colonialism and empowered nonstate groups representing peoples seeking independence. By implication, this created a crisis of coherence for the norm against nonstate violence, which was vigorously contested by advocates of self-determination. Using the rhetorical strategies I described in chapter 2, national liberation movements (NLMs) and their supporters emphasized not the only the moral justifiability of armed resistance to colonial authorities but also how powerful states in the international system had themselves supported violent nonstate actors in the past, thereby undermining the very norm those states now sought to protect. These efforts led to changes in international law and norms that, in effect, legitimized one specific but important form of nonstate violence: wars of national liberation against colonial rule or foreign occupation. In the third section, I examine the 1974–77 Diplomatic Conference in Geneva, which was intended to update the laws of armed conflict but was nearly derailed by a bitter split between Western and non-Western delegations over the subject of guerrilla warfare. Non-Western states insisted that the international commitment to decolonization logically and morally required that international law embrace the guerrilla tactics typically used by NLMs. Doing so, however, required contesting several long-standing norms that were integral to the underlying structure of existing law. The fourth section examines the broader outcomes of these episodes of contestation. I argue that the changes they produced in the legal and normative landscapes created tensions that were impossible to contain within a narrow legal or historical context and thus "spilled over" to create unintended consequences. These included an impetus toward separatism that now destabilizes many of the states created by decolonization, the proliferation (and normalization) of nonstate military actors on a significant scale, and the ubiquity of the irregular tactics of guerrilla warfare in contemporary international conflict.

Nonstate Violence and the Westphalian Order

As we have seen, Weber's definition of the state—"the form of human community that (successfully) lays claim to the monopoly on legitimate physical violence"—contains both material and ideational components. That is, it envisions a capacity for violence that is real and significant but also a shared sense that that capacity rests in the appropriate hands. It is easy to imagine situations in which neither condition exists or in which the first exists without the second. And indeed, Weber's definition is historically (and to some extent, geographically) bounded; the state as he describes it has existed only in certain places during certain historical eras. In the European context, the critical period of state-building was the sixteenth and seventeenth centuries and had its foundations in the chronic insecurity of European dynasts, who found their realms and personal power threatened by both external and internal forces. At this point, the distinction between legitimate and illegitimate violence was murky. Charles Tilly writes: "Early in the state-making process, many parties shared the right to use violence, the practice of using it routinely to accomplish their own ends, or both at once. The continuum ran from bandits and pirates to kings via tax collectors, regional power holders, and professional soldiers."[11] The nobility comprising this class of "regional power holders," moreover, represented a double-edged sword for monarchs in the defense of their lands from foreign invasion. "Many lords who did not pretend to be kings . . . successfully claimed the right to levy troops and maintain their owned armed retainers. Without calling on some of those lords to bring their armies with them, no king could fight a war; yet the same armed lords constituted the king's rivals and opponents, his enemies' potential allies. For that reason . . . disarming the great stood high on the agenda of every would-be state maker."[12] European governments accomplished this through various means. John Keegan writes that by the end of the eighteenth century, governments had "effectively demilitarized European society" "through a sustained policy of depriving the population of firearms, destroying the castles of the provincial grandees, appropriating their sons as regular officers . . . and monopolizing the production of battlefield weapons in state arsenals."[13]

Nevertheless, the physical crackdown on domestic violence was only part of what cemented the state's authority as *legitimate*. Of course, "legitimacy" in this sense is a relative judgment and does not necessarily imply a government's justice or magnanimity toward its people, much less the people's consent to the arrangement. While a philosophical examination of the just and proper relationship between a government and its citizens is beyond the scope of this project, what is important for our purposes is not a normative judgment but the empirical question of whether state governments are accepted (even if grudgingly and resentfully) as the legitimate political authorities by the bulk of the people living within their territories. For example, while Tilly sees legitimacy as an essential element of state power, he describes early state-makers as "coercive and self-seeking entrepreneurs" and likens the modern state to a criminal protection racket, using its citizens to its own purposes and "protecting" them from threats created in large part by the states themselves.[14] Moreover, he observes, "the distinctions between 'legitimate' and 'illegitimate' users of violence came clear only very slowly, in the process during which the state's armed forces became relatively unified and permanent."[15] This consolidation of power was accomplished not by material coercion alone but also through the construction and reinforcement of a norm (indeed, an entire system of norms) that delegitimized potential rivals, reserving to the state alone the right to wield military force.

One manifestation of this normative structure was the idea of the "divine right of kings" and the exaltation of the monarch him or herself, which made loyalty to the crown a religious as well as political obligation. A 1571 volume of sermons published by the Church of England contained "An Homily against Disobedience and Willful Rebellion" that was read regularly at church services, attendance at which was mandatory.[16] In fire-and-brimstone fashion, the sermon warned the congregants "what an abominable sin against God and man rebellion is, and how dreadfully the wrath of God is kindled and inflamed against all rebels, and what horrible plagues, punishments, and deaths, and finally eternal damnation, doth hang over their heads."[17] Similar messages came through literature and theater; Shakespeare turned frequently to the theme of the dangers of disorder that stem from rebellion, most notably in *Henry IV, Part 1*. In the play, set in 1403, Henry faces an ill-fated rebellion of northern nobles, a plot that scholars say Shakespeare's contemporaries would have recognized as a condemnation of the more recent 1569 northern rebellion against Elizabeth I, who still reigned at the time of the play's publication in 1598.[18] This message was strongly reinforced by criminal justice systems in most states, where taking up arms against the government was typically punished by death, with the sentence sometimes carried out publicly in gruesome and inhumane ways.[19]

The proscription applied to all acts of rebellion, regardless of their scale or the means by which they were pursued. Even if rebels were able to acquire the wherewithal to oppose the government in a way that outwardly resembled war, they were typically viewed as criminals, not combatants, and were entitled to none of the small mercies and acts of moderation that sometimes prevented war from becoming slaughter.[20] Geoffrey Best explains:

> No international jurist before the twentieth century dreamed of extending that regime of moderation into the realm of civil war, because to do so was felt to be a contradiction in terms. Law was something that civilized states existed within their own frontiers and to observe in their own dealings with one another, but not something that subjects in armed revolt against their normal lawgiver could claim the benefit of. . . . The all-important rule [was] that the law of war was international law, that government was government, rebels were traitors, and civilians had to be extra careful if they did not wish to have their status misunderstood.[21]

In terms of substate violence, moreover, no significant distinction was made between territory controlled by a state as a colonial or subordinate possession and the home territory of the state itself. This remained true through the flurry of imperialist expansion in the last decades of the nineteenth century, even as armed resistance to colonial rule became common. In terms of both domestic and international law, what came to be referred to in the metropoles as "imperial policing" remained a purely internal matter, though it more closely resembled fighting a war than subduing a lawless rabble.[22] As late as the beginning of World War II, Robert Jackson writes, "vast regions of Asia, Africa, and Oceania were still part of the domestic jurisdictions of certain Western states which has established formal empires over these areas."[23] For its part, international law reflected and reinforced the delegitimization of substate-actor violence by declining to deal with at all, since it was widely and uncontroversially assumed to belong entirely within the jurisdiction of national courts. In both institutional and legal terms, "war" was something that happened between states, not within them. As Heather Wilson writes, "by the close of the nineteenth century, sovereignty and the exclusive right to wage war were characteristics of a State so strongly established that to suggest otherwise would have seemed preposterous."[24]

Contestation in a Changing Normative Landscape

As I described in chapter 2, the decolonization movement that transformed the international system after World War II was decisively shaped by normative judgments and unsustainable contradictions between colonialism and principled beliefs that were gaining strength at the time. These factors made the international community, including most colonial powers themselves, increasingly willing to reject imperialism and recognize colonized peoples' right to independence. Just as decolonization was driven by the ripple effects of changes in other norms, the implications of decolonization itself proved to be complex and far-reaching. For example, recognizing that colonized peoples were entitled to independence inevitably raised the question of how they were to achieve it and whether they were entitled to pursue it through violent means. While the two issues may have been theoretically distinct, as an empirical matter they were linked from the start, since most of the colonies that gained their independence in the 1940s and 1950s did so through armed resistance. These included former French possessions Vietnam (independent in 1954), Tunisia, and Morocco (both 1956), former British possessions Malaya (1957) and Cyprus (1960), and former Netherlands possession Indonesia (1945). British colony Kenya would formally become independent in 1963, though fighting there had ended in 1956. By far the most influential liberation movement, however, was the Algerian Front de Libération Nationale (FLN), whose 1954–62 war to gain independence from France, in the words of George J. Andreopoulos, "contributed more than any other single event to the legitimation of national liberation movements in their quest for self-determination."[25]

What made the FLN so important was not just its effective mobilization of the Algerian people against French rule but also its engagement of the international community through a savvy diplomatic and public relations strategy. Recognizing that the struggle for self-determination hinged as much on global public opinion as it did local military success, in its first public proclamation in 1954 the FLN identified one of its primary objectives as the "internationalization of the Algerian problem."[26] The goal of the FLN's public diplomacy, in effect, was to gain global acceptance of NLMs by situating the new actors within established categories of international law—in essence, the "framing" strategy discussed in chapter 2. The FLN did this by arguing that it was not in fact merely a rebel movement but rather the representative of a sovereign people exercising its right to self-defense against an occupying force—thus evoking a scenario that was not only clearly covered by the UN Charter but that, less than a decade after World War II, remained salient for many nations, including France itself. The French government nevertheless rejected this claim, insisting that what was going on in Algeria was an entirely internal matter, and dealt with Algerian fighters (and civilians) under some of the more draconian provisions of the French penal code rather than the laws of armed conflict.[27] This stance, coupled with the brutality of French conduct, especially its torture of prisoners, generated opportunities for the FLN to underscore its bona fides as a responsible international actor. To this end, it courted the international media and set up political liaisons in other countries, with special emphasis on UN proceedings, and announced that it would abide by the laws of war, including the Geneva Conventions of 1949, which France itself had ratified a few years earlier.[28] In 1960, the FLN's New York office published a *White Paper on the Application of the Geneva Conventions of 1949 to the French-Algerian Conflict*, a monograph-length legal treatise whose central premises were that the FLN's struggle was an international conflict and that the FLN was a no less serious and accountable entity than the French government.[29] In fact, it claimed the moral high ground, asserting that French dismissal of international law in Algeria violated "humanitarian principles of justice and compassion [that should] govern and determine the treatment of man if *our* civilization is to be worthy of the name"—a stinging rebuke to a country that saw itself as the champion of the rights of man and portrayed its role in Algeria as a *mission civilisatrice*.[30]

By "internationalizing" its struggle, the FLN was skillfully structuring its public relations strategy to have sweeping implications beyond the Algerian case itself. To even take up the issue of decolonization under the UN Charter, member states had to determine that wars of independence fell under the UN's mandate "to maintain international peace and security" and were not "matters which are essentially within the domestic jurisdiction of any state" under article 2(7). This meant treating anticolonial wars as international conflicts rather than civil wars and in turn treating liberation movements as "belligerents" under international law rather than lawless rebels. What was less clear was exactly what legal status these movements should have, since they did not clearly fall under any of the existing categories of "subjects" of international law. How to resolve this ambiguity became a pivotal topic of contestation, with the FLN again reframing the problem to appeal to existing norms. It argued that sovereign state prerogatives were indeed what were at stake in Algeria but that in such a situation the legitimate bearer of those prerogatives was the liberation movement itself, not the colonial metropole seeking to deny it independence. Thus, it argued, the Algerian people should have the same right to use force as other UN member states and that in fighting against their oppressors they were exercising their right to act in self-defense under article 51 of the charter.[31]

The Algerian Revolution proved to be the decisive event in the international community's rejection of colonialism. It was no coincidence that mere days after passing the 1960 Declaration on the Granting of Independence to Colonial Countries and Peoples—widely considered to be a singularly important landmark in decolonization—the UN General Assembly approved Resolution 1573, which recognized "the right of the Algerian people to self-determination and independence" and "the passionate yearning for freedom of all dependent peoples and the decisive role of such peoples in the attainment of their independence."[32]

Nevertheless, the question of whether NLMs' use of military force could thenceforth be presumed to be legitimate remained unsettled. Unsurprisingly, newly independent countries and most others in the developing world, joined by the Soviet Union and other communist states, pushed for the recognition of a general right of armed national liberation. Western states, however, though mostly willing to accept decolonization, were wary of framing the issue so broadly, for at least two reasons. The first was the Cold War. Both the Western and communist blocs saw most independence movements as possible Soviet allies, and the West wished to avoid giving the Soviets legal justification to back "wars of liberation" around the world.[33] More generally, however, they wanted to avoid setting the precedent of recognizing nonstate actors as bearers of rights and responsibilities in international law, especially when it came to using military force. Moreover, Western states objected that the developing states' position would give NLMs the right to use force in circumstances not provided for by the UN Charter, thus actually putting them in a privileged position relative to states.[34] Adlai Stevenson, the American ambassador to the UN, stated categorically in 1961: "Resolution 1514 does not authorize the use of force for its implementation. It does not and it should not and it cannot, under the Charter."[35] Hoping to keep the question of self-determination separate and distinct from the right to use force in pursuit of that end, Western states took an ad hoc approach, supporting specific liberation struggles as they arose but remaining skeptical at best about the wisdom of endorsing them as a general principle. As Seymour Finger, the US representative to the UN Special Committee on Decolonization, explained: "It was not the U.S. view that peoples should be denied the right to resort to any means at their disposal, including violence, if armed suppression by a colonial power required it.... The difficulty lay in giving a general endorsement to the U.N.—an organization dedicated to peace—to such violence.... Such action could hardly be reconciled with the requirements of the Charter."[36] Nevertheless, in practical terms the inherent tension in this position could be avoided going forward only if all imperial powers quickly and willingly relinquished their colonies. Even after Algerian independence in 1962, however, the issue remained alive because of Portugal's intransigence in retaining its colonies, the repression of black populations by white-minority governments in South Africa and Rhodesia (which UN resolutions referred to as "racist regimes" and condemned on the same terms as colonial regimes), and, starting in 1967, Israel's occupation of territories captured in the Six-Day War.[37] These cases were thus to provide both the arena for and the impetus behind the continuing contestation of the norm against nonstate actor violence.

Facilitating this contestation was the fact that this norm was considerably less coherent by the 1960s than it had been decades earlier. Changes in international politics had begun to unsettle the normative framework on which the proscription on nonstate violence was based, making it more vulnerable to challenge. Among these changes were two that nonstate groups and their allies drew on significantly in trying to loosen the state's monopoly on military force and that interacted synergistically in contributing to the ultimate success of those efforts. The first was the victory of the principle of national self-determination itself and the moral and institutional implications that went with it. One obvious implication was the enhancement of the status of nonstate actors. Because decolonization by definition involved the rights of nonstate groups, it was difficult to support decolonization while continuing to treat these groups as invisible to international law. Furthermore, in practice these groups were defined by the very violence Western states sought to remain agnostic about. UN resolutions condemning colonialism typically used the term "peoples" to describe the unit to whom the right of self-determination attached. But who represented a "people"? While the term was not necessarily any more abstract than "states," the abstraction of a state usually at least came along with the more concrete reality of a government that purported to represent it. For non-self-governing peoples, the most relevant available agent was whatever armed group was able to fight the colonial government most effectively. While a people's right to self-determination therefore theoretically existed prior to and independent of an armed conflict to enact it, in practice it was not until a conflict existed that the right became politically salient. As in Algeria, the imperative to decolonize therefore elevated armed groups fighting for independence from rebels (who the colonial power was free to deal with at its discretion) to bearers of rights and responsibilities under international law. Moreover, even if the rejection of colonialism did not entirely place non-self-governing peoples on the same legal footing as existing states, it did place them on comparable—and in some cases stronger—moral footing. This heightened the perceived injustice of the continuing denial of self-determination to these peoples and also opened the door to the use of the same rationales and justifications for action that states themselves commonly appealed to. Here again analogical reasoning proved powerful, for if independence advocates appealed to principles states purported to embrace, it was hard to oppose them without seeming to deny the equal dignity of colonized peoples. This was especially true of the United States, which had won its own independence through armed resistance to a colonial master. An early example of such an appeal came less than a month after the end of World War II, when Ho Chi Minh began his Declaration of Independence of the Democratic Republic of Vietnam by quoting both the US Declaration of Independence and the French Declaration of the Rights of Man and the Citizen.[38] When the United States blocked discussion of the Algerian question at the UN in 1955 on the grounds that it was an internal French matter, an FLN spokesman said Algerians were "at a loss to understand why the United States should identify itself with a policy of colonial repression and bias contrary to American political traditions and interests."[39] Such appeals did not fall on deaf ears. In 1956, President Dwight Eisenhower suggested that continuing support for France would come back to bite the United States, and in July of the following year Sen. John F. Kennedy called on the United States to support Algerian independence.[40] Evoking America's own revolution, Kennedy argued that US support for French policy in Algeria

> is not a record to view with pride as Independence Day approaches. No matter how complex the problems posed by the Algerian issue may be, the record of the United States in this case is, as elsewhere, a retreat from the principles of independence and anti-colonialism, regardless of what diplomatic niceties, legal technicalities, or even strategic considerations are offered in its defense.... The United States must be prepared to lend all efforts to such a settlement, and to assist in the economic problems which will flow from it. This is not a burden which we lightly or gladly assume. But our efforts in no other endeavor are more important in terms of once again seizing the initiative in foreign affairs, demonstrating our adherence to the principles of national independence and winning the respect of those long suspicious of our negative and vacillating record on colonial issues.[41]

Algeria, Kennedy insisted, "is no longer a problem for the French alone—nor will it ever be again." After Kennedy's speech the United States stopped supporting France in UN votes on the Algerian matter, choosing instead to abstain.[42]

Framing their own plight as analogous to the experiences of Western states also allowed NLMs and their allies to call attention to a second source of pressure on the state monopoly on violence, which was that as an empirical matter the use of force by nonstate groups had been growing increasingly common for decades—often with the backing of the great powers themselves. Moreover, these precedents were important in more than one respect, since the circumstances in which they typically occurred were not unlike those facing colonized peoples: resistance to foreign occupation. A seminal event in this long-term trend was the emergence of armed groups of Spanish citizens fighting against French occupiers during the Peninsular War of 1808–14. These *guerrilleros* provided both a model for other resistance groups and a name—guerrilla warfare—for the tactics they employed. Similar groups played significant roles in the American Civil War and the Franco-Prussian War of 1870–71, the latter, according to Martin van Creveld, marking the first time residents of a territory annexed by force (Alsace-Lorraine) formally objected to the outcome.[43] Soon thereafter, the rights of citizens in occupied territories was an important agenda item at an 1874 conference in Brussels intended to produce a statement codifying the laws and customs of war—one of the first such conferences ever held. Until that time, international law and norms regarding belligerent occupation were consistent with the domestic prohibition of nonstate violence, with the occupying state more or less stepping into the shoes of the displaced government in terms of its authority over the territory's citizens.[44] Both the Union Army of the American Civil War and the Prussian army, for example, had followed customary practice in punishing nonuniformed fighters severely, often by execution.[45] The Brussels conference and the declaration it produced, however, reflected a shift in thinking caused largely by admiration in many quarters for the French *francs-tireurs* who had taken up arms against Prussia. While the Brussels Declaration did not overturn the general duty of obedience of citizens in territory already occupied by an invader, it recognized as legitimate combatants "militia and volunteer corps" and "the population of a territory which has not been occupied, who, on the approach of the enemy, spontaneously take up arms to resist the invading troops."[46] Although the declaration never came into force, it served as the model for the Hague Convention of 1907, which contained nearly identical provisions. At The Hague, some states wanted to go further by explicitly articulating a right of armed resistance to military occupation, with the British delegate introducing an article recognizing "the right which belongs to the population of an invaded country to patriotically oppose the most energetic resistance to the invaders by every legitimate means."[47] Other states, including Germany, strongly opposed this principle, and consensus on the matter was never reached, but the debate over the right of resistance signaled movement toward accepting the use of force by nonstate actors, even if only under narrowly defined circumstances. It is worth noting, of course, that recognition of the rights of occupied populations started to emerge once European populations found themselves in this predicament. Only then did European states, which remained disproportionately influential in the making of international law and norms, start to take the problem seriously. Moreover, there was little indication that these states viewed the topic as in any way applicable to their own colonial possessions, where they continued to put down resistance with sometimes shocking levels of violence.

In World War I, this increasing openness to nonstate actor violence on behalf of occupied populations happened to fit well with the strategic interests of the Allied Powers, who supported several such groups fighting against the Central Powers. Perhaps the most notable case was British support of the Arab Revolt against Ottoman rule in the Middle East, which proved in some senses a precursor to the post-1945 wars of national liberation, leading eventually to the creation of several new independent states—though, to be sure, Britain in no way intended the revolt to serve as a model or inspiration for universal decolonization, especially of its own possessions. Another case with murky implications for sovereignty was that of nationalists in Poland, which had not existed as a sovereign state since its partition in the late eighteenth century. While the Allies initially deemed Polish demands for independence to be an internal matter for its ally Russia, once Russia left the war in 1917 Allied governments recognized an autonomous Polish army under the authority of a Polish National Committee. In doing so, they formally accepted as a cobelligerent party an entity that was not yet a state and would not be recognized as one until November 1918.[48]

By far the most significant event in terms of setting a precedent for nonstate actor violence, however, was World War II. For the Allies, the central strategic task was the liberation of vast areas occupied by its enemies in Europe, Asia, and the Pacific, a task in which cooperation with indigenous resistance units would prove indispensable. Indeed, in almost every occupied area, irregular resistance forces played an important role and in some cases a decisive one. A century earlier these forces would have been seen as categorically illegitimate, yet by 1941 they constituted an important part of the Allied war effort. In certain cases it was possible to claim that resistance groups were not nonstate actors but rather the forces of the legitimate government in exile, but others clearly could make no such claim, and some were substate factions whose empowerment would inevitably lead to state instability in the future.[49] In any case, in rejecting the old norm of obedience to occupation, wartime resistance movements supplied a moral as well as a practical precedent for the decolonization movement. Indeed, some NLM forces were the very same groups that had fought against the Axis in World War II, including the Viet Minh, which would oust the French from Vietnam in 1954, and the National Organization of Cypriot Fighters (EOKA), which would lead Cyprus to independence in 1960. These and other NLMs claimed that their circumstances mirrored those facing the Western powers and their allies in the war: occupied by a foreign power, with their principles and very existence threatened.[50] By making the analogy explicit, NLMs framed the decolonization struggle in a familiar and compelling moral context that Western observers could not easily dismiss. Indeed, it was difficult to attack the analogy without falling back on the paternalism and racism that were becoming increasingly indefensible. References to World War II were thus common in NLMs' public statements. EOKA addressed its 1955 manifesto to "Diplomats of the World," urging them to apply the principles they purported to believe in to the Cypriot cause: "Look to your duty. It is shameful that, in the twentieth century, people should have to shed blood for freedom, that divine gift for which we too fought at your side and for which you, at least, claim that you fought against Nazism."[51] The quandary some Western governments faced is illustrated by a 1959 exchange between President Charles de Gaulle, who had famously led the French resistance against the Nazis in World War II, and one of his ministers, who had been approached about talks with FLN leaders. De Gaulle objected: "I don't want it; because the day after you've seen them they will say that I have recognized the FLN government. . . . Who are they, who nominated them?" His minister replied, "In 1940 people were asking exactly the same about you."[52]

These efforts at contesting the norm against nonstate violence produced resounding successes for decolonization. The 1960s witnessed a series of General Assembly resolutions endorsing resistance to Portugal's efforts to keep its colonies and the repression of black populations by white minority governments in South Africa and Rhodesia.[53] Although the General Assembly remained at the forefront of this movement, it was not only among developing states that resistance movements found support. In 1965, Britain called for intervention against the "illegal" white-minority government in Rhodesia and the following year joined with the United States in voting for a Security Council resolution reaffirming the right of Southern Rhodesians to independence and recognizing "the legitimacy of their struggle to secure the enjoyment of their rights."[54] Similarly, in 1972, the United States, Britain, and France declined to veto a Security Council resolution affirming "the legitimacy of [the] struggle" against Portuguese authority in Angola, Mozambique, and Guinea-Bissau.[55] Throughout this period, nevertheless, Western states hewed to their ad hoc approach. They resisted calls to recognize that liberation movements had a general legal right to resort to arms or a right of self-defense under the charter, since those rights, they argued, applied only to states.[56] A compromise of sorts was evident in a series of resolutions from 1965 to 1970 that "recognize[d] the legitimacy of the struggle by the peoples under colonial rule to exercise their right to self-determination and independence" but refrained from using the word "armed" to describe that struggle.[57] Heather Wilson notes that Western states further tried to walk the fine line their stance required by in some cases recognizing governments formed by liberation movements "prematurely"—that is, before they had effective control over territory or possessed other empirical attributes of states.[58] This allowed the West to evade the question of whether nonstate actors could justifiably use force, by saying that the groups using force in fact represented states already. In any event, while the vast majority of developing states made it abundantly clear that they interpreted "struggle" to mean *armed* struggle, Western states expressed support for armed liberation movements while backing away from endorsing the legitimacy of nonstate violence per se.

The National Liberation Struggle: From Ends to Means

By the late 1960s and early 1970s, therefore, a consensus (if only a tacit one) was growing that NLMs could legitimately use force to attain their goals. As profound a shift as this was in norms governing *who* could fight wars, in theory it did not in itself entail any changes to norms governing *how* wars could be fought. In practice, however, accepting a different kind of belligerent meant accepting a different kind of war. Because NLMs typically fought against forces with greater military resources, most adopted some version of guerrilla warfare, which emphasizes furtive strikes against enemy weaknesses rather than conventional battle and remaining hidden from the enemy between operations. Although the classic guerrilla model envisioned fighters exploiting a rural landscape they knew well, by the mid-twentieth century guerrilla tactics were increasingly adapted to urban settings. Guerrillas therefore sought to blend in amid the civilian population, effectively hiding in plain sight, unknown to the enemy even when they may have been entirely visible to them. This practice had, at best, an ambiguous relationship to the existing law of war, often referred to as international humanitarian law (IHL), which required troops to distinguish themselves from civilians—traditionally through the wearing of uniforms. It was obvious that a greatly inferior force would place itself at a significant disadvantage if it fought by those rules, but it was equally obvious that allowing guerrillas to blend in amid the population undermined the principle of distinction and had problematic implications for civilian immunity.

Even before the issue of NLMs' rights to use force had been settled, they and their supporters began pressing for a formal international endorsement of guerrilla warfare. At a 1968 UN human rights conference in Tehran, developing countries urged that NLM fighters be granted combatant status under the 1949 Geneva Conventions even though, as we shall see, it was doubtful they met their criteria. The following year, the legal status of "freedom fighters" arose as a prominent topic at a meeting of the International Committee of the Red Cross (ICRC), the international nongovernmental organization primarily concerned with IHL. This prompted the ICRC to convene two "conferences of government experts" in 1971 and 1972 to seek states' input on whether existing IHL was adequate to deal with the changing nature of war.[59] This in turn set the stage for the Diplomatic Conference that began in Geneva in January of 1974, which set out to update the 1949 Geneva Conventions to reflect developments in warfare since that time.[60] What happened at that conference provides valuable insight into the normative landscape prevailing at the time and the strategies of contestation employed by various actors with a stake in the outcome on the guerrilla question.

While the Diplomatic Conference was nominally intended to reaffirm and revise the Geneva Conventions of 1949, it in fact had the much more ambitious goal of thoroughly updating the entire body of IHL. Despite this expansive breadth, it was the few provisions relating to guerrilla warfare that proved to be by far the most contentious and time-consuming items on the agenda. Originally envisioned as a single five-week session, the conference took a total of thirty-five weeks over four years to produce its final products, and much of that time was spent in politically charged debates over the guerrilla question. As with the issue of the right of NLMs to use force, the fundamental division was between the Western powers and newly independent developing states, the latter backed by the communist bloc. Yoram Dinstein notes that the conference reflected "the then-prevailing zeitgeist: the confrontational mentality of the Cold War; the defiance of the West by a suddenly assertive and temporarily unified 'Third World'; the tendencies on the part of an entrenched majority in international organizations and forums to show no tolerance for the dissenting voices of a large and dissenting minority; and the cynical sacrifice of good sense (and good law) on the altar of political expediency."[61] Indeed, as British historian Geoffrey Best writes, the opening of the conference "happened to come at just about the climax of a sustained crescendo of liberationist agitation by the Third World and its First and Second World sympathizers [which was] essential to understanding what happened" there.[62]

One way in which the division among states was manifested was the degree to which their delegates viewed the conference as a political forum, as opposed to a more technical legal exercise. Most Western delegates were experts in international law who, while doubtless aware of the political stakes, approached the proceedings with a technocratic legalism.[63] Non-Western delegates, by contrast, took a more overtly political stance, seeing the conference not only as a means of ensuring that IHL did not neglect their interests but also as a venue for expressing grievances and demanding major change—treating it, in effect, as picking up where the General Assembly left off.[64] Of course, this mirrored the anti-Westernism prevalent at the time, but the hostility toward legalism also reflected a more specific theme in "the revolt against the West," which was the belief that international law itself was not a fair and neutral expression of lofty principles but rather a tool colonizers had used to exercise control and through which Western states were still trying to maintain their hegemony.[65] The Geneva Conventions themselves, as the Nigerian delegate reminded the conference, were "a product of European experience and history," which almost half the countries represented in 1974 had no role in creating.[66] Non-Western representatives, some of whom lacked legal training altogether, thus often proved impatient with Western insistence on purportedly apolitical principles of legal construction, while Western delegates were frustrated by the overtly political positions and fiery rhetoric of their counterparts.[67] One observer noted that the 1974 session "seemed to consist of two sets of delegations, which did not fully understand what the other side was talking about."[68]

Even before the discussion of substantive provisions began, the guerrilla issue arose in the form of disputes over whether NLMs would be permitted to send representatives to the conference. Western states opposed the idea, staking out the conventional Westphalian position that international law was, in essence, *interstate* law, and nonstate actors were neither parties to that law nor appropriate participants in defining and revising it. One problem with this argument, however, was that it ran contrary to the spirit—and the logic—of over a decade's worth of resolutions and other public statements in which the international community had endorsed the independence struggles of colonized peoples. The Sudanese delegate reminded the conference that "the United Nations had long since acknowledged such movements, and those who were trying to drown the issue in legal sophistry should remember that the representatives of the liberation movements could bring living experience of the sufferings which the Conference was trying to alleviate. The Conference could not claim to develop humanitarian law while refusing to acknowledge the right to self-determination."[69] A second problem facing the Western states was a practical one: the numbers at the conference were stacked against them, so if the question came to a vote they would lose badly. They therefore accepted the presence of NLMs without forcing a vote, which allowed over a dozen NLMs to participate at the conference, albeit in a nonvoting capacity.[70] There was a further logical implication of the participation of NLMs in Geneva, moreover, which was that the wars they were fighting should properly be considered international conflicts, rather than internal rebellions or civil wars.[71] This point was central to one of the key non-Western demands: that IHL should provide those fighting for self-determination with the same legal protections as soldiers in national armies, the most fundamental of which was, if captured, being treated as prisoners of war (POWs) instead of being charged (and possibly executed) as unprivileged combatants. Here again, Western states were in a bind: after a decade's worth of UN resolutions endorsing the premise that liberation struggles were indeed "international" conflicts, it was impossible to now deny that proposition. Moreover, the legal status of guerrilla fighters in NLMs simply meant less to the Western bloc than it did to other states, many of whom made it clear they were willing to scuttle the entire conference over the issue.[72] The Western states thus felt compelled to agree to language in article 1(4) of the first of the two additional protocols the conference produced specifying that the protocol was to apply to all international armed conflicts, including those "in which peoples are fighting against colonial domination and alien occupation and against racist régimes in the exercise of their right of self-determination, as enshrined in the Charter of the United Nations and the Declaration on Principles of International Law concerning Friendly Relations and Co-operation among States in accordance with the Charter of the United Nations."[73] This provision, along with the presence of NLM representatives in Geneva, was a clear sign of the salience of the guerrilla issue, but it also showed that for all intents and purposes the struggle over the legitimacy of NLMs' use of force was over—and that the NLMs had won, as Western states effectively consented to the proposition they had tried so cagily to evade.[74]

But, of course, legal fictions aside, the guerrillas fighting for self-determination were not soldiers in national armies, nor did they look or act like them. This meant that for article 1(4) to be taken seriously, the new rules had to make room for combatants who fought in unconventional ways. This represented a dramatic departure for IHL, which developed around the conventional model of direct combat between uniformed armies. Unsurprisingly, this caused considerable apprehension among traditional military powers such as the United States and Britain. Nevertheless, by 1974 the norm of uniformed combatancy was becoming increasingly anachronistic. Again, Western military powers had themselves contributed to its decline, and again the crucial precedent in this regard was Allied support for partisan and resistance groups in World War II. Moreover, the 1949 Geneva Conventions had recognized the World War II precedent by taking a step in this direction, recognizing "members of other militias and . . . other volunteer corps, including those of organized resistance movements," provided that they met certain conditions, including "carrying arms openly," "having a fixed distinctive sign recognizable at a distance," and "conducting their operations in accordance with the laws and customs of war."[75] The point of the 1949 provisions, of course, was to address the humanitarian challenges posed by fighters who were hard to distinguish from civilians. Still, they did this by requiring irregular fighters to take steps to make themselves identifiable as combatants rather than accepting the guerrilla's penchant for blending in with the civilian population as legally or morally permissible. There was fierce disagreement at the 1974 conference, however, about what it would take to accommodate what NLMs and their supporters called "freedom fighters" and exactly how far they should be allowed to depart from the traditional conventions of war. One bloc of Western states, including the United States, Britain, and Israel, argued that the 1949 provisions should be applied, insisting that the safety of the civilian population depended on "irregular" fighters clearly distinguishing themselves from civilians at all times. Others, led by the non-Western bloc, demanded more latitude for guerrillas, pointing to the realities of the situation facing NLM fighters. Poorly equipped and with a fraction of the resources of their enemies, if they were to remain identifiable as combatants even when they were not fighting, they would have no chance whatsoever. It was this type of asymmetry, after all, that gave rise to guerrilla tactics in the first place. As the Soviet delegate observed, "it is of the essence of guerrilla operations . . . that the *guerrillero* merges into the anonymity of the civilian population before and after his hostile act."[76] The delegate from North Vietnam expressed it more dramatically: "All the world knows that in guerrilla warfare a combatant must operate under the cover of night in order not to be a target for the modern weapons of the adversary. In such circumstances, does the spirit of humanity compel them to wear emblems or uniforms in order to 'distinguish themselves from the civilian population' in military operations? To do so would expose the combatant to the infernal fire-power of the imperialist aggressors who monopolize modern weapon techniques, and to sacrifice man to the war machine. It would be the opposite of humanity."[77]

So, the non-Western nations maintained that for NLM fighters to be fairly treated under IHL, they would have to be permitted to remain indistinguishable from the civilian population much of the time. Moreover, they pressed this controversial argument a step further by insisting that this prerogative should apply only to those fighting "against colonial domination and alien occupation and against racist regimes in the exercise of their right of self-determination."[78] Any other combatants—including not just soldiers in national militaries but also guerrillas fighting for any cause other than national liberation—would be expected to remain clearly identifiable as described in the 1949 Geneva Conventions. Their justification for this differentiated application of the rules was twofold. First, they argued, allowing NLM fighters to use guerrilla tactics to level the odds against regular armies would not work if regular armies were also allowed to use them.[79] Second, as noted earlier, governments in newly independent states feared that they themselves might eventually face armed resistance from insurgent or separatist groups (indeed, some already had) and wanted to deny those forces the privileges—and tactical advantages—they sought for NLMs.[80]

In trying to relax the rules as they applied to NLM fighters, and *only* NLM fighters, non-Western delegations employed the contestation strategies discussed in chapter 2. First, they frequently evoked events they saw as setting relevant precedents for their position, drawing on analogical reasoning to frame the situation faced by NLMs in favorable ways and to graft new normative interpretations onto existing or emerging ones. Second, they appealed to consequentialist moral logic—sometimes directly, sometimes indirectly—in ways that were revealing for what they suggested about how the terms of normative discourse in the international system were shifting.

In terms of relevant precedents for granting broad prerogatives to freedom fighters, World War II once again loomed large. Drawing parallels to this event allowed the non-Western bloc to frame the issue of guerrilla warfare, in both its jus ad bellum and jus in bello components, in terms the Western states could not help but take seriously. In the politically charged speech that opened the conference, the president of Mauritania told delegates that "when a nation was driven to the wall, it could not forget its right to self-determination. In Europe, during the Second World War, millions of resistance fighters had shed their blood to protect their freedom. Their memories made for a better understanding of the tragic situation of oppressed peoples who could not tolerate the indifference of mankind."[81] Of course, this line of argument gained considerable leverage from the fact that most of the precedents being cited were set by Western states themselves or by groups they had supported. While some of those groups had followed the convention of distinguishing themselves from civilians, many more had not—a fact that NLMs and their supporters argued demonstrated both guerrilla warfare's effectiveness and its legitimacy.[82] To this extent, the 1949 Geneva rules for "resistance movements" never accurately reflected how such movements had operated during the war, and even some Western states agreed it was unreasonable to expect NLM fighters to follow them.[83] In fact, France and Norway, both of which had been occupied by the Nazis, supported a relaxation of conventional standards for guerrillas. The French delegate remarked that countries that had experienced occupation "had placed the ashes of those underground fighters in their Pantheons" and noted that "nothing distinguished them, and nothing must distinguish them, from the civilian population."[84]

The consequentialist strand of the non-Western position at Geneva was most clearly apparent in the argument that the new treaty needed to provide freedom fighters with a good chance of actually winning the wars they were fighting. For as long as IHL had existed, it had contained provisions requiring combatants to distinguish themselves from civilians out of concern for civilians' safety. But if NLM fighters had to fight that way, they would lose. The rapporteur for the committee considering the matter noted the need to carve out an exception for situations "in which a guerrilla fighter could not distinguish himself [from civilians] throughout his military operations *and still retain any chance of success.*"[85] Michael Gross refers to this as the "fighting chance" argument and notes that what made it compelling in this case was that it was "integral to the idea of just cause. It makes little sense to acknowledge one group's right to fight oppression . . . and then use the law of armed conflict to deny [it] the means to do so."[86] But, of course, the effectiveness of the argument depends entirely on the importance of the cause being fought for. In this case, as we have seen, it was a principle almost all states had publicly embraced and that dozens of states saw as central to their very existence. The Nigerian delegate argued that to hold NLM fighters to the 1949 standard "would defeat the very purpose for which peoples took up arms in defense of the freedom which was the birth-right of every human being. To deny that reality was to undermine the progressive development of international humanitarian law . . . and the many resolutions of the United Nations General Assembly which had pronounced on the legitimacy of the armed struggles of national liberation movements."[87] Here again, the contestation of one norm was shaped by the earlier contestation of another. In fact, the "fighting chance" argument was a way of grafting a new jus in bello norm of permissive guerrilla warfare onto the recently established jus ad bellum norm of national liberation. If the international commitment to self-determination was to mean anything, the argument went, IHL had to change.

The analogy to World War II once more proved useful, as it supported the consequentialist case NLM supporters were making. For the West, the war had been seen as a struggle too important to lose—and this judgment had justified the bending of many long-standing rules and the complete obliteration of others. Georges Abi-Saab, Egypt's delegate to the Diplomatic Conference and perhaps the most influential proponent of the non-Western position at Geneva, argued that "the material situation [of a colonized people] would be identical to that of a State whose territory is wholly occupied, like most of the European countries during the Second World War, and where *the only possible internal resistance* to the occupant is through guerrilla operations."[88] If the goal of liberating Europe from the Nazis justified guerrilla warfare (among other measures), then it would be hypocritical to deny those seeking to liberate colonized peoples access to the same means. Indeed, Abi-Saab added, "against this background one can ponder over the irony of history that led the very States which championed this development to initiate attacks against the amendments and to question the 'motivations' of their sponsors."[89] Again, what made such reasoning effective were the stakes involved. It would not do for Western powers to cite extenuating circumstances as excusing their own behavior when what colonial peoples now faced was, in the words of one delegate, "a struggle in line with the one waged in the Second World War by many peoples of the world [against] . . . the menace of Hitler."[90]

In opposing the loosening of restrictions on NLM fighters, Western states appealed to two principles long seen as fundamental pillars of IHL. The first was that the safety of the civilian population should be a paramount concern. The United States delegate asserted that "if we are to give meaning to the protected status that we have conferred on civilians, it is vital that Protocol I deny a privileged status to combatants who violate the requirements that they must in some manner distinguish themselves from civilians."[91] The precedent of World War II cast a long shadow over this argument, however. In that conflict, not only had these states and their allies used the same tactics that they were now opposing, but also some of them had wrought large-scale carnage upon civilian populations, including the systematic destruction of cities by aerial bombing. In light of those actions, Western pleas on behalf of civilians seemed hypocritical and even incoherent. Geoffrey Best, writing in 1984, decried the

> self-serving . . . moral superiority implicitly claimed by governments and their armies, as if their own use of force for the alleged good of the

people placed in their charge were above criticism. Nasty truths about the actual performance of most governments and their armies were well enough known in most parts of the world before their moral bluff was called by the Second World War's display of the atrocious propensities of certain supposedly exemplary armed forces. No one in even the most "advanced" countries of the world could henceforth allege that guerrillas and rebels had a monopoly of atrocity.[92]

Of course, non-Western delegations were also eager to point to more recent events in questioning the sincerity of the Western commitment to civilians' safety. The Syrian and Palestine Liberation Organization (PLO) representatives accused Israel of bombing villages and refugee camps, and North Vietnam's delegate reminded the assembly of the massacre of Vietnamese civilians by American troops at My Lai in 1968.[93]

Some non-Western representatives responded to concerns about dangers to civilians by criticizing the distinction between fighters and civilians as it applied to "people's wars," in which fighters were the vanguard of the people themselves.[94] For the most part, however, the non-Western bloc did not directly contest the norm of civilian immunity, nor did it need to. In fact, some delegates argued that on balance, the guerrilla warfare provisions of Protocol I made civilians safer than before, since they would induce compliance by guerrilla forces, who, they pointed out, were still required to distinguish themselves from the civilian population while they are actually "engaged in an attack or in a military preparatory to an attack."[95] Given the narrow interpretation non-Western states gave to this phrase, the claim was specious, though in technical legal terms it was plausible.[96] More important to the outcome of the conference, however, was that the Western powers, by virtue of their own indifference to civilian victimization at other times, were seen as lacking the credibility to push the issue in Geneva.

The second principle to which Western states appealed in resisting the creation of rules specifically for NLM fighters was the customary separation of the jus in bello from the jus ad bellum. In other words, the cause for which a belligerent fought, however worthy, should not give it any special privilege in terms of *how* it fought or which rules applied to it. A closely related principle was that the same rules should apply to both sides in a conflict. The significance of these principles, they argued, extended beyond the issues of guerrilla warfare and national self-determination to the foundational structure of IHL itself. The separation of judgments about a war's cause from rules about its conduct had been articulated by Hugo Grotius in the seventeenth century and was one of the major advances of IHL over the medieval "just war" approach, which assigned the highest priority to the triumph of those fighting on the side of justice (in practical terms, the side given the imprimatur of the Catholic Church) and thereby justified all manner of atrocity in the service of a purportedly greater good.[97] The agnostic stance of IHL toward belligerents' war aims allowed it to focus on the humanitarian goal of reducing human suffering and (in theory anyway) kept its application from being hijacked by messy and indeterminate arguments about whose cause was just and whose was unjust. This was one reason Western delegates generally approached the conference from a more technical legal perspective and disapproved of the overtly political stance their non-Western and socialist counterparts adopted. The French delegate noted that

> the United Nations and the ICRC pursued their activities on entirely different levels. The United Nations was the political body whose role was to find political solutions to specific problems of the moment, whereas humanitarian law must provide protection for all war victims at all times and not be subordinated to subjective considerations of any sort. Consideration of elements such as motivation, justice and legitimacy, which it was quite normal to discuss in the United Nations, would be fatal in an assembly held under the auspices of the ICRC. Humanitarian law must remain free of the notion of political motivation or subjective judgment.[98]

Similarly, the British delegate argued that "legal and humanitarian protection should never vary according to the motives of those engaged in a particular struggle. Deviation from that principle would mean damaging the structure of the Hague and Geneva Conventions and would involve the need to reconstruct the whole of humanitarian law."[99] Even those Western states willing to accept more permissive rules for guerrilla forces balked at the idea of allowing them for one side in a conflict and not the other.[100]

The rift between the Western and non-Western blocs over differentiated rules reflected a shifting dynamic in international norms whose implications went beyond the status of guerrillas or indeed any issue addressed in Geneva. In chapter 2, I discussed the ascendance of consequentialist normative reasoning in the decades after World War II and how this created pressure on norms grounded in deontological (rule-based) judgments. An aspect of this, I noted, was skepticism that purportedly "neutral" rules and institutions in fact yielded results that were fair to all parties and the increasing willingness to apply different rules to different actors—a phenomenon I referred to as "normative asymmetry." This was justified because it produced more equitable outcomes but also in some cases because it helped to compensate for unjust treatment in the past. This was exactly the debate that played out at the Diplomatic Conference. The Western states appealed to the traditional structure of IHL, which emphasized deontological rules and the equal application of the rules to all parties, regardless of their cause or the resources at their disposal. Non-Western states, on the other hand, took the paradoxical position that providing equal protection for NLM fighters required different rules and that whatever rules emerged should be geared toward ensuring the success of decolonization.[101]

Several strands of thought converged in this debate, often becoming intertwined and conflated in delegates' statements. First, the rhetoric in Geneva clearly conveyed the prioritized status of the norm of self-determination and the international community's commitment to its success. This allowed for direct appeals to consequentialism in the form of reminders of the justness and significance of the cause of decolonization. Second, speakers frequently mentioned the material disadvantages faced by NLMs compared to their enemies, which it was argued gave them "no choice but to carry on a 'poor man's war,' by resorting to nonconventional or guerrilla warfare, which calls on man's ingenuity and cunning to beat the machine and compensate for material inferiority."[102] Given this reality, therefore, if the new protocol was to have any practical effect, it would have to meet the guerrillas where they were, by legitimizing how they fought rather than holding them to a stricter standard.[103] A third strand was skepticism of principles rooted in Western culture and experience. This was both an ideational and a political manifestation of the revolt against the West and manifested itself in Geneva as a rejection of deontological judgments in favor of a more consequentialist ethics animated by an ethos of redressing grievances. Finally, non-Western rhetoric reflected the deprioritization of the jus in bello regime relative to the jus ad bellum restrictions in the UN Charter—one of the two macronormative changes discussed in chapter 2. Simply put, struggling against "aggression" such as that committed by colonial powers was more important than regulating the conduct of those engaged in that struggle. The World War II experience that informed this judgment also undermined a major deontological premise undergirding traditional IHL—that opposing combatants should be treated as moral equals regardless of the cause they were fighting for. Given the odious ideologies that had driven the war, the premise of moral equivalence was difficult to reconcile with post-1945 sensibilities. The Romanian delegate thus expressed a common sentiment when he argued that in light of "the right of peoples resisting aggression in the exercise of their right to self-determination . . . humanitarian law must distinguish between the aggressor and the victim of aggression and must guarantee greater protection for the victim in the exercise of his sacred right of self-defense."[104]

An example of how these strands of thought came together is this statement by the North Vietnamese delegate, which touches on almost all of them:

> We understand that the condition of "visibility" . . . is justified in the war
> situations envisaged in The Hague Regulations of 1907 and the third

Geneva Convention of 1949, which have three essential characteristics: first, the two parties at war are industrialized countries of Europe at about the same level of economic and military development; second, these countries can retaliate on the enemy's territory: third, in the case of conventional war, the activities of armies such as militias or volunteer corps . . . are completely distinct from the life of the civilian population. These three characteristics of war situations which we would call conventional, are intrinsically linked together and determine among other things the rationality of the condition of visibility in question in paragraph 1 (b) of article 42 of the ICRC draft Protocol. But, at the present time, especially since the adoption of the 1949 Conventions, in the neo-colonial wars of the imperialist aggressors against the poor and ill-armed people of parts of Asia, Africa and Latin America who are fighting for their right to self-determination, other characteristics appear. International humanitarian law additional to the Geneva Conventions of 1949 should be conscious that the question concerns combatants of the ill-armed and aggressed party who must use all their bravery and intelligence in the place of weapons in order at least to escape or to defend themselves, or to hold in check the fire-power of the adversary equipped with the most modern and most cruel means of combat, and who, in addition, does not fear the law of retaliation against his own territory and his own civilian population. In these new unequal war situations, to demand similar conditions to those of equal war situations of which we spoke earlier, would manifestly result in injustice in the case of ill-armed and weak peoples who are attacked on their own territory.[105]

Although the non-Western position on differentiated obligations under IHL drew much of its power from weaving these strands around the cause of decolonization, the other elements of the argument were influential enough to give the idea life beyond that specific context. This reflected an increasingly progressive interpretation of international law based on a conception of "fairness" that focused on outcomes rather than processes and sought to protect or empower traditionally marginalized parties. This was evident not only among the non-Western bloc but also in the ICRC itself, whose official commentaries on Protocol I appeared to support the idea that one purpose of IHL is to "level the playing field" between belligerents of unequal military capabilities. The ICRC thus endorsed not only the "right to a fighting chance" but also the even more ambitious view that "in order to remain objective and credible, humanitarian law *must allow every party an equal chance* in combat."[106] Moreover, although Protocol I specified that all parties were required to comply with the laws of war, the ICRC (and many non-Western parties) envisioned that this could mean something different to the guerrilla than it did to his enemy: "It would be misguided to expect equality where inequality exists, and it is neither unreasonable nor unjust to postulate compliance with the rules in a less extensive and detailed manner when they are imposed upon guerrilla combatants than when they are imposed upon the so-called regular army."[107] In other words, the ICRC envisioned not just applying more permissive rules to NLM fighters than to their enemies but also giving them more leeway in following those rules.

This normative asymmetry—and indeed the entire idea that IHL should be an essentially redistributive enterprise—was a dramatic departure from the conventional understanding of international law. The idea was illustrated in a particularly striking way by two positions staked out by non-Western states at Geneva. One was the proposal by the delegate from Togo that in any war between a belligerent with an air force and a belligerent without an air force, the side with the air force should be forbidden to use it.[108] The other was the argument made by North Vietnam and China, among others, that soldiers fighting *against* NLMs could be denied POW status and tried as war criminals by virtue of their participation in a war of aggression.[109] Though both positions were a step beyond where even some non-Western delegates were willing to go, they reflected how significantly the terms of international normative discourse were changing. Certainly, the long-standing consensus regarding the neutrality and symmetrical application of IHL could no longer be assumed.

The non-Western nations' vigorous contestation of preexisting norms put the Western powers in a difficult spot. To be sure, the Diplomatic Conference was not a debating tournament; it was unlikely that many delegates, if any, could have been persuaded by canny rhetoric to change their position on these issues. Among other things, the simple fact that Western states were outnumbered was important.[110] As I have mentioned, the guerrilla issue was a much higher priority to the non-Western bloc than it was to the Western powers, and of course to the NLMs themselves it was paramount. What happened in Geneva reflected more than simply interest-driven geopolitics, however. For the non-Western states, the guerrilla issue was imbued with the spirit of the larger struggle from which they had emerged and that dominated their approach to foreign relations. As one author observed, the failure to adequately protect the interests of NLMs "would be a signal to the Third World nations that this Diplomatic Conference was to be another instance of an attempt by the developed nations to impose their wills on the underdeveloped and new nations and to maintain the colonial tradition."[111] Furthermore, the Western states were committed to getting a deal done in Geneva. Although the NLM and guerrilla provisions took the most time and got the most attention, they were only one element of a large project that on other subjects arguably constituted a significant advance for IHL. Simply going forward without non-Western support was not an option, since one goal of the conference was to get the newer states (which had not participated in the 1949 conference, much less the Hague conferences of 1899 and 1907) to buy into the IHL regime.[112]

Western states also had to consider the propaganda implications of allowing the conference to fail, and in this regard the cogency of the non-Western arguments did indeed matter. The more skillfully small states were able to portray themselves as champions of progressive principles, the worse it would look for powerful states to walk away from the table. This was especially true of the principle of national self-determination itself, since by 1974 few states wished to be seen as impeding decolonization. Suter notes that pressing the NLM issue would be "useful as a propaganda weapon against those governments which were still opposing liberation movements by the time that the Diplomatic Conference eventually adopted Protocol I. Those governments were hardly likely to ratify Protocol I . . . and this non-ratification would be used as yet another proof of how 'evil' they were."[113] What proved crucial was how the non-Western states were able to tightly link the right of self-determination with the narrower (and, to Western states, more troublesome) question of how much latitude guerrillas should be allowed in concealing their combatant status. When Western states tried to draw a bright line between the question of ends and the question of means, they found themselves outflanked by consequentialist and analogical arguments. In effect, they were victims of the "norm entrapment" discussed in chapter 2, unable to press their position without undermining their commitment to principles they had already endorsed.

For all these reasons, it was clear that if an agreement was to emerge from the conference, it would have to be one that accommodated guerrillas, at least those fighting for NLMs. The Western bloc eventually acceded to this outcome, albeit on terms it could describe as a compromise. The compromise consisted of two elements. The first was the addition of language to article 44 requiring guerrilla combatants to "carry arms openly" not just "during each military engagement" but also "during such time as he is visible to the adversary while he is engaged in a military deployment preceding the launching of an attack in which he is to participate."[114] This theoretically expanded the circumstances in which guerrillas would have to distinguish themselves from civilians. The second part of the compromise was that several Western states, including the United States and the United Kingdom, issued special declarations explaining that their agreement to the provision was based on an understanding that because it explicitly linked the permissibility of guerrilla tactics to self-determination struggles, it would apply to very few conflicts and would cease to be relevant altogether when the process of decolonization was complete.[115]

While this compromise was partly a face-saving measure, from the Western perspective it could be plausibly defended. The added phrasing in article 44 seemed to enhance civilian safety, and considered as a whole the protocol still imposed meaningful restrictions on guerrilla combatants. Even at the Diplomatic Conference, however, there were reasons to suspect that the Western interpretation was too sanguine. For one thing, various actors expressed dramatically different interpretations of what article 44 actually meant. Western states understood the requirement that a guerrilla carry arms openly "while he is engaged in a military deployment preceding the launching of an attack in which he is to participate" to include the time spent moving to the place from which the attack was to be launched. Others, including Egypt, Syria, and the PLO, thought it sufficient if a guerrilla produced a weapon and immediately began to fire it—an interpretation so narrow it practically negates the requirement altogether.[116] The Western belief that the era of self-determination struggles was winding down, on the other hand, was both reasonable and ultimately correct. Nevertheless, the assumption that guerrilla tactics would recede into irrelevance proved to be gravely mistaken, as I will explain in the next section.

Even if taken at face value, what emerged from Geneva in the form of Protocol I was a document that significantly strengthened the position of NLM fighters but also profoundly increased risks to civilians. Best observes that by allowing the guerrilla "to behave and look more like a civilian than ever before," the provisions "put the law of guerrilla warfare onto the knife-edge of delicacy. Given the legitimacy that guerrilla operations undoubtedly have, the law has to give them fair recognition. But the civilian's margin of safety in such circumstances has shrunk a good deal."[117] As Helen Kinsella writes, "broadening the category of combatant to include guerrillas and amending the strictures governing arms and uniforms created a more, rather than less, nebulous distinction [between combatants and noncombatants]. Far from tightening the distinction, Protocol I risks loosening it further."[118] Moreover, Kinsella notes, Protocol I contains no practical incentives for guerrillas to meet even the loose requirement to "carry arms openly" during attacks and preparations for attacks, since if captured they would receive equivalent treatment and judicial rights whether they technically qualified for POW status or not.[119]

Nonstate Actor Violence: Decolonization and Beyond

In this chapter, I have suggested that the debate over whether NLMs could legitimately use military force to pursue independence (a jus ad bellum question) was both historically and conceptually closely tied to the debate over what methods and tactics they were permitted to use while pursuing it (a jus in bello question). Furthermore, there are several significant parallels between these questions in terms of their status today. Neither was resolved clearly in terms of international law, and legal scholars still disagree about how they should be answered. Both addressed apparently narrow and historically specific circumstances, which should have limited their relevance beyond the decolonization process. Nevertheless, both have proved far more influential than these limitations would suggest in shaping the use of force in the contemporary international system.

Western states, recall, resisted explicitly affirming that NLMs had the same rights under international law as sovereign states, including the right to use force, although they implicitly affirmed it in agreeing to article 1(4) of Protocol I and in several cases endorsed the struggles of specific liberation movements through UN resolutions. Because of this ambivalent stance, legal experts remain divided on the question of whether NLMs possess jus ad bellum rights.[120] There is something closer to consensus, however, that the legal question has become largely moot, since it was relevant only to a specific historical episode—decolonization—that has more or less ended.[121] As Robert Jackson explains, the decolonization process rested on an interpretation of "self-determination" that jettisoned the earlier identification with "national" identities and limited independence movements to preexisting colonial boundaries. The intention, he argues, was to allow former colonies to gain independence without opening the door to further claims by domestic groups.[122] With the independence of former Portuguese colonies in the 1970s and the assumption of power by black majorities in Zimbabwe (formerly Rhodesia) and South Africa, by the twenty-first century there were few territories left to which the UN formulation applied.[123] Likewise, IHL scholars generally agree that because the guerrilla warfare provisions in Protocol I were specifically tied to wars of self-determination, they are of little legal relevance today.[124] Heather Wilson wrote in 1988 of article 1(4): "if it opens up a Pandora's Box at all, it is an unexpectedly small one."[125] W. Hays Parks, principal author of the US Defense Department's IHL manual, went so far as to say in 2010 that the provision governing the conduct of guerrilla forces "has had no play nor effect—none—since its incorporation into Protocol I in 1974."[126]

From the perspective of international law, these opinions are surely correct. Viewing the matter purely from a legal perspective, however, misses the true impact of the events I have been discussing. While the contestation of norms against nonstate violence may have yielded ambiguous and historically bounded legal results, from a practical political perspective it proved far more consequential. As I explained in chapter 2, international norms do not always accurately reflect international law, but they often have even stronger effects on behavior.

Because of the principle of normative coherence, norms can have "spillover" effects, shaping behavior in circumstances beyond those to which they originally are intended to apply and in ways that do not conform strictly to international law. For these reasons, technical legal analysis runs the risk of understating the real-world impact of changes in legal norms. Inis Claude recognized this as early as 1966, observing of the doctrine of national liberation that

> its claim to legal status is quite tenuous. But that is beside the point; it has been established by the political process of collective legitimization, and, while lawyers are free to brush it aside, statesmen are bound to take it into account as one of the facts of international political life. If the doctrine is illegal, its supporters would claim that this only convicts the law of legitimacy. In this respect at least, they attach greater weight to the political consensus of the [General] Assembly than to the established provisions of international law. Thus, in one of its aspects, collective legitimacy represents a revolt against international law.[127]

In this case, moreover, the normative changes associated with decolonization especially lent themselves to spillover effects because they replaced categorical judgments (nonstate actors may never justifiably take up arms; combatants must always distinguish themselves from civilians) with conditional judgments (certain nonstate actors may justifiably take up arms under certain circumstances; combatants may remain indistinguishable from civilians if they are fighting for a certain cause). The postcolonial normative regime thus shifted the focus from whether the actor using force was entitled to do so as a sovereign state to more fluid and contextual questions about the justness of the cause for which force was being used. Because such claims are harder to settle objectively and in a way that actors are likely to view as authoritative and legitimate, conditional norms tend to be much more susceptible to normative spillover than categorical norms.

Regarding the jus ad bellum question, what was on its face a narrow and conditional acceptance of the use of force by a particular subset of nonstate actors spilled over in significant ways. Although intended to be limited to the problem of colonialism, the norm of the "self-determination of peoples" had—and still has—implications that are hard to contain within a particular historical context. Taking this principle to its logical conclusions could help legitimize a broad range of secessionist and insurgent movements. The threat to global order posed by proliferating self-determination claims, indeed, was the primary reason states wanted to close the book on the right of national liberation.[128] But a "this far, but no further" approach to self-determination can appear hypocritical and arbitrary, especially when some movements (in Kosovo, East Timor, and South Sudan, for example) gain international support while others do not.[129] Consequently, in recent decades substate ethnonationalist and, increasingly, religious groups have demanded autonomy or independence, creating threats to stability in many postcolonial states. Even setting aside the moral logic of self-determination, it is harder than one might think to draw a historical line and declare the era of self-determination over. Christine Gray notes that while international law offers "no support for the right to use force to attain self-determination outside the context of decolonization or illegal occupation," even unlawful secessionist movements can become legitimate self-determination struggles if they are "met with forcible repression."[130] Moreover, ideological and geopolitical considerations sometimes lead governments to recognize armed groups in other states as legitimate "liberation movements," keeping the term in circulation in the hope of gaining for the groups in question the rights that go with it. One salient example is in Lebanon, where UN Security Council Resolution 1559 called for the elimination of armed substate groups in the interests of Lebanese self-determination, yet Syria, citing other UN resolutions, supports Hezbollah as a legitimate movement of national liberation from what is asserts is de facto Israeli occupation.[131] While the Ronald Reagan administration typically avoided the term "national liberation" because of its association with socialist revolutions, Reagan frequently referred to US-supported guerrillas in Afghanistan and Nicaragua as "freedom fighters," and at least one prominent American legal scholar argued that Afghan groups fighting Soviet occupation constituted an NLM for the purposes of international law.[132] More recently, nationalist allies of Vladimir Putin in the Duma defended Russia's 2014 annexation of Crimea as a case of national liberation and promised more to come: "National liberation is a global process, a fight that 99 percent of the world's population depends on. Russia, with Putin at its head, is a vanguard in the war against the American colonial system. . . . Our goal is to reclaim the sovereignty Russia lost in 1991—the right to determine how we live and operate. We are fighting to free the nation from foreign occupation."[133] In the 2000s, fundamentalist cleric Moqtada al-Sadr invoked the idea of "war until liberation" in opposing the US military presence in Iraq, and in 2009 Sudanese president Omar al-Bashir responded to his indictment for war crimes by the International Criminal Court by decrying the West and claiming that he was leading "a liberation movement against this new colonization."[134] In recent years the vocabulary of national liberation has been employed by, among others, Kurds, Basques, Abkhaz, South Ossetians, Ogaden, Kashmiris, and the Afghan Taliban.[135] Self-determination may therefore be a genie that is hard to return to its bottle, especially after Kosovo's controversial declaration of independence in 2008.

Similarly, the most significant effect of the guerrilla provisions in Protocol I had less to do with the challenges involved in applying the new legal rules than with how those rules spilled over beyond decolonization, ultimately pushing the boundaries of guerrilla war itself. Some delegates at the Diplomatic Conference in fact foresaw that Protocol I's endorsement of guerrilla tactics was likely to have an impact beyond wars of self-determination. Several states that had been occupied during World War II saw guerrilla war not as an exceptional short-term accommodation but rather, in the Austrian delegate's words, "a very general method of combat which has been used many times in the past in inter-state conflicts and which will lose none of its significance in the future, not even when the transitional era of decolonization is over."[136] Likewise, the Colombian delegate was convinced that the application of article 44 "could not be confined within any specific ideological doctrine."[137] Moreover, several in the non-Western bloc suggested that although the article 1(4) criteria could not apply to separatist groups within postcolonial states, it was consistent with its purposes to interpret those criteria flexibly in other cases going forward.[138] The PLO representative gave clear notice of his organization's intention to do just that, claiming that the territories it sought to liberate were not just those occupied by Israel since the 1967 Six-Day War but also the entire territory of the state of Israel itself.[139] Indeed, just as many groups since the early 1970s have claimed the jus ad bellum rights intended for NLMs, these groups have almost always employed tactics that article 1(4) of Protocol I legally reserves for fighters "against colonial domination and alien occupation and against racist regimes." Furthermore, the close association between national liberation and guerrilla warfare not only imbued NLM status with privileges in terms of permissible tactics but also gave nonstate groups another lever for seeking legitimacy, by invoking IHL to signal that they were responsible international actors. This ploy, pioneered by the FLN in Algeria, was eventually emulated by a wide range of militant groups, including the Symbionese Liberation Army, the American Indian Movement, and the Black Panthers.[140]

More generally, moreover, the normative changes associated with decolonization and the precedent set by the acceptance of NLMs and their tactics opened the door to a broad proliferation of armed nonstate groups that continue to shape international politics. While some still evoke self-determination, either sincerely or as pretext, others pay no obeisance at all to the principle. Nonstate military forces have simply become, in many parts of the world, an accepted part of the landscape. To be sure, this situation is not only a product of changes in international norms. As we have seen, one common problem is state weakness, which impedes the building of strong national armies and allows alternative power centers to emerge. Of course, even this material fact has been shaped by ideational factors since many weak states were born of decolonization, which was firmly rooted in normative judgments. Nevertheless, militias and other armed groups have arisen even in states with relatively capable militaries, sometimes working in common cause with governments and sometimes operating as a sort of parallel authority, neither openly in conflict with the government nor reliably beholden to it.[141] In a similar way, the normative acceptance of guerrilla warfare—far from falling into disuse as colonialism waned, as the United States and United Kingdom expected (or at least hoped)—has in fact been so broad that today few see the need to defend it. It has simply become taken for granted that these methods are part and parcel of contemporary warfare. This is certainly true in conflicts pitting modern national forces against insurgencies, such as US operations in Somalia, Iraq, and Afghanistan, Soviet/Russian campaigns in Afghanistan in the 1980s and Chechnya in the 1990s, and Israel's wars against Hamas and Hezbollah since 2000.[142] What is perhaps surprising is that these tactics have also been used by states themselves, such as Russia in Ukraine since 2014 and the Federal Republic of Yugoslavia (Serbia) during the 1999 Kosovo conflict, in which Serbia quartered some of its uniformed forces in civilian dwellings and interspersed military and civilian vehicles on the roads to avoid attack.[143] Indeed, many US experts advise that the American military should emphasize "irregular" warfare in its operational planning, in part because of the continuing prevalence of intrastate conflict but also because in the future "the strategies and tactics of Russia and China, not to mention Iran or ISIL, may have more in common with insurgent forces than the kind of conventional air or naval engagements the U.S. military expects in a great power showdown."[144] In any event, in the words of a 2014 RAND Corporation study, "a continuing high incidence of irregular or hybrid warfare, whether conducted by states or nonstate actors," is likely to be "the new normal."[145]

Conclusion

An important theme of this book is that normative change is complicated. Although agents such as norm entrepreneurs can shape norms in ways that bring about salutary changes in international politics, norm change often also brings about unintended consequences, which are not always salutary. A related theme is that norms are resistant to incoherence. So, trying to carve out narrow exceptions to a norm for particular circumstances, or making a norm conditional instead of categorical, cannot help but undermine the coherence of the norm and expose it to contestation by those who want it changed or wish to be exempted from it themselves. When some European powers expressed support for resistance movements at Brussels in 1874 and The Hague in 1907, they were by no means thinking in terms of their own colonies—in fact, at the time some were themselves aligning with nonstate militias to maintain order in those colonies.

Likewise, the Allies in World War II did not see their support for partisan and resistance forces as a nail in the coffin of colonialism, nor did Western states in the 1960s and 1970s, in recognizing the right of colonial peoples to govern themselves, intend to open the door to the broader use of force by nonstate actors. Nevertheless, as I have described in this chapter, the logic of normative coherence contributed to these unintended consequences, as evidenced by the strategies used by NLMs and their allies in contesting preexisting norms governing the use of force.

At the heart of the process, of course, was the macronormative phenomenon of decolonization, which delegitimized one of the central institutions in the international system and provided a normative imperative so powerful that it forced a reexamination of the meaning of sovereignty itself. Although decolonization was the lodestar, several of what I described in chapter 2 as subsidiary and ancillary normative changes also played important roles. The normative "revolt against the West" that was both a foundation of and an adjunct to decolonization was apparent not just in the rejection of Western rule over colonies but also in the repudiation of principles that Western states used to justify the status quo, from the benevolent paternalism and mission civilisatrice of colonialism, to the requirements of "chivalry" in the conduct of war, to the purported neutrality of international law.[146] The ethos of this "revolt" pervaded the Diplomatic Conference of 1974–77, contributing to the adoption of provisions in IHL that further blunted the material advantages many Western states possess in the military realm. Moreover, the withdrawal of deference to state discretion and the related contextualization of the right to use force (both of which I described in chapter 2 as accompanying the macronormative retreat from the raison d'état after World War II) combined to redefine the prerogative of political violence from one that presumptively resided in states to one limited to circumstances in which force was being used to advance a just cause—even if those seeking to advance it were not in fact states themselves. This shift was indispensable in vesting nonstate actors seeking self-determination with jus ad bellum rights—especially since doing so amounted to the creation of a new exception to the UN Charter's prohibition on the use of force.

The ascendance of consequentialist normative reasoning, another of the post-1945 ancillary normative changes I discussed in chapter 2, proved similarly crucial in the successful contestation of norms by and on behalf of nonstate actors. Consequentialist logic was implicit, and sometimes explicit, in arguments that the right of self-determination was meaningless unless accompanied by the right to take up arms to pursue it. The same logic, moreover, was at the core of the non-Western position at the Diplomatic Conference on the need for IHL to accommodate guerrilla warfare. Western objections thus were characterized as hostility to the decolonization project itself—a rhetorical gambit so powerful that it succeeded in winning legal acceptance of guerrillas, even though doing so required undermining several long-standing principles of international law. Finally, the enhanced normative authority of new actors was both a contributing cause and a lasting consequence of the events described in this chapter. Buoyed by the rising acceptance of ideas about human rights and racial equality, groups fighting on behalf of colonized peoples were seen by the late 1950s not only as aggrieved parties but also as legitimate bearers of rights under international law. Decolonization itself further empowered these groups, putting many at the helm of new sovereign states and enhancing the legitimacy of those still struggling for independence. Clearly, the participation of dozens of NLMs at the Diplomatic Conference both reflected and signaled a level of normative authority that violent nonstate actors of earlier generations never remotely approached. Decoloniza- tion also benefited from, and enhanced, the authority of another type of non- state actor: the UN General Assembly. It played a vital role in providing a forum for debates over self-determination and forming consensus on the matter and subsequently became more central to the UN, and international politics more generally, as its ranks swelled with newly independent states.

As I have argued, the acceptance of the use of force by NLMs had effects that extended well beyond decolonization. Most significantly, it was a breach in the wall of Weberian sovereignty: after that, it could no longer be said that the use of military force by nonstate actors was categorically illegitimate. Instead, it was now permissible under certain conditions. These conditions were, on their face, narrowly defined, but knowing whether they were or were not present in a given case nevertheless required further information and invited further debate. This opening proved deceptively large and, when combined with the similar opening in jus in bello norms revealed at the Diplomatic Conference, would have fateful implications for how, and by whom, force would be used in the international system.

4

ONE MAN'S FREEDOM FIGHTER?

Normative Change and the Geopolitical
Construction of Terrorism

Transnational terrorism is perhaps the defining security challenge of the early twenty-first century. Many states devote enormous resources to fighting terrorists and preventing attacks, and opinion polling in Western states shows that fear of terrorism looms large in the minds of the general public.[1] The reason for the fixation on terrorism is obvious, as is the date on which it emerged: September 11, 2001. The shock of that day played out again many times in the years that followed, as attacks in London, Madrid, Istanbul, Nairobi, Riyadh, Casablanca, Baghdad, Jakarta, and Paris, among other places, focused attention on newly emboldened groups willing to use deadly force against urban populations and the vulnerabilities they were able to exploit. Moreover, the scale and scope of terrorist groups has grown in recent years. The Institute for Economics and Peace (IEP) reports in its Global Terrorism Index that both the intensity and geographic reach of terrorism has increased since the late 1990s, with the impact of terrorism increasing in every region in the world from 2002 to 2017.[2] Over the same period the percentage of terrorist attacks producing fatalities has increased significantly, resulting in over two hundred thousand deaths since 2002.[3]

One important development has been the increasingly transnational character of terrorism, as organizations are able to recruit, fundraise, and plan operations across national borders. Richard H. Shultz, Douglas Farah, and Itamara V. Lochard described this in 2004 as a "revolution in terrorist affairs" analogous to the technology-driven "revolution in military affairs" occurring at the same time: "like their state counterparts, armed groups can now acquire the capacity to execute violent strikes that can have a strategic impact on even the most powerful nation-state. This capacity is new."[4] One indication of the increasing size and potency of large terrorist organizations is that just four groups—ISIS, the Taliban, al-Shabaab, and Boko Haram—were responsible for over 56 percent of the almost nineteen thousand deaths from terrorism in 2017. Ten years earlier—a decade that saw "the largest surge in terrorist activity in the past fifty years"—the same four groups were responsible for just six percent of terrorism deaths.[5] These four groups do not even include the organization most often associated with this new paradigm: al-Qaeda. The al-Qaeda case shows that the trend toward large and powerful terrorist groups predated the twenty-first century; by the time it carried out the 9/11 attacks in 2001, al-Qaeda was a shockingly well-resourced entity, having trained some eighteen thousand people in its bases in Afghanistan over the previous five years and with access to billions of dollars in funds.[6] While efforts by the United States and other countries in the years after 9/11 put the organization on the defensive and diminished its capabilities, it adapted by becoming more organizationally flexible, turning into, in Bruce Hoffman's words, "a networked transnational constituency rather than the monolithic, international terrorist organization with an identifiable command and control apparatus that it once was."[7] The IEP reported in late 2018 that al-Qaeda "has spent recent years strategizing and rebuilding. With upward of 30,000 active fighters dispersed throughout [the Middle East, South Asia, and Africa] and active in at least 17 countries, Al Qaeda's renewed presence poses a continuing threat."[8] The most dramatic example of this trend, however, is ISIS, which started as one of many insurgent groups within Iraq in the 2000s but eventually transcended the category of "terrorist organization," actually governing large swaths of land within the territories of two sovereign states.[9] Even while imposing a reign of terror in the lands under its control, it carried out numerous attacks abroad, including the November 2015 attacks in Paris that killed 130 people and the Easter 2019 attacks in Sri Lanka with over 300 fatalities. Almost half (46 percent) of all deaths from terrorism in Western Europe and North America from 2013 to 2017 were in attacks committed or inspired by ISIS.[10] Although by 2019 ISIS had been driven from the territory it occupied in Syria and Iraq, the threat it posed had not disappeared.[11] One sobering statistic was that over forty-one thousand fighters from eighty countries joined the organization from 2013 to 2018, of whom over seven thousand had returned to their home countries by the end of 2018.[12]

It is thus understandable that terrorism should command attention from both the general public and scholars. Nevertheless, the topic also gives rise to some considerable gaps between perception and reality. First, the growth in terrorist activity notwithstanding, the perceived dangers of terrorism in many societies, including the United States, are dramatically out of proportion to the actual risks it poses. Steven Pinker observed in 2011 that terrorism generates "a cockeyed ratio of fear to harm," citing statistics that show Americans are less likely to die in terrorist attacks than from accidental falls, drowning, accidental poisoning, bee stings, and peanut allergies.[13] Cognitive psychology might help explain this disjuncture; surely, horrific images of attacks loom large in the psyche, and frequent references to terrorism by national leaders and in the press likely reinforce this bias. But this in turn raises the question of why Western leaders continue to prioritize the problem and portray it as an unprecedented and potentially existential threat to their societies.

Certainly, while there has been an enormous amount written about the topic, it remains plagued by conceptual confusion. It seems almost obligatory in works on terrorism to discuss how hard it is to define the term and how little consensus exists about what its essential characteristics are. This confusion in the literature parallels a similar difficulty in international politics itself, where agreement about what does and does not constitute terrorism is evasive, as we shall see. However, there is one point of almost universal agreement: to be called a terrorist is not a compliment. The term has overwhelmingly negative connotations and is perhaps the most damning description that can be applied to any political group. It is no surprise that it has become a go-to epithet for governments wishing to paint their enemies as illegitimate and dangerous. As Brian Jenkins notes, "the term implies a moral judgment, and if one party can successfully attach the label *terrorist* to its opponent, then it has indirectly persuaded others to adopt its moral viewpoint."[14] What Jenkins describes is not simply a matter of one party trying to persuade others that its adversary's actions are morally wrong but rather the applicability of the term itself, which already has moral condemnation built into it. Moreover, groups will go to great lengths to avoid association with the term, including what Hoffman describes as "convoluted semantic obfuscations to sidestep terrorism's pejorative overtones."[15]

It would be a mistake, however, to see all attempts to affix or avoid the label of "terrorist" as merely cynical semantic games. This is because the problem of terrorism in contemporary international politics cannot be understood without first understanding how the term is defined and how that definition has changed over time. The act of defining a term is often intensely political and can create significant real-world implications. Prominent terrorism scholar Martha Crenshaw writes: "Politics involves competition to define terms, as actors attempt to impose their own interpretations of history. In contemporary politics, calling adversaries 'terrorists' is a way of depicting them as fanatic and irrational so as to foreclose the possibility of compromise, draw attention to the real or imagined threat to security, and promote solidarity among the threatened."[16] Given the strongly negative connotations of the term "terrorism" and the political costs that come along with it, the stakes involved in defining the term are high. Make no mistake, defining terrorism is a political matter, not merely a semantic one.[17] As Ben Saul observes, "the struggle over the representation of a violent act is a struggle over its legitimacy."[18]

In this chapter, I examine how contestation of the definition of "terrorism" became a critical part of the political landscape associated with the problem and shaped norms regarding what constituted permissible conduct by inferior forces in asymmetrical conflicts. The chapter contains five sections. In the first section, I briefly review the literature on terrorism. While this work is richly detailed and informative, scholars have struggled to generate causal explanations for terrorism, which occurs across a vast range of conditions. I suggest that this difficulty reflects limitations in the way the term is typically defined. The problem is not that scholars of terrorism are imprecise in their definitions; it is rather that the concept itself has become so thoroughly contested and politicized that definition has become a political rather than a scholarly act. Furthermore, because the designation rests fundamentally on a choice of certain methods of violence rather than an actor's characteristics, it describes a wide variety of actions that is hard to capture in causal explanations. In the second section, I discuss the use of the term "terrorism" before it became the subject of contestation in the early 1970s. I make two points that might surprise contemporary readers. First, for most of the twentieth century there was a consensus about what "terrorism" meant; the essence of it was violence directly targeted at civilians in a variety of contexts and by a variety of actors, including states themselves.[19] Second, it was not uncommon for individuals and groups to admit to "terrorism" or to refer to themselves as "terrorists." Indeed, the term was typically used as an objective description and even occasionally as a badge of pride.

This started to change around 1970, and again at the heart of that change was the contestation of norms whose coherence had been damaged by the macro-normative changes that followed World War II. In this case, contestation proceeded along two closely related tracks. The first, described in chapter 3, aimed at legitimizing the use of guerrilla tactics by groups fighting for independence from colonial powers. The second involved expanding the scope of what was deemed acceptable in guerrilla warfare, which entailed effectively redefining "terrorism." In this chapter's third section ("Beyond Guerrilla Warfare"), I explain the logical nexus between these tracks, which is rooted in guerrilla warfare's implications for the treatment of civilian populations. While it is possible to conduct guerrilla warfare without targeting civilians, inherent in its very nature is the instrumental use of civilians as means to achieve military and political ends. Historically this has manifested itself in a variety of practices that put civilians at risk, from guerrillas living amid the population, to commingling military and civilian equipment and using "human shields" to deter attack, to directing mass violence against civilians themselves. Furthermore, accepting the legitimacy of guerrilla warfare undermined several norms governing the use of force in ways that made it easier to rationalize such ethically problematic tactics. The fourth section ("Contesting 'Terrorism'") recounts the second track of contestation described above, which built upon the normative assumptions inherent in the push to legitimize guerrilla warfare to reconfigure the international discourse relating to "terrorism" itself. The pivotal event in this process was the UN General Assembly debate following the killing of eleven Israeli athletes by Palestinian militants at the 1972 Olympics. The contentious exchanges in the General Assembly staked out positions that produced a bitter division between Western and non-Western states that continues to demarcate the terrorism issue today. Both groups departed from preexisting conceptions of terrorism in ways that served their own ends. The non-Western bloc insisted on exempting from any definition of terrorism the actions of groups fighting for national liberation, effectively seizing on weaknesses in existing norms to contest the prerogatives of powerful states. Western states (especially the United States) came to insist on politically charged definitions of their own, treating "terrorism" less as a coherent description of a global problem than a geopolitical cudgel to wield against their adversaries. The effect of both positions was to shift the definitional focus of "terrorism" away from the use of certain violent means and toward the ends for which violence was being used and the identity of the party using it.

In the chapter's fifth section, I examine how this impasse shaped the trajectory of international terrorism in recent decades. By the 1980s, the terrorism "debate" had descended into an exercise in political and moral relativism, as both non-Western and Western states supported organizations that employed tactics that in earlier eras clearly would have been described as terrorism. This diminished the impact of normative criticism of these actions, reducing the disincentives for both terrorist organizations and their sponsors and allowing these groups to grow stronger than similar groups in earlier eras. Although since 9/11 the interests of disparate states may be converging toward an international antiterrorism regime, progress toward that end has been slow and continues to be impeded by fundamentally incompatible conceptions of the problem. Thus, despite nearly universal condemnation of "terrorism," the term is used by different people to mean different things, and there are deep divisions over who is properly considered a terrorist and who is not. This has contributed to a normative environment that is amenable to the nonstate use of violence and in which it is difficult to forge effective international legal or regulatory responses to the problems such violence presents.

Explaining Modern Transnational Terrorism

The volume of both popular and scholarly literature on terrorism has seen two significant spikes: in the 1970s and in the years after the attacks of September 11, 2001. In both cases, attempts to explain the causes of terrorism ranged far and wide across academic disciplines. An extensive review of this literature would be difficult and also too diffuse to be of much use here. For example, if one seeks to explain broad trends that have changed the landscape of international politics, micro-level analyses are less helpful than those that focus on broader systemic variables.[20]

That being said, scholars have struggled to identify what causes terrorism. Two variables researchers have examined in seeking to understand modern terrorism are economic conditions and governmental regime type. The findings, however, have been at least somewhat counterintuitive. Whereas common popular explanations posit that extreme poverty and/or severe governmental repression are likely to spawn violent resistance, evidence suggests otherwise. Terrorism is relatively rare in the world's poorest societies, and where it is more common, terrorist organizations rarely draw from society's poorest and most deprived. Indeed, studies have found that terrorists are typically better educated than most of their countrymen and tend to come from middle-class backgrounds.[21] Although undoubtedly an extreme case, Osama bin Laden was a scion of a wealthy and influential Saudi family. Similarly, states with the most repressive regimes have produced relatively little terrorism, while liberal democracies have occasionally produced a lot.[22] Data suggests that terrorism is in fact most likely to emerge in states transitioning from authoritarianism to democracy or those with some limited democratic institutions but few protections for civil rights. Even here, however, correlations have been too inconsistent to generate confident causal conclusions.[23] Like others studying violent nonstate actors, terrorism scholars have pointed to an abundance of weak states as contributing to terrorism. Weak governments, they argue, are less able to take action against militant groups in their territory, allowing these groups to operate more freely.[24] Weak states also often cannot provide social services for their citizens, allowing nonstate actors with adequate resources to court local support and boost recruiting by building schools, hospitals, orphanages, and infrastructure, as Hamas did in the West Bank and Hezbollah did in southern Lebanon.[25] Others question this link, however, noting that the correlation between weak states and terrorism is inconclusive.[26] Moreover, some of the most important militant organizations based in weak states, such as al-Qaeda in Afghanistan and Lashkar-e-Taiba in Pakistan, have operated with the active support and cooperation of the host nations, not because the governments were too weak to expel them. The search for structural causes or even reliable correlates of terrorism has thus yielded disappointing results. As Walter Laqueur writes, "terrorism in the contemporary world has occurred in all kinds of conditions—in times of economic prosperity and decline; it has occurred in big cities and in small towns; and it has affected people of various social classes. . . . It has happened in countries that were ethnically homogeneous, as well as heterogeneous. Terrorism has been sponsored by the left as well as the right."[27]

In light of these difficulties, it is worth asking whether part of the problem might lie in how the topic itself is typically conceptualized. Scholars often note that defining terrorism is notoriously difficult. Hoffman spends the entire first chapter of his book *Inside Terrorism* on matters of definition, as do Alex P. Schmid and Albert J. Jongman, who in their *Political Terrorism* discuss 109 different definitions of the term from scholars, organizations, and government agencies.[28] One difficulty is that the term can refer to a wide range of actions, as Walter Laqueur observes at the beginning of his widely cited book *The Age of Terrorism*, noting (somewhat puzzlingly) that "no definition of terrorism can possibly cover all the varieties of terrorism that have appeared throughout history."[29] The challenge of defining terrorism is not an entirely technical one, however, for as many commentators point out, it is impossible to define the term in a way that does not invite controversy.[30] The definition problem, in other words, is largely a political one: the interpretation and application of "terrorism" are so vigorously contested that the word means very different things to different audiences. What is interesting is that few authors regard this as a fundamental obstacle to scholarly analysis. Instead, most either settle on a particular definition in the interests of analytical clarity or acknowledge the impossibility of a single workable definition and forge ahead anyway. Again, Laqueur: "Ideally, all discussions of terrorism . . . should start with a clear, exact and comprehensive definition of the subject. For unless there is broad agreement on the definition of the subject, there is the risk that everyone will interpret it in a different way. . . . Unfortunately, such a comprehensive and universally accepted definition does not exist." He says that this need not be a problem, however: "even if there is no agreed definition of socialism or Fascism, it would be absurd to argue that the subject cannot be studied, for much progress has been made in these fields—as in the study of terrorism."[31]

I wish to suggest that the difficulties in defining terrorism are not so easily overcome, for they reflect the fundamentally unsettled nature of the subject itself.

No amount of analytical precision is likely to yield reliable causal explanations of terrorism because the topic does not lend itself to precision. At its core are bitterly contentious disputes not just about terminology but also about elemental questions that go to the heart of international politics. The definitional morass that confronts those studying terrorism is thus in fact a clue that the dependent variable is too unstable to ground coherent conclusions upon. One must understand that although terrorist practices have existed for centuries, "terrorism" as a distinct international phenomenon and a subject of expert analysis dates back only to the early 1970s. Both emerged from a series of militant attacks in the late 1960s and early 1970s and, as important, from the maelstrom that ensued when nations assembled to address those attacks.[32] Before that time, "terrorism" typically referred to a means of political violence characterized primarily by targeting civilians in order to instill a general sense of fear. For reasons I explain in this chapter, this usage was too broad to describe the particular practices emerging as an international concern, which involved nonstate actor attacks that, although they fit the existing definition, constituted only one narrow subset of possible terroristic actions. Because analyzing these practices required treating them as a distinct and intellectually tractable phenomenon, scholars began defining terrorism in ways that spoke to the concerns of the moment, typically limiting the term to actions by nonstate groups.[33] This corresponded to the way in which Western governments were approaching the subject in the UN and other arenas. To be clear, many scholars (and some Western states) explained that doing this was necessary to treat the subject coherently and that doing so in no way excused states for atrocities of their own.[34] Nevertheless, framing the terrorism problem in terms of not only the actions committed but also the type of actor committing them would have far-reaching consequences for both the terrorism literature and, as I will argue, practices of transnational terrorism itself because it tied both to a discourse that from the beginning was hotly contested and thoroughly politicized. The goal of objective, value-neutral analysis was stymied by the fact that there was no way of conceptualizing the dependent variable that did not amount to taking sides in an ongoing international controversy. Indeed, from 1972 onward, the term itself was so geopolitically loaded that dispassionate analysis was extremely difficult.

Besides its inescapably political implications, a problem with conceptualizing the study of terrorism in this way is that it shifts the focus away from the fact that at its core it hinges on the choice of specific methods of violence. This skews the moral question, but it also frames the problem both too narrowly to be universally acceptable (for the reasons just discussed) and too broadly to be analytically useful. As Charles Tilly observes, "the term sprawls across a wide range of human cruelties," and this fact requires the terrorism literature to grapple, within a single analytical framework, with a variety of events shaped by widely disparate circumstances, even if only nonstate actors are considered.[35] This helps to explain the elusiveness of causal explanations Laqueur refers to and points to the difficulties inherent in approaching terrorism as a sui generis field of study. Tilly argues, "Social scientists who attempt to explain sudden attacks on civilian targets should doubt the existence of a distinct, coherent class of actors (terrorists) who specialize in a unitary form of political action (terror) and thus should establish a separate variety of politics (terrorism)."[36]

To be clear, I am not arguing that terrorism is "all about" discourse. Most emphatically, I am not suggesting that "there is no such thing as terrorism." Whether it ultimately hangs together as a coherent analytical category or not, what many in the West call "terrorism" describes something real and troubling. I do intend to suggest, however, that it is hard to disentangle these practices from the political discourse that arose around them. Moreover, I argue that this discourse in turn actually shaped these practices by changing norms about what actions were acceptable and unacceptable in various circumstances, thus helping to make the methods customarily associated with terrorism more prevalent. This is best understood by returning to the question of why actors choose certain means of violence and specifically why they opt to target civilians. We must start from the assumption that they have some reason for doing so. The common portrayal of terrorism as an irrational manifestation of hatred can obscure the fact that it is pursued with an instrumental purpose in mind. As Martha Crenshaw reminds us, violence is "a willful choice made by an organization for political and strategic reasons."[37] Even suicide terrorism, Hoffman writes, "is neither irrational nor desperate, as is sometimes portrayed; rather it is an entirely rational and calculated choice, consciously embraced as a deliberate instrument of warfare."[38] A second premise is that these organizations care what others think of them and want to be perceived as legitimate. This, too, goes against the grain of much mainstream coverage in the West but is obvious when one reflects on the extensive public information campaigns they often carry out and that almost all vigorously deny they are "terrorists" because of the stigma attached to the term.[39] In fact, Audrey Kurth Cronin argues that appeals to legitimacy are "at the heart of terrorism."[40] Furthermore, these groups seek to be well regarded not only by the people they claim to be fighting for but also by a broader audience comprising at least some foreign governments and global public opinion. This in part reflects the legacy of the skillful courtship of international opinion by the FLN discussed in chapter 3, which was cited as a model by PLO leader Yasser Arafat and other militant leaders.[41]

The value these organizations attach to legitimacy is, of course, consistent with my discussion in chapter 2 about the power of norms and "the logic of appropriateness" to shape behavior. However, it also raises a puzzle. In short: killing civilians seems like an odd way to win friends. It violates one of the oldest principles in the law of war, offends moral sensibilities that exist across cultures, and seems to risk public condemnation and blowback. I have argued elsewhere that in the decades after World War II belligerents increasingly avoided bombing civilians in wartime, in large part to avoid the negative political consequences they feared they would suffer for violating an important ethical norm.[42] The frequent targeting of civilians by militant nonstate groups over the same time period flies in the face of this logic and begs for explanation. Clearly, not only are these groups not terribly bothered by targeting civilians—they believe that many others will not be either and that doing so will not seriously damage their legitimacy with their desired audiences.

Tackling this puzzle requires us to remember that modern "terrorism" as we know it is the product of a particular historical moment. Crenshaw insists that a "general theory [of terrorism] based on conditions is impossible because the final decision depends upon the judgments individual political actors make about these conditions. There is nothing automatic about the choice of terrorism. . . . It is thus necessary to recognize that an important aspect of terrorism is its social construction, which is relative to time and place, thus to historical context."[43] This historical context, I argue, helps us understand the normative incongruity of modern terrorism. While the norm against targeting civilians is not dead and still in fact significantly constrains Western states in many cases, its vigorous contestation by nonstate groups and their allies significantly diminished its power over certain types of actors in certain circumstances. Thus, as these groups became increasingly empowered to use violence by the processes described in chapter 3, further normative changes made available to them methods that had long been condemned and the normative arguments to justify them. Paradoxically, even as this occurred, the term "terrorist" became a more damning epithet that ever before.

Defining "Terrorism" before 1972

Although it is hard to imagine today, in an earlier time the definition of "terrorism" was not contested, nor did groups always object to being labeled as "terrorists." The term was first used in connection with the Jacobin Reign of Terror that followed the French Revolution in the late eighteenth century. This specific historical connection remained until the Russian underground anarchist group People's Will adopted the term in the late 1800s. People's Will members embraced and even romanticized the "terrorist" moniker, with one contending that "the terrorist . . . is noble, terrible, irresistibly fascinating, for he combines in himself the two sublimities of human grandeur: the martyr and the hero."[44] People's Will was one of the first of a wave of anarchist organizations that sought to destabilize governments through violence, starting with attacks on high-ranking government officials and facilities but evolving, in Martin Miller's words, to "unlimited warfare against sectors of the governing order in which the line between society and the state was completely obliterated."[45] One French anarchist explained at his trial for the 1894 bombing of a railway station: "We do not spare bourgeois women and children, because the wives and children of those they love are not spared either. Are not those children innocent victims who, in the slums, die slowly of anemia because bread is scarce at home; or those women who grow pale in your workshops and wear themselves out to earn forty *sous* a day, and yet are lucky when poverty does not turn them into prostitutes?"[46] While this sense of "terrorism" was different from that used by the Jacobins—notably, one was a method of governmental rule, the other a means of bringing down a government—the core element in each was the premise that even limited acts of violence could have political effects that resonated far more broadly by breeding fear and insecurity. Indeed, the word itself captures the idea that the objective of terrorism is not the death and destruction it causes directly but the dread that spreads among others as a result. Not coincidentally, while in the nineteenth century dictionaries typically defined "terrorism" in ways that specifically evoked the French Reign of Terror, by the early twentieth century definitions had broadened to include actions by both governments and those opposing governments and to focus on the psychological impact of the actions. A typical entry from 1931 defined it as "a system of government or opposition to government by methods which excite fear."[47]

This sense of "terrorism" as hinging on the impact of indirect psychological effects of violence was adopted by those codifying the law of war in the early twentieth century, especially in the years after World War I. In this context, the defining criterion of "terrorism" was violence against civilians. Military forces had long employed violence against enemy civilians as a means of subjugating occupied populations. By the early 1900s, however, this morally troubling practice was growing, for two reasons. One was that occupying forces saw it as a means of deterring guerrilla violence by local resistance groups, which as we have seen was a growing trend at the time. The second was the advent of manned flight, which made it possible to intimidate an enemy's population without occupying its territory. Both these practices occurred in World War I, which contributed to the unprecedented toll the conflict took on civilians. This problem of "terrorism," then, was high up the list of concerns at international conferences and newly established international organizations aimed at updating and reinvigorating IHL in the years after the war. Among the first was the Commission on the Responsibility of the Authors of the War and on Enforcement of Penalties, which in its 1919 report listed among the war crimes committed by the Central Powers "systematic terrorism" of civilians, by which they "had deliberately sought to strike terror into every heart for the purpose of repressing all resistance."[48] The phrase "systematic terrorism" was later used by the UN War Crimes Commission in 1945 and appeared frequently in the proceedings of the Nuremberg International Military Tribunal that tried Nazi officials in 1946.[49] In those cases "terrorism" was used primarily to describe German actions in occupied territories, specifically "indiscriminate attacks on civilians, intended to put them in grave fear, and thereby to subdue resistance to Nazi rule."[50]

In its application to aerial bombing, too, "terrorism" was associated with attacks on civilians, though efforts to outlaw the practice proved more complicated. In 1923, an international Commission of Jurists proposed a set of Draft Rules of Aerial Warfare, which prohibited "aerial bombardment for the purpose of terrorizing the civilian population."[51] The rules were never adopted, largely because several of the great powers were intrigued by the possibilities of strategic bombing and did not wish to limit their options going forward.[52] What is noteworthy for our purposes is that bombing proponents did not shrink from recognizing that "terrorizing the civilian population" was exactly the goal they sought. Giulio Douhet, perhaps the most influential of the interwar theorists of airpower, described one of the important tasks of the air force in coming wars as being "to terrorize the capital and sow destruction in its suburbs."[53] Airpower would be decisive in the future, he wrote, because it would "cut off the enemy's army and navy from their bases of operation, spread terror and havoc in the interior of his country, and break down the moral and physical resistance of his people."[54] Similarly, Hugh Trenchard, the first commander of Britain's Royal Air Force, argued that while it would be unacceptable to target the civilian population as a whole, it would be entirely legitimate "to terrorize munitions workers (men and women) into absenting themselves from work . . . through fear of air-attack upon the factory or dock concerned."[55] To be sure, as Trenchard's position suggests, proponents sometimes recognized that "terror bombing" raised serious moral concerns, and even during World War II leaders typically avoided the phrase and, for that matter, admitting to directly targeting civilians. Still, in this case it was the moral stigma attached to targeting civilians itself, rather than the term used to describe it, that leaders sought to avoid. By the end of World War II, then, there was little indication that the meaning typically attached to "terrorism" had changed significantly from the early interwar years. Most fundamentally, it referred to particular means or methods (targeting civilians or civilian installations) chosen with a particular intent (to intimidate, demoralize, or spread terror within a population). Indeed, the two most common uses of the term during World War II—describing the Nazi abuse of civilians in occupied territories and indiscriminate aerial bombing operations—underscored the notion that the targeting of civilians was at the essence of the concept. Finally, it is important to note that the definitions and usage of the word "terrorism" at the time make clear that it was not something that was limited to a specific type of actor. It was, for example, abundantly clear that terrorism was something of which sovereign states as well as nonstate actors could be guilty, since most uses of the term during World War II referred to states.

The NLMs fighting for independence in the decades after World War II varied widely in terms of their resources and military capabilities, but a considerable number employed tactics that clearly met the definition of "terrorism" in use at the time. Among the first to do so were two groups fighting to create an independent Israeli state: the Fighters for the Freedom of Israel (better known by its acronym Lehi) and the Irgun. In campaigns that began before the end of World War II, both groups targeted Arab civilians, officials of the British mandatory authority that governed Palestine, and those deemed to be in collaboration with them.[56] Moreover, both groups openly and unapologetically described their tactics as "terrorism." Lehi leader (and future prime minister of Israel) Yitzhak Shamir wrote in 1943: "Neither Jewish ethics nor Jewish tradition can disqualify terrorism as a means of combat. We are very far from having any moral qualms as far as our national war goes. . . . First and foremost, terrorism is for us a part of the political battle being conducted under the present circumstances, and it has a great part to play: speaking in a clear voice to the whole world, as well as to our wretched brethren outside this land, it proclaims our war against the occupier."[57] Similarly, the FLN, while keenly mindful of global opinion and skillful in appealing to it, nevertheless referred to some of its operations as terrorism, depending on whether they primarily targeted civilians.[58] South African resistance leader Nelson Mandela employed the same sense of the word in a statement at his 1964 trial, soberly assessing the relative merits of terrorism and other tactics:

> Four forms of violence are possible. There is sabotage, there is guerrilla warfare, there is terrorism, and there is open revolution. We chose to adopt the first method and to test it fully before taking any other decision. In the light of our political background the choice was a logical one. Sabotage did not involve loss of life, and it offered the best hope for future race relations. Bitterness would be kept to a minimum and, if the policy bore fruit, democratic government could become a reality. . . . But we in Umkhonto [weSizwe, Mandela's organization] weighed up the white response with anxiety. The lines were being drawn. The

whites and blacks were moving into separate camps, and the prospects of avoiding a civil war were made less. The white newspapers carried reports that sabotage would be punished by death. If this was so, how could we continue to keep Africans away from terrorism?[59]

The 1960s Brazilian revolutionary Carlos Marighella, whose *Minimanual of the Urban Guerrilla* influenced many neo-Marxist and Maoist groups, explicitly embraced "terrorist" tactics and cast the term in a positive light: "To be called . . . a terrorist in Brazil is now an honor to any citizen, for it means he is fighting, with a gun in his hand, against the monstrosity of the present dictatorship and the suffering it causes."[60] Well into the 1960s, therefore, "terrorism" was not simply an epithet but was also widely understood to refer to a particular means of political violence characterized by targeting civilians.[61]

Beyond Guerrilla Warfare

This consensus on the meaning of terrorism started to erode in the early 1970s. The catalyst was again decolonization and the series of contentious disputes over the rights of NLMs discussed in chapter 3. A pivotal step was the success of non-Western efforts to legitimize guerrilla warfare, which originated in the mid-1960s and culminated in the Diplomatic Conference in Geneva in 1974 and the subsequent conclusion of Protocol I. This constituted one of two tracks of contestation that redefined what methods were acceptable for groups struggling toward national liberation. The second, which I discuss in the next section, was the debate over the meaning and application of the concept of "terrorism" itself. Logically speaking, the first track was prior to the second in that the expansion of guerrilla methods depended on the acceptance of guerrilla warfare itself. Nevertheless, there was considerable overlap between the two tracks, and both occurred more or less simultaneously.

The Diplomatic Conference revealed much about the varying trajectories of several important norms and showed that three crucial and long-standing distinctions in international norms were in deep trouble. The first, of course, was the central distinction between civilians and combatants in times of war. As I have noted, there is a practical aspect of this problem, as soldiers who cannot tell their enemies from civilians are likely to kill more civilians, even if their intentions are good. But more fundamentally, although Protocol I purported to simply adapt the duty to distinguish fighters from civilians to the realities of guerrilla warfare, this neglects the extent to which modern guerrilla warfare is itself, inescapably and by design, premised on blurring this line. Of course, as Mandela's typology suggests, terrorism and guerrilla tactics are not the same thing. It is possible to carry out guerrilla warfare without targeting civilians, and some guerrilla groups carefully avoided doing so. Mandela's Umkhonto weSizwe refrained from attacking civilians into the 1980s, and famed South American revolutionary Che Guevara counseled against "terrorism" as "a measure that is generally ineffective and indiscriminate in its results, since it often makes victims of innocent people and destroys a large number of lives that would be valuable to the revolution."[62] Nevertheless, as discussed in the last chapter, by their very nature guerrilla tactics subject civilians to risks they might not face in conventional warfare. These dangers existed well before the twentieth century, as demonstrated by the plight of civilians in areas where guerrillas operated in the American Revolution, Napoleon's Peninsular Wars, and the American Civil War, and only worsened with the increasing urbanization of guerrilla operations in the late twentieth century.[63] While in most cases civilians suffered at the hands of the uniformed forces fighting against guerrillas, often guerrilla forces themselves targeted the people they fought among. Notwithstanding the revolutionary tenet that guerrillas represent the people as a whole, in many conflicts the population has been battered and coerced into submission by insurgents and counterinsurgents alike, including the Vietnam War, the Algerian Revolution, and the twenty-first-century wars in Afghanistan, Iraq, and Syria. Despite the apparent irony, this sad outcome seems a natural consequence of the instrumentalist approach toward civilians that is inherent in the nature of guerrilla warfare itself. As Richard Hartigan points out, "neither the guerrilla nor his antagonist accords the civilian the highest priority as a category of persons who should be protected and spared. In guerrilla combat the neutral civilian is merely a means to be used, or if necessary, abused, to attain victory."[64] Legitimizing guerrilla warfare therefore not only made it harder to discern where to draw the line between combatants and civilians but also opened to question the relevance of that line to begin with. This was especially problematic in light of the populist ideologies behind most liberation movements, which saw the distinction between "the people" and those fighting for them as illusory. This made it all too easy for belligerents to rationalize that "there are no real civilians" among the population—a rationalization frequently used to justify terrorism, as we shall see.[65]

Second, in accepting the argument that allowing guerrillas to blend with the population was the only way to give them a chance to win, Protocol I signaled the declining coherence of the distinction between civilian immunity and military necessity. A timeless conundrum in warfare is what Michael Walzer refers to as the tension between "winning" and "fighting well": the imperative to achieve victory, balanced against the legal and ethical rules that keep war from descending into slaughter. The danger in deferring to military necessity, Walzer explains, is that both logically and in practice it tends to subsume all other considerations: "The doctrine justifies not only whatever is necessary to win the war, but also what is necessary to reduce the risks of losing, or simply to reduce the losses or the likelihood of losses in the course of the war. In fact, it is not about necessity at all; it is a way of speaking in code, or a hyperbolical way of speaking, about probability and risk."[66] For this reason, if the rules are to be at all effective, international law must presumptively resolve this tension in favor of restraint. Protocol I, to the contrary, accepts the consequentialist logic of military necessity and incorporates it into IHL itself, at the cost of compromising the integrity of the principle of distinction in guerrilla wars. This undermines not only the civilian immunity norm but also the normative structure on which the entire project of IHL is based, and it invites belligerents to start down the slippery slope Walzer describes.[67]

Finally, in making this concession only for a specific category of belligerents, Protocol I applied different rules to different sides in the same conflict, making the legitimacy of certain means conditional upon the ends for which they are used. It therefore not only undermined but also explicitly rejected the long-standing distinction between questions of cause and conduct reflected in the categories of jus ad bellum and jus in bello. As I have mentioned, keeping these inquiries distinct had long been seen as fundamental to IHL, which could not survive if exceptions were allowed for those fighting in a just cause—or who claimed they were. To be sure, belligerents have often tried to justify their conduct based on the moral stakes of their struggle, but formally and explicitly endorsing such exceptionalism, as Protocol I does, cannot help but create significant problems for international law. It is here, in opening IHL to claims of special privilege based on the justness or importance of one's cause, that Protocol I may have set the most troublesome precedent since it undermines the obligatory nature of international law itself. Even beyond endorsing asymmetry in the content and application of the law, this constituted a step toward accepting that the ends can justify the means, which is a principle fraught with troubling implications.

A crisis for any of these norms would have been significant in its own right, but the combined effect of all three was to create a context in which a large spillover of the approach to the rules of guerrilla warfare reflected in Protocol I was almost inevitable. The breakdown of these three distinctions brought a consequentialist ethos to norms regarding the treatment of civilians, all in the service of the greater good of national liberation. Moreover, all this played out in a political milieu where, as seen in chapters 2 and 3, nonstate actors were newly empowered, states' interests were increasingly constrained, and anticolonialism was morphing into anti-Westernism. This, then, was the permissive normative environment in which the second track of the contestation of jus in bello norms played out.

While there is undeniably a significant leap from some guerrilla tactics to the overt, even ostentatious, targeting of civilians by organizations such as al-Qaeda, ISIS, and Boko Haram, they are different points on the same normative arc.

To appreciate this, it is useful to consider how frequently belligerents strategically exploit the norm of civilian immunity. To start with, any form of guerrilla warfare in which fighters rely for protection on their indistinguishability from civilians implicitly makes strategic use of this norm. The phenomenon extends far beyond this, however. In almost every conflict since 1990 (and some before then) pitting a strong state against a militarily inferior adversary, the weaker party has used tactics designed to exploit the norm of noncombatant immunity, not only taking refuge among the civilian population but also locating military objects in heavily populated areas, conducting military operations from residences, schools, or other protected sites, and in some cases using civilians as unwilling "human shields" (see table 4.1). The choice thus left to the adversary is to forgo

TABLE 4.1 Examples of use of civilian-centric tactics

YEAR(S)	CONFLICT	BELLIGERENT(S) USING CIVILIAN-CENTRIC TACTICS
1963–75	Vietnam War	North Vietnam; Viet Cong[a]
1991	Gulf War	Iraq
1992–94	UNITAF, UNOSOM II[b]	Somali irregulars[c]
1994–2000	Chechen Wars	Chechen separatists[d]
1999	Kosovo Conflict	Federal Republic of Yugoslavia[e]
2001	Afghanistan invasion	Afghanistan (Taliban government)[f]
2001–	Afghanistan insurgency	Taliban and al-Qaeda insurgents[g]
2003	Iraq War	Iraq[h]
2003–11	Iraqi occupation/insurgency	Iraqi insurgents; al-Qaeda in Iraq
2002	Jenin (Israel vs. Palestinians)	both sides[i]
2006	Israel vs. Hezbollah	Hezbollah[j]
2007	Pakistan vs. Taliban	Taliban[k]
2008–9	Gaza War (Israel vs. Hamas)	both sides[l]
2008–9	Sri Lanka vs. Tamil Tigers	LTTE (Tamil Tigers)[m]
2011	Libyan Civil War	Qaddafi regime[n]
2011–	Syrian Civil War	Assad regime, rebels, ISIS[o]
2014	Gaza War (Israel vs. Hamas)	Hamas[p]
2016	Iraqi siege of Mosul	ISIS[q]

Note: It is a sign of the intense politicization of the civilian casualties issue that almost all accounts are contested and there is no source that all parties will recognize as neutral. Here I rely heavily on the reports of Human Rights Watch, an organization that, based on its methodology (which in many ways pioneered humanitarian battle-damage assessment) and its record of relative even-handed willingness to criticize both sides in a conflict, has a better claim than most to authoritative status.

[a] Among the tactics employed by the North Vietnamese Army was placing antiaircraft batteries on dams and dikes, which US aircraft crews were under orders not to attack.

[b] The Unified Task Force (UNITAF) was the UN-sanctioned multinational force charged with delivering humanitarian relief in Somalia from December 1992 to May 1993. It was replaced by the United Nations Operation in Somalia II (UNOSOM II), which operated under an expanded mandate that included restoring peace in the country.

[c] Sebastian Kaempf, *Saving Soldiers or Civilians? Casualty Aversion versus Civilian Protection in Asymmetric Conflicts* (Cambridge: Cambridge University Press, 2018), 133–35.

[d] Barry Renfrew, "Chechnya," in *Crimes of War 2.0* (2007), crimesofwar.org/thebook/chechnya.html (site discontinued), accessed February 8, 2010.

[e] Human Rights Watch, "Civilian Deaths in the NATO Air Campaign," 2000, https://www.hrw.org/reports/2000/nato; Human Rights Watch, "Kosovo Human Rights Flash #33: Civilians at Risk by Yugoslav Use of Civilian Property for Military Purposes," April 30, 1999), https:www.hrw.org/campaigns/kosovo98/flash5.shtml.

[f] William Branigan, "Taliban's Human Shields," *Washington Post*, October 24, 2001.

[g] Human Rights Watch, "Troops in Contact: Airstrikes and Civilian Deaths in Afghanistan," September 8, 2008, https://www.hrw.org/report/2008/09/25/troops-contact/airstrikes-and-civilian-deaths-afghanistan.

[h] Human Rights Watch, *Off Target: The Conduct of the War and Civilian Casualties* (New York: Human Rights Watch, 2003), 67–69.

[i] Human Rights Watch, "Jenin: IDF Military Operations," May 2, 2002, https://www.hrw.org/en/reports/2002/05/02/jenin-0.

[j] Human Rights Watch, "Why They Died: Civilian Casualties in Lebanon during the 2006 War," September 5, 2007, https://www.hrw.org/en/node/10734. The HRW report concludes, however, that although Hezbollah did use human shields in some cases, "these cases were far less numerous than Israeli officials have suggested."

[k] Human Rights Watch, "Pakistan: Taliban, Army Must Minimize Harm to Civilians," May 18, 2009, https://www.hrw.org/en/news/2009/05/18/pakistan-taliban-army-must-minimize-harm-civilians.

[l] Human Rights Watch, "Country Summary: Israel / Occupied Palestinian Territories," January 2010, https://www.hrw.org/en/node/87711.

[m] Human Rights Watch, "War on the Displaced: Sri Lankan Army and LTTE Abuses against Civilians in the Vanni," February 19, 2009, https://www.hrw.org/report/2009/02/19/war-displaced/sri-lankan-army-and-ltte-abuses-against-civilians-vanni. The Liberation Tigers of Tamil Eelam (LTTE) was a militant separatist group operating in northern and eastern Sri Lanka from 1976 until its defeat in 2009.

[n] "Report: Gadhafi Forces Perched Children on Tanks to Deter NATO Attacks," MSNBC, August 30, 2011, https://www.nbcnews.com/id/wbna44323971; "NATO: Gadhafi Using Mosques, Children's Parks as Shields," MSNBC, June 19, 2011, https://www.nbcnews.com/id/wbna43451301.

[o] "Syrian Children Used as Human Shields, Says UN Report," BBC, June 12, 2012, https://www.bbc.com/news/world-middle-east-18405800; "Syrian Rebels Using Caged Civilian Captives as 'Human Shields,'" *Telegraph* (UK), November 2, 2015, https://www.telegraph.co.uk/news/worldnews/middleeast/syria/11971269/Syrian-rebels-using-caged-pro-Assad-captives-as-human-shields.html; Agence France-Presse, "ISIS Uses 2,000 Civilians from Northern Syria as 'Human Shields,'" PRI, August 12, 2016, https://www.pri.org/stories/2016-08-12/isis-uses-2000-civilians-northern-syria-human-shields.

[p] Although accusations by the Israel Defense Forces (IDF) that Hamas used human shields were generally dismissed as groundless, there was ample evidence that Hamas located rockets and other military objects in civilian sites. There were also reports that the IDF used human shields, but such accusations were fewer and more problematic. United Nations Human Rights Council, *Human Rights Situation in Palestine and Other Occupied Arab Territories: Report of the Detailed Findings of the Independent Commission of Inquiry Established Pursuant to Human Rights Council Resolution S-21/1*, June 23, 2015, https://ohchr.org/Documents/HRBodies/HRCouncil/ColGaza/A_HRC_CRP_4.doc.;

[q] United Nations Office of the High Commissioner for Human Rights, "Battle for Mosul: ISIL Forces Thousands of Civilians from Their Homes and Executes Hundreds," October 28, 2016, https://ohchr.org/EN/NewsEvents/Pages/DisplayNews.aspx?NewsID=20783&LangID=E.

taking action against hostile forces—even those actively engaged in shooting at them—or to risk killing civilians and the considerable political consequences that go with it. These practices, which I will call "civilian-centric tactics," in effect constitute the weaponization of civilian immunity.

An implicit assumption behind such behavior is that the norm against killing civilians is strong enough to constrain actors in this way; if civilian deaths could be brushed off with little thought, these tactics would be ineffectual and incoherent.[68] Indeed, it is difficult to imagine the prospect of killing civilians as serving as much of a deterrent in military operations throughout most of history, especially in conflicts like World War II, which saw civilian populations deliberately targeted on a large scale. As I have argued elsewhere, only since World War II has the injunction against killing civilians evolved into a norm that, while far from perfect, significantly impacts the behavior of states.[69] Even in recent conflicts, however, the effect of this norm has varied widely, and in some cases (such as Rwanda and Congo) the wholesale slaughter of civilians has been central to the conflict itself.[70] This implies that the strategic logic of civilian-centric tactics is context-specific: they make sense only in certain times, in certain wars, and against certain adversaries. It also suggests that although "asymmetrical warfare" typically refers to an imbalance in material military capabilities, one of the most important ways in which a conflict may be asymmetrical is *normative* asymmetry: a situation in which the opposing sides are constrained by different norms or by the same norms to significantly different degrees. After all, if the norm were applied symmetrically, belligerents who deliberately placed civilians at risk would face considerable political fallout for doing so, and that knowledge itself would make such tactics unattractive or even politically unacceptable. When such asymmetry exists, it favors the weaker side over the conventional army, which, Walzer explains, "gets no circumstantial exemption from the old rules; it is expected above all to maintain the distinction between combatants and civilians, even if the insurgents deliberately blur the distinction."[71] In most cases, the weaker belligerent is also from the non-Western world—not an incidental fact in light of the discussion of normative asymmetry in chapter 2, as well as the dynamics recounted in chapter 3.

To be clear, Protocol I did not legalize using human shields, using schools as armories, or firing mortars from mosques, nor did it directly "cause" these things to happen. But the normative underpinnings of such practices are clearly evident in the protocol and the political dynamics that produced it. The normative spillover of the legitimization of guerrilla tactics went even further, however, not just making such tactics increasingly common but also underpinning efforts to redefine the boundaries of what guerrilla warfare permitted. This is the second track of contestation I referred to earlier, the core element of which was the contestation of the norm of civilian immunity itself. The second track, which played out over much the same time as the first and grew from the same unsettled normative landscape, would create the ideational framework for the growth of transnational terrorism.

Contesting "Terrorism"

The seminal event in this second track—what could be called the contestation of "terrorism"—was the kidnapping and murder of eleven Israeli athletes and officials by Palestinian militants at the 1972 Olympics in Munich. However, the tactics and goals of the Munich attack were not new but followed a pattern that began after the Six-Day War of 1967 and the subsequent Israeli occupation of the territories of the West Bank, Gaza, and the Sinai Peninsula. While the years after Israeli independence in 1948 had seen both cross-border attacks on Israelis by displaced Palestinians and Israeli reprisal raids against Palestinian villages, the 1967 war galvanized militant Palestinian opposition and led to a change in tactics. Hoffman traces the beginning of "modern, international terrorism" to July 22, 1968, when three gunmen associated with the PLO hijacked an Israeli commercial airliner, demanding the release of Palestinians imprisoned in Israel.[72] The event was pivotal, Hoffman argues, because it internationalized both the scope of operations and their intended "audience." Especially in light of the technological improvements that allowed television news to air on-location footage, "terrorists rapidly came to appreciate that operations perpetrated in countries other than their own and directly involving or affecting foreign nationals were a reliable means of attracting attention to themselves and their cause."[73] As a PLO official explained in 1976, "the first several hijackings aroused the consciousness of the world and awakened the media and world opinion much more—and more effectively—than twenty years of pleading at the United Nations."[74]

From the late 1960s, then, Palestinian militancy was in an important sense a battle for international public opinion. This battle was waged with both dramatic acts of violence and words and ideas disseminated through the media and through debate at international conferences and the UN. Indeed, it is hard to overstate the significance of the Israeli-Palestinian conflict in shaping the current state of law, politics, and rhetoric regarding transnational terrorism. For one thing, throughout the 1970s, Palestinian terrorist groups were the most active in the world, making them the focal point for the issue.[75] As important, however, was that the Palestinian position attracted support from newly independent states, who for reasons of both principle and politics saw the Palestinians' struggle as their own. This meant that the Palestinian position had not only a good deal of rhetorical support but also sometimes the votes to command a majority in the

UN General Assembly, which, as I explained in chapter 2, can play an important role in effecting normative change. For these reasons, the plight of Palestinians in refugee camps and in the occupied territories provided the political backdrop against which much of the contestation of "terrorism" took place. Nevertheless, this contestation dynamic did not take shape immediately. Most non-Western states condemned the 1968 El Al hijacking, albeit perfunctorily. More hijackings followed, the most dramatic in September 1970 when members of the Popular Front for the Liberation of Palestine (PFLP) hijacked four commercial airliners and held their passengers and crews hostage for several days before releasing them in exchange for several PFLP members in British custody. Again, the reaction among non-Western states was circumspect, and the UN Security Council unanimously condemned the action, with several communist and African states, as well as an Arab state (Syria), joining in.[76]

Munich and the General Assembly Debate, 1972

Things were altogether different after the Munich Olympics attack in 1972, which came just three months after an even deadlier attack on civilians at Tel Aviv's Lod Airport by Japanese gunmen working for the PFLP. Two days after the Munich incident, UN secretary-general Kurt Waldheim proposed that the General Assembly, whose fall session was to begin two weeks later, address the problem of "terrorism." What followed was an acrimonious debate pitting Western against non-Western states, with both sides staking out positions that have defined the international discourse on terrorism ever since.

Two factors combined to make this debate so pivotal in the contestation of "terrorism." The first was the forum in which it occurred. As I have mentioned, the General Assembly was an intensely political body, where by 1972 the influence of postcolonial states, and the anti-Western ethos that went with it, had reached unprecedented levels. Already a venue perfectly suited to the sort of symbolic politics and rhetorical argument that are central to normative contestation, the General Assembly in 1972 was primed to play a key role in shaping the terms of the debate over terrorism. The second factor was the terminology itself: the fall 1972 General Assembly session marked the first time the international community addressed the problem of "terrorism" per se since World War II. Although it seems surprising today, pre-1972 incidents such as the 1968 El Al and 1970 Dawson's Field hijackings were very rarely described as "terrorism," either by the press or by political leaders. Media accounts typically described the perpetrators as "guerrillas" or "commandos." At the time of the El Al hijacking, an official statement by the Israeli government condemned it as an "act of piracy in the air," and Prime Minister Levi Eshkol called it "highway robbery," but neither statement used any form of the word "terrorism."[77] Remi Brulin writes that until 1972, "no American president had used the term 'terrorism' or 'terrorist' to refer to hijackings or bombings of commercial aircraft" and notes that US government documents "referred to members of the PFLP as 'guerrillas' or 'fedayeen.'"[78] Using terms other than "terrorism" did not reflect a value judgment but simply that the term was not at the time routinely used to describe these acts. Waldheim's framing of the Olympics attacks as "terrorism," combined with Western states' determination to conclude a resolution (or perhaps even a treaty) requiring states to take measures to prevent such actions, convinced non-Western states that the West was in effect using the terrorism issue as a Trojan horse to discredit and ultimately criminalize self-determination movements.[79]

For the Western countries in the General Assembly in 1972, the focus did not—and should not, they argued—stray far from the events in Munich. The Olympics attack illustrated what made the recent trend so disturbing: not only the humanitarian outrage of the deaths of innocent civilians but also the ubiquitous danger to international interactions of all sorts. US secretary of state William Rogers told the General Assembly:

> The issue is not an issue of war—not war between States, not civil war or revolutionary war. The issue is not the strivings of people to achieve self-determination and independence. Rather, it is whether millions of air travelers can continue to fly in safety each year. It is whether a person who opens his mail can open it without fear of being blown up. It is whether diplomats can safely carry out their duties. It is whether international meetings, like the Olympics, like this General Assembly, can proceed without the ever-present threat of violence. In short, the issue is whether the vulnerable lines of international communications—the airways and the mails, diplomatic discourse and international meetings—can continue, without interruption, to bring nations and peoples together. All who have a stake in this have a stake in decisive action to suppress these demented acts of terrorism.[80]

The non-Western bloc, however, saw the West's moralistic stand against "terrorism" as an opportunistic attempt to undermine liberation movements and refused to accede to any measure that would constrain those struggles or cast them in a negative light. In shaping this position, it was surely important that the precipitating event pitted Palestinians against Israelis, a conflict that had become the single most contentious issue between Western and non-Western blocs. It did not help that among those states denouncing these nonstate "terrorists" were not only Israel but also Portugal and South Africa, whose own policies had turned them into international pariahs and which did indeed describe resistance movements within their own territories as terroristic.[81] Non-Western states therefore resented what they viewed as an effort to distract the international community from the injustices perpetrated by colonial states that created the grievances these "terrorists" were trying to redress. Before the item even came to the floor, therefore, they insisted that Waldheim's proposal to examine "measures to prevent international terrorism which endangers or jeopardizes fundamental freedoms" be amended to include "and study of the underlying causes of those forms of terrorism and acts of violence which lie in misery, frustration, grievance and despair which cause some people to sacrifice human lives, including their own, to effect radical changes."[82] By this, they hoped to place the focus back on the conditions that gave rise to nonstate violence and also on "state terrorism," which included not just colonialism and foreign occupation but also the conduct of war by Western states against non-Western peoples, such as the United States in Vietnam.[83]

The essence of the non-Western position, however, was not simply a normative justification of terrorist actions carried out in a just cause, such as those provided in earlier times by Russian anarchists, Lehi, the FLN, and others. It was instead a denial that actions taken by those resisting Western oppression could properly be called "terrorism" at all. The Moroccan foreign minister put it this way: "First of all, what is terrorism? We exclude from the definition that people are now trying to work out any act motivated by the defense of a legitimate and inalienable right which the law has failed to protect. This principle, in our view, applies as much as to an individual as to a group and, *a fortiori*, to an entire people. An objectively violent act may have legitimate motivations and, speaking of the actions of Palestinians, let us clearly say that this involves the expression of one of the most painful aspects of the crisis in the Middle East, namely, that where there is aggression there is necessarily resistance."[84] Similarly, the Indonesian delegate argued that

> a distinction should be drawn between terrorism perpetrated for personal gain and other acts of violence committed for political purposes. Although recourse to violence must ultimately be eliminated from relations between peoples, it must be borne in mind that certain kinds of violence were bred by oppression, injustice, the denial of basic human rights, and the fact that whole nations were deprived of their homeland and their property. It would be unjust to expect such peoples to adhere to the same code of ethics as those who possessed more sophisticated means of advancing their interests. It was unacceptable for acts committed by common criminals to be identified with acts committed by those who resisted oppression and injustice by all possible means in

order to achieve independence and regain their dignity. Such acts could not be classified as terrorism; on the contrary, they were to a certain extent to be regarded as anti-terrorist acts aimed at combatting a much more repulsive kind of terrorism, namely colonialism and other forms of domination. These forms of violence were legitimate, being founded on the right to self-determination proclaimed in the Charter and often reaffirmed by the United Nations.[85]

The Syrian ambassador went so far as to assert that "the international community is under the legal and moral obligation to promote the struggle for liberation and to resist any attempt to depict this struggle as synonymous with terrorism and illegitimate violence."[86]

Western states, on the other hand, wished to draw a clear distinction between acts of violence and the political causes that inspired them. Most insisted that they remained committed to self-determination but that even in the service of a worthy cause certain actions were categorically unacceptable, especially those that targeted civilians.[87] Canada's foreign minister noted, "When we agree that the cause is noble, we are tempted to condone the terror. But are we wise to do so? The act we condone today may be the one we regret tomorrow, when it is turned against us, for terrorism in the end affects everyone: it is an attack on civilization at large."[88] Abba Eban, Israel's ambassador to the UN, remarked, "Once the deliberate and unprovoked murder of unarmed civilians is justified by reference to the murderers' 'motives' or 'frustrations,' we might as well include murder amongst the legitimate indulgences of a permissive society and wipe the sixth commandment off the tablet of man's ethical history."[89]

The United States anticipated resistance from states sympathetic to NLMs but nevertheless hoped the General Assembly session might produce a treaty requiring states to act against terrorism. It therefore submitted a draft convention that sought a compromise, seeking to curtail only "the dangerous recent trend to internationalize terrorism," addressing violent acts "which occur both outside the State of nationality of the perpetrator and outside the State against which the act is directed"—a formulation that would have included the Munich attack but not the Lod Airport massacre.[90] As one scholar has observed, the proposal "focused on an extremely small set of violent acts."[91] By limiting the scope of the terrorism covered by the draft convention, the Americans hoped to avoid being cast as opponents of national liberation struggles but also to keep those struggles contained within their respective territories. This formula, they thought, might "isolate a specific threat common to the international community as a whole, which all could agree on, regardless of ideology or alignment."[92] To that end, the US draft convention sought to punish only those acts "committed neither by nor against a member of the armed forces of a State in the course of military hostilities."[93] The rationale for excluding national armed forces was not that such forces should be free to do as they pleased but rather that they were already subject to an established body of international law—IHL—which, as we have seen, already forbade the targeting of civilians, sometimes using the term "terror" in describing it. The purpose of the exclusion was thus technocratic and mundane, not to forever fix "terrorism" as an exclusively nonstate phenomenon. As a US official explained, the draft convention "did not seek to define terrorism in the abstract" but instead sought to focus the General Assembly's attention on a specific subset of terroristic acts.[94]

The US approach was ambitious in proposing that the international community's response to the problem be codified in treaty form but limited in the relatively narrow scope of offenses it sought to address. For this it was criticized by some other Western states, including the United Kingdom, Israel, and South Africa, all of which faced insurgencies within territories they controlled.[95] But while the draft convention did not go far enough to satisfy some other Western states, in the eyes of the non-Western bloc it went much too far. The proposal gained practically no traction with these states, who persisted in turning the spotlight back toward the policies of Western countries in the Middle East, Africa, and Asia. They were particularly critical of the Western insistence on distinguishing between "international terrorism" and the actions of state military forces, however brutal or inhumane. While the Americans insisted that their proposal did not amount to a condemnation of nonstate violence generally or NLM operations specifically, non-Western states objected to what they saw as singling out methods used by liberation fighters while remaining silent about far more destructive practices employed by developed states. Indeed, Chile's foreign minister accused the United States of "systematic and highly-mechanized terrorism" in Vietnam, while Libya's called attention to "the terror with which we all live, while the weapons of destruction are stockpiled in the warehouses of the superpowers, threatening the total ruin of the world."[96] The Syrian delegate complained that "the imperialist, colonialist and Zionist forces were unceasing in the use of their war machine, which conferred, as it were, an official status on the terrorism they were practicing."[97]

The impasse between these contending positions proved impossible to break. Finally, in December the General Assembly produced a resolution that reflected the upper hand the non-Western bloc had gained by its increasing numbers in the body. Resolution 3034 not only contained no mention whatsoever of Munich but also specifically "condemn[ed] the continuation of repressive and terrorist acts by colonial, racist and alien regimes" while affirming "the inalienable right to self-determination and independence of all peoples under colonial and racist régimes and other forms of alien domination and uphold[ing] the legitimacy of their struggle, in particular the struggle of national liberation movements"— language that echoed Security Council and General Assembly resolutions endorsing the jus ad bellum rights of NLMs. The resolution also created an Ad Hoc Committee on International Terrorism, comprising representatives of thirty-five states, to study the problem further. Seventy-six states voted for Resolution 3034, including every communist state and all but a handful from Africa and the Middle East, seventeen abstained, and thirty-five opposed it, including Israel, the United Kingdom, and the United States.

The debate Waldheim and the Western powers had sought on how to address the problem of international terrorism, therefore, became instead a battle over the meaning of the term "terrorism" itself. The non-Western bloc, by dint of rhetorical contestation, went a long way toward shifting the long-standing definitional core of the term away from a choice of means and toward the ends for which those means were used, in order to shield NLMs from stigmatization. This could be characterized as a cynically self-interested distortion of diplomatic discourse, but there was more to it than that. In fact, these states had a keener sense of the normative implications of the debate, and its inescapably political nature, than did the Western bloc. They understood that because this was the first time the UN was to address "terrorism" per se, the meaning the General Assembly attached to the term in that context was likely to frame the issue going forward. As the Yemeni delegate put it, under the circumstances any debate on terrorism could not help but "unintentionally expose the liberation movements in the world to trial by a world court."[98] Thus, in a pattern that would be repeated at the Diplomatic Conference in Geneva a little over a year later, Western states, especially the United States, approached the problem from a narrow legalistic perspective, while non-Western states insisted on treating it as part of a broader narrative about colonialism and great power arrogance. By refusing to engage the US proposal on its own legalistic terms, the non-Western states were not misunderstanding it but rather reframing it in a way that allowed them to highlight the apparent hypocrisy of the great powers.[99] So, by using "terrorism" as the rubric under which to discuss Munich and similar incidents, Waldheim unwittingly set in motion events that would fix a previously broad and generic term as an enduring focus of fractious relations between Western and non-Western countries.[100]

Indeed, the positions espoused in the General Assembly in 1972 only hardened in the years that followed. The Ad Hoc Committee on International Terrorism created by Resolution 3034 predictably accomplished little. Non-Western delegates focused their attention on state terrorism, applying the term to a broadening array of actions, including "oppression, serfdom, hegemony, use of defoliants, [and] economic destruction."[101] They remained insistent that the term was inapplicable to those fighting against colonial or racist regimes, whose activities were instead "a negation of terrorism."[102] Western states, following the US position in the General Assembly, argued that because state actions were already widely regulated, the committee should limit its focus to nonstate violence. The committee issued reports in 1973, 1977, and 1979, none of which ever defined "terrorism," which the committee described as a "highly emotional" and "loaded term" that was "liable to diverse interpretations."[103] It was not until the 1979 report that the committee actually condemned terrorism per se, but even this was a tepid measure, given that the absence of consensus on definition meant that various states were in fact condemning entirely different things.[104] As cynical and unproductive as this "condemn it but don't define it" approach may have been, it would serve as the model for UN resolutions dealing with terrorism going forward.[105] Even then, non-Western states made sure that General Assembly resolutions included language specifically exempting the actions of those struggling against colonialism or racism. This typically led Western delegates to abstain in their voting, allowing them to express grave but very general concerns about terrorism without endorsing the non-Western position.[106]

Strategies of Contestation

The contestation of the meaning of "terrorism" continued in the years after 1972, both through diplomatic channels and in the work of journalists, academics, international lawyers, and others sympathetic to liberation movements (especially the Palestinians), who made their case in various media, at conferences, and in journals. In these efforts, the arguments and rhetorical strategies used in the 1972 General Assembly session were clearly influential. At the core of most arguments was an unapologetic consequentialism. Indeed, the power of the moral imperative of decolonization was so great that it often effectively preempted direct consideration of the means used in the struggle to advance it. This meant that although what was ultimately being contested in these debates was the norm against deliberately targeting civilians, focusing on the injustices of colonialism and occupation often allowed NLMs and their allies to avoid having to directly confront that unpleasant fact. The most obvious example of this was the approach to the terminology itself: by refusing to even allow the word "terrorism" to be applied to liberation movements, the non-Western bloc obviated discussion of whether the cause of national liberation was sufficient to justify tactics that theretofore had defined the term. The implicit judgment about ends and means that underlay this argument therefore seldom had to be openly expressed in ways that subjected it to scrutiny. Sometimes this was done by invoking, directly or indirectly, the UN resolutions endorsing liberation movements. One PLO official

described a 1978 attack on a bus that killed 34 Israeli civilians as "a heroic operation stemming from the right of our people and our revolution to employ all
forms of struggle," his language mirroring various UN resolutions.[107] More generally, Hezbollah's 1985 manifesto described its core mission as "a veritable war
of resistance against the Occupation forces."[108] Ibrahim Abu-Lughod, a Palestinian American professor, conveyed the argument concisely: "It is quite obvious
that the successful implementation of [decolonization], which is superior to the
objective of the colonizer or settler, will not be carried out voluntarily or as a
consequence of the good wishes of the United Nations. The strenuous effort of
the liberation movements is the only means of implementation."[109] The rejection
of the "terrorist" tag for those involved in this effort was sometimes implicit but
not always. Lebanese cleric Sayyid Muhammad Husayn Fadlallah, the spiritual
leader of Hezbollah, said: "We don't see ourselves as terrorists, because we don't
believe in terrorism. We don't see resisting the occupier as a terrorist action. We
see ourselves as mujihadeen who fight a Holy War for the people."[110]

On those occasions when militant groups or their supporters were indeed
forced to confront the problematic nature of their methods, the consequentialism inherent in their position could become overt. This was sometimes expressed
in terms similar to the just war criterion of "last resort," with those fighting for
liberation claiming to be forced into adopting extreme measures by their lack
of resources and the absence of peaceful means of pursuing political change.[111]
As one PLO official put it: "How else are we to bring pressure to bear on the
world? The deaths are regrettable, but they are a fact of war in which innocents
have become involved."[112] Similarly, M. Cherif Bassiouni, an Egyptian American
legal scholar who would later consult to the US State Department and play a
pivotal role in the founding of the International Criminal Court, argued in 1974:
"The present situation leaves no alternative but to resort to 'terror-violence' to
accomplish what is sometimes a legitimate end based on legitimate rights, but
which find no legal or peaceful remedy for their redress. . . . The 'terror-violence'
of colonization cannot be condoned while the 'terror-violence' of liberation is
condemned."[113] Fadlallah explained in 1985: "Oppressed nations do not have the
technology and destructive weapons America and Europe have. They must thus
fight with special means of their own. [We] recognize the right of nations to use
every unconventional method to fight these aggressor nations, and do not regard
what oppressed Muslims of the world do with primitive and unconventional
means to confront aggressor powers as terrorism. We view this as religiously
lawful warfare against the world's imperialist and domineering powers."[114] Of
course, this was the same argument that would be used at the Geneva Diplomatic Conference to justify legitimizing guerrilla tactics, relying on the same—
often unstated—premise that the ends for which violence was being used were

so important that any qualms about the means being used to pursue them would have to be set aside. Also often unstated, but clear nonetheless, was the implication that ultimate moral responsibility for these actions should lie with those who oppressed and ignored colonized peoples rather than those acting on their behalf. Pakistani political scientist Eqbal Ahmad said in 1998:

> The Palestinians, for example, the superterrorists of our time [Ahmad used the term facetiously], were dispossessed in 1948. From 1948 to 1968 they went to every court in the world. They knocked at every door in the world.... Nobody was listening to the truth. Finally, they invented a new form of terror, literally their invention: the airplane hijacking. Between 1968 and 1975 they pulled the world up by its ears. They dragged us out and said, Listen, Listen. We listened. We still haven't done them justice, but at least we all know.[115]

When apologists for these groups directly confronted the uncomfortable fact of targeting civilians, they justified it using a range of arguments. Some used formal legal reasoning, including Bassiouni, who argued that that under the circumstances IHL should be interpreted to allow a relatively wide variety of civilians to be legitimate objects of attack.[116] More commonly, those contesting the norm turned to moral reasoning, questioning the assumptions that supported protecting civilians in the first place: that civilians were innocent, harmless, or not complicit in the circumstances driving the conflict. Moreover, the argument for expanding the class of permissible targets for attacks was analogous to the ideology of "the peoples' war" that animated many NLMs. If wars of liberation were in effect fought by and on behalf of not just a small group but an entire people, then by the same token the enemy they were fighting was not just an oppressive government but the entire people that government represented— especially those among the people who were seen as unjustly "occupying" contested territory. Applying this logic, Hamas, Hezbollah, and the PLO all refused to make any distinction between Israel's military forces and Israeli civilians. Arafat declared in 1972, "Civilians or military, they're all equally guilty of wanting to destroy our people."[117] Even when Arafat nominally renounced terrorism in 1988, he excluded from that term "any operation against any Israeli occupying my country," military or civilian, defining the occupied country as not just the territories occupied since 1967 but also all of Israel.[118] To be sure, the rhetorical strategy of broadly assigning moral culpability or complicity to civilians was not new; it was used by nineteenth-century anarchists and revolutionaries to justify attacks on industrialists, merchants, and bureaucrats—even clergy.[119] Militants in the late twentieth and early twenty-first centuries often applied this strategy with a very broad brush. In some formulations, the fact that civilians paid taxes made them accountable for their government's actions—reasoning applied by Osama bin Laden to Americans and Chechen militant leader Shamil Basayez to Russians.[120] Although it is difficult by any standard to attribute responsibility to the very young, the deaths of children in militant attacks was nevertheless sometimes excused by claiming that they were unintended by-products of legitimate attacks—not coincidentally the same reasoning that in IHL excuses what is typically referred to as "collateral damage."[121] Sheikh Yusuf al-Qaradawi, one of the leaders of the Muslim Brotherhood, justified suicide bombings against Israeli civilians by arguing that "Israeli society is militaristic in nature. Both men and women serve in the army and can be drafted at any moment. On the other hand, if a child or an elderly person is killed in such an operation, he is not killed on purpose, but by mistake, and as a result of military necessity. Necessity justifies the forbidden."[122] On a similar note, the president of Sinn Fein, the political wing of the Irish Republican Army (IRA), described the death of seventeen-month-old girl in a bombing as "one of the hazards of urban guerrilla warfare."[123] In some cases, however, even this strained logic was dispensed with, as in the horrifying example of a Phalangist militiaman who justified the slaughter of hundreds of Palestinians, including women and children, in refugee camps in Lebanon in 1982 by claiming, "Pregnant women will give birth to terrorists; the children when they grow up will be terrorists."[124]

Apart from the consequentialism that underlies almost all contestation of "terrorism," the most common strategy used by liberation movements and their sympathizers was once again an appeal to analogical reasoning. This had been a significant theme in the General Assembly debates in 1972, as non-Western delegates drew parallels between contemporary resistance groups and examples from Western states' own national experiences. The Syrian ambassador queried: "Were not Jefferson and Benjamin Franklin and George Washington in their time the leaders and commanders of terrorism in the view of the ruling colonial Power? Were not the heroes resisting Nazi and Fascist occupation in Europe 'terrorists' in the eyes of the Nazi and Fascist leaders?"[125] Likewise, the delegate from the Peoples' Republic of the Congo reminded Western delegates of their revolutionary roots: "In the official education it provides for its children the Christian and bourgeois West has found it proper to devote pages of tributes to the terrorists who liberated their countries by harassing the invaders. . . . If the Europeans of 1972 no longer blow up trains and bridges, it is because their countries are free."[126] More than two decades later, Northern Irish Catholic activist Bernadette Devlin McAliskey said of a 1993 bombing that killed a three-year old and a twelve-year old: "It was a terrible action, but then the American War of Independence was not won with feather dusters either. . . . I refuse to condemn those who are forced by the system to resort to violence, but if I actually supported violence I would use it."[127]

Liberation movements themselves drew some of the same parallels, pointing to earlier resistance forces as relevant precedents both for the justice of their cause and for their methods. The implications of this logic could be startling, as in a 1973 manifesto by the Provisional Irish Republican Army, in which it provided a litany of targets, most of them civilian, that it considered acceptable to attack:

> military and police barracks, outposts, customs offices, administrative and government buildings, electricity transformers and pylons, certain cinemas, hotels, clubs, dance halls, pubs, all of which provide relaxation and personal comforts for the British forces; also business targets e.g., factories, firms, stores . . . owned in whole or in part by British financiers or companies, or who in any way are a contributory factor to the well-being of Her Majesty's invading forces, and in certain instances residences of people known to harbor or be in league with espionage personnel or *agents provocateurs*. . . . In many ways this campaign is reminiscent of that carried out by the underground Resistance in France during World War II.[128]

Moreover, supporters of NLMs could point to several national leaders, including Kenya's Jomo Kenyatta, Cyprus's Archbishop Makarios, Algeria's Ahmed Ben Bella, and even French president Charles de Gaulle, who had themselves led resistance groups that used tactics similar to those now at issue.[129] The numerous examples of this transition from "terrorist" to "statesman" undermined Western condemnations of terror tactics as self-defeating and unacceptable.

The most important precedent for the use of terrorism in national liberation, especially in the Palestinian case, was Israel itself. This was true in both rhetorical and strategic terms; Hoffman notes that "the Irgun's campaign . . . established a revolutionary model that thereafter was emulated and embraced by both anti-colonial- and postcolonial-era terrorist groups around the world."[130] Indeed, it was difficult to meaningfully distinguish between the tactics employed by Palestinian terrorists of the 1970s and those of the Irgun and Lehi that had helped achieve Israeli independence in 1948. For critics of Israel, the precedent included not only events leading up to independence but also the actions of the Israeli state afterward, including the reprisals policy that killed thousands of Palestinians from 1949 to 1956.[131] In the General Assembly in 1972, the Saudi Arabian representative thundered:

> Who murdered Lord Moyne? Who hanged British Tommies from trees in Palestine? Who blew up the King David Hotel in Jerusalem and tried repeatedly to kill the British High Commissioner in Palestine, Sir Harold MacMichael, and succeeded in wounding him? Who murdered Count

Folke Bernadotte and his French assistant in Jerusalem? And have we forgotten the highly organized Zionist terrorist gangs such as the Irgun Z'vai Leumi, the Stern gang, the Haganah and other splinter terrorist organizations, acting in concert or independently? And who can forget the massacre of Deir Yasin, whose population was subjected to total genocide? It was that horrible massacre which terrorized helpless people and forced them to leave their homes, thereby enabling the Zionists to establish themselves in Palestine.[132]

In the same forum, the Tunisian delegate quoted at length a statement about "Palestinian terrorism," only at the end revealing its author to be former French premier Léon Blum, speaking in 1947 in favor of the establishment of Israel:

> A few months ago, I said what I thought about Palestinian [i.e., Zionist] terrorism. I spoke out freely. Inevitably, you provoke terrorism when you reduce fanatical believers in a just cause to a hopeless situation. But the people I am talking about are not terrorists. They are simply martyrs. They will die with their weapons in their hands as heroes, as did the martyrs of the Warsaw ghetto. Like the Christian martyrs in the Coliseum, they have no weapon but their faith, but their decision to stand without flinching and accept the supreme sacrifice. In making this act of faith, this willingness, this act of will to sacrifice themselves, they are not humbled; they grow in stature. . . . We must put an end to this. The universal appeal for justice is irresistible. We must ask mercy on these unhappy persons who, after so many tribulations and sufferings, legitimately and naturally seek the refuge of a homeland, their homeland. It is natural that in emerging from so many trials they dream of an asylum in a land which would be theirs, where they would find themselves among their equals with other free men and where they might at last be able to count on breathing, working and seeing their children grow up in a secure and brotherly atmosphere.[133]

The legacy of preindependence Zionist terrorism remained salient for decades, in large part because some of its primary architects became the leaders of Israel itself. Menachem Begin, the leader of the Irgun, was prime minister from 1977 to 1981, and Yitzhak Shamir, the leader of Lehi, served in the same position from 1983 to 1984 and 1986 to 1992. One Palestinian author noted the irony that in his memoirs "Begin describes his terrorism—including the wholesale massacre of innocent women and children—in righteous (and chilling) profusion. . . . Yet a few weeks after his election in May 1977 he emerged in the press with his terrorism forgotten, as a 'statesman' with implied comparison to Charles de Gaulle."[134]

Defenders of militant movements also drew on analogy more generally to highlight what they saw as the hypocrisy of the West. Some states now vociferously criticizing the targeting of civilians, they pointed out, had themselves used far more objectionable methods in fighting their own wars. Again, the conduct of World War II provided abundant examples, though not the only ones. Abu-Lughod described the General Assembly debate and the US draft proposal in these terms: "The question that has been posed for discussion certainly does not have the terroristic practices of states, especially Western states, as a background. It is obvious that the recent acts committed on behalf of the Palestinian Resistance and intended to advance the interests of the Resistance have given rise to the presumed search for a remedy; and with alacrity a spokesman for a state that has been the chief practitioner of terror bombing assumed a leadership role in attempting to stampede the world organization to adopt an ill-conceived draft of a treaty for the so-called prevention of terrorism."[135] Bassiouni argued along the same lines in 1974: "However abhorrent all forms of violence are, the 'terrorism' we know today is probably the beginning of a new historical cycle. If such acts of violence are to replace wars . . . then 'terrorism' is welcome because its harmful consequences are minimal in comparison to the well-known consequences of war. A single bombing raid in World War II or Viet Nam caused more damage, harm, and destruction than all the consequences of 'terrorism' during the last quarter of a century."[136] Three years before 9/11, Osama bin Laden also evoked World War II: "Throughout history America has not been known to differentiate between the military and the civilians, between men and women, or adults and children. Those who hurled atomic bombs and used weapons of mass destruction against Nagasaki and Hiroshima were the Americans. Can the bombs differentiate between military and women and infants and children?"[137]

While accusations of Western hypocrisy were wide-ranging, a frequent focus was the West's (and especially the United States') support of Israel, whose policies continued to create grievances among the Palestinian population. Although the PLO predated the Six-Day War of 1967, the resulting occupation of Gaza and the West Bank invigorated the organization, enhanced its standing, and sharply increased its recruiting and funding. From 1968 to 1985, PLO groups carried out over eight thousand attacks, hundreds of them outside Israel and the territories, and killed over 650 Israelis (the large majority of them civilians) as well as hundreds of citizens of other countries.[138] Another critical episode was Israel's military incursion into southern Lebanon in 1982 and its role in abetting the massacre of hundreds, perhaps thousands, of Palestinian refugees by Phalangist militia forces in the camps at Sabra and Shatila in September of that year. This event was pivotal in the formation of Hezbollah, which mentioned it prominently in its founding manifesto.[139] Several years later, in 1987, Sunni

Palestinians in Gaza founded Hamas, an organization unaffiliated with the PLO but devoted to similar ends, including the "liberation" of Palestine from Israeli control.[140] Hamas "military" operations consisted in large part of suicide bombings of Israeli civilian targets and, after 2001, mortar and missile attacks on Israeli towns. While Western governments consistently condemned these tactics, these organizations and their supporters complained that the West turned a blind eye toward the Israeli actions that purportedly provoked them. Khaled Meshaal, the political leader of Hamas, maintained in a 2008 interview that "martyrdom operations are part of the response to Israeli massacres. So why do people in America, or the West, or the world in general, criticize what is being done by Hamas, or the Palestinian people, but they do not criticize Israel's behavior?"[141] Edward Said, an influential Palestinian American scholar, identified this hypocrisy as the central element in the Western narrative of the Palestinian problem. While Said took a nuanced view, neither denying nor justifying Palestinian terrorism (and referring to it as such), he nevertheless objected to "the ways in which the whole grisly matter is stripped of all its resonances and its often morally confusing detail, and compressed simply, comfortably, inevitably under the rubric of 'Palestinian terror.' . . . The planting of bombs in Israel or the West Bank and Gaza must be understood in the context of day-to-day coercion and the brutality of a long military occupation. Besides, there is nothing in Palestinian history, absolutely nothing at all to rival the record of Zionist terror against Arabs, against other Jews, against United Nations officials, against the British."[142]

One of the best-known examples of the contestation of "terrorism" was Arafat's address to the UN General Assembly in November 1974. He was the first representative of a nonstate entity to address the General Assembly, and his appearance itself, vociferously opposed by the United States and Israel, reflected the ascendance of developing and postcolonial states in the UN at the time. Arafat's speech, which drew on almost all of the rhetorical strategies I have described, is worth quoting at length:

> Those who call us terrorists wish to prevent world public opinion from discovering the truth about us and from seeing the justice on our faces. They seek to hide the terrorism and tyranny of their acts, and our own posture of self-defense.
>
> The difference between the revolutionary and the terrorist lies in the reason for which each fights. For whoever stands by a just cause and fights for the freedom and liberation of his land from the invaders, the settlers and the colonialists cannot possibly be called terrorist, otherwise the American people in their struggle for liberation from the British colonialists would have been terrorists; the European resistance

against the Nazis would be terrorism, the struggle of the Asian, African and Latin American peoples would also be terrorism, and many of you who are in this Assembly hall were considered terrorists. This is actually a just and proper struggle consecrated by the United Nations Charter and by the Universal Declaration of Human Rights. As to those who fight against the just causes, those who wage war to occupy, colonize and oppress other people, those are the terrorists. Those are the people whose actions should be condemned, who should be called war criminals: for the justice of the cause determines the right to struggle.

Zionist terrorism which was waged against the Palestinian people to evict it from its country and usurp its land is registered in your official documents. Thousands of our people were assassinated in their villages and towns; tens of thousands of others were forced at gunpoint to leave their homes and the lands of their fathers. Time and time again our children, women and aged were evicted and had to wander in the deserts and climb mountains without any food or water. No one in 1948 witnessed the catastrophe that befell the inhabitants of hundreds of villages and towns—in Jerusalem, Jaffa, Lydda, Ramle and Galilee—no one who has been a witness to that catastrophe will ever forget the experience, even though the mass black-out has succeeded in hiding these horrors as it has hidden the traces of 385 Palestinian villages and towns destroyed at the time and erased from the map. The destruction of 19,000 houses during the past seven years, which is equivalent to the complete destruction of 200 more Palestinian villages, and the great number of maimed as a result of the treatment they were subjected to in Israeli prisons cannot be hidden by any black-out. . . .

The only description for these acts is that they are acts of barbarism and terrorism. And yet, the Zionist racists and colonialists have the temerity to describe the just struggle of our people as terror. Could there be a more flagrant distortion of truth than this?[143]

Finally, as Arafat's speech shows and contrary to what critics sometimes claimed, those contesting terrorism—and even those practicing it—were by no means rejecting moral argumentation. As Mervyn Frost says of the rejection of the "terrorist" label, "if it is important for such groups to be described in one way rather than another then they have indicated their participation in the business of moral argument."[144] Similarly, philosopher Robert Fullinwider writes, "It is false to say that the revolutionary terrorist has no moral limits; but it is true that he or she repudiates the conventional boundaries that guide our actions."[145] But even this is not entirely true or at least depends on which of "our actions" are being referred to. As I have argued, one of the strategies used by those contesting "terrorism" was to use analogical reasoning to hold a mirror up to their accusers in the hope of forcing them to see in the terrorists' practices some of their own actions and the sometimes tenuous moral arguments used to justify them. Although they may repudiate prevailing interpretations of certain principles or judgments about priorities among principles, contestation requires that they draw on a recognizable moral frame of reference. Likewise, when Frost asserts that most terrorists "reject the legitimacy of the law (or of the legal system as a whole)," he is only partly right because he overlooks those who reject not the law itself but interpretations of the law hinging on what they claim to be specious distinctions, especially when they reinforce advantages Western states already possess.[146] As one FLN official put it, "I see hardly any difference between the girl who places a bomb in the Milk-Bar and the French aviator who bombards a *mechta* (village) or who drops napalm on a *zone interdite* (free-fire zone)."[147]

Of course, arguments of this sort also reflect the salient role played in the contestation of terrorism by what I have called "the revolt against the West." Given the close connection between the terrorism debate and the repudiation of Western colonialism, this is unsurprising. But they also remind us that this revolt did not always entail a thoroughgoing rejection of any and all normative frames of reference Westerners found meaningful. After all, the normative linchpin of decolonization was the ability to turn Western norms back against their authors, reminding governments and societies that purported to value human dignity and freedom that they were not practicing what they preached. Different manifestations of the revolt against the West therefore suggest a spectrum, with varying degrees of acceptance and rejection of legal and normative premises. At one end of the spectrum are religious extremists who described the Western-dominated order as fundamentally incompatible with, and hostile to, the divine commands that guided them. Many of the pronouncements of twenty-first-century extremist organizations such as al-Qaeda and ISIS fit this description but so too did the rhetoric of the Iranian government after the 1979 fundamentalist revolution. As Iran's first postrevolution defense minister, Mostafa Chamran, proclaimed: "We are not fighting within the rules of the world as it exists today. We reject all those rules."[148] More typical, however, and more relevant to the international process of contestation, were appeals to shared norms and principles that spoke both to those aggrieved by the Western order and to Westerners themselves. An arresting example came from the Saudi delegate in the 1972 General Assembly: "A civilization is something of the spirit. We have witnessed in two world wars that people who were advanced materially and who went to church on Sunday and prayed to the Prince of Peace—none other than Jesus—on Monday cut one another's throats. What kind of civilization is that?"[149]

The Western Response

It was not only NLMs and their supporters, however, that tried to shape the understanding of "terrorism" in ways that advanced their own priorities. Over time Western states, led by the United States, increasingly did the same thing, primarily by employing definitions that explicitly framed the terrorism problem in terms of nonstate actors. While the 1972 US draft convention had excluded state conduct from its definition of terrorism, this was done for reasons of legal precision, as I have explained; American government officials and legal scholars agreed that in general there was nothing in the concept of "terrorism" per se that precluded applying the term to states' actions.[150] Even at that time, to be sure, Western states such as Britain and Israel that had faced violent anticolonial movements were more likely to emphasize the nonstate aspect of terrorist violence.[151] By the 1980s, however, the nonstate aspect of the terrorism problem moved to the very center of the Western—especially the US—position in the terrorism debate.

A pivotal development was the election of Ronald Reagan in 1980. Reagan brought to the White House unstinting support for Israel, a skeptical stance toward international law and institutions, and a determination to make fighting terrorism a foreign policy priority. These factors converged in the administration's handling of Protocol I, which Reagan's predecessor Jimmy Carter had signed in 1977 but never submitted to the Senate for ratification, largely because of the US military's misgivings about its guerrilla warfare provisions. The Reagan administration was strongly hostile to the protocol, going beyond previous expressions of concern to condemn it as, in the words of one official, "a pro-terrorist treaty that calls itself humanitarian law."[152] In recommending its rejection by the Senate in 1987, Reagan asserted it "would endanger civilians among whom terrorists and other irregulars attempt to conceal themselves."[153] Reagan's stance had bipartisan support and was endorsed by both the *New York Times* and the *Washington Post*, down to its description of the treaty as a shield for terrorists.[154] To the extent that the administration's position purported to be based on the actual terms of Protocol I, it was an inaccurate and logically flawed interpretation. As some critics noted, the administration was in effect equating guerrillas with terrorists, despite the fact that the protocol placed restrictions upon the tactics that guerrillas could use and contained many provisions that ostensibly enhanced the protection of civilians.[155] In fact, the US conflation of guerrilla warfare and terrorism had less to do with what the protocol said than with the political process that had produced it and the actors whose interests it best served. Among the NLMs at the Diplomatic Conference were some the United States regarded as terrorist organizations, including the PLO and the South West Africa People's Organization (SWAPO), and that indeed targeted civilians in their operations.

As flawed as the legal reasoning behind Reagan's rejection of Protocol I may have been, it was attentive to the political and normative implications of the treaty's legitimization of NLMs. The overly broad brushstrokes with which the administration tarred Protocol I was in fact the antithesis of the narrow legalism that had characterized the American approach at the Diplomatic Conference and the General Assembly a decade earlier. In this sense, the United States was playing the same game the non-Western bloc had been playing since 1972. In doing so, it moved the West toward a position in the terrorism debate that, like the non-Western position it opposed, focused less on the nature of violent actions and whether they targeted civilians and more on the identity of the actor carrying them out. If, in its pre-1972 sense, "terrorism" had described a practice that could be employed by both state and nonstate actors, the United States now used it to refer to an exclusively nonstate problem—and in fact, a problem that was centrally defined by the nonstate status of the actors involved. Secretary of State George Shultz highlighted this in condemning Protocol I, writing that the treaty "undermines the principle that the rights and duties of international law attach principally to entities that have those elements of sovereignty that allow them to be held accountable for their actions, and the resources to fulfill their obligations."[156] In 1983, the Department of State and the Department of Defense adopted definitions of "terrorism" that excluded overt state action, with the Defense Department version referring specifically to "the unlawful use or threatened use of force or violence *by a revolutionary organization* against individuals or property with the intention of coercing or intimidating governments or societies, often for political or ideological purposes."[157] The State Department version, which remains in use, would play an especially significant role in shaping US policy, serving as the basis for its annual reports listing "foreign terrorist organizations" (FTOs) and "state sponsors of terrorism"—the latter designation carrying with it a bruising range of sanctions.[158] The State Department defined terrorism as "premeditated, politically motivated violence perpetrated against non-combatant targets by subnational groups or clandestine agents, usually intended to influence an audience."[159] While the reference to "noncombatant targets" seemed to conform to the essence of most pre-1972 usage, a footnote defined this phrase extremely broadly, "to include, in addition to civilians, military personnel who at the time of the incident are unarmed and/or not on duty. . . . We also consider as acts of terrorism attacks on military installations or on armed military personnel when a state of military hostilities does not exist as the site, such as bombings against US bases in Europe, the Philippines, or elsewhere."[160] Of course, the very question of whether "a state of military hostilities" exists is often a point of contention between nonstate groups and their governmental foes. Depending on how this phrase is interpreted, almost any politically motivated violence by a nonstate group could be deemed terrorism. At the least, the State Department definition includes actions that would not be forbidden to national military forces under IHL. The result is a formula that clearly condemns nonstate violence but otherwise invites arbitrary and politicized interpretations, as illustrated in this exchange in a congressional subcommittee between Rep. Lee Hamilton and State Department official Ned Walker:

> HAMILTON: Well, how do you define terrorism, do you define it in terms of non-combatants?
>
> WALKER: The State Department definition which is included in the terrorism report annually defines it in terms of politically motivated attacks on non-combatant targets.
>
> HAMILTON: So an attack on a military unit in Israel will not be terrorism?
>
> WALKER: It does not necessarily mean that it would not have a very major impact on whatever we were proposing to do with the PLO.
>
> HAMILTON: I understand that, but it would not be terrorism.
>
> WALKER: An attack on a military target. Not according to the definition. Now wait a minute; that is not quite correct. You know, attacks can be made on military targets which clearly are terrorism. It depends on the individual circumstances.
>
> HAMILTON: Now wait a minute. I thought that you just gave me the State Department definition.
>
> WALKER: Non-combatant is the terminology, not military or civilian.
>
> HAMILTON: All right. So any attack on a non-combatant could be terrorism?
>
> WALKER: That is right.
>
> HAMILTON: And a non-combatant could include military?
>
> WALKER: Of course.
>
> HAMILTON: It certainly would include civilian, right?
>
> WALKER: Right.
>
> HAMILTON: But an attack on a military unity would not be terrorism?
>
> WALKER: It depends on the circumstances.
>
> HAMILTON: And what are those circumstances?
>
> WALKER: I do not think it will be productive to get into a description of the various terms and conditions under which we are going to define an act by the PLO as terrorism.[161]

The politicization inherent in the US position on terrorism was evident not only in its exclusive focus on nonstate actors but also in a selective application of the standard, condemning some violent nonstate actors while praising others. A notorious example was Reagan's embrace of the Nicaraguan Contras (whose campaign to oust a socialist regime comprised mostly attacks against civilian targets) as "the moral equivalent of our Founding Fathers and the brave men and women of the French Resistance." In the same speech, Reagan praised the Afghan mujahideen, whose operations against the Soviets in Afghanistan included attacks on both soldiers and civilians, as "our brothers, these freedom fighters, and we owe them our help."[162] When asked in 1984 whether the administration was applying a double standard in its use of these terms, Secretary Shultz indignantly replied, "It is not hard to tell, as we look around the world, who are the terrorists and who are the freedom fighters"[163] This selectivity in identifying terrorists shaped policy as well as rhetoric, from funding for the Contras and mujahideen in the 1980s to the State Department's state sponsors of terrorism list, which from its inception in 1979 has reflected transparently political priorities, with states moving on and off the list as various administrations sought to punish, reward, or engage them, irrespective of their relationship to terrorist activities.[164]

Over time, other Western states adopted similarly contextualized approaches. The United Kingdom's approach to defining terrorism and designating terrorist organizations is similar to the US approach, in terms of most of the specific groups listed and the political calculations that inform the choices made.[165] Britain's official list of banned terrorist organizations includes many separatist and insurgent groups that plague British allies, while excluding similar (and even closely associated) groups that make life difficult for governments Britain wishes to isolate. In the 1990s and early 2000s, for example, Britain excluded from its list Kurdish and Shi'ite organizations working to undermine the Saddam Hussein government, while banning their affiliated organizations in other states.[166] Israel, a state exceptionally impacted by militant attacks, designates any armed resistance to its presence in or power over the territories of Gaza and the West Bank as terrorism, regardless of who or what is targeted—in effect, mirroring the militant Palestinian claim that the entire state of Israel constitutes hostile occupation of Palestinian territory.[167] Moreover, it has shown a willingness to embrace "a disproportionate response to dissuade terrorists from further attacks."[168] Former Israeli deputy national security adviser Charles Freilich describes one aspect of Israel's counterterrorism policy as "indirectly pressing terrorist organizations to cease attacks against Israel, by exerting pressure on the civilian populations in which they are embedded, and/or on the host governments."[169] Indeed, Israel was criticized by various human rights organizations and the UN for inflicting disproportionately heavy civilian casualties in its operations against Hamas in 2008–9 and 2014 and Hezbollah in 2006.[170] Freilich's description of Israel's counterterrorism measures, however, suggest that this was at least partly by design, as does his assessment that the country's "tough response to the Second Intifada turned Palestinian public opinion at least partially against violence, not in principle, but because of the heavy costs incurred. The 2006 Lebanon War had a similar deterrent effect on the Lebanese population."[171] The Israeli approach to terrorism thus reflects less overarching and universal moral principles than the particular political judgments and priorities of the country in prevailing circumstances.

Both the politicization of the US definition of "terrorism" and the propensity to equate it with nonstate violence figured prominently in American policy and rhetoric after the 9/11 attacks in 2001. One place this was evident was the military commissions in which dozens of persons captured in the "war on terror" were tried. These commissions were governed by a 2003 Department of Defense "instruction" that defined their jurisdiction and the crimes that fell under it. Although the instruction purported to be consistent with existing international law, it defined the offense of "terrorism" in ways that departed considerably from it. Notably, the instruction included in the definition not just deliberate attacks on civilians but also conduct "intended to intimidate or coerce a civilian population, or to influence the policy of a government by intimidation or coercion." This dramatically expanded the scope of possible terrorist action, since it could include even "an attack against a lawful military objective" unless carried out "by military forces of a State in the exercise of their official duties."[172] This approach—of broadening the range of conduct that could be considered "terrorism" but narrowing the application of the term to only nonstate actors—was also commonly found in US government statements about the Iraq War, especially after it degenerated from successful "major combat operations" in 2003 into a long and grinding counterinsurgency. Although this period saw a spike in attacks that would properly be considered terrorism by any definition, US authorities also applied the label to actions that many international lawyers would deem to be acceptable modes of international armed conflict, including "irregular forces resisting occupation, or . . . civilians *levée en masse*."[173] In such cases the word "terrorism" was used not in a formal legal sense but rather as a rhetorical device to frame ongoing US and allied efforts in a way most likely to elicit support and enhance claims to legitimacy. One commentator surmised that frequent American references to terrorism "derive from earlier unsubstantiated links between Iraq and terrorism, and paradoxically address the appearance of non-State terrorism in Iraq where, pre-invasion, there was none."[174]

To be clear, neither the United States nor other Western states explicitly claimed that actions committed by sovereign states could never legally be considered terrorism. Indeed, in at least one case the United States led the push for a

UN Security Council resolution condemning a state for its involvement in "acts of international terrorism," in response to Libya's role in the Lockerbie airliner bombing in 1988.[175] Nevertheless, the sense of state terrorism contemplated under the American usage comprised only acts that were, in the language of the State Department definition, carried out by "clandestine agents." This was an extremely limited subset of state action that categorically excluded almost anything national armed forces did. This reinforced the association of "terrorism" with small-scale, shadowy, and subversive operations—the very antithesis of the large-scale application of national military might, however terrible and indiscriminate it might be. The Donald J. Trump administration's April 2019 designation of Iran's Islamic Revolutionary Guard Corps (IRGC) as an FTO marked an apparent departure from this practice and was the first time an element of a foreign government had been so designated. Even in that case, however, what the administration deemed objectionable was the IRGC's support for nonstate FTOs and its role in clandestine bombing and assassination plots rather than large-scale conventional military operations that targeted civilians—such as those carried out by Russian and Syrian forces in Syria and Saudi Arabian forces in Yemen.[176] And, surely, the IRGC designation only underscored the overtly political nature of the FTO process.

The fact that Western states followed their non-Western counterparts in focusing on the identity of these violent actors rather than their choice of methods reflects how poorly positioned the West was to appeal to moral arguments about the evils of targeting civilians. As Ian Lustick writes, "if the innocence or noncombatant status of the specific targets of threats or violence are used as the main criteria for identifying terrorism, this will tend to cast states in the main terrorist role—states that, because they operate on a larger scale and employ armies and air forces that wreak 'accidental' havoc as an inevitable corollary of their use, usually kill, injure, or terrorize many more 'innocents' than even the most 'successful' nonstate terrorists."[177] Moreover, the "accidental" effects Lustick speaks of pale in comparison to the quite deliberate havoc powerful states wreaked in the twentieth century, of which the area bombing in World War II was a preeminent example. Michael Walzer, though a vocal critic of terrorism, acknowledges that "terrorism in the strict sense, the random murder of innocent people, emerged as a strategy of revolutionary struggle only in the period after World War II, that is, only after it has become a feature of conventional war."[178] Drawing moral distinctions between the actions of groups such as the PLO and things Western states had done in other contexts required narrowing the terrorism discourse to a specific subset of wanton violence: that committed by groups that seemed to threaten the established order. This was essentially a retrograde argument, based on norms that had become embattled in the years since World War II and hard to sustain in the face of the emerging acceptance of nonstate violence in various settings. By focusing on who committed acts of violence rather than the methods of violence chosen, Western states were in effect contesting "terrorism" on the turf staked out by their adversaries. Their argument was further undermined by the selectivity (one might say hypocrisy) with which it was applied. By turning a blind eye to atrocities committed by groups they supported, countries such as the United States seemed to accept the premise they had rejected in the General Assembly in 1972: that worthy ends justified dubious means and that the categories of "terrorists" and "freedom fighters" were mutually exclusive. What purported to be a principled argument, therefore, could be easily dismissed as a politically expedient exercise in name-calling. So, while it was by no means logically or historically inevitable that one person's terrorist would be another person's freedom fighter, by the 1980s this cynical maxim accurately captured the state of international discourse on the problem.

Terrorism: The Normative Picture Today

Several factors helped transnational terrorism grow in scope and influence from the 1970s onward, including unsettled political conditions (both within and among nations) in the postcolonial world. Through it all, however, the impasse on how to respond to this problem—indeed, on whether it even *was* a problem—contributed to conditions that facilitated and encouraged that growth. Most important, it prevented the creation of meaningful disincentives to engage in terrorist actions or support groups that did so.

In fact, throughout the 1970s and 1980s, some organizations that used terrorist tactics were becoming increasingly accepted as responsible actors in the international community, especially if they claimed the status of NLMs. The UN General Assembly granted special observer status to the PLO in 1974 and to SWAPO in 1976 and affirmed in a later resolution that the participation of such groups in the UN "helps to strengthen international peace and co-operation."[179] By 1980, the PLO, whose role in the terrorism debate was seminal, enjoyed formal diplomatic relations with more countries than did the state of Israel.[180] In the 1980s, judges in several countries, including the United States, refused to extradite suspects charged in terrorist attacks because of a provision in international law forbidding extradition for "political offenses."[181] In one case, the Greek government released a member of the notorious Abu Nidal group on the grounds that "the actions for which he was being accused fall within the domain of the struggle to regain the independence of his homeland and consequently suggest action for freedom." Those actions were the bombing of a synagogue in

Rome that killed a two-year-old boy and wounded thirty-four others.[182] More generally, over time some of these groups emerged as important political actors, both within national electoral systems (Hezbollah in Lebanon, for example) and as stakeholders whose participation in political processes was necessary to make progress toward peace (the IRA's role in the Good Friday Accords comes to mind).

Another telling sign that no significant opprobrium attached to terrorist tactics was that so many states actively supported organizations that employed them. According to Daniel Byman, "during the 1970s and 1980s, almost every important terrorist group had some ties to at least one supportive government."[183] At times this reflected Cold War politics: PLO operatives, for example, were trained in the Soviet Union, East Germany, Romania, China, Vietnam, North Korea, Pakistan, and various Arab states.[184] The success of Iran's fundamentalist revolution in 1979 ushered in a period of even more energetic state sponsorship, marked by support for Islamist opposition movements throughout the Middle East and parts of Asia. Iran played a central supporting role in the 1983 bombings of the US embassy and Marine barracks in Beirut and by the mid-1990s was spending $100 million annually to support militant fundamentalist groups.[185] Along with Iran, Syria, Sudan, and Iraq funded the PLO, Hamas, and other Islamist groups throughout the region, and Pakistan has supported Kashmiri and Punjabi separatist groups in India since the early 1980s. Libya assisted an ideologically and geographically disparate set of organizations, ranging from militant Palestinian groups to the Provisional IRA to Maoist rebels in the Philippines.[186] State sponsorship bolstered the resources and effectiveness of such organizations, allowing them to mount larger and more lethal operations; one study found that attacks by state-sponsored organizations during the 1980s produced eight times more fatalities than attacks by groups lacking state support.[187] The most notorious example of state sponsorship (at least to US observers) was Afghanistan's support for al-Qaeda in the years leading up to the 9/11 attacks, when the country was ruled by the Taliban. Again, however, this case reminds us that a balanced assessment of state sponsorship of terrorism would also include the United States, given the roots of both al-Qaeda and the Taliban in the US-armed and -financed mujahideen of the 1980s—a group that, along with the Contras, could easily have been designated a terrorist organization had it been targeting an American ally rather than a foe.[188] US sponsorship of terrorism may have been even more direct in a 1985 episode in Beirut, in which a car bomb exploded outside the residence of Islamic cleric Fadlallah, killing scores of civilians.[189] Louise Richardson observes: "It's not only the bad guys who use terrorism as an instrument of their foreign policy. Sometimes the good guys do too."[190] Support for the mujahideen, certainly, had profound consequences, as the group served as the model for, and the core of, several Islamist organizations that emerged as threats to the United States and its allies in the 1990s and 2000s, including the Taliban, al-Qaeda, and Ansar al-Islam. Indeed, Richardson points to the success of the mujahideen against the Soviets as the single most important event in the emergence of Islamic fundamentalist terrorism.[191] Of course, while Islamic fundamentalism has been the most common and most consequential impetus behind religion-based terrorism in recent decades, it has by no means been the only one, as deadly attacks have been carried out in the name of religion by militant Jews, American Christian white nationalists, and Catholic members of the IRA, among others.[192]

Systemically, state sponsorship of terrorism presents a puzzle, as one would not expect states to willingly empower actors that threaten their institutional monopoly on violence. Nevertheless, states sponsor terrorism for the same reason some militant groups practice it: because it makes sense to do so. Hoffman argues that for state sponsors, "terrorism remains a useful and integral tool of foreign policy: a clandestine weapon to be wielded whenever the situation is appropriate and the benefits tangible, but one to be kept sheathed when the risks of using it appear to outweigh the potential gains and the possible repercussions are likely to prove counterproductive. For the state sponsor, much as for the terrorist group itself, terrorism—contrary to popular perception—is not a mindless act of fanatical or indiscriminate violence; rather it is a purposefully targeted, deliberately calibrated method of pursuing specific objectives at acceptable cost."[193] Furthermore, this method is not always clandestine: Crenshaw describes state involvement after the 1980s as "open and deliberate," and Byman notes that Iran and Taliban-era Afghanistan "openly boasted" of their support for anti-Western groups.[194] This partly reflects the fact that sponsoring militant groups can not only serve foreign policy interests but also strengthen a government's position by appealing to national or regional constituencies. This has long been a salient factor in sponsorship of Palestinian groups, as support for Palestinian nationalism has been consistently strong throughout most of the Middle East and West Asia. This also explains what Byman describes as the United States' "passive" sponsorship of the Provisional IRA in the 1970s, when the group was permitted to conduct significant fundraising activities in the United States with minimal government interference.[195]

Hoffman's mention of risks, repercussions, and acceptable costs highlights the point that whatever reasons states have for supporting terrorist groups, they typically do not face strong disincentives to do so. First, it is obvious that the tactics these groups use do not give rise to a sufficiently powerful stigma that supporting them is categorically foreclosed as an option, in the way that the use of biological weapons or assassination of foreign leaders has been at various times.[196] In fact, some of the benefit states derive among their constituencies by supporting these groups may be because of, not in spite of, such tactics. Beyond stigmatizing certain actions, another way in which a norm can shape behavior is that actors that value the norm can impose tangible costs on transgressors. The more widely held the norm, the greater the number of actors (especially powerful actors) willing to enforce the norm, and the more actors are willing to sacrifice to enforce it, the more effective these measures are likely to be. Broadly multilateral sanctions for state sponsorship of terrorism have been rare, however. Since 1979, the United States has unilaterally sanctioned countries it designates as state sponsors of terrorism (SSTs), but it has seldom been successful in persuading others, even among its close allies, to join in these measures. When President Bill Clinton tried to garner overseas support for a new round of sanctions on Iran in 1995, several European states rebuffed him, favoring engagement with the Tehran regime.[197] Only Israel, El Salvador, and Ivory Coast joined the sanctions regime. Furthermore, US sanctions against SSTs have rarely had much impact. No state unilaterally sanctioned by the United States has significantly curtailed its support for militant groups; the only two cases in which sanctions yielded moderate success were Libya and Sudan, both of which were subject to UN as well as US sanctions.[198] The case for sanctioning Libya was especially strong, as the country not only supported militant nonstate groups but also actively engaged in terrorist operations in its own right, including the 1986 Berlin disco bombing and the 1988 Lockerbie attack.[199] Nevertheless, even many US allies strongly condemned the April 1986 American bombing raid on Tripoli in response to the Berlin attack. Ironically, American efforts to isolate states it accuses of sponsoring terrorism have often led to the relative isolation of the United States itself.

As we have seen, the 1970s and 1980s was a time particularly poorly suited for forging an international consensus on the terrorism question. Two later developments, however, seemed to hold out promise for progress. The first was the end of the Cold War. For ideological and fiscal reasons, Russia abdicated the former Soviet role of patron to NLMs in the developing world, and soon thereafter it and other post-Soviet states were threatened by separatist movements in their own countries. Indeed, in the 1990s and 2000s, several communist and postcommunist states moved noticeably closer to the American position on terrorism. The 1999 treaty of the Commonwealth of Independent States and the 2001 Shanghai Cooperation Organization (SCO) Convention on Combating Terrorism, Separatism, and Extremism both moved emphatically away from the exaltation of self-determination movements that characterized these countries' earlier positions.[200] Easing tensions between the Cold War blocs also brought less reflexive opposition in the UN, allowing for the Security Council sanctions on Libya and Sudan mentioned earlier. The second development was 9/11. The shocking nature of the attacks made it hard for states to equivocate in condemning them, and soon afterward the Security Council unanimously passed Resolution 1373 requiring member states to take steps to suppress terrorism, including freezing assets and blocking financing, preventing the free movement of suspected terrorists, and preventing their territories from being used as havens for terrorists.[201] In the year or two after 9/11, some saw signs of growing common interests among countries on opposite sides of the debates of the 1970s and 1980s, as decolonization receded into memory and groups such as al-Qaeda (which could hardly be considered an NLM) seemed to threaten both Western and non-Western regimes.[202]

In both cases, however, there was less than meets the eye to these signs of a convergence of international views about terrorism. Postcommunist states did in fact change their stance after the Cold War, but their former client states in the Middle East, Africa, and Asia did not follow suit. Indeed, the rift turned bitter in 2004, when Arab states refused to condemn Chechen rebel attacks as "terrorism," largely because they saw parallels between the Chechen and Palestinian cases.[203] A telling sign that significant differences remained was the failure to include terrorism as an offense under the 1998 Rome Statute, which founded the International Criminal Court, because no definition could be agreed upon.[204] Signs of growing solidarity after the 9/11 attacks were also misleading. While the Security Council condemned the attacks the day after they occurred, it took the General Assembly nearly a week to do so and only after debates showing that discord on anything related to terrorism remained very much alive.[205] Resolution 1373 itself, intended to serve as a statement of common cause against terrorism, overstated the degree of consensus even in the Security Council in the days after September 11, since its passage could only be assured if it refrained from defining "terrorism" itself.[206] The apparent success of US efforts to secure Pakistan's cooperation in fighting terrorism, viewed by some as a reason for optimism, did not stop Islamabad from supporting Lashkar-e-Taiba in its 2008 attacks in Mumbai or harboring key elements of the Afghan Taliban and—almost certainly knowingly—Osama bin Laden. Most revealing was the continued insistence by developing states that terrorism be understood to exclude "the legitimate struggle of peoples under colonial or alien domination and foreign occupation, for self-determination and national liberation." This language dating back to the 1960s appeared consistently in UN debates and statements and conventions of organizations such as the Organization of the Islamic Conference and the Non-Aligned Movement, which together comprise 124 states.[207] In light of this continuing impasse, it is not surprising that little meaningful progress has been made toward concluding a comprehensive convention on international terrorism, even though a General Assembly ad hoc committee devoted to that purpose has been in existence since 1996.[208]

The absence of a consensus on what constituted "terrorism" or what to do about it created a permissive and relatively low-cost normative environment for these groups and their supporters. One effect of this was that terrorist tactics not only proliferated but also sometimes proved successful in accomplishing at least some of their political goals. An often-cited example is international awareness of, and support for, the Palestinian cause since 1968.[209] Similarly, Martin Kramer observes that Hezbollah's suicide bombings in the mid-1980s "met with astonishing success in bringing about policy reassessments" by some Western states.[210] The number of terrorist organizations also increased dramatically beginning in the late 1960s. One notable database identified eleven international terrorist groups operating in 1968; by 1978, the number had grown to fifty-five, and by 2008 there were well over six hundred.[211] New groups benefited from the support of both states and other militant organizations, which passed on expertise, resources, and an operational model whose many facets included strategies of political contestation of norms governing the legitimate use of force.[212]

The apotheosis of the trend toward militant organizations with substantial scale and transnational impact has been al-Qaeda and ISIS, both of which followed a model that other organizations developed in the preceding decades, benefiting from the permissive normative milieu regarding nonstate violence prevailing at the time. Both received state support in their early stages (although states have disputed reports of assisting ISIS), and both had roots as nonstate jihadist resistance to foreign occupation. Both made good use of telecommunication technology, updating the public affairs playbook of militant organizations by turning to modern social media to boost their recruiting and propaganda efforts. This allowed them to recruit on an international scale: like both the Afghan mujahideen and al-Qaeda before them, ISIS attracted fighters from abroad.[213] Although the capabilities and territorial acquisitions of ISIS went far beyond the usual profile of a "terrorist group," the ways in which ISIS and al-Qaeda differed from earlier militant organizations in the post-1968 period were less significant than their similarities. And while countries on different sides in the debates of the 1970s have recently found some common ground in condemning these groups (sometimes even coordinating military and intelligence efforts against them), it would be a mistake to conclude these steps represent significant movement toward international consensus that the model of nonstate violence they embody should be abolished.

The state of play, then, is this. The international community fervently condemns "terrorism"—but remains deeply and perhaps intractably divided over how the term should be defined, who it applies to, and exactly why it poses a problem.[214] Much of the non-Western world remains insistent on carving out exceptions from the definition, nominally grounded in support for "the inalienable right to self-determination and independence of all peoples under colonial and racist régimes and other forms of alien domination." Always a tenuous position, today it is especially ironic for two reasons. First, as I explained in chapter 3, this inalienable right is legally nearly irrelevant, since there are very few cases left that meet the conditions in which it would arise. Here we see how long a shadow the Israeli-Palestinian dispute casts in global politics. In legal terms, the territories occupied by Israel since 1967 are not colonial possessions, falling instead under the international law of belligerent occupation.[215] Again, however, legal analysis is often beside the point. Politically and normatively, the right to self-determination is now inextricably entangled in the Palestinian case. The second irony is that in other ways as well, the practices associated with wars of national liberation have spilled over far beyond the privileges the international community granted to liberation movements, to shape the nature of modern conflict itself. Guerrilla warfare, intended to be a mode of combat reserved for the very few, is now the norm, used by states as well as nonstate groups, without regard for the type or merits of the *cassus belli*. Moreover, as we have seen, the guerrilla ethos was widely corrupted, first to justify civilian-centric tactics that use civilians as pawns and then to rationalize targeting them directly. Finally, to the extent that there was a terrorist ethos that reserved such tactics for the oppressed and downtrodden, that too has eroded, as civilians are victimized by violent actors of all descriptions, including states themselves. The norm governing current practice seems to be that belligerents (both state and nonstate) engaging in asymmetrical warfare against more powerful adversaries have the license to target civilians to serve their ends. Tragically but predictably, this license often gives rise to a general disregard for civilian life altogether, whether one is the weaker party or not. The ironic ubiquity of these methods is illustrated by the fact that Hezbollah, which perpetrated one of the deadliest vehicle bombings ever in 1983, killing 241 US service personnel, had transformed by the 2010s into a formidable nonstate army and was itself the target of car bombings on a regular basis, including one carried out by US and Israeli operatives.[216]

Western powers, too, share responsibility for this sorry state of affairs. Their own politicization of the terrorism discourse has painted them into a corner, unable to coherently define "terrorism" outside of the context of their specific foreign policy goals. Moreover, their frequent neglect of the principles upon which any such definition might be based undercuts the prospects for international progress on addressing the problem. The incoherence implicit in the Western focus on terrorism as a nonstate phenomenon has, especially in the United States, manifested itself as a proclivity in both policy and academic circles to define what constitutes acts of terrorism only *after* defining or otherwise reaching a judgment about who the "terrorists" are, leading to logically circular formulations of the problem that often amount to something akin to "terrorism is what terrorists do."[217] Apart from the obvious logical problems, this tendency mirrors the same non-Western strategy that many Western states find so objectionable. Consider the predicament the Council of the European Union faced in 2001 as it struggled to define the crime of terrorism in a way that did not expose veterans of World War II resistance movements to criminal liability. Eventually it adopted the same approach the Palestinians had thirty years earlier, carving out an exemption for actions taken in a worthy cause. The council specified that "terrorism" was meant to describe the actions of "individuals whose objectives constitute a threat to their democratic societies respecting the rule of law and the civilization upon which these societies are founded" but not "the conduct of those who have acted in the interest of preserving or restoring these democratic values, as was notably the case in some member states during the Second World War."[218] As Saul notes, this position "is not dissimilar to the exclusion of liberation violence from the anti-terrorism treaties of the Arab League, the Organization of the Islamic Conference, and the African Union—even though such an exemption is the main sticking point between those organizations and western states in the negotiation of a comprehensive anti-terrorism treaty."[219]

Conclusion

The events I described in chapter 3 as creating a breach in the wall of Weberian sovereignty were more than simply a prelude to those that contributed to the growth of transnational terrorism in the late twentieth and early twenty-first centuries. In fact, the two sets of events were closely related and in some ways parts of one larger process. Similarly, the macronormative and normative changes discussed in chapter 2 shaped the debate over terrorism in much the same way they shaped the general debate over nonstate violence. At the core of these debates was the overarching imperative of decolonization, which dominated nearly every aspect of both. First, it contributed directly to the enhanced normative authority of new actors. Just as new states, NLMs, and reinvigorated international organizations were central to the extension of jus ad bellum rights to nonstate actors, so, too, were they important in the expansion of those actors' jus in bello privileges, both through formal discussions at the UN General Assembly in 1972 and the Geneva Diplomatic Conference starting in 1974 and in general efforts at contesting preexisting norms through other channels. Also crucial was the fact that many of the groups associated with terrorism were, or described themselves as, NLMs, which after the events recounted in chapter 3 had legal and moral standing in the international system.

Moreover, the moral imperative of decolonization was so powerful that it often trumped other norms through the application of consequentialist normative reasoning. In debates over the merits of competing moral claims, consequential-ism is the proverbial gun in a knife fight, and this was its effect in the General Assembly debates of 1972. The widespread appeals by non-Western officials to the paramount value of self-determination showed that the international embrace of national liberation was able to transform the parameters of an entirely differ-ent debate, one in which the main principle at stake was the norm of civilian immunity. The result was to throw open the very definition of terrorism: what had before been fundamentally about a choice of violent means came to rest instead on the ends that violence was being used to pursue. This was a stunning demonstration of consequentialist reasoning, one that would be reprised at the Diplomatic Conference soon thereafter. There, consequentialist logic in the ser-vice of decolonization produced the introduction of normative asymmetry into rules governing the use of force, as non-Western delegates insisted that national liberation fighters be allowed to fight differently than their adversaries. This posi-tion, which hinged on a denial of (or obliviousness to) the distinction between the jus ad bellum and the jus in bello, was formally embodied in the treaty that emerged from the conference, Protocol I.[220]

As I have argued, however, it would be a mistake to dismiss the non-Western arguments as cynical and politically self-interested hypocrisy. They clearly spoke to the deep and justified sense of alienation that pervaded most of the non-Western (especially the colonial and postcolonial) world and to the frustration with purportedly principled Western institutions that seemed only to perpetuate an unjust status quo. Moreover, the fact that these arguments could gain purchase in the international system revealed that they resonated with a broader range of peoples and governments. As important, the relative success of these efforts reflected the compromised moral authority of the West itself. While this moral authority had always been an adjunct to Western economic, military, and techno-logical might, the decades after World War II showed it to be a waning resource, largely because of Western nations' own actions. In particular, after World War II and wars in the years that followed, these nations were in a weak position to base their appeals in the terrorism debate on the norm of civilian immunity, the coherence of which had been badly damaged. Consequently, Western arguments often seemed no less hypocritical and self-interested than their adversaries'.

It is worth pondering whether, and to what extent, things could have gone differently. What if the United States in the 1980s and 1990s had been defter and more capable of thinking past the geopolitical moment? What if Israel's Arab adversaries had not opted for war in 1967—or if in victory Israel had remained content with its existing borders? What if Black September had decided in 1972 to confine its operations to Israeli territory—or Israeli military targets? Would any of this have left intact a bit more common ground on which the international community could build when transnational terrorism gradually evolved into a force that, while no more existentially dangerous than before, was more omni-directional and threatening to a greater variety of societies and peoples? Might there have been a deeper reservoir of moral credibility for Western powers to draw on as the more egregious abuses of the twentieth century receded further in the past? Might "terrorism" be something closer to a categorical taboo rather than a nearly meaningless pejorative? Of course, we can never know the answers to these questions or whether a strong and universally held norm against killing civilians under any circumstances would have significantly changed the trajec-tory of transnational terrorism in the past fifty years. Nevertheless, the actions that constitute international politics are products of human choices—whether to launch an attack, who to target, how to respond when an attack occurs, how to address rising levels of both violence and grievance—and human choices are never entirely predetermined. This should remind us that ideas, including nor-mative judgments, are important and their influence should not be underesti-mated, especially in understanding something as strongly driven by ideas (about justice, values, and responsibility, among others) as terrorism.

FROM SOLDIERS OF FORTUNE TO FORTUNE 500

Normative Contestation and the Return of Entrepreneurial Violence

The most significant shots fired by Americans in a twenty-first-century war zone were fired not by US troops but by private citizens. On September 16, 2007, private security guards from the US-based company Blackwater Worldwide opened fire in a crowded intersection in Baghdad known as Nisour Square, killing seventeen Iraqi civilians. The guards claimed that they were fired on first, while witnesses called the contractors' actions reckless and unprovoked.[1] The incident had immediate and far-reaching consequences, heightening the Iraqi population's distrust of Americans and ultimately hastening the withdrawal of US forces from Iraq at the end of 2011—creating a vacuum in which ISIS forces were able to establish a caliphate a few years later.[2]

The Nisour Square episode is but one illustration of a dramatic trend. Around the world, civilian contractors are doing jobs that until recently were done by soldiers: supplying forces in the field, guarding military bases, gathering intelligence, and defending headquarters, government officials, and supply convoys. In some cases, they have literally taken the place of national armed forces, planning and fighting military campaigns on behalf of clients who pay handsomely for their work. These services are offered not by ragtag individual adventurers but by sophisticated companies with corporate governance structures and slick, state-of-the-art marketing and PR strategies. All the more remarkable, this has happened mere decades after the use of military force by private actors would have constituted an almost unthinkable violation of international norms. Private military force, once a common feature of international politics in the forms of mercenaries, privateers, pirates, and overseas mercantile companies, was all but eliminated from the scene by states wishing to consolidate their power and lend order to their relations abroad.[3]

In this chapter, I offer an explanation of the rise of private military and security companies. The chapter contains four sections. In the first section, I discuss the decline of private force in the nineteenth century and its resurgence in recent years. In the second section, I review the literature that attempts to explain this resurgence. Following my critique of rationalism in chapter 2, I argue that while these accounts identify several important causes of the PMSC phenomenon, their theoretical assumptions lead them to neglect the influence of changes in norms governing the use of force. The third section revisits the twin macronormative transformations of the post–World War II system—the change in international norms surrounding decolonization in the 1950s and 1960s and the post-1945 change in international law regarding the legitimate resort to force—and explores their implications for the proscription of private force, especially in the form of mercenaries. I show how this changed normative landscape not only contributed to material conditions that created fresh demand for mercenaries but also caused the norm against mercenaries to be narrowed and its application circumscribed. This "contextualization" diminished the norm's previously formidable power, leading to a crisis of coherence for the norm. In the fourth section, I detail how this crisis was exploited by purveyors and proponents of privatized force, who vigorously and often shrewdly contested the state monopoly on violence. I argue that these contestation efforts have largely succeeded, staving off attempts to abolish the private military and security industry, distancing it from the negative connotations of "mercenarism," and swinging international consensus toward a relatively permissive regime of regulation and oversight.

The Fall and Rise of Entrepreneurial Violence

Viewed over the broad sweep of history, private forces probably have been more the rule than the exception. As P. W. Singer observes, "hiring outsiders to fight your battles is as old as war itself. Nearly every past empire, from the ancient Egyptians to the Victorian British, contracted foreign troops in some form or another."[4] In Europe, from the Middle Ages into the seventeenth century, forces typically consisted of ready-made military (and, often, naval) units assembled and led by entrepreneurs. These ranged in size from the company level or smaller to as many as one hundred thousand, as in the case of the "Great Company" of mid-fourteenth-century Italy and the army of Albrecht von Wallenstein in the early seventeenth century.[5] States, moreover, were not the only entities to employ private forces, as chartered mercantile companies such as the Dutch East India Company, the English East India Company, and the Hudson's Bay Company controlled what were in essence corporate armies, navies, and police forces.[6]

Things changed drastically, however, starting around the turn of the nineteenth century. Among the pivotal events were the French Revolution and the Napoleonic Wars, which, Singer writes, "signaled the end of hired soldiers playing a serious role in warfare, at least for the next two centuries."[7] Napoleon's Grande Armée, which conquered most of Europe, is widely considered the first true national army, comprising primarily French citizens who were animated by revolutionary spirit and national pride. The ensuing decades saw a widespread move among other states away from forces procured on the open market toward citizen armies. At roughly the same time, states took steps to eliminate the institutions of privateering and chartered mercantile companies, while reinforcing the marginalization of mercenaries by enacting neutrality laws that outlawed enlisting in or recruiting for foreign armies.[8] In a relatively short time, therefore, states effectively gained a monopoly on international force, all but ending practices that had thrived throughout history.

This dramatic transformation was caused by a propitious fit between material and ideational factors. Clearly, one important impetus toward the creation of citizen armies was the self-interested desire of governments to build strong militaries, which led to the emulation of the successful French model.[9] Bringing vast numbers of citizens into military service, however, would have been impossible without changing ideas about the relationship between the state and its citizens. The late eighteenth and early nineteenth centuries saw the decline of dynasticism and the rise of social contract theory, which emphasized the importance of the political community and bound citizens and their government together as partners in the national enterprise. This implied not only new ideas about the state's obligations to its citizens but also about citizens' obligations to the nation, including the duty to fight on its behalf.[10] Indeed, an important benefit of citizen armies was that they could harness the power of nationalist ideology, which was a growing, and potentially destabilizing, force throughout Europe in the nineteenth century.[11] Similarly, state interest in getting rid of privateers and mercantile companies was driven largely by the rise of the new statehood paradigm, which held governments responsible for the actions of their citizens abroad, thus creating conflicts between states over actions that were beyond any government's effective control.[12]

Significantly, this change in the control over military force coincided with, and was reinforced by, the rise of a strong norm against the use of violence by nonstate actors. According to Sarah Percy, this norm drew on a long-standing moral disdain of those who fight for money, which in the nineteenth century became particularly compelling when contrasted with the growing power of the idea that fighting for the nation was a noble cause.[13] Private purveyors of force such as mercenaries and privateers did not merely fall into disuse, therefore; they were stigmatized by the growing belief that what they did was illegitimate. In fact, the idea that only national governments should be permitted to use force, both within and outside their own territories, became inextricably associated with evolving definitions of state sovereignty, to the point where it came to be viewed as the essence of the institution of sovereignty in the modern international system. This norm proved to be a powerful and effective bar to the use of private force for well over a century. Percy writes: "Mercenaries largely disappeared from the international system after the Crimea [1854]. . . . The shift away from mercenary use in the nineteenth century was so absolute that mercenaries did not appear on the international stage again until the 1960s."[14] And when mercenaries did appear in the 1960s, it was in the form of individuals and small groups hired to fight in the colonial and civil wars that plagued Africa and not as part of large enterprises providing military services on a significant scale.[15]

Among the first clear signs that that private force was making a significant comeback was the role of private military companies (PMCs) in internal conflicts in several developing countries in the 1990s.[16] A South Africa–based company called Executive Outcomes provided training and support services, and sometimes directly participated in combat, under contracts with the governments of Angola, the Central African Republic, Rwanda, and Sierra Leone, and UK-based Sandline International did much the same for Sierra Leone and Papua New Guinea.[17] For all intents and purposes these firms were throwbacks (albeit on a smaller scale) to the *condottierri* of Renaissance Italy, providing trained units that openly used military force on a contractual basis. In the context of the late-twentieth century, however, their appearance generated controversy, as many observers found the application of a sterile business model to the provision of lethal violence jarring.[18]

By the early 2000s, however, there were other manifestations of the privatization trend, one of the most important of which was the increasing prevalence of contractors in the US-led campaigns in Afghanistan and Iraq. To be sure, the United States had always employed considerable numbers of contractors in fighting its wars, but two things changed in the wars of the twenty-first century. The first was the relative numbers involved. The ratio of contractors to uniformed military personnel in major American wars before 2000 ranged from 1:2.5 (Korea) to 1:20 (World War I), most commonly falling around 1:6

or 1:7. From the early days of the conflicts in Afghanistan and Iraq, however, contractors were far more heavily represented, actually outnumbering troops in each theater even when force levels were near their peaks. The ratio only increased as the United States drew down its forces, with about three times as many contractors as troops in Afghanistan by 2016, and thousands remaining in Iraq after the departure of combat forces in 2011.[19] The second change was the types of jobs these contractors were hired to do. Historically the vast proportion of contractors provided relatively mundane support and logistical services. While this was true of most contractors in Afghanistan and Iraq, there was nevertheless a sharp increase in the proportion of armed contractors performing "security" roles, and a significant number of these found themselves in situations closely resembling combat. One reason for this is that modern warfare has made the distinctions between combat and noncombat roles far less distinct than in the past. This is especially true in a counterinsurgency setting, as insurgents are often indistinguishable from civilians and eschew large-scale combat with enemy forces in favor of ambushes and hit-and-run attacks on more vulnerable targets such as government officials and supply convoys—exactly those likely to be guarded by private contractors. The Blackwater team involved in the September 2007 Nisour Square incident, for example, was a security escort detail protecting State Department officials. In Iraq and Afghanistan, convoy-protection missions became notoriously volatile. By 2007, US officials estimated that 50 to 60 percent of all supply convoys in Iraq were being attacked; one PMSC alone experienced nearly three hundred "hostile actions" against its convoys in the first four months of that year.[20] "Static" security details, too, sometimes gave rise to hostile engagements. In one firefight in April 2004, Blackwater contractors protecting the Coalition Provisional Authority headquarters in Najaf not only fought off Mahdi Army insurgents for three-and-a-half hours, firing thousands of rounds of ammunition, but in effect commanded active-duty US soldiers who participated.[21] A senior Blackwater executive, while insisting that the incident was not combat but a rather a "security operation," admitted: "The line is getting blurry. . . . This is a whole new issue in military affairs. Think about it. You're actually contracting civilians to do military-like duties."[22] Reflecting this reality were rules issued in 2006 by the Defense Department permitting contractors to use "deadly force" not only in self-defense but also "when necessary to execute their security mission to protect assets/persons, consistent with the mission statement contained in their contract."[23] Ironically, the same year US ground forces adopted a new counterinsurgency doctrine whose emphasis on avoiding civilian casualties led to rules of engagement limiting commanders' use of force *even in self-defense*, requiring that there be "no other options . . . available to effectively counter the threat."[24] Ironically, therefore, soldiers on patrol in an offensive mission in rural Helmand Province had stricter limits on when they could fire their weapons than did private contractors protecting a convoy in Kabul. When US forces withdrew from Iraq at the end of 2011, the number of contractors in the country jumped sharply, with the State Department doubling its contractor contingent.[25] The contractors remaining in Iraq not only continued to do jobs they did since 2003 but also in some cases stepped into roles vacated by the military, including flying helicopter gunships over Baghdad and serving on "quick reaction forces" to rescue civilians in danger from insurgent or sectarian violence.[26]

One sobering illustration of the changing role of contractors in these wars was casualty numbers. By mid-2015, about sixteen hundred contractors had died in the war in Afghanistan, compared to about twenty-two hundred American troops.[27] Moreover, contractors were facing relatively more danger as the wars progressed: the Congressional Research Service reported in May 2011 that in 2009–10, "a PSC employee working for DOD [the Department of Defense] in Afghanistan is 2.75 times more likely to be killed in action than uniformed personnel."[28] This high level of risk, combined with the growing role of private security, meant that by early 2010 more contractors than US troops were dying in Iraq and Afghanistan—a situation unprecedented in American history.[29] Nor have contractors been spared the psychological costs of war. A 2013 RAND Corporation study of a multinational sample of contractors found that 25 percent tested positive for posttraumatic stress disorder, a considerably higher rate than was found among US service members (8–20 percent).[30]

There is more to the privatization of force, however, than the increasingly violent atmosphere facing contractors in Afghanistan and Iraq. In recent years private firms have assumed not just support roles but also roles at "the tip of the spear," performing missions previously clearly within the domain of government forces. In the US experience in Afghanistan and Iraq, this often took the form of contractors participating in paramilitary operations under contract to the CIA. From 2004 to 2009, for example, the United States engaged Blackwater to work with the CIA in tracking and killing al-Qaeda officials, missions so sensitive they had to be authorized by a presidential "special finding."[31] It was also revealed in 2009 that Blackwater employees had routinely participated alongside CIA operatives in "snatch and grab" raids to capture or kill insurgents in Pakistan and Iraq.[32] Blackwater founder Erik Prince would later claim that in the years after 9/11 "the company became a virtual extension of the CIA because we were asked time and again to carry out dangerous missions, which the Agency either could not or would not do in-house."[33] In other theaters, too, PMSCs under US contract participated in hostilities. Singer writes that DynCorp International contractors employed by the United States in Colombia, although purportedly only there in a supporting role, regularly "engaged in combatant roles, fighting in counterinsurgency operations against the Colombian rebel groups."[34] Even in purportedly noncombat capacities, PMSCs ventured into activities that are integral to military operations, with far-reaching results. An often-cited example is the role of the American firm Military Professional Resources International (MPRI) in the Croatian Army's victories over occupying Serb forces in 1995. It is widely believed that MPRI training went well beyond the relatively mundane matters of military professionalism spelled out in its contract, extending into tactics, operations, and campaign planning, with some observers claiming that MPRI personnel even accompanied the Croats into battle.[35] And although he provides few details, former DynCorp employee Sean McFate writes that he and other DynCorp personnel under contract to the US government played a significant, if unspecified, role in helping to repel a rebel assault on the capital of Burundi in 2004.[36]

Other states have employed PMSCs in yet larger and more ambitious operational roles. One notable success story was Nigeria's decision in 2015 to turn to private forces (led by the former head of Executive Outcomes) in its struggle against the jihadist group Boko Haram, which proved effective in temporarily neutralizing it.[37] Near the forefront of the trend has been the United Arab Emirates. While the UAE had long employed foreign soldiers in its armed forces, it went a significant step further in 2010 when it hired Reflex Responses, a company run by Prince after he sold Blackwater, to build an eight-hundred-man battalion of foreigners, whose responsibilities were to include special operations, urban combat, and quelling internal revolts.[38] In 2015, the Emirati government sent troops from this force, by that time nominally integrated into the country's military but comprising mostly fighters from Colombia, to fight alongside progovernment forces in Yemen's civil war.[39] Starting in 2010, the UAE also funded a contract between the semiautonomous Somali state of Puntland and South Africa–based company Saracen International to assemble a force of nearly a thousand contractors to conduct counterpiracy operations.[40] Reports also emerged in 2017 that UAE-based companies employing mostly American pilots were providing air support for the embattled regime in Libya, flying not only cargo and transport missions but also bombing rebel forces.[41] Most stunning was the revelation that the Emirati government employed Spear Operations Group, a US-based company employing former US military personnel, to kill Yemeni opposition leaders and clerics. Spear's founder told one journalist, "There was a targeted assassination program in Yemen. I was running it. We did it. It was sanctioned by the UAE within the coalition."[42]

Even more consequential has been Russia's recent use of private forces. Russian-backed contractors have seen extensive combat in eastern Ukraine and played a central role in the 2014 annexation of Crimea.[43] Hundreds have also reportedly seen action in the Central African Republic, Burundi, Libya, Mozambique, and Sudan, where they fought the government of Omar al-Bashir in the country's civil war.[44] Most significantly, they have been deployed to Syria in several locations, in numbers reportedly in the thousands.[45] In March 2016, some twenty-five hundred Russian contractors, some operating tanks and other heavy weapons, fought alongside Syrian national forces in retaking Palmyra from ISIS.[46] Almost two years later, several hundred Russians working for a firm called the Wagner Group took part in an assault on a Kurdish-held oil field being protected by a detachment of US Marines and US Army Special Forces troops.[47] The defenders repelled the attack with the help of US air strikes, resulting in scores of Russian deaths in what was likely the largest instance of combat between Americans and Russians since US intervention in the Russian Civil War in 1920.[48]

Another trend with potentially significant implications for state sovereignty is PMSCs working not just for national governments but also for many nonstate clients, including multinational corporations, nongovernmental organizations, and international organizations such as the UN. Although corporations have long had transnational business interests, not since the mid-eighteenth century have they had the option of advancing those interests through the independent use of armed force. The list of companies that have employed PMSCs is too long to recount, but a sense can be gained from a partial list of corporate clients for one British firm, Defence Systems Limited, in the years before the wars in Afghanistan and Iraq: DeBeers, Texaco, Chevron-Schlumberger, British Gas, Amoco, Exxon, Ranger Oil, Mobil, BP, Bechtel, BHP Minerals, American Airlines, and Shell Oil.[49] In some cases PMSCs have fallen under the same corporate ownership structure as, or had joint venture agreements with, companies they served, arrangements that resemble the integration of commerce and arms that characterized the chartered mercantile companies of past centuries.[50] While the UN has in many ways struggled to come to terms with the privatization phenomenon, it, too, has frequently been a PMSC client. Agencies such as the UN High Commissioner for Refugees, the United Nations Children's Fund, and the UN Development Programme have all used private security. The UN also administered US-funded DynCorp training contract in Liberia, and as Deborah Avant notes, every multilateral peacekeeping mission sanctioned by the UN since 1990 has used PMSCs.[51] Perhaps most surprising has been the degree of reliance upon private security by NGOs, especially those providing humanitarian aid. A report based on a 2008 survey of aid organizations revealed that "no major humanitarian provider—UN, NGO or Red Cross—can claim that it has never paid for armed security. According to their headquarters respondents, over the past year at least 41% of the major humanitarian organizations contracted some form of armed protective services (guards, escorts or bodyguards) for one or more of their operations."[52]

Perhaps most striking, the encroachment of the private sector into roles and missions previously reserved for military forces is evident not only in what PMSCs have done but also in what they have aspired to do. One impressive vision was Blackwater's 2006 proposal to assemble a seventeen-hundred-man "contractor brigade" that could be deployed anywhere in the world in a matter of weeks.[53] The plan was striking not only for its unabashed vision of marketing private forces for combat operations but also for its scale, which would have been larger than the combat contingents supplied by Executive Outcomes and Sandline in the 1990s. But even this proposal paled in comparison to the plan Prince and DynCorp owner Stephen Feinberg presented to US officials in 2017, which called for privatizing most aspects of the US war in Afghanistan, including both operational and training missions.[54] The plan envisioned four thousand contractors to train and fight alongside Afghan troops on the ground and another two thousand to provide an airpower component, flying both noncombat and combat missions.[55] The aviation component of Prince's plan was noteworthy both for its ambition and because it apparently formed the basis of proposals he had made to other governments to provide what amounted to a private air force or, as he described it to the Afghan government, a "turnkey air wing."[56] Another one of Prince's companies, Frontier Services Group, is providing security services in support of China's Belt and Road Initiative, and reportedly operates two facilities in China "to train and deploy an army of Chinese retired soldiers who can protect Chinese corporate and government strategic interests around the world, without having to involve the Chinese People's Liberation Army."[57]

In sum, since the end of the Cold War, private contractors have performed a host of missions that not long before clearly would have been done by national militaries—and some that not even they would have done. Of course, this has generated much debate, not only about whether it is a trend to be applauded or lamented but also about what it portends for the future and what it means for the state monopoly on the legitimate means of violence. At the least, it seems to represent, as one scholar puts it, "a marked reversal in the progressive centralization of control over armed force and the strengthening of the norm against mercenarism over the past three centuries."[58]

Explaining the Return of Entrepreneurial Violence: Beyond Supply and Demand

Scholars who have tried to explain the reemergence of private armed force usually agree on several points. The first is that the phenomenon dates to the beginning of the 1990s, with the end of the Cold War.[59] Beyond the question of timing, however, they also agree that many of the important causes of the new military privatization can be traced to that event. Several influential works, including those by P. W. Singer and Deborah Avant, portray changes brought on by the end of the Cold War as variables affecting the supply and demand in the market for private force, which led to its increasing prevalence.[60] On the supply side, two main factors are seen as contributing to an abundance of trained former military personnel, who provide PMSCs with their employee base.[61] One was the post–Cold War reductions in the size of many national militaries, especially those in the United States and the countries of former Soviet bloc. Adding to the excess supply of military veterans was the 1994 transition to a postapartheid government in South Africa, after which many members of the old regime's South African Defence Force left and found work with PMSCs, including both Executive Outcomes and Sandline.[62] Worldwide, over six million personnel left military service in the 1990s.[63] Another supply-side factor often cited is the profusion of cheap arms that started to become widely available in the 1990s, which not only lowered the costs of doing business for PMSCs but also facilitated the use of force by other types of nonstate actors such as militias and insurgent groups.[64]

Mirroring these developments on the supply side, commentators argue, were factors that increased the demand for the services of PMSCs. Among the most important was the growing number of weak states, including many with limited resources that had been supported by superpowers during the Cold War, that were left to fend for themselves after that support dried up.[65] Exacerbating this was the increase in conflict within and among such states, as ethnic and sectarian rifts that had been suppressed during the Cold War flared and opportunistic actors saw the potential for political or economic advantage.[66] This combination of limited state capacity and new types of conflict was, and remains, most prevalent in Africa, where many regimes struggle with scarce resources and tenuous political control, but has been seen in parts of Europe and Asia as well.

Demand has not been limited to weak states, however. Indeed, the biggest and most lucrative PMSC contracts have been with major powers, with the United States leading the way.[67] This is commonly attributed to two things. First, the size of major militaries after the end of the Cold War shrunk faster than the need for military forces, as new roles, missions, and conflicts emerged to at least partly take the place of old ones. For the United States, the wars in Afghanistan and Iraq clearly strained the manpower of its armed services. While neither entailed conventional warfare on the scale envisioned during the Cold War, both evolved into prolonged counterinsurgencies that required the continuing presence of large numbers of troops. These wars, combined with what Avant refers to as "the new threat environment" after 9/11, spiked demand for manpower-intensive capabilities in a military that only a few years earlier was striving to become less reliant on manpower. The second factor was increasing sophistication and specialization, both in the jobs that military units and personnel are called upon to perform and in the weapons themselves. As Singer explains, "at the high intensity level of warfare, the requirement of advanced technology has dramatically increased the need for specialized assistance, which often must be pulled from the private sector."[68] Consequently, even states with large and high-quality militaries turned increasingly to PMSCs to fill gaps, augment capabilities, and on occasion do things they would rather not have their uniformed militaries do.

This combination of reduced supply and increased demand, experts argue, was pivotal in the return of entrepreneurial violence. In Singer's words, "when the Berlin Wall fell, an entire global order collapsed almost overnight. The resultant effect on the supply and demand of military services created a 'security gap' that the private market rushed to fill."[69] In using the conceptual framework of market economics as its explanatory linchpin, of course, the PMSC literature situates itself squarely within the rationalist tradition, emphasizing the choices and outcomes that emerged from changes in material conditions. Nevertheless, the literature also uniformly identifies one important ideational, perhaps even ideological, change that contributed to the PMSC trend. This is what Singer calls "the power of privatization and the privatization of power": the increasing faith, especially in Western democracies and international institutions, in the ability of the private market to deliver efficient solutions to policy challenges, and the restructuring of governmental and societal institutions based upon that faith.[70] Perhaps most closely identified with the rhetoric and policies of the Margaret Thatcher and Ronald Reagan administrations in the United Kingdom and United States, respectively, this change was fundamentally rooted in ideas, and as Christopher Coker points out, marked the reversal of a century-long trend toward ever-greater bureaucratization and government involvement in the identification and provision of public goods.[71] This "neoliberal" preference for market-oriented solutions has driven a wave of privatization of formerly governmental functions that, combined with the factors of supply and demand discussed above, has proved a boon to the PMSC industry.

Given the importance of the ideology of privatization in these accounts of the rise of PMSCs, it would be inaccurate to say that the literature neglects ideational variables altogether. What is ironic in this case, however, is that the ideational variable in question actually reinforces the rationalist orientation of the literature. These accounts explain changes in behavior by adopting the paradigm of market economics, departing from that paradigm only to tout the role of the politicization of market economics as the normative principle driving military privatization. While there is no doubt that neoliberal ideology has played an important role in the rise of PMSCs, this is not the only normative assumption that needs to be accounted for in this story. Many of the same authors, after all, agree that the disappearance and prolonged absence of private force from international politics in the 175 years prior to the end of the Cold War reflected not just material changes but also norms of legitimacy, which foreclosed or stigmatized certain options.[72] The reemergence of private force, therefore, constitutes not just a dramatic change in practices but also a dramatic change in attitudes. The literature on PMSCs, however, says curiously little about this change in attitudes. To the extent that it is addressed at all, the norm against nonstate violence is portrayed as fragile, quickly fading with the emergence of the supply of and demand for PMSCs. Singer writes: "The provision of security has long been recognized as the most important function of government. By the start of the twentieth century, state control over the means of violence had been institutionalized through a process that spanned centuries. But as long as it took to develop, this cartelization of state power has proven to be short-lived. . . . With the growth of the global military services industry . . . the state's role in the security sphere has now become deprivileged."[73] Avant describes the causal sequence in similar terms: "As the demand for non-state service has increased, the collective monopoly [of states on the use of force] has broken down."[74] Elke Krahmann, while noting that the growth of PMSCs suggests "a transformation of the norm of the state monopoly on violence," argues that this normative shift occurred subsequent to, and as a result of, changes in practice prompted by material conditions and "the Neoliberal paradigm."[75] In these accounts, norms governing who may or may not legitimately use force are treated as merely epiphenomenal reflections of more important material conditions prevailing in the international system, exercising little or no independent influence.[76] This is strikingly inconsistent, however, with the notion that the same norms shaped the conduct of war for generations prior to 1990. Certainly, it is strange that norms viewed as powerful enough to stave off mercenarism for nearly two cataclysmic centuries, and which protected the most valuable prerogative of national governments, would fade so quickly and quietly into irrelevance.

I do not mean to suggest that the causes identified in the privatization literature were irrelevant. The post–Cold War changes in material conditions were important, as was the ascendance of market ideology. Nevertheless, the neglect of the causal role played by norms governing the use force leads to an understanding of the return of private violence that is both incomplete and, on some key points, inaccurate. Most fundamentally, these accounts get one crucial causal sequence backward: the booming market for private force did not begin to erode a robust state monopoly on violence; rather, the market was able to develop because the norm that states should exercise a monopoly on violence had already started to lose its power. Indeed, aspects of the privatization trend were present before its dramatic explosion in the 1990s and 2000s. This is because, like the rise of militia forces and terrorist organizations discussed in previous chapters, it had its roots in the transformation of international macronorms that occurred in the decades after 1945.

Contextualization and Crisis: Sources of Pressure on the Norm against Private Force

The macronormative changes I discuss in chapter 2—the retreat from raison d'état in the use force and decolonization—along with the growing influence of consequentialist ethics all contributed significantly to the return of private violence in the late twentieth century. In this section, I describe how this reorientation of the international normative landscape led to what I refer to as the contextualization of the norm against mercenaries, narrowing the scope of its application in such a way as to create distinctions between permissible and impermissible uses of private force. I also describe small and incremental steps toward privatization in Britain and the United States in the later decades of the Cold War, which did not directly challenge the antimercenary norm but nonetheless contributed to the increasing pressure it faced. I then discuss how failed attempts to address the mercenary problem through international conventions in the 1970s and 1980s revealed that even before the end of the Cold War, the norm against private military force was already experiencing a crisis of coherence.

Decolonization and the Contextualization of Mercenarism

When private violence reappeared after its long absence from the international system, it was in the form of mercenaries fighting in the decolonization struggles of the 1960s. This fact decisively shaped the response to the mercenarism problem, and that response in turn shaped the way the problem would eventually be viewed. What emerged was not a clear endorsement of the long-standing norm against mercenaries but instead a narrowed interpretation of the norm that defined the problem in terms of the specific context in which it arose.

The issue began to attract international attention in the Congo Crisis of the early 1960s, which saw mercenaries employed by both Katangan separatists (aided by Belgium) and the fledgling government fighting against them.[77] The Congo episode presaged the complexity of the problem, as mercenaries were used both by European states resisting independence movements and trying to destabilize newly independent states and by the new states themselves, which had no capable militaries at their disposal. It was against this backdrop that the international community, acting through the UN, came to address the return of mercenarism. The Security Council typically couched the problem in terms of the danger mercenaries posed to the autonomy of fragile new postcolonial states, passing resolutions in the 1960s and early 1970s denouncing the presence of mercenaries in Congo, the Democratic Republic of Congo, and Guinea.[78] The General Assembly, reflecting the views of the developing and newly independent states that now swelled its ranks, went beyond the Security Council's concern for fragile sovereign states to decry mercenaries as a threat to NLMs' prospects for success and therefore as an affront to the principle of self-determination itself. The connection between the two issues was seen as so integral that language condemning mercenaries was included in many of the same declarations and resolutions through which the General Assembly cemented its role as the champion and catalyst of self-determination struggles. Significantly, however, rather than denouncing mercenarism generally or for its troublesome implications for sovereignty, these documents embedded the problem specifically within the issue of decolonization. The 1968 Implementation of the Declaration on the Granting of Independence to Colonial Peoples and Countries, for example, defined as a criminal offense not mercenarism per se but "the practice of using mercenaries against movements for national liberation and independence."[79] The General Assembly reaffirmed this formulation several times in the following years, and in the 1973 resolution that sought to establish combatant status for guerrillas fighting for NLMs, it offered an updated but still explicitly contextualized condemnation of "the use of mercenaries by colonial and racist regimes against the national liberation movements struggling for their freedom and independence from the yoke of Colonialism and alien domination."[80]

Framing the issue in this way might have done little to undermine the preexisting antimercenary norm had mercenaries not represented an opportunity as well as a danger to decolonizing peoples. But as in the Congo Crisis, in the 1960s and 1970s new states (and some separatist movements, asserting their own self-determination claims) often turned to mercenary forces themselves. Indeed, some of the same states pushing for a ban on mercenaries fighting against self-determination movements were using them in other settings.[81] Framing the problem in a context-specific way in the UN, however, would allow mercenaries to be banned in some settings and permitted in others without flagrantly violating the principle of normative coherence. The General Assembly's actions, while drawing on and apparently reinforcing the stigma against mercenaries, in fact narrowed the stigma, which, as international jurist Antonio Cassese explains, was "not on mercenaries as such . . . but on those mercenaries who fight against national liberation movements or attack the integrity and independence of sovereign States."[82]

The contextualization of the norm against mercenaries therefore reflected both the political milieu in which the norm was being applied and the interests of the actors who were most heavily vested in the issue—and who had newfound clout in international institutions. Just as clearly, however, it reflected the implications of the macronormative transformations in the international system since 1945. The connection to the decolonization upheaval, of course, was critical and manifested itself in both obvious and subtle ways. As I have argued, decolonization provided both the preeminent political objective and the dominant discursive paradigm for the developing world. Its macronormative status meant that other specific policy goals, and other normative prescriptions or prohibitions, could be supported only insofar as they did not undermine the overarching objectives of self-determination. Because mercenaries threatened self-determination in some cases but advanced it in others, conflict with the categorical antimercenary norm was inevitable. The discursive frame of decolonization, however, provided a lens through which the two norms could be viewed as complements rather than competitors but only by narrowing the context in which mercenaries were deemed problematic. This contextualized interpretation gained credibility from the fact that mercenarism had reemerged in the milieu of decolonization, thus allowing it to be addressed as a subset of the colonialism problem rather than a more general problem with broader implications.

The contextualization of mercenarism thus marked a fundamental departure from previous practice. The norm that had evolved since 1815 was a general proscription on a category of fighters, whose status depended neither on who employed them nor on the cause for which they fought.[83] A mercenary was a mercenary, and mercenaries were by definition illegitimate. By defining the problem explicitly in terms of the threat it posed for the self-determination of newly independent states rather than the threat it posed to the institution of state sovereignty per se, the approach adopted by the General Assembly effectively narrowed the definition of mercenarism itself. Moreover, in shifting from a categorical prohibition on a major form of nonstate violence to what was in effect a conditional one, the norm became not only narrower but also less compelling. Because of the peremptory effect categorical norms have on actors' behavior, they are more readily internalized and embedded in policymaking, whereas conditional norms invite calculations and exceptions.[84] The contextualized norm not only dramatically weakened the prohibition, but to the extent that it allowed self-determination movements and new states to use mercenaries themselves, it was also not truly a norm against mercenaries at all but rather a norm against using force for certain purposes or against certain actors. In effect, the taboo against private violence was subsumed under an entirely different, more compelling normative concern.

The General Assembly's resolutions of the 1960s and 1970s did not eradicate the norm against private violence. Powerful norms do not change easily, and the efforts to contextualize the prohibition reflected a distinctly developing country perspective (supported by the socialist bloc) rather than a universal consensus.[85] Nevertheless, as we have seen, although General Assembly resolutions are not legally binding, the body can sometimes exercise influence disproportionate to its formal institutional powers. This was the case here, especially because the norm against private violence was pitted against the extremely powerful macronormative force of decolonization. So, while the old norm still existed, its power and coherence were gradually undermined by its contextualization, which proved influential in shaping the terms of the debate over mercenaries—including the question of what constituted mercenarism itself. This approach was also adopted by the Organization of African Unity's 1977 Convention for the Elimination of Mercenarism in Africa, which defined as a necessary element of the crime of mercenarism "the aim of opposing by armed violence a process of self-determination stability or the territorial integrity of another State," while reserving to African states themselves the right to use mercenaries.[86] Another important legacy of this contextualization was to permanently situate the UN's handling of the mercenary issue (and by extension issues pertaining to PMSCs) in bureaucratic bodies dealing with self-determination. Since 1987, when the UN created a "Special Rapporteur on the use of mercenaries as a means of impeding the exercise of the right of peoples to self-determination," the mercenary issue has fallen under the Commission on Human Rights / Human Rights Council and (since its creation in 1993) the Office of the High Commissioner for Human Rights. Moreover, the mandate for bodies addressing the issue, including the current "Working Group on the use of mercenaries as a means of violating human rights and impeding the exercise of the right of peoples to self-determination," has remained couched in the language of decolonization and postcolonialism.[87]

"Privatization Creep" in Britain and the United States

The contextualization of mercenarism specifically as a challenge to self-determination was one important source of pressure on the norm against private violence. Another, surprisingly, came from the practices of two of the leading Western powers, Britain and the United States, both of which took steps toward privatization in the 1960s and 1970s. In neither case did this involve coming to terms with the antimercenary norm directly, either by repudiating it or trying to contextualize it, as in the General Assembly. Instead, security policy in both countries experienced what could be called "privatization creep," as a series of developments led them down paths that, while distinctly different, would eventually converge in the PMSC boom of the 2000s.

Britain's path to privatization began almost as early as the mercenary wave in Africa, when in early 1963 the UK government secretly sent four dozen former Special Air Service (SAS) officers, recruited by SAS founder David Stirling, to aid royalist forces in the North Yemeni Civil War. The choice of private forces was prompted not by a desire to supplement capabilities but rather to conceal British involvement, which if discovered would have ruffled feathers both in the Arab world and with American allies. The operation itself arguably represented only a minor, and ambiguous, departure from the norm against mercenaries: the troops were UK citizens, working directly for their country on a mission not very different from others in the framework of proxy wars that was coming to define the Cold War. The crucial legacy of the Yemen episode in terms of privatization, however, was that it inspired Stirling to create Watchguard International, which was incorporated in 1967 and is widely recognized as the first PMC.[88] Stirling envisioned Watchguard serving as a regular resource for the British government when it wished to act "without any direct identification."[89] When government contracts failed to materialize, Watchguard sought other clients, including corporations. This precedent opened the door for several other private firms that would become more profitable than Watchguard, including Control Risks Group (established in 1975), Keenie Meenie Services (1977), and Defence Systems Ltd. (1981). Long before the end of the Cold War, such firms were prospering with business models much like those of contemporary PMSCs. As Christopher Kinsey writes, "by the middle of the 1970s these newly formed private military/security companies were transforming the role of private military security through taking commercial security operations. More importantly, they started to distance themselves from the clandestine operations that had been the hallmark of British mercenaries during the 1960s and 1970s."[90] They also eventually won a fair number of contracts with the British and US governments, including training military forces in several client states and assisting the mujahideen resistance in its war against the Soviet Union in the 1980s.[91] One journalist reported in 1988 that over 40 percent of British special operations personnel were joining "private protection companies" upon leaving the military.[92]

Moreover, by the mid-1970s there were other signs in Britain of pressure on the norm against mercenaries. Telling in this regard was the 1976 report of the Diplock Commission, which was tasked with examining "whether sufficient control exists over the recruitment of United Kingdom citizens for service as mercenaries [and] to consider the need for legislation."[93] The commission described the difficulty of defining "mercenaries" in any way that did not include fighters whose legitimacy was generally accepted, such as the Nepalese Gurkha regiments that had been part of the British Army since the early nineteenth century and the "soldiers of conscience," such as those "who served in the International Brigade in the Spanish Civil War, United States citizens who joined up in the British Air Forces before their own country entered World War II, and British Jews who fought in the Israeli army against the Arabs."[94] The commission went a step further, however, by defending the right of an individual to serve as a mercenary if he wished and opposing "any attempt to impose such a prohibition upon him by law as involving a deprivation of his freedom."[95] This was a sentiment rarely encountered in the late nineteenth and early twentieth centuries, when many countries, including the United Kingdom, enacted legislation forbidding their citizens from enlisting in foreign armies.[96] The commission therefore concluded not only that existing practice and precedent made it difficult to apply the anti-mercenary norm coherently but also that by the late twentieth century the coherence of the norm itself was less than obvious.[97]

If Britain's privatization creep grew from connections between the country's political elite and its special operations community, the US version was more technocratic in its origins and more circuitous in its path. While the PMSC literature emphasizes such events as the neoliberal turn to market solutions in the 1980s, the 1990s endorsements of privatization by the Congressional Commission on Roles and Missions and the Defense Department's Defense Science Board, and the contracts awarded under the Logistics Civil Augmentation Program (LOGCAP) starting in 1995, significant steps toward privatization were in fact taken considerably earlier.[98] Particularly important was the wave of civilian contractors sent to train foreign militaries starting in the early 1970s, initially a by-product of the dramatic increase in US arms sales to developing countries during the Richard Nixon and Gerald Ford administrations.[99] Sending arms overseas was nothing new for the United States, nor was sending American troops to train foreign armies. The fiasco in Vietnam, however, led to the Nixon Doctrine, which sought to limit military commitments abroad and shift more of the burden for the defense of US allies to the allies themselves. This in turn prompted the United

States to convert most of its arms transfers from military assistance to foreign military sales—in other words, selling weapons to its client states rather than giving them away. The commercialization of arms transfers was soon followed by a commercialization of the training required to operate and maintain the weapons. By 1977, nine of the ten largest US training and technical assistance projects (all of them in Iran and Saudi Arabia) were run by private firms, and over 80 percent of training and technical assistance personnel were contractors.[100]

Although this practice represented a significant shift away from uniformed troops and toward private contractors, several factors prevented it from appearing to pose a direct challenge to the norm against mercenarism. Because the contractors were in most cases adjuncts to larger transactions (arms sales), they attracted less attention in their own right. Indeed, unlike their British counterparts, the first US-based companies to employ sizable numbers of former soldiers on overseas contracts were primarily in other lines of business, typically arms or engineering. This contributed to a sense of incrementalism that belied the significance of the trend. A telling episode was the brief controversy surrounding the February 1975 report that the Vinnell Corporation had been awarded a $77 million contract to train the Saudi Arabian National Guard. The contract, which was to send to Saudi Arabia one thousand US military veterans, many with special operations backgrounds, was the first to entail contractors training foreign forces in general ground-warfare tactics and operations rather than simply the use of particular weapon systems.[101] Responding to calls from US senators Hubert Humphrey and Henry Jackson, as well as press reports describing the contractors as "mercenaries," the Senate Armed Services Committee held hearings to investigate.[102] Government officials effectively defused the controversy by emphasizing the contract's consistency with existing practices. They rejected the assertion that the Vinnell deal raised greater concerns than training programs that accompanied weapon sales, observing that contractors had taught Saudi armed forces to fly fighter aircraft and fire antiaircraft missiles.[103] They also pointed to the United States' long-standing practice of providing military training for friendly governments. Outsourcing this training from uniformed troops to the private sector, they argued, avoided the diversion of scarce resources and was simply a more cost-effective way doing what had always been done.[104] Finally, Vinnell spokesmen noted that the company had a long history of Defense Department contracts, including in war zones in Korea and Vietnam.[105] On all three points the contract in question differed in key details from the precedents cited to defend it, but the overall effect blunted the fear that it was a venture into new and problematic territory. Congress allowed the contract to stand, and the tempest did little to slow the privatization trend, which only accelerated with the ascendance of free-market ideology in the 1980s.

It is no doubt ironic that great powers such as the United States and the United Kingdom would do anything to undermine the norm against mercenarism since they are the sort of states who would seem to benefit the most from its existence: wealthy, militarily capable states that do not need to turn to the private market to provide for their security needs. In both countries, however, the turn to privatization was incremental enough that there was never a single decision point about whether privatization would do more harm than good to national interests over the long run.[106] By the same token, it was never necessary in either case to directly confront the norm against private violence in its most robust and unconditional form. Nevertheless, both countries' actions, taken even as many of the nations of the developing world were pressing for a narrowed and contextualized reading of the norm, contributed to the growing crisis of coherence for norm.

A Crisis of Coherence

The growing incoherence of the antimercenary norm was brought into relief in the mid-1970s and 1980s during two attempts to create binding restrictions on mercenaries. The first was part of the comprehensive updating of the 1949 Geneva Conventions that culminated in 1977's Protocol I, where talks were dogged by difficulties in arriving at a widely acceptable and workable definition of "mercenary." The impasse in fact reflected the inevitable challenges in coherently expressing a prohibition that was once unconditional but that now required distinguishing between unacceptable and acceptable forms of private force. Delegates at the Diplomatic Conference took two approaches to this problem. One was to focus on motives. Since it was no longer sufficient to define mercenaries as foreigners to the conflict who were not in the armed forces, the drafters added a provision that a mercenary must be "motivated by private gain."[107] This, it was thought, would exclude those who fought on behalf of national liberation and self-determination, as well as ideologically driven foreign "volunteers" of the sort who had fought against fascism in the Spanish Civil War and World War II.[108] While some states expressed doubts about the practicability of a definition hinging on motive, several developing states were concerned that the provision did not go far enough in protecting those fighting for national liberation and wanted to carve out a more explicit exception for such individuals.[109] Although such an exception did not make it into Protocol I, the idea arose again a few years later when the UN undertook to create a freestanding treaty against mercenaries. This task, prompted largely by what many saw as the unsatisfactory resolution of the issue in Protocol I, would prove just as onerous and no more satisfactory. Again negotiations stalled on matters of definition, and again some states sought a specific exclusion for national liberation fighters. By the mid-1980s, the general idea of excluding NLMs was widely enough accepted that, starting in 1986, it was endorsed in the General Assembly's annual resolution condemning mercenaries, which reaffirmed "the legitimacy of the struggle of peoples and their liberation movements for their independence, territorial integrity, national unity and liberation from colonial domination, apartheid and foreign intervention and occupation, *and that their legitimate struggle can in no way be considered as or equated to mercenary activity*."[110] In fact, such an exclusionary clause only made explicit what was already implicit in the contextualized version of the norm and which was bound to become clear when it became necessary to codify it. The starkness with which this clause exposed the differentiated application of norms inherent in this version was unpalatable to enough states to prevent its inclusion in the final draft of the convention in 1989, but there was little doubt that it reflected the position of dozens of states. Ultimately it took nine years to conclude the convention and twelve more years to obtain the ratifications necessary for it to enter into force. By January 2019, only thirty-five states had become parties, with only three new signatories since 2008.[111]

The clear absence of an international consensus on how to handle the mercenary issue was a telling sign that, by the end of the 1980s, the old norm against private violence was experiencing a crisis of coherence. This was the normative landscape in which the PMCs of the 1990s emerged, at which time the contestation of the norm began in earnest.

Contestation and Change

The mercenaries who appeared in Africa in the 1960s and 1970s did little to contest either the norm against private force or their negative public image. Mike Hoare, who led mercenaries in Congo and the Seychelles and wrote books about both experiences, was straightforward about the nature of the trade: "By and large we were there for one reason only—money. Having accepted the mercenary calling the only principle I insisted upon was a reasonable standard of behavior. If there were more than five percent of us who had carefully considered the moral implications of fighting for money I would have been surprised."[112] The British and US corporations that ventured into the private security realm soon thereafter, however, did not have the luxury of being indifferent to their reputations. Of course, these firms (especially the US firms) offered somewhat different services than the ad hoc bands of mercenaries, but more important, they were based on different business models. They sought contracts with Western governments and in many cases had shareholders to answer to—two factors that required some semblance of respectability. For most of the 1970s and 1980s, the quest for legitimacy did not require aggressively contesting the norm against private force but only attempting to place particular practices within the context of accepted precedents, as in the 1975 Vinnell episode. However, as the material changes at the beginning of the 1990s created more opportunities for contracts increasingly close to involvement in combat, the more it became necessary to address the antimercenary norm itself and the attendant perception that the very nature of the business was illegitimate. During the 1990s, this work was done primarily by PMSCs themselves, with varying degrees of success. Since 2000, a larger role has been played by trade associations representing the interests of the private security industry, most prominently the US-based International Stability Operations Association (ISOA, known until 2010 as IPOA—the International Peace Operations Association) and, in the United Kingdom, the British Association of Private Security Companies (BAPSC) as well as, since 2011, the Security in Complex Environments Group (SCEG). Although a relatively small percentage of the PMSCs operating on the market are members of these associations, they play an important role in representing the industry as a whole to national legislatures, international and nongovernmental organizations, the media, and the general public.[113]

Both individual PMSCs and professional associations draw on a range of public affairs and governmental relations tools, including writing op-eds and letters to the editor, publishing their own periodicals, testifying before legislative bodies, and lobbying legislators and government officials.[114] In this way the private security industry resembles scores of others. What is different, and what makes these efforts even more important than for most industries, is that in this case part of what is at stake is the legitimacy—even the very existence—of the industry itself. The industry and its supporters have therefore needed to shape not only perceptions about PMSCs and the tasks they can perform but also the parameters of the debate about ethical limits on who may use force.[115] What they have done, in other words, is nothing less than contest the norm against private violence in the international system. In this they have been aided by the fact that the norm had been sufficiently compromised to make the entire enterprise of private security plausible and to make several strategies for contestation available to them.

One such strategy is to highlight and exploit the incoherence of the norm by pointing to precedents for the use of private security, emphasizing PMSCs' similarities with past practice while glossing over discontinuities. As mentioned earlier, industry figures in the United States commonly evoke the use of contractors during the American Revolution, and Prince often cites the Flying Tigers as a relevant precedent.[116] A regular feature of ISOA's bimonthly journal is a column recounting historical events in which private contractors played key roles, such as delivering mail on the US frontier, fighting fires in nineteenth-century London, and transporting the convicts who would settle Australia.[117] As the number of contractors in Afghanistan and Iraq swelled, ISOA president Doug Brooks wrote: "We should . . . remember that large numbers of contingency contractors are not new. Hundreds of thousands of contractors were employed in the Second World War, and as many as 80,000 in Vietnam at one point."[118] Furthermore, as the privatization trend gathered momentum in the 2000s, there were more and more precedents to cite, each serving to further chip away at the norm against private force. In a 2010 article criticizing a draft UN convention that would monitor and regulate PMSCs, an ISOA official warned of "a danger that the United Nations, through this Convention, might end up handicapping itself. After all, U.N. peacekeeping operations have become increasingly dependent on the private sector, particularly in terms of logistics and support."[119]

A second strategy PMSCs pursue is to disassociate themselves from the negative connotations attached to "mercenaries," an approach that by the 1990s meant disavowing not just the rogue image evoked by mercenaries of the 1960s and 1970s but also the word itself. This strategy was decisively shaped by the earlier contextualization of the antimercenary norm. The effect of contextualization, remember, was not to remove the stigma from "mercenarism" but rather to narrow the definition of that term so that not all providers of private force fell under it. The term itself therefore still had strongly pejorative connotations, but its association with colonialism and the move toward a definition hinging on motive had opened considerable space to contest its meaning and application. In a 1996 interview the CEO of Executive Outcomes, which was providing combat services to clients on a contract basis, said, "We don't consider ourselves mercenaries. Mercenaries are the type of guys . . . who have overthrown legal governments. We don't do that. We will only work for legal governments, governments in place."[120] This strategy has been aggressively pursued by the private security trade associations. One ISOA official, in bemoaning the use of what he called "the 'm' word," wrote: "The term 'mercenary' is commonly used to describe the private peace and stability operations industry by opponents and those who lack a fundamental understanding of exactly what it is that the industry does. Regardless, it is a popular pejorative term among those who don't particularly care for the private sector's role in peace and stability operations."[121] Prince dismissed it as a "slanderous term, an inflammatory word they use to malign us," and told a US House Oversight Committee hearing in 2007 that "the Oxford dictionary defines a mercenary as a foreign soldier working for a foreign government. And Americans working for America is not it."[122]

A third contestation strategy is to emphasize the respectability of the contemporary private security industry by appealing to principles valued by other participants in the debate over the legitimacy of private force, including national governments and international and nongovernmental organizations. This allows PMSCs to further differentiate themselves from the "dogs of war" mercenaries and to present themselves in ways that resonate with the contextualized, postdecolonization version of the norm against private force. For example, given the concern that private forces will destabilize weak states by hiring themselves out to the highest bidder regardless of the cause, PMSCs often stress that they choose their clients judiciously, working only for legitimate governments and not for insurgent movements.[123] PMSCs also highlight themes of professionalism, efficiency, and cost-effectiveness, thus appealing to the market-oriented principles so central to the move toward privatization in Western nations. Perhaps most striking, especially against the backdrop of UN documents that define the mercenary problem in terms of the threat it poses to human rights, the industry has positioned itself as an enthusiastic champion of humanitarianism, ready to take on humanitarian intervention and peacekeeping missions when states lack the will or ability to do so themselves. Even back in the 1990s, Executive Outcomes referred to their employees as "privatized peacekeepers," trying not only to avoid the stigma of mercenarism but to identify with a type of military mission consistent with the UN Charter framework and widely viewed in favorable terms.[124] Blackwater linked its 2006 "contractor brigade" proposal to aggressive lobbying efforts by many PMSCs and the IPOA to use private force to respond to humanitarian crises such as the one then unfolding in the Sudanese region of Darfur.[125] Similarly, ISOA founder Doug Brooks said in 2007: "The humanitarian potential is just enormous. . . . The big money is still in Iraq and Afghanistan doing stuff for the US military, but I think what our industry will most be known for is the humanitarian side. It's revolutionary."[126] Brooks noted in terms of what constitutes appropriate missions for contractors: "We try to push the envelope a bit. I mean, it's frustrating to me that it's perfectly acceptable to use private security to protect an oil field, extractions, gold mines, copper mines, whatever else—nobody bats any eye on that, really. . . . But God help you if you use the same guys to start protecting a refugee camp or an IDP [internally displaced persons] camp. All of a sudden [people say,] 'Oh, you can't do that—those are mercenaries.'"[127]

This strategy represents a logical extension of the contextualization of concerns about mercenarism in the 1960s and 1970s. Because the dangers posed by mercenaries were expressed relative to self-determination and Third World stability, PMSCs can plausibly claim that fears about mercenaries in general do not apply to them. They can thus focus their PR efforts on contextual factors— their expertise, their corporate structure, and the burgeoning demand for their services—without having to contend with a powerful categorical prohibition on nonstate violence per se. Along the same lines, some PMSCs have themselves endorsed the regulation of their industry, and ISOA, the BAPSC, and SCEG have adopted codes of conduct for their members.[128] These codes of conduct and the keenness to participate in the crafting of regulations serve multiple purposes. They create standards of professionalism that enhance the reputation of the industry and probably lead to higher-quality services and convey a sense of transparency at odds with the shadowy image of mercenaries. However, they also ensure an active industry role in determining the future of private force and provide alternatives to more restrictive legislative or regulatory regimes, or even prohibition.

An excellent case study of contestation is the brief but eventful existence of Sandline International, whose CEO Tim Spicer may be the single most important figure in the contestation of the antimercenary norm after 1990. Sandline was founded in 1996 by Spicer (a retired British Army officer) and former employees of Executive Outcomes. The company quickly found controversy, first in 1997 when Spicer and others were arrested in Papua New Guinea by military officers resentful of the government's decision to employ Sandline and again in 1998 when it violated a UN arms embargo on Sierra Leone as part of its effort to help ousted president Ahmad Tejan Kabbah regain power.[129] Spicer claimed that the firm's involvement in Sierra Leone had been approved by the British Foreign Office, triggering an investigation in the House of Commons. Both the Papua New Guinea and Sierra Leone cases received heavy media coverage, much of it critical of the involvement of "mercenaries." Eschewing a low profile, Spicer used the attention to conduct an aggressive public campaign to defend the existence of firms like Sandline. The company hired a PR consultant and released a series of publications (including Spicer's autobiography) that featured all three of the contestation strategies described above.

Spicer described Sandline as a logical and legitimate step in a progression of private military force that built on numerous precedents. He claimed the company was inspired not only by Executive Outcomes but also by the precedents of "contract officers" serving in the armed forces of Oman and Rhodesia and loaned or "seconded" officers provided by the British Ministry of Defence to foreign armies.[130] He also cited David Stirling's Watchguard, "the forerunner of the modern PMC [whose] methods and outlook also contributed to my thinking in setting up Sandline."[131] Most interesting was Spicer's evocation of the "long and honorable history" of "mercenary soldiering," while trying to distance himself and his company from the "squalid modern image" it had acquired.[132] This image, he claimed, dated back only to 1960 and the mercenary "thugs" who plagued Africa and "gravely damaged the reputation of mercenaries as professional soldiers."[133]

Despite Spicer's insistence on the merit of "traditional mercenaries" (which, to be sure, was based on a selective reading of history), it became clear that the term itself was a liability. At its founding Sandline had coined the term "private military company," and soon after it hired a PR consultant during the Papua New Guinea affair, the phrase began appearing in press reports.[134] In February 1999, Sandline published an open letter objecting to characterizations of the firm as mercenaries: "Sandline is as different to [recent mercenaries] as apes are to man."[135] The letter listed eight characteristics that distinguished PMCs from mercenaries:

1. They [PMCs] have a public persona in the form of a corporate identity.
2. They work out of or have representative offices in first world countries.
3. They abide by a stated code of conduct.
4. They are selective about the clients for whom they will work.
5. They operate to the standards of first world armies.
6. Their operating principles are strictly applied.
7. They work within the framework of national and international laws.
8. They are prepared to be regulated.[136]

By late 1999, Spicer was insisting that Sandline employees be referred to as "contract soldiers": "The word mercenary conjures up a picture in people's minds of a rather ruthless, unaligned individual, who may have criminal, psychotic tendencies. We are not like that at all. All we really do is help friendly, reasonable governments solve military problems."[137]

As illustrated by the criteria in the open letter, Sandline also sought to appeal to principles that would assure observers of the company's—and indeed the entire industry's—professionalism and acceptance of international norms. It endorsed regulation as a step that would distinguish between reputable and "rogue" companies as well as legitimize the industry as a whole.[138] Finally, it portrayed the essence of its business as protecting, not threatening, weak governments, which it said were being abandoned by the international community. Lamenting the "failed first world interventions" in Somalia, Rwanda, and Sierra Leone, Sandline's open letter continued: "If the international community is unwilling to provide real support then these governments must be entitled to seek out an alternative and it is far better that it takes the form of a recognized entity than an anonymous group of individuals. . . . If that choice is to hire a PMC then, arguably, the international community has abdicated its entitlement to object as a result of its own lack of help."[139] Spicer argued that PMCs "can help stop the killing in [places such as] Sierra Leone and Rwanda when nobody else is prepared to do it."[140] This way of framing the market for private security not only appealed to humanitarian ideals but also aligned the industry's interests with those of an international community that was eyeing it warily.

In the end, the parliamentary investigation of the so-called arms-to-Africa affair yielded inconclusive results, determining that Sandline had violated the embargo but had done so unknowingly and with the tacit approval of UK government officials.[141] More important, however, were the conclusions about the private military industry. The report not only adopted the term "private military companies" but also endorsed their existence, noting that "these companies are on the scene and look likely to stay on it" and "are entitled to carry on their business within the law and, for that purpose, to have the access and support which Departments are there to provide to British citizens and companies."[142] This did not settle the matter once and for all in the court of public or international opinion, but it portended a generally permissive approach toward the burgeoning industry.

The Nisour Square Backlash

Of course, the contestation of the norm against private force has not been an entirely one-sided affair. Strong norms do not die—or change—easily, and material and normative conditions notwithstanding, there has been considerable resistance to the reintroduction of entrepreneurial violence. This resistance has been strongest in the wake of controversial incidents that have allowed critics to focus attention on some of the more problematic aspects of PMSCs, such as their autonomy from governmental control and the difficulty in holding contractors accountable for their actions. If the Sandline tempest of the late 1990s was the best example of this in the United Kingdom, the closest US equivalent was the backlash against PMSCs after the 2007 Nisour Square shootings. Even before this incident, the privatization phenomenon was attracting growing attention and concern, leading to calls from critics for greater regulation and the clarification of contractors' rules of engagement.[143] Nisour Square crystallized these concerns and brought them dramatically to the fore. In the months that followed, Blackwater and the private security industry faced harsh media attention and strong criticism in Congress; in a rare display of bipartisanship, the House voted 389 to 30 to bring contractors in foreign combat zones under the jurisdiction of US courts.[144] Both the State Department and the Defense Department instituted new procedures to improve the supervision of contractors and tightened the rules governing their conduct.[145] The General Accountability Office, the Congressional Budget Office, and the White House Office of Management and Budget all issued reports aimed at taking stock of the privatization trend, including whether the United States had crossed the line into improperly contracting out "inherently governmental functions."[146]

Blackwater and other advocates for PMSCs responded vigorously to this heightened scrutiny, highlighting the themes that had defined the industry's contestation efforts since the 1990s. Blackwater hired a leading PR firm to minimize the damage, and Prince, who had previously preferred to keep a low public profile, gave interviews on several national television outlets and wrote an op-ed piece defending the firm and its employees.[147] The company also disseminated on its email distribution list "A Request for Your Support" urging recipients to contact their congressmen and congresswomen to "tell the Blackwater story and encourage your representatives to seek the truth instead of reading negative propaganda and drawing the wrong conclusions." It included "suggested themes" to mention, such as "cost efficiency of Blackwater" and "professional population of service veterans and mature law enforcement personnel."[148] The IPOA continued to stress the value and professionalism of PMSCs, while objecting to the selective media coverage that it claimed was feeding a "global war on contractors": "We should not expect *The New York Times* to print a headline declaring that despite war, abysmal infrastructure and countless other hindrances the military operations in Afghanistan and Iraq are the best supported and supplied in history. You are far more likely to read of a contractor accidentally running over someone's goat."[149]

There was no question that Nisour Square was a setback for the industry, reinforcing the image of contractors as reckless cowboys and undermining the themes of control, accountability, restraint, and humanitarianism that were central to its contestation efforts. The damage was felt most acutely by Blackwater itself. With the spotlight now fixed on the company, reports surfaced of other alleged improprieties. More than a dozen government agencies launched investigations of Blackwater, and a 2008 raid by the Bureau of Alcohol, Tobacco, Firearms and Explosives on its North Carolina headquarters resulted in five senior company officials (Prince not among them) being indicted on federal weapons and conspiracy charges.[150] The heat over Nisour Square also led to a rift between Blackwater and the rest of the industry. When IPOA's Standards Committee started an investigation of the incident, Blackwater withdrew from the association, which company executives believed had betrayed them.[151] Soon other companies sought to distance themselves from Blackwater, portraying it as a rogue outfit that flouted industry standards.[152] Most damaging of all, the controversy ultimately cost Blackwater its lucrative and high-profile contract with the State Department, which was canceled in January 2009 after Iraq refused to renew the company's license to operate in the country. A month later, in an effort to rebrand, Blackwater changed its name to Xe Services, and soon thereafter Prince and company president Gary Jackson resigned from their posts.[153] By the end of 2010, with company revenues having declined 40 percent since Nisour Square, Prince had sold his ownership stake and moved to the UAE, complaining bitterly about the "giant proctological exam" prompted by the incident.[154] In December 2011, the company changed its name again, to Academi, a moniker the new CEO said conveyed its goal of becoming "boring."[155]

Contestation Successful? The Norm Today

The troubles faced by Sandline and Blackwater notwithstanding, the weight of the evidence suggests that efforts at contesting and reinterpreting the norm against private force have largely been successful. This is apparent in three significant ways. First, there has been a general shift away from efforts to prohibit private force and toward attempts to regulate it—and these attempts at regulation have yielded underwhelming results. The two main international instruments intended to outlaw mercenaries—article 47 of Protocol I and the 1989 UN convention—have languished. Article 47 is one of the few provisions of Protocol I for which state practice and interpretation is so unsettled that it is not widely considered to enjoy the status of customary international law.[156] As noted earlier, the UN convention has attracted little support, and most commentators view it as an unqualified failure.[157] Another example was the 1996 revision of the International Law Commission's Draft Code of Crimes against the Peace and Security of Mankind. Acting mainly at the urging of Western states, the ILC removed all provisions assigning criminal responsibility for mercenary activity, which had been a part of the previous draft code in 1991.[158] Likewise, despite calls from some states, the 1998 Rome Statute, which established the International Criminal Court, did not include the crime of mercenarism.[159] Even the goal of devising a scheme of regulation and accountability for PMSCs has proven elusive. As I discuss below, several different approaches taken by the UN since the mid-1980s have been fruitless. The most meaningful steps toward regulation have come through "multishareholder initiatives" (MSIs), which have brought together national governments, PMSCs, and civil society representatives to develop guidelines for the industry. Initiatives spearheaded by the ICRC and the Swiss government produced the 2008 Montreux Document and the 2010 International Code of Conduct (ICoC), which largely mirror the voluntary codes of conduct written by organizations such as ISOA and the BAPSC. While violations can serve as the basis for breach-of-contract claims by governments who have written the codes into their contracting provisions, they are not punishable under international or civil law, and only a handful of governments have signed the documents.[160]

The aversion to both prohibition and restrictive regulation has prevailed at the national as well as the international level. A telling event in this regard was the UK Foreign and Commonwealth Office's 2002 green paper titled *Private Military Companies: Options for Regulation*.[161] The report grew out of the investigation of Sandline's activities in Sierra Leone, which requested that "in respect of mercenary activities, the Government publish a Green Paper outlining options for the control of private military companies." While ostensibly intended only to present the range of available options, the green paper made clear that banning private force altogether was neither a viable nor a desirable outcome. Strikingly, it echoed many of the arguments Spicer and Sandline had made in the previous few years. It adopted both the term "private military company" and the distinctions between PMCs and mercenaries Sandline had outlined, and it agreed that the private sector was "a cost effective way of procuring services which would once have been the exclusive preserve of the military" and "might have a role in enabling the UN to respond more rapidly and more effectively in crises."[162] It also cited recent trends and precedents to question the feasibility of prohibition, at one point arguing that "in one sense the United Nations already employs some mercenary forces [because] at least some countries who contribute to UN peacekeeping do so largely for financial reasons."[163] After the green paper, there was little doubt that at least insofar as British policy was concerned, the private military and security industry had notched a significant victory. If steps toward the privatization of security were irreversible by the time the British government took stock of it, it was even more so in the United States. Because the US private security industry emerged gradually from the privatization of logistics, training, and procurement, the regulation of PMSCs evolved by accretion in a disorganized, ad hoc process.[164] The closest US parallel to the process that produced the green paper was the scrutiny of the industry that followed the Nisour Square incident. From 2007 to 2011, bills were introduced in the House and Senate that proposed measures ranging from enhancing transparency and government oversight of PMSCs to "phasing them out" altogether. None even made it out of committee, and no coherent and systematic approach to regulation emerged through any other channels.[165]

A second sign that contestation efforts have worked is that the attempt to disassociate the private security industry from the terminology of "mercenarism" has overwhelmingly succeeded. In his 1999 book, Spicer noted: "The word 'mercenary' appears less frequently; the term 'military consultant' is more widely employed—and people can see the difference. In part this is due to an extensive public-relations exercise that we have undertaken, orchestrated by [PR consultant] Sara Pearson and her team."[166] Still, in the late 1990s and into the 2000s, describing PMSCs as "mercenaries" was not uncommon in media and academic accounts, even among those who supported their use.[167] After the 2002 green paper, however, the term was rarely used in any but the most polemical critiques. Scholars especially, even those critical of private security, typically take care to emphasize the distinctions between PMSCs and mercenaries, most of which follow the model of Sandline's 1999 open letter.[168]

Of course, the primary implication Sandline hoped to convey with these distinctions was that PMSCs, unlike mercenaries, were legitimate actors. By the 2000s, industry figures were going a step further by redefining the terms, building judgments about legitimacy and legality into the very definitions themselves. By 2006, Spicer, who a few years earlier accepted that he was technically a "mercenary" while lamenting the stigma attached to the word, rejected the term altogether, saying that mercenaries were individuals whose actions are illegal, while PMSCs did lawful work within a corporate structure.[169] In a 2007 column, a senior IPOA official took issue with a blogger's description of DynCorp contractors in Somalia as "mercenaries" by noting that they were "hired by the U.S. government on behalf of the UN, after all. You want legitimacy? You've got legitimacy."[170] This essentially tackles the problem of defining "mercenaries" by starting from the assumption that mercenaries are illegitimate and working backward, making the term's negative connotation part of the definition itself. Interestingly, some scholars have adopted this approach. Krahmann, for example, argues that of the criteria differentiating private force providers, "foremost is the corporate nature of private security and military firms and their resulting legal status, which contrasts with mercenaries who operate outside national and international law," and that "mercenary forces are composed ad hoc and, frequently, for illicit purposes."[171] Similarly, Percy writes that "two basic factors make mercenaries different from other fighters: mercenaries lie outside legitimate control and are not motivated to fight by an appropriate cause."[172] As some of these examples suggest, the presence of a corporate structure—mentioned by Sandline in 1999 as one way in which PMSCs differ from mercenaries—has likewise become a commonly cited criterion for excluding an actor from mercenary status.[173] In this case, contestation not only narrowed the application of the norm against mercenaries—it seems to have changed the meaning of the word itself.

As a result, a vestige of the old norm survives in the strongly pejorative connotations of the term "mercenarism," but the term itself has become increasingly incoherent. It is worth noting how closely this trajectory resembles that of the term "terrorism." In each case, the meaning of the term was at one time uncontroversial, and there was a strong norm against the practice it described. When that norm became less coherent, part of the contestation that followed involved the narrowing and politicization of the term itself. The result in each case was a strongly pejorative term whose application in practice follows from one's prior judgment of whether the actor in question is legitimate or illegitimate. The acceptability of private force, therefore, is inextricably tied to the language used to describe it. For example, former UN secretary-general Kofi Annan noted that in responding to humanitarian crises, "some have even suggested that private security firms . . . might play a role in providing the United Nations with the rapid reaction capacity it needs. When we had need of skilled soldiers to separate fighters from refugees in the Rwandan refugee camps in Goma, I even considered the possibility of engaging a private firm. But the world may not be ready to privatize peace."[174] On the other hand, when someone raised the prospect of employing "respectable mercenary organizations" for peacekeeping, Annan indignantly replied, "I don't know how one makes a distinction between respectable mercenaries and non-respectable mercenaries," while admitting that in Goma he had considered "the possibility of bringing in other elements—not necessarily troops from Governments."[175] Annan's apparent ambivalence, and the notion that "private firms" and "mercenaries" are distinctly different entities even when they are performing the same functions, shows the critical role of language in the debate over private violence.

A third piece of evidence that the contestation of the norm against private force has succeeded is the very frequency and scale of its use. As I discussed earlier in the chapter, states are turning to the private sector for military services more frequently and in a widening range of circumstances. Ulrich Petersohn observes that while the first decade or so of the twenty-first century saw the norm against mercenaries become "reconstructed" so as to allow contractors to use force in situations that could be interpreted as "self-defense," since about 2013 it has become more common for PMSCs to engage in more full-fledged military operations.[176] "Combat contracting is not an insignificant random event," Petersohn argues. "On the contrary, contracting combat services is a frequent pattern, and the contracts are significant in size."[177] To be sure, many states remain outwardly opposed to hiring contractors to engage directly in combat, a position that is expressed in both the Montreux and ICoC documents. Nevertheless, only very rarely do states even take public notice of the practice when it occurs—a silence that, Petersohn notes, reflects the relatively low stakes most states have in the violation of the norm itself and the weak incentives they have to enforce it.[178] Furthermore, "audience costs" are typically low; that is, the problematic practice generates little outrage—or even attention—from the "watchdogs" that monitor the use of private force, such as the ICRC, the UN Working Group, and the press.[179] This fact itself suggests that the use of private force is seen as less novel and less troubling than in the past—a sign that the antimercenary norm has been diminished. The travails of

Sandline and Blackwater may therefore be red herrings, illustrating not a robust stigma against private force but rather how PMSCs can get into trouble even in a context in which private force is increasingly accepted. Both firms came a cropper only after multiple controversies revealed specific acts of misfeasance or malfeasance—because of what they *did*, in other words, not what they *were*. Moreover, although Spicer was unable to save Sandline, in terms of his contestation efforts he lost the battle but won the war. He went on to found Aegis Defence Services, which by 2008 had won over $750 million worth of contracts from the Defense Department for intelligence and security services in Iraq.[180] As Spicer said in 2006, what he was "doing ten years ago was way ahead of its time."[181] For his part, Prince's proposal to privatize America's longest war suggests at the least an abundance of confidence both that the market for PMSCs was strong and that the aversion toward private force had receded significantly. His efforts to sell his plan have incorporated all the contestation strategies I have discussed, rolled into a multi-media PR and lobbying blitz in both the United States and Afghanistan.[182] Apart from frequent mentions of the Flying Tigers and similar contractor contingents, in a *Wall Street Journal* op-ed Prince evoked the "centuries-old approach" of the English East India Company, which "for 250 years prevailed in the [Afghanistan] region through the use of private military units [that] lived, patrolled, and—when necessary—fought shoulder-to-shoulder with their local counterparts."[183] Prince insisted, moreover, that although his plan envisioned contractors sometimes engaging in offensive combat operations, as a matter of definition they would not be "mercenaries" because of their status as adjuncts of the Afghan military.[184] Finally, he emphasized the benefits of privatization in terms of efficiency and cost-effectiveness, contrasting it with the failure of US and NATO forces since 2001. "Afghanistan is an expensive disaster for America," Prince wrote, later adding that he knew President Trump was "frustrated. He gave the Pentagon what they wanted . . . and they haven't delivered."[185] Although Trump rejected the proposal under strong pressure from the then secretary of defense James Mattis, Prince continued to publicly lobby for it, saying in 2020 that "the public advice I offered the president in 2017 still applies, there is a way to rationalize U.S. presence there." He recommended "letting veterans go back in and contract to the Afghan government and provide them the essentials that they need at a fraction of the cost and a fraction of the numbers there now."[186]

A Norm in Flux: The UN and Mercenaries

An enlightening illustration of the success of contestation is the progression of the UN's stance on the issue of private security since the early 1980s. As

I have discussed, that decade began with a mandate to draft a convention banning mercenaries, but the process was plagued by discord, taking nine years
to conclude an agreement that still has scant international support. In 1987,
continuing responsibility for the mercenary issue was given to the special rapporteur, whose mandate fell under the Commission on Human Rights and was
tied to self-determination. The special rapporteur's annual reports provide
an intriguing overview of the evolving view of private force. For ten years the
reports made no real distinction between mercenaries and other private security
providers. In 1997, however, Special Rapporteur Enrique Bernales Ballesteros
spoke directly to the increasing use of PMSCs and the tensions they created with
long-standing norms. The report clearly conveyed Ballesteros's frustration with
how the "new operational model" of PMSCs was undermining antimercenary
efforts.[187] He conceded that it was hard to classify employees of firms such as
Executive Outcomes as mercenaries because of the earlier contextualization of
the mercenary problem, lamenting "the restrictive approach adopted in various United Nations resolutions which link mercenaries with concerted acts of
violence aimed at violating the right of peoples to self-determination."[188] Nevertheless, he was strongly critical of their activities, calling Executive Outcomes
"a legally constituted private company behind whose façade is hidden mercenary
activities, which have been changed and modernized in the legal configuration
of its operations without ceasing to be essentially mercenary in nature."[189] While
acknowledging that "attitudes appear to be changing towards the mercenary
issue," Ballesteros suggested that the growing use of PMSCs might be occurring without a clear appreciation of its implications: "Is not responsibility for a
country's internal order and security an inalienable obligation that a State fulfils
through its police and armed forces? Is it not a grave infringement of that State's
sovereignty to hand over such responsibilities to companies registered in third
countries which sell security services staffed by foreigners, presumably mercenaries?"[190] The question, he argued, called for a systematic thinking through of
the effects of private force on state sovereignty.[191] Until then, he wrote, "contradictions are . . . likely to arise between declarative statements formally condemning mercenary activities and practical concessions to the provision of efficient
services by persons or groups of persons and businesses with a mercenary past
and strong suspicion about and mistrust of the activities they are carrying out
at present."[192]

Ballesteros remained critical of PMSCs until the end of his tenure in 2004 but
was forced to concede that the existing legal instruments provided little basis for
banning them and that their increasing use demonstrated that much of the international community did not *want* them banned. Having apparently determined
that the old antimercenary regime was dead, in 2003 Ballesteros proposed a new

definition of mercenary that seemed intended to reverse some of the effects of the contextualization of the decolonization era while acknowledging that the privatization trend was to a large degree irreversible. He suggested expanding the scope of what constituted mercenarism, considering activity "not only in relation to the self-determination of peoples but also as encompassing a broad range of actions, including the destabilization of constitutional governments, various kinds of illicit trafficking, terrorism and violations of fundamental rights."[193] At the same time, however, he acceded to narrowing the definition to apply only to "persons with military training who offer paid professional services *to take part in criminal activity*," which would include the "direct participation in military operations" by civilians.[194] By making criminal activity an element of mercenarism, Ballesteros was essentially striking a compromise: PMSCs would be accepted as legitimate international actors, but they were not to engage in combat, and their employees could not hide behind the edifice of their legally constituted corporate structure if they committed criminal actions. Ballesteros's proposed definition was nevertheless seen as still too restrictive and has not been taken up seriously since.

In 2004, Ballesteros was replaced by Shaista Shameen, and the following year the Commission on Human Rights terminated the mandate of the special rapporteur, replacing it with the Working Group, composed of experts.[195] These steps moved the UN further from a prohibitionist stance toward PMSCs and toward accepting them as legitimate entities distinct from mercenaries. Shameen's final report in 2005 called for a "practical approach" that accepted PMSCs as a fact of life in the international system, raised the possibility of scrapping the 1989 convention, and endorsed the industry's suggestion that a voluntary code of conduct was, for the time being, the best practicable way to regulate PMSCs. Shameen also recommended that the UN convene a round-table to discuss these issues and reconcile older institutions and statements with more recent changes in practices and attitudes toward private force.[196] "A paradigm shift," she wrote, "needs to occur with respect to the mandate."[197] The Working Group has continued in this direction, affirming that the 1989 convention does not apply to PMSCs and proposing a separate international convention specifically aimed at regulating them, while at times signaling a qualified and reluctant willingness to accept private forces engaging in hostilities.[198] To be sure, the Working Group and the private security industry remain at odds over many issues, including the adequacy of the Montreux and ICoC documents as a means of regulating PMSCs and the need for an international convention.[199] Still, there is no doubt that the UN approach has grown more amenable to private security over time. As an IPOA official noted in 2010, "now that even the most virulent in the 'mercenary regulation' camp (such as the UN Working Group on Mercenaries) have become more realistic in their views, there seems to be some progress on the horizon."[200]

The UN experience also illustrated the shift in the meaning of the term "mercenarism" itself. In a 2005 letter, a group of "peace and security companies" asked that the term "mercenaries" be eliminated from the Working Group's name and mandate: "This derogatory term is completely unacceptable and is too often used to describe fully legal and legitimate companies engaged in vital support operations for humanitarian peace and stability operations."[201] While the UN rejected this request at the time, the 2007 report of the Working Group reflected a sense of weary resignation on the issue: "The problem with the current definition [of mercenarism] is twofold: either nearly everyone engaged privately in armed conflict in covered by the definition, or no one is, thus making the Convention very difficult if not impossible to implement. . . . Member States need to decide what the international community will accept as State responsibility for the use of force. Activities of PMSCs which will not be permitted can be defined as mercenarism."[202] What was remarkable was the forthrightness with which the Working Group acknowledged that its mandate had become inescapably arbitrary: successive reconceptualizations of mercenarism since the 1960s had produced a term that was almost meaningless except for its connotations of illegitimacy.

Finally, it is worth noting that although the UN sometimes expresses misgivings about PMSCs, it *does* in fact use them. While the UN has thus far rejected the large-scale use of PMSCs for intervention and peacekeeping, for example, it has frequently used them for smaller missions, including delivering supplies and providing escorts for officials in dangerous areas.[203] Humanitarian NGOs, too, have professed unease about private security firms, but not only do NGOs regularly employ them, but some NGO officials have also expressed support for using them for humanitarian intervention.[204]

Conclusion

In this chapter, I have emphasized the significance of the macronormative change that made decolonization an almost unparalleled priority in the 1950s through 1970s. It should be noted, however, that other subsidiary normative changes I discuss in chapter 2 also were influential. The reassessment of core sovereign functions that was an aspect of decolonization, recall, deemphasized an effective military apparatus as an indispensable defining element of state sovereignty.

If one effect of this reassessment was to validate the idea that actors other than sovereign states may possess military capabilities, as we saw in chapter 3, another was to legitimize the practice of governments turning to outside actors to meet their military needs, which chipped away at the opprobrium associated with mercenaries.

The changes that accompanied the macronormative retreat from the raison d'état following World War II also contributed to these events. First, the withdrawal of deference to state discretion created pressure on the antimercenary norm by challenging the correlation between sovereignty and the exclusive control over military force, thus toppling one of the pillars on which the norm had long rested. If nonstate actors could legitimately use force in some circumstances, then the sweeping categorical prohibition of mercenaries was bound to come under scrutiny. Even more important was the contextualization of the right to use force that was logically inherent in the circumscription of states' prerogatives after the war. We saw in chapter 3 how self-determination movements were able to successfully contest the state monopoly on violence in part by exploiting the new regime's shift in focus from who used force to the cause for which it was used. The contextualization of the mercenary problem not only drew directly on this effort—it was in some ways actually part of it, finding expression in the same influential debates and documents in the UN.

Also important was the acceptance of normative asymmetry that grew from the ascendance of consequentialist normative reasoning in international politics after World War II. The contextualization of the antimercenary norm entailed just such an asymmetrical judgment, since it deemed mercenaries to be a pernicious and criminal force if they fought for one side but a progressive force if they fought for the other. Finally, the demilitarization of society discussed in chapter 2 played a role in helping to reshape ideas about the relationship between national citizenship and military service, which had been important in the stigmatization of mercenarism that emerged in the nineteenth century.[205] This change entailed not only moving away from the idea of serving in one's national military as an obligation of citizenship but also recognizing the right to serve in other militaries, and for other causes, as a valid expression of personal liberty—a position articulated as early as 1976 in the Diplock Report.[206]

To be sure, the antimercenary norm is not entirely dead; there is still reticence about embracing private violence in various forms. We have not seen a return to massive mercenary armies, and we may not see one anytime soon. Moreover, as I have explained, for the time being the term "mercenary" itself remains pejorative.[207] Nevertheless, governments—as well as international organizations and businesses—employ private force to a degree that would have been unthinkable several decades ago. While there are still steadfast opponents of privatization in the media, academia, government, and NGOs, their concerns seldom command headlines in the ordinary course of events, nor have they halted the growth of the private security industry. This fact, and the increasing openness with which military entrepreneurs champion a broader return to old practices, suggests a significant change in international norms has already occurred and that an even larger one may be in the offing.

WHAT'S AT STAKE?

The Implications of Nonstate Actor Violence

We are witnessing significant changes in how—and by whom—violence is used in the international system. In the preceding three chapters, I have shown that these changes had their foundations in systemic and normative transformations that occurred in the decades after World War II. These transformations some-times contributed to material conditions favoring the rise of nonstate violence, but as important was their reshaping of norms governing when such violence was deemed legitimate. Through processes of normative contestation, nonstate actors and their allies succeeded in further weakening already compromised state prerogatives concerning the use of force and assuaging concerns about private military actors. The result has been a reconfiguration of the landscape of transnational violence into something that would have been unrecognizable several decades ago—but that might have seemed familiar three or four centu-ries earlier.

The cases in chapters 3, 4, and 5 describe three distinct trends, each impor-tant in its own right. The central argument of this book, however, is that taken together they constitute a single phenomenon whose significance goes beyond any of its parts: that nonstate actor violence has become both a more frequent and a more accepted feature of international politics. In this chapter, I return to considering this central argument and its implications for international politics. I begin by discussing some of the connections among these and other types of nonstate violence, including transnational organized crime. I then examine the question of control over, and accountability for, transnational violence. While it is important not to overstate the degree to which sovereign states themselves are always held accountable for the violence they employ, they are nevertheless subject to pressures that can sometimes induce restraint. Nonstate actors, on the other hand, are more often beyond the reach of such measures. This is patently obvious in some cases (terrorist groups for example) but, for reasons I explain, is often true even when one might expect control to be less problematic. This in turn raises the prospect of violence without accountability, which is worrisome even on a small scale but on a widespread basis can threaten to significantly undermine international order. Finally, I consider some policy implications of nonstate actor violence. Although it is unlikely that the trend toward increased nonstate actor violence can be entirely reversed, the crucial role played by norms in its return should remind us that human agency remains relevant, which points the way toward certain policy choices that might slow the trend and ameliorate some of its more pernicious effects.

A Tangled Web

The three cases of nonstate actor violence examined in the book are bound together, first, by the fact that they all emerged from the same set of macronormative transformations in the years after 1945, as I have explained. Second, they all have the same significant implications for international relations theory. Even if we acknowledge that state sovereignty has in practice seldom matched the classical Weberian definition, the growth in the frequency and impact of nonstate actor violence is noteworthy. So, too, is the increasing acceptance of this violence as legitimate. As we have seen, states and international organizations often supply these actors with material and rhetorical support and in some cases with legal recognition as well. There have been, in other words, not just changes in the practices of international violence but also in attitudes toward such practices. A third sign that these various forms of nonstate violence should be viewed as parts of a common whole is how often they converge and intersect in practice. Of course, clearly distinguishing among categories of violent nonstate actor can be difficult, as I have argued, but even when the distinctions appear clear-cut, different types of actors frequently interact and collude. While militias and terrorist organizations may typically be motivated by political, ideological, or religious goals, they often make common cause with transnational organized crime (TOC) enterprises to fund their endeavors. Illegal narcotics have been a major source of funding for Hamas, Hezbollah, and al-Qaeda, as well as the FARC and the National Liberation Army in Colombia and the Shining Path in Peru.[1] Al-Qaeda was also involved in the illicit diamond trade (with the assistance of the regime of Liberian president Charles Taylor), as were Hezbollah, UNITA in Mozambique, and the Revolutionary United Front in Sierra Leone.[2] Indian mob boss Dawood Ibrahim, in many ways a classic underworld don, involved in narcotics, gambling, and even the Bollywood film industry, also reportedly has ties to al-Qaeda, helped finance terrorist bombings in Mumbai in 1993 and 2005, and lives in Pakistan under the protection of the Pakistan military's Inter-Services Intelligence Directorate (ISI).[3] Moreover, criminal organizations' involvement in politics can sometimes be more than simply convenient means of making money. The group that funded the March 2004 Madrid train bombings, which killed almost two hundred people and injured two thousand more, began as a drug-trafficking ring in Morocco but adopted a militant Islamist agenda when its members became radicalized.[4] And in places such as the Caribbean, criminal street gangs have become important political actors and power brokers, providing public goods and services where governments are too weak to do so and tipping the balance toward certain parties and candidates. This puts the gangs in the position of a "parallel power" to governments willing to accommodate them and a potential insurgent force against governments seeking to crack down on them.[5]

PMSCs, too, have at times worked with other types of violent nonstate actors as well as with governments pitted against them. In several African countries in the 1990s and 2000s, both governments and antigovernment rebels employed private firms.[6] Latin American drug cartels and antigovernment militias also reportedly hired private military firms, and in the 2000s there were extensive ties among PMSCs, warlords, and drug traffickers in Afghanistan.[7] In Russia the lines delineating PMSCS from militias, terrorists, and organized crime can be blurry. Both the Wagner Group and its predecessor, Slavonic Corps, had close ties to nationalist militias, many of which in turn are associated with criminal syndicates and in some cases—unsurprisingly, given the kleptocratic nature of Russian politics—the government itself.[8] The fuzziness of distinctions between PMSCs and other nonstate actors is not limited to Russia, however, as illustrated by the case mentioned in chapter 3 that saw the US State Department employing warlord-led militias in a PMSC role to provide embassy security and by the role of local warlords and militias in US Defense Department supply chains in Afghanistan.[9] Categorization becomes even more difficult if one considers the already elusive line between PMSCs that engage in combat and "mercenaries." A July 2020 report in *Der Spiegel* detailed Iran's assembly of a "mercenary network" that took the form of "a monstrous apparatus of militias from half a dozen different countries . . . that can rapidly assembly ever-changing groups of fighters in division-sized units."[10] Among the groups fighting for the Bashar al-Assad regime in Syria is the Shabiha, which multiple human rights NGOs and other analysts refer to as mercenaries.[11] The Shabiha nevertheless fits the definitions of several types of violent nonstate actor: a sectarian group that started out (and remains) heavily involved in robbery and the smuggling of commodities, drugs, and arms, it evolved into a brutal proregime militia that directly targets civilians to terrorize the population into submission.[12] Another group that is difficult to categorize is Malhama Tactical, which has been called "the Blackwater of jihad."[13] Malhama is a small but profitable firm that uses multiple social media platforms to slickly market its services to militant Sunni Islamist nonstate groups, merging fundamentalist ideology with profit-driven enterprise.[14] Even this model of the terrorist/mercenary hybrid is not entirely new, however. Bruce Hoffman describes how during the 1980s the Abu Nidal Organization became "terrorists for hire," as it "progressively relinquished its original revolutionary/political motivations in favor of activities devoted almost entirely to making money."[15] By 1988, the group reportedly had assets of about $400 million, including large sums invested in commercial enterprises and real estate.[16] The lines among categories of violent nonstate actors, then, tend to be fluid, and seemingly quite different groups often have more in common than it might initially seem.[17]

Violence and Accountability

The question of who is legitimately permitted to use force in the international system is significant because it is tied to who can be held accountable for its use and ultimately to the degree to which violence can be limited or controlled. Of course, it is important not to overstate either of these connections, including the extent to which sovereign states themselves are always held fully accountable for the violence they employ. State violence (both within and outside national borders) has long been far more lethal and destructive than nonstate violence and remains so today. Surely, the world wars that marked the apotheosis of state power in the twentieth century were horrific beyond compare. Nevertheless, as we have seen, in response to that nightmare states themselves wrought normative changes that conceded that the raison d'état was untenable as the sole criterion for resort to war and reflected a collective willingness to be tethered to some sense of principle and collective good. While limiting transnational state violence remains a very imperfectly realized goal, today even powerful states typically must give account of their decisions to use force, and this, too, is important. States that use force irresponsibly rarely do so with impunity, despite what critics claim. Such actions usually entail consequences, from coercive enforcement under the UN Charter (such as Iraq faced in response to its 1990 invasion of Kuwait), to economic and diplomatic sanctions (such as those imposed on Russia after its 2014 annexation of Crimea), to damage to beneficial relationships, disapprobation, public pressure, and diminished international standing (all of which the United States experienced after its invasion of Iraq in 2003).[18] As Christine Gray observes, "states argue and negotiate to try to avoid condemnation; the price may be intangible, but it is one that states using force do not want to have to pay."[19] An interesting example has been Hamas's behavior since winning Palestinian elections in 2006 and becoming the de facto governing authority for Gaza—events that effectively turned a violent nonstate actor into something like a state actor. While Hamas has officially refused to accept Israel's right to exist or to renounce violence, in practice "Hamas's survival instinct also pushed it toward moderation. Paradoxically, Hamas's formal integration into the political process has done more to limit its room for maneuver in its relations with Israel than any other development since 1993. After 2005–6, Hamas and its government often refrained from using violence, preferring immediate political survival over 'resistance.' Indeed, Hamas's commitment to its declared and undeclared ceasefire arrangements with Israel has been relatively stable even when they failed to force public concessions, or exact the intended price, from the Israelis."[20] To be clear, Hamas's relative restraint (and it is only relative—the group has engaged in two sizable conflicts with Israel since 2007) is not a function of altruism or exemplary international citizenship but rather the pragmatism and caution with which self-interested states must concern themselves.[21]

The avenues of influence that can be exerted on states are often unavailable in dealing with nonstate actors. This is most clearly true of antigovernment groups that are not beholden to state sponsors but can also be true of nonstate groups that are bound closely to states. First, the plausible deniability that nonstate actors provide can make it hard to control them simply by pressuring their sponsors. More fundamentally, however, the actual control that sponsors have over nonstate groups can be very tenuous. Regimes relying on militias to bolster their power have often found them to be unmanageable and prone to pursuing their own priorities to the detriment of government interests. This has been a problem in Iraq since the fall of Saddam Hussein in 2003 and in Libya since the fall of Moammar Qaddafi in 2011, and there are signs it will plague the Assad regime in Syria in the future.[22] It became an existential crisis for Colombia, which passed legislation in 1968 allowing the government to organize and arm "self-defense units" to fight rebels, only to strike down the law in 1989 after these units grew beyond control and turned on the government, terrorizing both the nation's judiciary and much of its rural population.[23] The United States itself has cautionary tales to draw on, including the aftermath of its support of mujahideen rebels in Afghanistan in the 1980s and of Sunni militias during the Anbar Awakening in Iraq in the late 2000s. In both cases, the erstwhile allies turned to stridently anti-Western forms of fundamentalist militancy. And while relationships based on mutual political expediency have often proved unreliable, even ideological or religious allegiances can be fragile and short-lived.[24]

PMSCs are typically portrayed as easier to control than other types of violent nonstate actors. Because they often operate more in public view, follow a more explicitly business-oriented model, and are bound by the terms of their contracts with clients, there are more means of holding PMSCs accountable for their actions and commensurately less risk of unauthorized violence.[25] Nevertheless, there are reasons to doubt that control over PMSCs is always as secure as the industry suggests. Since 2000, many experts have detailed the failure to meaningfully regulate the industry, the difficulties in holding contractors accountable under legal codes, and how these shortcomings have contributed to incidents in which force has been used in morally, legally, or politically problematic ways.[26] PMSCs have their own priorities, driven by the logic of the market rather than that of national interest, national or institutional loyalty, the common good, or wider interests in peace and stability. This fact has several potentially troublesome implications. One is that PMSCs often view their mission in narrow contractual terms and disregard the wider political consequences of their actions. Even when performing services under contract, therefore, they sometimes act in ways that undermine the interests of their clients. The Nisour Square incident is the best-known example but far from the only one. A Brookings Institution study authored by P. W. Singer in 2007 concluded, "When we evaluate the facts, the use of private military contractors appears to have harmed, rather than helped, the counterinsurgency efforts of the U.S. mission in Iraq, going against our best doctrine and undermining critical efforts of our troops."[27] In another case, Afghan PMSCs subcontracted by a British firm in the 2000s were connected to "murder, kidnapping, bribery, and anti-coalition activities," damaging efforts to win the trust of the population.[28] Indeed, the disjuncture between incentives driving contractors and the interests of their employers can create unintended consequences. PMSCs hired to shut down illicit diamond-trading in Africa harassed local civilians, secretly imprisoned and murdered suspected illicit traders, and laid land mines that ended up killing both diamond smugglers and innocent people.[29] In one case, subsidiaries of a single PMSC reportedly worked for both sides at the same time in the civil war in Sierra Leone in the late 1990s.[30] And a 2010 House of Representatives report found pervasive problems in the system of contracts supplying US forces in Afghanistan, which "put responsibility for the security of vital U.S. supplies on contractors and their unaccountable security providers. This arrangement has fueled a vast protection racket run by a shadowy network of warlords, strongmen, commanders, corrupt Afghan officials, and perhaps others."[31] Most troubling was that much of the money generated by this "protection racket" likely ended up in the hands of the Taliban, the very enemy US forces were fighting.[32]

Another implication of the incentive structure of the PMSC industry has to do with what happens when contracts expire and demand subsides. PMSCs themselves often remain intact and search for new opportunities, but the number of individuals they employ may decline dramatically. What remains, then, is a large number of unemployed contractors with a particular set of skills that can make them very useful or very dangerous, depending on the circumstances. A 2018 analysis of the Russian private security market noted that "in the past several years dozens of Russian PMCs have popped up, many of them short-lived. When a PMC goes defunct, its personnel often splinter into new groups and proliferate, as in the case of Tigr Top-Rent Security that was established in 2005 and went defunct the very next year."[33] Companies founded by former Tigr employees subsequently operated in Afghanistan, Syria, and several African countries.[34] Despite Vladimir Putin's apparent enthusiasm for PMSCs, other government officials and Duma members have been wary of such long-term effects of supporting the industry, and legislation to formally legalize private military firms has failed repeatedly despite Putin's support. Officials of the country's security agency and Defense Ministry both expressed fears that such measures might one day lead to "tens of thousands of uncontrollable Rambos turning their weapons against the government."[35] Scholar Tor Bukkvoll comments that, ironically, one useful purpose served by the use of Russian firms like the Wagner Group in Syria is that it keeps well-trained but angry and disaffected men out of Russia, where they could stir up trouble.[36] The chaotic decline of the Puntland Maritime Police Force produced just such a scenario in Somalia, as the company assembling and training the force abruptly abandoned the project, leaving about five hundred "half-trained and well-armed members of the Puntland Maritime Police Force . . . to fend for themselves at a desert camp carved out of the sand, perhaps to join up with the pirates or Qaeda-linked militants or to sell themselves to the highest bidder in Somalia's clan wars—yet another dangerous element in the Somali mix."[37] Indeed, some experts see what might happen in the aftermath of large military operations as a particularly fraught aspect of heavy reliance on PMSCs. Sean McFate describes the pattern that followed US draw-downs in Iraq and Afghanistan: "What happens to these sub[contractor]s when the big contractor goes home? In some notable, alarming cases, they go into business for themselves, breeding mercenary markets in the wake of a U.S. intervention."[38] Consequently, a policy intended to serve US interests and enhance the security of the region over the long term can undercut both those goals.

PMSCs and their supporters have argued that fears of unaccountable companies and contractors are overblown because they fail to recognize that PMSCs are typically closely linked to their home country, employing individuals who are not only responsible professionals but patriotic citizens who would never act against the interests of their home states. Blackwater's Erik Prince testified to a House of Representatives committee in 2007 that "the people we employ are former U.S. military and law enforcement people, people who have sworn the oath to support and defend the Constitution against all enemies, foreign and domestic. They bleed red, white and blue. So the idea that they are going to suddenly switch after having served honorably for the U.S. military and go play for the other team, it is not likely."[39] Such assurances are less than persuasive, however, for several reasons. First, PMSCs and national militaries are very different sorts of institutions, as we have seen. Swati Srivastava points out that PMSCs challenge Samuel Huntington's model of "objective civilian control" over the military because they are "a hybrid entity that does not face the same loyalty tests as the military or the same scrutiny as civilians."[40] Second, many PMSCs employ contractors, and engage subcontractors, who are not citizens of the country in which the PMSC is based, making bonds of national loyalty a potentially complicating factor rather than a reassuring one. Third, these claims understate the extent to which the PMSC industry has been shaped by the processes of globalization, producing companies that in many cases are difficult to identify with any single country, much less assume are bound to any country by bonds of patriotic allegiance. Moreover, these firms often contract not only with their nominal "home country" but with other governments as well—along with multinational corporations—which exemplify the increasingly stateless character of commercial enterprise.

To understand the shortcomings of Prince's argument, one need look no further than Prince's own business dealings. Three years before assuring the House committee of the patriotic bona fides of Blackwater, Prince established a Blackwater affiliate called Greystone Limited. Billing itself as "an international security services company that offers your country or organization a complete solution to its most pressing security needs," Greystone was registered not in the United States but in Barbados and claimed to have recruited employees from nine non-US countries who would be available for "ready deployment in support of national security objectives as well as private interests."[41] Later, after selling Blackwater in the wake of the Nisour Square controversy, Prince himself moved to the United Arab Emirates and helped establish the company Reflex Responses, which contracted with the UAE government to provide an eight-hundred-man battalion comprising mostly Colombian ex-soldiers.[42] Since then, Prince is reported to be involved with companies based in Austria, Bulgaria, Hong Kong, South Africa, and the UAE, among others, which have sought or received contracts with the UAE, Afghanistan, Puntland, several African governments, and the United

States.[43] Since 2014, Prince has partnered with the Chinese government through Hong Kong–based FSG to provide security for Chinese installations in Africa and also reportedly to train and deploy a private force of former Chinese soldiers for the government's use.[44] Given China's status as one of the United States' most formidable strategic challengers, Prince did in fact effectively "go play for the other team." Certainly, Prince's post-Blackwater career shows that PMSCs are often now largely stateless entities—a fact also illustrated by the murky status of the Wagner Group, which to this point works for and trains its personnel in Russia but is registered in Argentina and Hong Kong.[45] In a confluence of these two notorious actors, Prince reportedly met in 2020 with Wagner officials with an offer to support Wagner operations in Mozambique and Libya, an arrangement that would have had Prince effectively working for Russia. Wagner is said to have rejected the proposal.[46]

There are therefore reasons to worry that PMSCs might already—and increasingly in the future—raise some of the same problems of "violence without accountability" as other violent nonstate actors.

Policy Implications

In this book, I have argued that many factors, both material and ideational, contributed to the reemergence of nonstate violence over the last several decades. It would be impossible to simply hit the reset button and return to the days when the state's monopoly on force was relatively more secure—nor, given the many welcome changes in the international system over the same time, would it be desirable to do so. Still, human agency in the form of policy choices made by states and other actors did play an important role in eroding this monopoly and will continue to shape state and nonstate prerogatives in the future. It is therefore worth considering the policy implications of these trends and offer recommendations going forward.

Nonstate actor violence presents both narrow and broad challenges for states. The first and most obvious narrow challenge is that attacks by nonstate actors can undermine their citizens' security and their own interests. While 9/11 remains the clearest example of the harm these attacks can do, armed nonstate groups are acquiring new capabilities, including perhaps the ability to exploit vulnerabilities in data systems to launch attacks that could cause "nation-state type effects."[47] Moreover, nonstate actions could trigger events that threaten even more dire consequences. Here it is worth returning to Janice Thomson's account of how the state monopoly on force arose in the first place. Thomson explains that armed nonstate actors used to be common features of international politics and often were supported by states themselves, who used them in service of their own interests. Because states only had tenuous control over these actors, however, supporting them had the unintended consequence of dragging states into disputes and conflicts that grew out of their nonstate allies' provocative actions. This eventually led states to delegitimize and ban these actors, not as part of a concerted effort to abolish nonstate violence per se but rather as a series of responses to specific foreign policy problems that nevertheless had the general effect of creating a state monopoly on the use of force, thus redefining the institution of state sovereignty.[48] Although levels of nonstate violence have not returned to those seen in the seventeenth and eighteenth centuries, states have again found supporting armed nonstate groups to be a relatively cheap and easy means of pursuing foreign policy goals. Predictably, some of the old problems have emerged. I have mentioned several examples of nonstate actors doing things that have undercut their sponsors' interests, including the role played by US-employed PMSCs in alienating the Iraqi people and leadership and by the Colombian militias that began as government allies and ended up terrorizing much of the country, including the regime itself.

One of the most potentially disastrous incidents involving an unruly nonstate group was one that largely escaped attention: the February 2018 firefight between US troops and Russian contractors from the Wagner Group discussed in chapter 5. Given escalating tensions between the countries, a pitched battle between Americans and Russians in which scores of Russians die is fraught with dangerous possibilities. What makes it especially ominous, however, is that the Wagner unit apparently initiated the attack without the approval of Russian military authorities and may have defied official instructions to stand down.[49] The group's profile is troubling: Russian fighters deployed by Russia to support Russian objectives but not fully under Russian control and with incentives that may lead them to act recklessly, risking conflict that could easily escalate catastrophically. In that sense, Wagner seems to occupy the same shadowy gray area in which Thomson situates the privateers, mercenaries, and merchant companies of the eighteenth century and presents many of the same dangers.

The broad challenge to states posed by nonstate violence is its threat to state power over the intermediate to long term. Just as the series of decisions Thomson describes helped strengthen the institutional status of states in international politics two centuries ago, so has the gradual return of violent nonstate actors helped diminish state prerogatives in the contemporary world. Again, some of this has been intentional and positive, contributing to trends such as greater restraint in the use of force and increased emphasis on multilateralism and international institutions. These trends have for the most part made states and their citizens more secure and more prosperous, allowing them to pursue their goals in a more stable and peaceful environment. Other manifestations of declining state power could be more pernicious, however. The less that legitimate violence remains the sole domain of the state, the less central a role states will play in shaping the global environment, setting norms for those operating in it and determining the future of the international order. Moreover, although it is common to distinguish sharply between the state and "civil society," it is through states that citizens in many countries, including the United States, have the best opportunity to weigh in on important decisions about whether and how force is used across national borders. The growing influence of nonstate actors thus threatens to further marginalize citizens' concerns and exacerbate a growing democratic deficit in decision-making on vital issues.[50] Finally, empowering violent nonstate actors will cause problems for states domestically as well as internationally. We have seen that this has happened in countries such as Libya, Iraq, and Colombia, but the United States also suffers from this problem. The preoccupation with international terrorism in American political rhetoric obscures the fact that domestic terrorism is far more common.[51] This is largely a product of far-right militancy, which has saddled the country with a militia problem of its own. These militias have been involved in numerous attacks on and armed standoffs with law enforcement authorities, provided paramilitary "security" for the white supremacist marchers in Charlottesville, Virginia, in August 2017, unilaterally detained migrants at the border with Mexico, caused the closure of the Oregon state legislature in June 2019 by threatening its Democratic members, plotted to kidnap Michigan governor Gretchen Whitmer in 2020, and, most notoriously, played a leading role in the insurrection at the US Capitol on January 6, 2021.[52] Domestic nonstate violence, then, already endangers American citizens and challenges US government sovereignty in fairly significant ways.

All this points to two interrelated policy recommendations for states, especially powerful states like the United States. The first is to recognize the risks posed by nonstate actor violence and refrain from taking steps to accelerate a trend that will almost surely harm their interests in the long run. Certainly, it suggests that states should be less eager to ally themselves with nonstate actors in addressing foreign policy problems, especially those involving national security. To be sure, reversing this trend will not be easy and will pose political challenges for national leaders—and their constituents—who have gotten comfortable with shunting tasks away from government institutions, where they receive less attention and are less likely to generate public debate. But as we have seen, outsourcing delicate or dubious tasks is not the same thing as avoiding them. It may defer consequences but is unlikely to allow them to be escaped altogether—and when they come, they may be worse than they otherwise would have been. Of course, perspective, sound judgment, and the ability to think past the crises of the moment would be helpful here. The shock of 9/11 notwithstanding, for example, terrorism per se is not an existential threat to the United States, and some of the measures adopted to combat it could have effects more harmful than those of terrorism itself. Among other things, there has been a tendency to ignore that other actors are likely to assert the same prerogatives America claims for itself. In this regard, the failure of the United States to think through the effect of the precedents it sets when it relies on nonstate actors is striking. As one study of Russia's use of PMSCs observes, "the example set by the U.S. in particular, and its extensive use of PMSCs in the military operations in Iraq and Afghanistan, is likely to have been a source of inspiration for many other countries interested in expanding their war fighting repertoire and defense industries," including Russia.[53] It is noteworthy that there has been no public response by the US government to the UAE's hiring of American firm Spear Operations Group to kill Yemeni opposition leaders and clerics, a case mentioned in chapter 5.[54] Assessing reports that the CIA knew in advance of the operation, Deborah Avant writes:

> From the outside any U.S. action is taken to be representative of U.S. policy. News of the United States allowing the export of hit squads will thus weaken more normal U.S. efforts. . . . President Vladimir Putin and his allies can more easily dismiss [US criticism] as flagrant hypocrisy. . . . It [also] sets a very bad precedent for rogue operators. . . . If the industry comes to believe that the world's largest consumer of military and security services has an appetite for rogue behavior, more will move in that direction. More PMSCs willing to work outside the rules will feed into the designs of similarly inclined leaders.[55]

This admonition is worth keeping in mind as the United States weighs policy options, especially in countering terrorism, for which experts and legislators have recommended such practices as reviving the eighteenth- and nineteenth-century practice of privateering and collaborating with transnational criminal organizations.[56] While these may be tempting in the moment, when it comes to the use of force both American and global interests would be better served by brightening, rather than blurring, the line between states and nonstates.

The second policy recommendation is to remember that in the long game that is foreign policy, norms matter more than is often supposed. This points to the importance of taking norms seriously and protecting those that embody valued principles or serve important interests. It should be remembered, too, that the principle of normative coherence means that violating or even temporarily exempting oneself from a norm can be as harmful as explicitly repudiating it. Carving out exceptions to norms based on current exigencies makes it difficult to later cite them as meaningful international standards or to appeal to them in criticizing the behavior of others. I described in chapter 2 how since 1945 it has become more common to use consequentialist reasoning to justify setting aside existing norms in the service of a compelling moral objective. This dynamic played a role in all three case studies, most commonly employed by non-Western states or nonstate actors seeking to disrupt the status quo. Nevertheless, strong states such as the United States have themselves made frequent use of the same logic. We saw in chapter 4 that US leaders eventually followed the non-Western world in politicizing the debate over transnational terrorism, thus contributing to the devaluation of the term and the dilution of its normative power. Consequentialist reasoning has been more common since 9/11, when US policy became fixated on terrorism as its central foreign policy concern. One example was the Bush Doctrine's dramatic expansion of the doctrine of preemptive self-defense, which justified the 2003 invasion of Iraq but also set a precedent that could support aggression in a wide range of circumstances and was later cited by Russia in explaining its 2008 intervention in Georgia and its evolving military strategy against NATO and the United States in particular, in which preemption would include "non-military measures" such as "information warfare."[57] Another is the occasional indifference of American officials to civilian casualties caused by US operations. This was evident in Secretary of Defense Donald Rumsfeld's remark in a 2001 press conference: "We did not start this war. So understand, responsibility for every single casualty in this war, whether they're innocent Afghans or innocent Americans, rests at the feet of the al Qaeda and the Taliban."[58] It was memorably on display in Trump's comment that "when you get these terrorists, you have to take out their families."[59] But it was also implicitly present in various US policies in all three post-9/11 administrations that marginalized noncombatant immunity to serve perceived strategic needs.[60] Of course, one's own purposes will always seem more noble and legitimate, and one's own crises more dire, than other countries'. Nevertheless, it is shortsighted to ignore norms that help maintain order and restraint in an international system that is historically prone to chaos.

Conclusion

The decline of Westphalian sovereignty has long been foreseen. Even before World War II, E. H. Carr wrote that "the concept of sovereignty is likely to become in the future even more blurred and indistinct that it is at present . . . [and] the effective group unit of the future will in all probability not be the unit formally recognized as such by international law."[61] In 1977, Hedley Bull devoted a chapter of his classic *The Anarchical Society* to considering the prospective "decline of the states system."[62] While he concluded at the time that talk of such a decline was premature, he argued that one sign it was under way in the future would be "the resort to violence on an international scale by groups other than the state, and the assertion by them of a right to commit such violence."[63] The 1990s produced a number of important works noting the increasing prominence of nonstate actors of all sorts in global politics, including James Rosenau's seminal work on "postinternationalism," which he described as a "trend in which more of the interactions that sustain world politics unfold without the direct involvement of states."[64] By 2001, P. W. Singer saw a system in which states were becoming "like dinosaurs toward the end of the Cretaceous period: powerful but cumbersome, not yet superseded, but no longer the unchallenged masters of their environment."[65]

Many scholars and activists have welcomed the postinternationalist move as ushering in a more enlightened and democratic form of world politics, citing progress in human rights, environmental policy, and other issues.[66] Indeed, given that the "Westphalian order" has often been sanguinary and, for that matter, not terribly orderly, it is reasonable to ponder whether we should continue to trust states with the keys to the international system. Martin van Creveld muses that "the devil's bargain that was struck in the seventeenth century, and in which the state offered its citizens much improved day-to-day security in return for their willingness to sacrifice themselves on its behalf if called upon, may be coming to an end. Nor, considering that the number of those who died during the six years of World War II stood at approximately thirty thousand people *per day*, is its demise necessarily to be lamented."[67] Nevertheless, the relative decline of the state is a complex and multifaceted phenomenon and brings with it an enormous range of effects, both good and bad. In this book I have called attention to some of these potentially dangerous effects, and in this chapter I have suggested that, as complex as these changes are, it is not entirely beyond the power of states, and others, to shape their future course. I propose that there is wisdom in recognizing that states themselves are complex and multifaceted and, as villainously as they sometimes behave, are not always villains. To be sure, private individuals and institutions should continue to work toward holding states accountable and demanding that they live up to their promises, both domestic and international. Still, it is a mistake to reflexively vilify them or the principles that define the system they built. Allison Stanger argues that "state-centric principles . . . have served the world well since the end of the Thirty Years' War" and "became the foundation on which collective-security enterprises such as the UN were built."[68] While any ledger sheet for the Westphalian world would be intricate and hotly contested, it is imprudent to categorically reject the entire system, especially when one considers some of the norms and practices that might step in to replace it.[69] This willingness to think flexibly and contextually can also guard against the danger of embracing principles that can have very different consequences in one setting than they might in another. A clear example is the principle of national self-determination, a positive and emancipatory force at various historical junctures but in recent decades a retrograde and destabilizing force that can inspire both separatism and irredentism.[70] A narrower example is the preference for privatizing government functions that is so important in the PMSC case. In some circumstances, certainly, privatization can help provide public goods more effectively and economically than the government itself. Nevertheless, to assume that privatization will yield such benefits for all services under any circumstances is not practicality but rigid dogmatism.

Nuanced and prudent thought will be indispensable in the coming years in navigating what promises to be a stormy period for international politics. The use of violence by transnational nonstate actors is but one challenge, but the stakes involved are high, and the prevalence of such actors is likely to feed norms that contribute to the diffusion of interstate violence. This is a prospect that should be of concern to all, not just sovereign states themselves.

Notes

1. THE FALL AND RISE OF NONSTATE VIOLENCE

1. A few examples among many are Thomas L. Friedman, *The World Is Flat: A Brief History of the Twenty-First Century* (New York: Farrar, Straus and Giroux, 2005); Jessica T. Mathews, "Power Shift," *Foreign Affairs* 76, no. 1 (January/February 1997); and several works by Saskia Sassen, notably *A Sociology of Globalization* (New York: W.W. Norton, 2006).

2. Deborah D. Avant, Martha Finnemore, and Susan K. Sell, eds., *Who Governs the Globe?* (Cambridge: Cambridge University Press, 2010).

3. See, e.g., Margaret Keck and Kathryn Sikkink, *Activists beyond Borders* (Ithaca, NY: Cornell University Press, 1998); Richard Price, "Reversing the Gun Sights: Transnational Civil Society Targets Land Mines," *International Organization* 52, no. 3 (Summer, 1998): 613–44; and Andrew Hurrell, *On Global Order* (Oxford: Oxford University Press, 2007).

4. Alex J. Bellamy, *The Responsibility to Protect: Towards a "Living Reality,"* United Nations Association-UK, 2013, https://una.org.uk/sites/default/files/The%20Responsi bility%20to%20Protect%20Towards%20a%20Living%20Reality%20-%20Professor%20 Alex%20Bellamy.pdf; Ban-Ki Moon, *Implementing the Responsibility to Protect: Report of the Secretary General*, UN General Assembly, Doc. A/63/677 (January 12, 2009), http:// responsibilitytoprotect.org/SGRtoPEng%20(4).pdf.

5. These and other cases are discussed in chapter 5. The term "private military company" (PMC) was common in the 1990s, but in the 2000s many companies added the word "security" to emphasize that they performed functions other than combat operations. As I explain in chapter 5, other terms have since proliferated, and what these companies should be called is a fiercely contested question. In this book, I use "PMSC" as a general descriptor because it is the most widely used and recognized term, especially within scholarly work.

6. Max Weber, "Politics as a Vocation," 1, accessed February 14, 2017, http://anthro pos-lab.net/wp/wp-content/uploads/2011/12/Weber-Politics-as-a-Vocation.pdf.

7. Norms can be defined as "collective understandings of the proper behavior of actors." Jeffrey W. Legro, "Which Norms Matter? Revisiting the 'Failure' of Internationalism in World War II," paper presented at the annual conference of the American Political Science Association, Chicago, August 31–September 3, 1995, 2. Norms are therefore both *prescriptive* and *descriptive*: prescriptive in identifying certain behavior as "proper" and descriptive because "collective understandings" can only form if there is a certain level of regularity of such behavior among relevant actors.

8. Norms are reflected in events and institutions throughout international politics, including international law. Nevertheless, norms and law are not the same thing and can differ considerably. Norms are sometimes more permissive than law, but they can also be more restrictive. I discuss the relationship between norms and law in more detail in chapter 2.

9. See, e.g., Ben Saul, *Defining Terrorism in International Law* (Oxford: Oxford University Press, 2008), and several chapters in Tony Coady and Michael O'Keefe, eds., *Terrorism and Justice: Moral Argument in a Threatened World* (Victoria: Melbourne University Press, 2002).

10. Janice E. Thomson, *Mercenaries, Pirates, and Sovereigns: State-Building and Extraterritorial Violence in Early Modern Europe* (Princeton, NJ: Princeton University Press, 1994).

11. Thomson, *Mercenaries, Pirates, and Sovereigns,* chaps. 4–5; Martin van Creveld, *The Rise and Decline of the State* (Cambridge: Cambridge University Press, 1999), 170.

12. Stephen D. Krasner, *Sovereignty: Organized Hypocrisy* (Princeton, NJ: Princeton University Press, 1999).

13. See chap. 3, passim; Thomson, *Mercenaries, Pirates, and Sovereigns,* chaps. 4–5, and Program on Humanitarian Policy and Conflict Research (hereafter PHPCR), *Transnationality, War and the Law: A Report on a Roundtable on the Transformation of Warfare, International Law, and the Role of Transnational Armed Groups,* April 2006, Harvard Humanitarian Initiative, https://hhi.harvard.edu/publications/transnationality-war-and-law-roundtable-report, 7.

14. In the 1930s and 1940s, 33 percent of all wars were interstate wars. Since the 1950s, that proportion has steadily declined: 1950s, 33 percent; 1960s, 21 percent; 1970s, 18 percent; 1980s, 14 percent; 1990s, 14 percent; 2000–7, 8 percent. *Meredith Reid Sarkees and Frank Wayman, Resort to War: 1816–2007 (Washington, DC: CQ Press, 2010), app. A.*

15. Annyssa Bellal, *The War Report: Armed Conflict in 2018* (Geneva: Geneva Academy of International Humanitarian Law and Human Rights, April 2019), https://www.geneva-academy.ch/joomlatools-files/docman-files/The%20War%20Report%202018.pdf, 32–34.

16. Keith Krause and Jennifer Milliken, "Introduction: The Challenge of Non-State Armed Groups," *Contemporary Security Policy* 30, no. 2 (2009): 205.

17. "Armed Groups' Holdings of Guided Light Weapons," *Small Arms Survey* (December 2014), 2.

18. Neil A. Englehart, "Non-State Armed Groups as a Threat to Global Security: What Threat, Whose Security?," *Journal of Global Security Studies* 1, no. 2 (May 2016).

19. Richard H. Shultz, Douglas Farah, Itamara V. Lochard, "Armed Groups: A Tier-One Security Priority," INSS Occasional Paper no. 57, USAF Institute for National Security Studies, September 2004.

20. PHPCR, *Transnationality, War and the Law,* 6.

21. For examples of each, see chaps. 3 and 4.

22. Phil Williams, "Violent Non-State Actors and National and International Security," International Relations and Security Network, 2008, 4.

23. Williams, "Violent Non-State Actors," 8–17.

24. Shultz, Farah, and Lochard use a taxonomy with four categories (insurgents, terrorists, militias, organized crime), but the distinctions among them are difficult to sustain. For example, they describe terrorists as having an "operational approach that increasingly focuses on targeting non-combatants" but also say that both insurgents and militias often employ these tactics as well. Shultz, Farah, and Lochard are themselves critical of the incoherence of the categories used by the Non-State Actors Working Group, which are "rebel groups, irregular armed groups, insurgents, dissident armed forces, guerrillas, liberation movements, and *de facto* territorial governing bodies." Shultz, Farah, and Lochard, "Armed Groups," 14, 21–23.

25. Anne Barnard, "Hezbollah's Role in Syria War Shakes the Lebanese," *New York Times,* May 20, 2013, https://www.nytimes.com/2013/05/21/world/middleeast/syria-developments.html?pagewanted=all&_r=0.

26. David Daoud, "Hezbollah's Latest Conquest: Lebanon's Cabinet," *Newsweek,* January 12, 2017, https://www.newsweek.com/hezbollahs-latest-conquest-lebanons-cabinet-541487; Barnard, "Hezbollah's Role."

27. Eric Schmitt, David D. Kirkpatrick, and Suliman Ali Zway, "U.S. May Have Put Mistaken Faith in Libya Site's Security," *New York Times*, September 30, 2012, https://www.nytimes.com/2012/10/01/world/africa/mistaken-sense-of-security-cited-before-envoy-to-libya-died.html?pagewanted=3&ref=world.

28. Williams, "Violent Non-State Actors," 11–12. For an overview of how recent literature defines "militia," see Romain Malejacq, "Pro-Government Militias," Oxford Bibliographies, last modified July 26, 2017, http://www.oxfordbibliographies.com/view/document/obo-9780199743292/obo-9780199743292-0213.xml.

29. Sudarsan Raghavan, "Surge in Fighting among Libya's 'Super Militias' Imperils Western Peace Efforts," *Washington Post*, October 2, 2018, https://www.washingtonpost.com/world/surge-in-fighting-among-libyas-super-militias-imperils-western-peace-efforts/2018/10/01/54969c5c-c0d0-11e8-9f4f-a1b7af255aa5_story.html?utm_term=.98e1bf94d206; David D. Kirkpatrick, "Libya Struggles to Curb Militias, the Only Police," *New York* Times, October 13, 2012, https://www.nytimes.com/2012/10/14/world/africa/libyan-government-struggles-to-rein-in-powerful-militias.html?nl=todaysheadlines&emc=edit_th_20121014&_r=0.

30. Monika Sieradzka "Paramilitary Groups Ready to Defend Poland," Real Clear World, June 13, 2016, http://www.realclearworld.com/articles/2016/06/13/paramilitary_groups_ready_to_defend_poland_111906.html; Siddhartha Mahanta, "These Baltic Militias Are Readying for War with Russia," *The Atlantic*, November 26, 2017, https://www.theatlantic.com/photo/2017/11/baltic-anti-russian-militia/545465/.

31. As of January 2019, the US State Department designated sixty-seven groups as "foreign terrorist organizations." US Department of State, "Foreign Terrorist Organizations," accessed January 25, 2019, https://www.state.gov/j/ct/rls/other/des/123085.htm.

32. Important works include Christopher Coker, "Outsourcing War," in *Non-State Actors in World Politics*, ed. Daphné Josselin and William Wallace (London: Palgrave, 2001), 189–202; P. W. Singer, *Corporate Warriors: The Rise of the Privatized Military Industry*, Cornell Studies in Security Affairs (Ithaca, NY: Cornell University Press, 2004); Daniel Bergner, "The Other Army," *New York Times*, August 15, 2005; Deborah D. Avant, *The Market for Force: The Consequences of Privatizing Security* (Cambridge: Cambridge University Press, 2005); and Sean McFate, *The Modern Mercenary: Private Armies and What They Mean for World Order* (Oxford: Oxford University Press, 2015).

33. Deborah Avant, "The Privatization of Security and Change in the Control of Force," *International Studies Perspectives* 5, no. 1 (Winter 2004): 154; Avant, *Market for Force*, 86–113.

34. These activities are described in more detail in chapter 5.

35. Ase Gilje Ostensen and Tor Bukkvoll, *Russian Use of Private Military and Security Companies: The Implications for European and Norwegian Security*, Norwegian Defence Research Establishment, September 11, 2018, 7, https://www.ffi.no/no/Rapporter/18-01300.pdf.

36. P. W. Singer, remarks at the Carnegie Council on Ethics and International Affairs, December 5, 2005, https://www.carnegiecouncil.org/studio/multimedia/20051201-corporate-warriors-the-privatized-military-and-iraq.

37. Avant, *Market for Force*, 171. This incident is detailed in chapter 5.

38. Avant, chaps. 3–4; Patrick Cullen, "Keeping the New Dog of War on a Tight Leash: Assessing Means of Accountability from Private Military Companies," *Conflict Trends* 2000, no. 1 (June 2000): 38.

39. See chap. 5; Ostensen and Bukkvoll, *Russian Use of Private Military*; and Ulrich Petersohn, "Chequing Private Force? The Re-Emergence of the Combat Market for Force," unpublished manuscript, 2018.

40. Singer, remarks at Carnegie Council.

41. Thomas Gibbons-Neff, "How a 4-Hour Battle between Russian Mercenaries and U.S. Commandos Unfolded in Syria," *New York Times*, May 24, 2018, https://www.nytimes.com/2018/05/24/world/middleeast/american-commandos-russian-mercenaries-syria.html.

42. Quoted in Ostensen and Bukkvoll, *Russian Use of Private Military*, 34.

43. See, e.g., Williams, "Violent Non-State Actors"; PHPCR, *Transnationality, War and the Law*; Shultz, Farah, and Lochard, "Armed Groups," and the special issue of the journal *Contemporary Security Policy* devoted to nonstate armed groups, issue 30, no. 2 (2009).

44. Williams, "Violent Non-State Actors," 5–8; Shultz, Farah, and Lochard, "Armed Groups," 5–10.

45. Shultz, Farah, and Lochard, "Armed Groups," 8.

46. Martha Crenshaw, "Why America? The Globalization of Civil War," *Current History* 100, no. 650 (December 2001): 429; Martha Crenshaw, "Thoughts on Relating Terrorism to Historical Contexts," in *Terrorism in Context*, ed. Martha Crenshaw (University Park: Pennsylvania State University Press, 1994), 16–17.

47. Jori Breslawski, "Terrorists, Militants and Criminal Gangs Join the Fight against the Coronavirus," The Conversation, April 10, 2020, https://theconversation.com/terrorists-militants-and-criminal-gangs-join-the-fight-against-the-coronavirus-135914; Sukanya Podder, "Understanding the Legitimacy of Armed Groups: A Relational Perspective," *Small Wars and Insurgencies* 28, nos. 4/5 (2017): 687–91; Louise Richardson, *What Terrorists Want: Understanding the Enemy, Containing the Threat* (New York: Random House, 2006), 57.

48. P. W. Singer, "Corporate Warriors: The Rise of the Privatized Military Industry and Its Ramifications for International Security," *International Security* 26, no. 3 (Winter 2001–2002): 193–97. See also Avant, *Market for Force*, 30–38.

49. Zeev Maoz and Belgin San-Akca, "Rivalry and State Support for Non-State Armed Groups (NAGs), 1946–2001," *International Studies Quarterly* 56 (2012): 732.

50. Williams, "Violent Non-State Actors," 6.

51. United Nations Office on Drugs and Crime, *The Use of the Internet for Terrorist Purposes* (New York: United Nations, 2012), https://www.unodc.org/documents/frontpage/Use_of_Internet_for_Terrorist_Purposes.pdf; Michael Jacobsen, "Terrorist Financing on the Internet," *CTC Sentinel* 2, no. 6 (June 2009), https://ctc.usma.edu/terrorist-financing-on-the-internet/.

52. Avant, *Market for Force*, 32.

53. Avant, 144.

54. See my discussion of the literature on the rise of PMSCs in chapter 5.

55. James G. March and Johan P. Olsen, *Rediscovering Institutions: The Organizational Basis of Politics* (New York: Free Press, 1989), esp. chap. 2.

56. PHPCR, *Transnationality, War and the Law*, 6; Williams, "Violent Non-State Actors," 5–6.

57. Williams, "Violent Non-State Actors," 6–7; Richardson, *What Terrorists Want*, 55–56.

58. Williams, "Violent Non-State Actors," 8.

59. In the context in which he wrote, Weber's use of the broad phrase "legitimate physical violence" referred most clearly to armed policing in a domestic setting and military force in a transnational one. Since my subject here is transnational violence, I will use the terms "military force" or "armed force" to refer to the actions of states and the nonstate actors I am writing about, although some of these might not be commonly associated with "military" operations. This fact itself, of course, reflects the state-centric nature of how we traditionally understand transnational violence.

60. See, e.g., Coker, "Outsourcing War," 189, 200; Singer, "Corporate Warriors," 187; and Sarah Percy, *Mercenaries: The History of a Norm in International Relations* (Oxford: Oxford University Press, 2007).

61. Thomson, *Mercenaries, Pirates, and Sovereigns*, 145–46.

62. See, e.g., Keck and Sikkink, *Activists beyond Borders*; Richard Price, *The Chemical Weapons Taboo* (Ithaca, NY: Cornell University Press, 1997); and Martha Finnemore, *National Interests in International Society* (Ithaca, NY: Cornell University Press, 1996).

63. For an extensive explanation of constructivism, see Alexander Wendt, *Social Theory of International Politics* (Cambridge: Cambridge University Press, 1999). For a concise one, see Finnemore, *National Interests*, chap. 1, or Ward Thomas, *The Ethics of Destruction: Norms and Force in International Relations* (Ithaca, NY: Cornell University Press, 2001), chap. 1.

64. Finnemore, *National Interests*, 24–26; Thomas, *Ethics of Destruction*, 12–13.

65. On the various elements contributing to the construction of international norms, see Thomas, *Ethics of Destruction*, 27–40.

66. Daniel Philpott, *Revolutions in Sovereignty: How Ideas Shaped Modern International Relations* (Princeton, NJ: Princeton University Press, 2001).

2. COHERENCE AND CONTESTATION

1. Kenneth Waltz, *Theory of International Politics* (Reading, MA: Addison-Wesley, 1979).

2. Michael C. Desch, "It's Kind to be Cruel: The Humanity of American Realism," *Review of International Studies* 29, no. 3 (2003): 417.

3. Deborah D. Avant, "The New Institutional Economics and Norms of Warfare," paper presented at the Annual Meeting of the International Studies Association, Washington, DC, March 28–April 1, 1994; Ted Hopf, "The Promise of Constructivism in International Relations Theory," *International Security* 23, no. 1 (Summer 1998): 180–81.

4. Martha Finnemore and Kathryn Sikkink, "International Norms and Political Change," *International Organization* 52, no. 4 (1998): 894.

5. Finnemore and Sikkink, "International Norms and Political Change," 894; Price, "Reversing the Gun Sights"; Neta Crawford, *Argument and Change in World Politics: Ethics, Decolonization, and Humanitarian Intervention* (Cambridge: Cambridge University Press, 2002).

6. Keck and Sikkink, *Activists beyond Borders*; Thomas Risse, Stephen C. Ropp, and Kathryn Sikkink, eds., *The Power of Human Rights: International Norms and Domestic Change* (Cambridge: Cambridge University Press, 1999); Finnemore, *National Interests*, chap. 3; Price, "Reversing the Gun Sights"; Thomas Risse-Kappen, "Ideas Do Not Float Freely: Transnational Coalitions, Domestic Structures, and the End of the Cold War," *International Organization* 48, no. 2 (March 1994).

7. Finnemore and Sikkink, "International Norms," 888.

8. Finnemore and Sikkink, 909; Robert C. Ellickson, "The Evolution of Social Norms: A Perspective from the Legal Academy," in *Social Norms*, ed. Michael Hechter and Karl-Dieter Opp (New York: Russell Sage Foundation, 2001), 49–51; Jeffrey W. Legro, "The Transformation of Policy Ideas," *American Journal of Political Science* 44, no. 3 (July 2000).

9. Deborah Avant, "From Mercenary to Citizen Armies: Explaining Change in the Practice of War," *International Organization* 54, no. 1 (Winter 2000); Thomas U. Berger, *Cultures of Antimilitarism: National Security in Germany and Japan* (Baltimore: Johns Hopkins University Press, 2003); J. Samuel Barkin and Bruce Cronin, "The State and

the Nation: Changing Norms and the Rules of Sovereignty in International Relations," *International Organization* 48, no. 1 (Winter 1994).

10. Kowert and Legro refer to this as the "good norms" problem. Paul Kowert and Jeffrey Legro, "Norms, Identities, and Their Limits: A Theoretical Reprise," in *The Culture of National Security*, ed. Peter Katzenstein (Ithaca, NY: Cornell University Press, 1996). Finnemore and Sikkink note that some scholars argue that norms will grow and prosper to the extent they represent "moral progress." Finnemore and Sikkink, "International Norms," 906.

11. Part of Harald Müller's definition of "norm initiators" is that they are "benevolent individuals." Harald Müller, "Security Cooperation," in *Handbook of International Relations*, ed. Walter Carlsnaes (London: SAGE, 2002), 497. On the "exogenous shock" literature, see note 9, above.

12. Finnemore and Sikkink, "International Norms," 901–5. See also Wayne Sandholtz, *Prohibiting Plunder: How Norms Change* (New York: Oxford University Press, 2007), chap. 1.

13. John Mueller, *Retreat from Doomsday: The Obsolescence of Major War* (New York: Basic Books, 1989), 9–12; Keck and Sikkink, *Activists beyond Borders*; Sandholtz, *Prohibiting Plunder*, 270–71.

14. See, e.g., Robert K. Merton, "The Unanticipated Consequences of Purposive Social Action," *American Sociological Review* 1, no. 6 (December 1936); Robert Jervis, *System Effects: Complexity in Political and Social Life* (Princeton, NJ: Princeton University Press, 1997).

15. Merton, "Unanticipated Consequences," 897–901.

16. Jervis, *System Effects*, 61.

17. See, e.g., Ann Florini, "The Evolution of International Norms," *International Studies Quarterly* (Fall 1996): 376, and Finnemore and Sikkink, "International Norms," 908.

18. Florini, "Evolution of International Norms," 376.

19. Price, "Reversing the Gun Sights," 623.

20. Robert H. Jackson, "The Weight of Ideas in Decolonization," in *Ideas and Foreign Policy*, ed. Judith Goldstein and Robert O. Keohane (Ithaca, NY: Cornell University Press, 1993), 113.

21. Crawford, *Argument and Change*, 110.

22. Finnemore and Sikkink, "International Norms," 891; Thomas Biersteker and Cynthia Weber, eds., *State Sovereignty as Social Construct* (Cambridge: Cambridge University Press, 1996).

23. Michael J. Glennon, *Limits of Law, Prerogatives of Power: Interventionism after Kosovo* (New York: Palgrave Macmillan, 2001), 8.

24. Robert H. Jackson, *Quasi-States: Sovereignty, International Relations, and the Third World* (Cambridge: Cambridge University Press, 1990), 74.

25. Jackson, *Quasi-States*, 74.

26. Crawford, *Argument and Change*, 104–5.

27. Quoted in Robert W. Tucker and David C. Hendrickson, "The Sources of American Legitimacy," *Foreign Affairs* 83, no. 6 (November/December 2004).

28. Mark Landler and Michael R. Gordon, "Air War in Kosovo Seen as Precedent in Possible Response to Syria Chemical Attack," *New York Times*, August 23, 2013, https://www.nytimes.com/2013/08/24/world/air-war-in-kosovo-seen-as-precedent-in-possible-response-to-syria-chemical-attack.html?pagewanted=all&_r=0; Robert Pape, "The New Standard for Humanitarian Intervention," *The Atlantic*, April 4, 2011, http://www.theatlantic.com/international/archive/2011/04/the-new-standard-for-humanitarian-intervention/73361/.

29. Jackson, *Quasi-States*, 190.

30. Thomas, *Ethics of Destruction*, 7, 41–43. Even customary international law, which is based on patterns of state practice, envisions a lag time between when a norm starts to reliably dictate state behavior and when that behavior can be considered legally obligatory.

31. Thomas, 72–77.

32. Finnemore, *National Interests*, 135.

33. Thomas, *Ethics of Destruction*, chap. 2.

34. March and Olsen, *Rediscovering Institutions*, 44.

35. See, e.g., Finnemore and Sikkink, "International Norms," 899, and Price, "Reversing the Gun Sights," 622–33.

36. Sandholtz, *Prohibiting Plunder*, 22.

37. Sandholtz, 14.

38. Sandholtz, 15.

39. Finnemore and Sikkink, "International Norms," 897. For examples of how norm entrepreneurs have used framing in their efforts on the issues of decolonization and climate change, see Neta C. Crawford, "How Previous Ideas Affect Later Ideas," in *The Oxford Handbook of Contextual Political Analysis*, ed. Robert E. Goodin and Charles Tilly (Oxford: Oxford University Press, 2006), and Loren Cass, *The Failures of American and European Climate Policy* (Albany: State University of New York Press, 2006), respectively.

40. Price, "Reversing the Gun Sights," 629.

41. "'Marriage Equality' and the Civil Rights Movement," National Public Radio, August 26, 2011, http://www.npr.org/2011/04/26/135741226/marriage-equality-and-the-civil-rights-movement; Michael Joseph Gross, "Gay Is the New Black?" *Advocate*, November 16, 2008, http://www.advocate.com/news/2008/11/16/gay-new-black?page=full.

42. Loren Cass, "Norm Entrapment and Preference Change: The Evolution of the European Union Position on International Emissions Trading," *Global Environmental Politics* 5, no. 2 (May 2005): 39.

43. Price, "Reversing the Gun Sights," 617.

44. The principle of noncombatant immunity "prohibits directly intended attacks on noncombatants and nonmilitary targets." Albert C. Pierce, "Just War Principles and Economic Sanctions," *Ethics and International Affairs* 10 (1996): 101. Of course, this simple description belies a dizzying level of complexity; almost every word in it has been parsed and contested repeatedly over centuries.

45. By "macronorms," I mean broadly overarching constitutive norms that define institutions, relationships, and roles within a system.

46. Anthony Clark Arend and Robert J. Beck, *International Law and the Use of Force: Beyond the UN Charter Paradigm* (London: Routledge, 1993), 15–17. One international legal treatise spoke of "the traditional right of a State to resort to war for a good reason, a bad reason or no reason at all." Herbert W. Briggs, ed., *The Law of Nations* (New York: Appleton-Century-Crofts, 1952), 976.

47. Van Creveld, *Rise and Decline of the State*, viii.

48. The Nuremberg defendants objected that the charge was invalid because it created an offense ex post facto. The argument was rejected, however, because Germany had signed the 1928 Kellogg-Briand Pact outlawing aggressive war. While the pact therefore provided legal precedent, it had little impact on the attitudes and actions of nations in the years before 1945.

49. "Affirmation of the Principles of International Law Recognized by the Charter of the Nurnberg Tribunal," Audiovisual Library of International Law, accessed June 19, 2012, http://untreaty.un.org/cod/avl/ha/ga_95-I/ga_95-I.html.

50. Article 2(4) of the charter states the central proscription on force, article 51 spells out the right of self-defense, and chapter VII details enforcement actions authorized by the Security Council.

51. K. J. Holsti, *Taming the Sovereigns: Institutional Change in International Politics* (Cambridge: Cambridge University Press, 2004), 284.

52. International Court of Justice, *Nicaragua v. United States*, 1986, para. 190, http://www.icj-cij.org/docket/files/70/6503.pdf; Michael Byers, *War Law: Understanding International Law and Armed Conflict* (New York: Grove, 2005), 6.

53. Van Creveld, *Rise and Decline of the State*, 259.

54. A poll taken in the late 1990s showed that only 31 percent of US citizens trusted their government "all or most of the time." Van Creveld, 411.

55. Van Creveld, 414.

56. Ban-Ki Moon, "Responsible Sovereignty: International Cooperation for a Changed World," July 15, 2008, http://www.globalpolicy.org/component/content/article/154/26074.html.

57. Thomas, *Ethics of Destruction*, 38.

58. Jimmy Carter, "Just War—or a Just War?" *New York Times*, February 9, 2003, https://www.nytimes.com/2003/03/09/opinion/just-war-or-a-just-war.html.

59. The vote on the declaration was 89–0, with nine abstentions. Jackson, *Quasi-States*, 77.

60. UN website, accessed July 24, 2006, https://www.un.org/Overview/growth.htm.

61. Jackson, *Quasi-States*, esp. chaps. 3 and 4; Crawford, *Argument and Change*. See also Jackson, "Weight of Ideas."

62. Geoffrey Barraclough, *An Introduction to Contemporary History* (New York: Basic Books, 1964), 155.

63. Jackson, *Quasi-States*, chap. 2.

64. Jackson, chaps. 1–2.

65. Jackson, 38–39; Van Creveld, *Rise and Decline of the State*, chap. 3.

66. Stephen Peter Rosen, "Military Effectiveness: Why Society Matters," *International Security* 19, no. 4 (Spring 1995): 6.

67. Jackson, *Quasi-States*, 77–78.

68. Quoted in Rosen, "Military Effectiveness," 28.

69. Rosen, 30.

70. Of the twenty-five "least peaceful" states in the Global Peace Index 2020 rankings, seventeen gained their independence after the end of World War II. Vision of Humanity, accessed November 29, 2020, https://www.visionofhumanity.org/ the-2020-global-peace-index-a-brazil-focus/.

71. Van Creveld, *Rise and Decline of the State*, 419.

72. The phrase "the revolt against the West" has been commonly used by scholars of the "English School" to describe resistance to the hegemony of Western norms. See, e.g., Barraclough, *Introduction to Contemporary History*, chap. 6, and Hedley Bull, "The Revolt against the West," in *The Expansion of International Society*, ed. Hedley Bull and Adam Watson (Oxford: Oxford University Press, 1985).

73. See, e.g., Siba N. Grovogui, *Sovereigns, Quasi Sovereigns, and Africans: Race and Self-Determination in International Law* (Minneapolis: University of Minnesota Press, 1996), and Paul Keal, "'Just Backward Children': International Law and the Conquest of Non-European Peoples," *Australian Journal of International Affairs* 49, no. 2 (November 1995).

74. Bull, "Revolt against the West," 217 (emphasis in original).

75. Bull, 222.

76. Examples include the flexibility allowed developing states to manufacture and import generic drugs under the 2001 Doha Declaration, the forgiveness of debt owed by poor countries under the Heavily Indebted Poor Countries initiative of 1996 and the Multilateral Debt Relief Initiative of 2005, and the exemption of developing states from

emissions-reductions requirements of the Kyoto Protocol of 1997. In chapter 3, I examine the influence of this idea on the Law of Armed Conflict.

77. Ramesh Chandra Thakur, *The United Nations, Peace and Security* (Cambridge: Cambridge University Press, 2006), 281. In 1979, Louis Henkin observed that "the demands of Third World solidarity and the desire to maintain it even at high cost has sometimes led the Third World to condone violations by its neighbors even of laws that are not ideologically disputed and are generally favored, especially when 'the victim' is a developed state." Louis Henkin, *How Nations Behave: Law and Foreign Policy*, 2nd ed. (New York: Columbia University Press, 1979), 134.

78. Jackson, *Quasi-States*.

79. Bull, "Revolt against the West," 223–24.

80. Grovogui, *Sovereigns, Quasi Sovereigns*.

81. Charles Tilly, "Reflections on the History of European State-Making," in *The Formation of National States in Western Europe*, ed. Charles Tilly (Princeton, NJ: Princeton University Press, 1975).

82. Anthony A. Giddens, *A Contemporary Critique of Historical Materialism, Vol. 2: The Nation-State and Violence* (Berkeley: University of California Press, 1985), 210.

83. Paul Fussell argues that World War I was in fact the pivotal event in the deromanticization of war. Paul Fussell, *The Great War and Modern Memory: 25th Anniversary Edition* (New York: Oxford University Press, 2000).

84. Van Creveld, *Rise and Decline of the State*, 336–37.

85. Martin Shaw, *Post-Military Society: Militarism, Demilitarization and War at the End of the Twentieth Century* (Philadelphia: Temple University Press, 1991), viii.

86. Robert Kagan, "Power and Weakness," *Policy Review* no. 113 (June 2002), https://www.hoover.org/research/power-and-weakness.

87. Kagan, "Power and Weakness."

88. Quoted in Kagan.

89. Kagan; Shaw, *Post-Military Society*.

90. A central point in Kagan's argument is that American and European attitudes toward the use of force are fundamentally different.

91. Van Creveld, *Rise and Decline of the State*, 412; Shaw, *Post-Military Society*, 84–87.

92. See Coker, "Outsourcing War," 196; Edward N. Luttwak, "Where Are the Great Powers? At Home with the Kids," *Foreign Affairs* 73, no. 4 (July/August 1994).

93. Or, to be precise, by the consequences it can reasonably be expected to bring about.

94. See Michael Walzer, *Just and Unjust Wars*, 5th ed. (New York: Basic Books, 2015), 264–68.

95. While both the United States Conference of Catholic Bishops and the International Court of Justice expressed concern over this aspect of nuclear deterrence, both bodies nevertheless cautiously endorsed deterrence because of its effectiveness in preventing war. United States Conference of Catholic Bishops, *The Challenge of Peace: God's Promise and Our Response*, 1983, 30–36, http://old.usccb.org/sdwp/international/TheChallengeofPeace.pdf; International Court of Justice, *Legality of the Threat or Use of Nuclear Weapons*, advisory opinion of July 8, 1996, paras. 37–50, https://www.icj-cij.org/public/files/case-related/95/095-19960708-ADV-01-00-EN.pdf.

96. Jackson, *Quasi-States*, 40.

97. At this point, a question presents itself: How is this normative asymmetry consistent with what I have said about the principle of normative coherence? In the short term, the answer is that it merely reflects the inevitability of occasional conflict between norms and the priority given to the norms associated with the two macronormative shifts I have described. More broadly, however, the prioritization itself suggests that

norms that are applied asymmetrically have already been devalued and that their uneven application will continue to create pressure on them. Over the long term, in fact, the concern is precisely that the logic of normative coherence will continue to degrade the norms that are asymmetrically applied, in the same way that the great powers' violation of norms under claims of exceptional circumstances degraded those norms. Asymmetrical application is thus both the sign of a damaged norm and a portent that the norm is at risk of further decline.

98. Thomas, *Ethics of Destruction*, 30–33.

99. Henkin, *How Nations Behave*, 121.

100. Thomas, *Ethics of Destruction*, chap. 5; *Sarah B. Sewall, Chasing Success: Air Force Efforts to Reduce Civilian Harm* (Maxwell AFB, AL: Air University Press, 2016), chaps. 5–6; Colin H. Kahl, "In the Crossfire or the Crosshairs? Norms, Civilian Casualties, and U.S. Conduct in Iraq," *International Security* 32, no. 1 (2007); Bruno Pommier, "The Use of Force to Protect Civilians and Humanitarian Action: The Case of Libya and Beyond," *International Review of the Red Cross* 93, no. 884 (December 2011).

101. Thomas Risse, "Let's Argue! Communicative Action in World Politics," *International Organization* 54, no. 1 (2000): 22.

102. Inis L.Claude Jr., "Collective Legitimization as a Political Function of the United Nations," *International Organization* 20, no. 3 (Summer 1966).

103. Richard Falk, "The Quasi-Legislative Role of the General Assembly," *American Journal of International Law* 60, no. 4 (October 1966). See also Henkin, *How Nations Behave*, 127.

104. Mathews, "Power Shift"; Price, "Reversing the Gun Sights."

105. Bull, "Revolt against the West," 227.

3. PARTISANS, LIBERATORS, AND MILITIAS

1. Geneva International Center for Justice, *Syrian Civil War: Six Years into the Worst Humanitarian Tragedy since World War II* (Geneva: CICJ, 2017), http://www.gicj.org/images/2016/pdfs/Final-Report-Syria_June-2017.pdf; Amnesty International, "Syria: The Worst Humanitarian Crisis of Our Time," April 7, 2015, AI, https://www.amnesty.org.nz/syria-worst-humanitarian-crisis-our-time; Alia Chughtai, "Syria's War: Who Controls What?," Al Jazeera, March 13, 2019, https://www.aljazeera.com/indepth/interactive/2015/05/syria-country-divided-150529144229467.html.

2. Lenka Butíková, "The Radical Right in Eastern Europe," *The Oxford Handbook of the Radical Right* (February 2018), http://www.oxfordhandbooks.com/view/10.1093/oxfordhb/9780190274559.001.0001/oxfordhb-9780190274559-e-28; Ronald F. Inglehart and Pippa Norris, "Trump, Brexit, and the Rise of Populism: Economic Have-Nots and Cultural Backlash," HKS Working Paper no. RWP16-026, 2016, Kennedy School of Government, Harvard University.

3. "Guide to the Syrian Rebels," BBC News, December 13, 2013, https://www.bbc.com/news/world-middle-east-24403003; Podder, "Understanding the Legitimacy," 697.

4. Podder, "Understanding the Legitimacy," 695.

5. Michael Pregent and Erica Hanichak, "Countering Iran Means Sanctioning Terrorist Militias," *The Hill*, September 27, 2018, https://thehill.com/opinion/international/408741-countering-iran-means-sanctioning-terrorist-militias; Kheder Khaddour, "Syria's Troublesome Militias," Diwan, Carnegie Middle East Center, November 5, 2018, https://carnegie-mec.org/diwan/77635; Haid Haid, "Troublesome Allies: How the Syrian Regime is Reintegrating Loyalist Militias," *Middle East Eye*, September 11, 2018, https://www.middleeasteye.net/opinion/troublesome-allies-how-syrian-regime-reintegrating-loyalist-militias; Jonathan Spyer, "Syria's Civil War Is Now 3 Civil Wars," *Foreign Policy*, March 18, 2019, https://foreignpolicy.com/2019/03/18/syrias-civil-war-is-now-3-civil-wars/.

6. States supporting the Assad regime and progovernment groups include Russia, Iran, and Iraq. Support for antigovernment factions has come from the United States, the United Kingdom, France, Saudi Arabia, Qatar, and Jordan. Turkey has supported some antigovernment groups and actively fought against others.

7. Williams, "Violent Non-State Actors," 10–12; Shultz, Farah, and Lochard, "Armed Groups," 9–27; Podder, "Understanding the Legitimacy," 697; John Buchanan, *Militias in Myanmar* (Yangon: Asia Foundation, 2016), https://asiafoundation.org/wp-content/uploads/2016/07/Militias-in-Myanmar.pdf.

8. For example, Williams and Shultz, Farah, and Lochard use the term to refer to progovernment forces. Williams, "Violent Non-State Actors," 8–17; Shultz, Farah, and Lochard, "Armed Groups," 14. On the other hand, see Sabine C. Carey and Neil J. Mitchell, "Pro-Government Militias and Conflict," Oxford Research Encyclopedia of Politics, October 2016, http://oxfordre.com/politics/view/10.1093/acrefore/9780190228637.001.0001/acrefore-9780190228637-e-33, and Malejacq, "Pro-Government Militias."

9. See Richard English, *Armed Struggle: The History of the IRA* (Oxford: Oxford University Press, 2003), and Tony Geraghty, *The Irish War* (London: HarperCollins, 1998).

10. Podder, "Understanding the Legitimacy," 698; Maoz and San-Akca, "Rivalry and State Support."

11. Charles Tilly, "War Making and State Making as Organized Crime," in *Bringing the State Back In*, ed. Peter B. Evans, Dietrich Rueschemeyer, and Theda Skocpol (Cambridge: Cambridge University Press, 1975), 173.

12. Tilly, "War Making and State Making, 173.

13. John Keegan, *A History of Warfare* (New York: Vintage Books, 1994), 50.

14. Keegan, *History of Warfare*, 169.

15. Keegan, 173.

16. Barbara Hodgdon, *The First Part of King Henry the Fourth: Texts and Comments* (Boston: Bedford Books, 1997), 173–74.

17. Hodgdon, *First Part of King Henry*, 175.

18. Hodgdon, 169–72.

19. In Britain, burning at the stake was the punishment for treason until 1790, when it was replaced by hanging. Lizzie Seal, "A Brief History of Capital Punishment in Britain," History Extra, March 2018, https://www.historyextra.com/period/modern/a-brief-history-of-capital-punishment-in-britain/.

20. Noelle Higgins, "The Application of International Law to Wars of National Liberation," *Journal of Humanitarian Assistance* (2004): 12–14, http://sites.tufts.edu/jha/files/2011/04/a132.pdf.

21. Geoffrey Best, "Civilians in Contemporary Wars," war studies lecture at King's College, University of London, 1983, accessed April 23, 2006, https://www.airpower.maxwell.af.mil/airchronicles/aureview/1984/mar-apr/best.html (inactive link).

22. Charles W. Gwynn, *Imperial Policing* (London: Macmillan 1934).

23. Jackson, *Quasi-States*, 17.

24. Heather A. Wilson, *International Law and the Use of Force by National Liberation Movements* (Oxford: Clarendon Press, 1988), 15.

25. George J. Andreopoulos, "The Age of National Liberation Movements," in *The Laws of War: Constraints on Warfare in the Western World*, ed. Michael Howard, George J. Andreopoulos, and Mark R. Shulman (New Haven, CT: Yale University Press, 1994), 192.

26. Quoted in Alistair Horne, *A Savage War of Peace: Algeria 1954–1962* (New York: Viking Press, 1977), 95.

27. Luis Lema, "Torture in Algeria: The Report That Was to Change Everything," *Le Temps*, August 19, 2005, https://www.icrc.org/en/doc/resources/documents/article/other/algeria-history-190805.htm; Andreopoulos, "Age of National Liberation Movements," 202–5.

28. Helen M. Kinsella, *The Image before the Weapon: A Critical History of the Distinction between Combatant and Civilian* (Ithaca, NY: Cornell University Press, 2011), 129. It must be noted that notwithstanding this public stance, the FLN's observance of the laws of war was spotty at best. Even in the best of times, it interpreted noncombatant immunity narrowly and in any case carried out many attacks that directly targeted civilians. Kinsella, *Image before the Weapon*, 133; Martha Crenshaw Hutchinson, *Revolutionary Terrorism: The FLN in Algeria, 1954–1962* (Stanford, CA: Hoover Institution Press, 1978).

29. Algerian Office, *White Paper on the Application of the Geneva Conventions of 1949 to the French-Algerian Conflict* (New York: Algerian Office, 1960).

30. Quoted in Kinsella, *Image before the Weapon*, 131 (emphasis in original).

31. Wilson, *International Law*, 130–34; Andreopoulos, "Age of National Liberation Movements," 201–2.

32. UN General Assembly, Resolution 1573, Question of Algeria, A/RES/1573 (December 19, 1960), https://undocs.org/en/A/RES/1573(XV).

33. Andreopoulos, "Age of National Liberation Movements," 192–93.

34. Andreopoulos, 197.

35. Quoted in Wilson, *International Law*, 94.

36. Quoted in Wilson, 134.

37. Christine Gray, *International Law and the Use of Force* (Oxford: Oxford University Press, 2004), 53.

38. Ho Chi Minh, "Declaration of Independence of the Democratic Republic of Vietnam," September 2, 1945, Liberté, Égalité, Fraternité: Exploring the French Revolution, http://chnm.gmu.edu/revolution/d/583/.

39. Quoted in John F. Kennedy, "Remarks of Senator John F. Kennedy in the Senate," Washington, DC, July 2, 1957, John F. Kennedy Presidential Library and Museum, https://www.jfklibrary.org/archives/other-resources/john-f-kennedy-speeches/united-states-senate-imperialism-19570702.

40. Kinsella, *Image before the Weapon*, 132.

41. Kennedy, "Remarks of Senator John F. Kennedy."

42. Wilson, *International Law*, 110.

43. Van Creveld, *Rise and Decline of the State*, 349–50.

44. Richard Baxter, "The Duty of Obedience to the Belligerent Occupant," *British Yearbook of International Law* 27 (1950). Violation of this "duty of obedience" to the occupying authority could be punished as "war treason" under customary international law until about the time of World War II. Bowen Lee, "Safer in Danger: How War Treason Can Rescue the Principle of Noncombatant Immunity," unpublished paper, December 2016.

45. Lester Nurick and Roger W. Barrett, "Legality of Guerrilla Forces under the Laws of War," *American Journal of International Law* 40, no. 3 (July 1946): 574.

46. International Declaration Concerning the Laws and Customs of War, Brussels, August 27, 1874, International Committee of the Red Cross, https://ihl-databases.icrc.org/ihl/INTRO/135.

47. Quoted in Wilson, *International Law*, 18–19.

48. Wilson, 92–93.

49. Wilson, 92. The postwar history of Central and Eastern Europe provides several illustrations of this dynamic.

50. On similar claims made by the South West Africa People's Organization (SWAPO), the Palestine Liberation Organization, and the Mozambique Liberation Front, see Kinsella, *Image before the Weapon*, 137.

51. Quoted in Bruce Hoffman, *Inside Terrorism: Revised and Expanded Edition* (New York: Columbia University Press, 2006), 54.

52. Quoted in Horne, *Savage War of Peace*, 384–85.

53. Gray, *International Law*, 52–58.

54. Jackson, *Quasi-States*, 107; UN Security Council, Resolution 232, Southern Rhodesia, S/RES/232 (December 16, 1966), https://undocs.org/S/RES/232(1966).

55. UN Security Council, Resolution 312, Territories under Portuguese Administration, S/RES/312 (February 4, 1972), https://undocs.org/S/RES/312(1972).

56. Wilson, *International Law*, 95–97.

57. Wilson, 95–97.

58. Wilson, 104–17.

59. Keith Suter, *An International Law of Guerrilla Warfare: The Global Politics of Law-Making* (New York: St. Martin's, 1984), chaps. 2–4.

60. Adam Roberts and Richard Guelff, *Documents on the Laws of War*, 2nd ed. (Oxford: Clarendon Press, 1989), 387. The official title was the Diplomatic Conference on the Reaffirmation and Development of International Humanitarian Law Applicable in Armed Conflicts.

61. Yoram Dinstein, "Comments on Protocol I," *International Review of the Red Cross* 320 (1997): 515.

62. Geoffrey Best, *War and Law since 1945* (Oxford: Clarendon Press, 1994), 344.

63. The US delegation's willingness to subordinate political to legal principles was illustrated, for example, by the criticism it received from American military authorities for failure to take the military's perspective into account and from officials in the Reagan administration, which refused to submit Protocol I to the Senate. Abraham Sofaer, "The Rationale for the United States Decision," *American Journal of International Law* 82 (1988).

64. Kinsella, *Image before the Weapon*, 134; Suter, *International Law of Guerrilla Warfare*, 128.

65. Jackson, *Quasi-States*, 61.

66. *Official Records of the Diplomatic Conference in Reaffirmation and Development of International Humanitarian Law Applicable to Armed Conflicts: Geneva 1974–1977*, 17 vols. (Bern, Switzerland: Federal Political Department, 1978) [hereafter *Official Records*], vol. 5, 118.

67. Kinsella, *Image before the Weapon*, 134.

68. Suter, *International Law of Guerrilla Warfare*, 128.

69. *Official Records*, vol. 5, 63.

70. Roberts and Guelff, *Documents on the Laws of War*, 387. The United States managed to salvage a small victory by preventing the seating of a representative of the provisional communist government of South Vietnam. Suter, *International Law of Guerrilla Warfare*, 138.

71. This placed the provisions relating to NLM fighters in Protocol I rather than Protocol II, which addressed only internal conflicts.

72. Best, *War and Law since 1945*, 345; Michael Bothe, Karl Josef Partsch, and Waldemar A. Solf, *New Rules for Victims of Armed Conflicts: Commentary on the Two 1977 Protocols Additional to the Geneva Conventions of 1949* (Boston: Martinus Nijhoff, 1982), 247.

73. *Protocol Additional to the Geneva Conventions of 12 August 1949, and Relating to the Protection of Victims of International Armed Conflicts* (hereafter Protocol I), article 1(4), https://ihl-databases.icrc.org/applic/ihl/ihl.nsf/Article.xsp?action=openDocument&documentId=6C86520D7EFAD527C12563CD0051D63C.

74. Stefan Oeter, "Terrorism and 'Wars of National Liberation' from a Law of War Perspective," *Heidelberg Journal of International Law* 49, no. 3 (1989): 471; Georges Abi-Saab, "Wars of National Liberation in the Geneva Conventions and Protocols," *Recueil des Cours* 165, no. 4 (1979): 389–92.

75. *Geneva Convention Relative to the Treatment of Prisoners of War, 12 August 1949* (Geneva Convention III), article 4(A)(2), https://ihl-databases.icrc.org/applic/ihl/ihl.nsf/Treaty.xsp?documentId=77CB9983BE01D004C12563CD002D6B3E&action=openDocument.

76. *Official Records*, vol. 14, 361.

77. *Official Records*, vol. 14, 464. Similar arguments were made by the delegates from Ghana (vol. 14, 454), Algeria (vol. 14, 365), Nigeria (vol. 14, 370), Lesotho (vol. 14, 500), Burundi (vol. 5, 116), Ivory Coast (vol. 14, 373), and the Zimbabwe African National Union (vol. 14, 555–56).

78. Of course, by definition this description could apply to only one side in a conflict.

79. See, e.g., comments of the delegate from North Vietnam, *Official Records*, vol. 14, 464.

80. *Official Records*, vol. 14, 453 (statement of the delegate from Pakistan); Suter, *International Law of Guerrilla Warfare*, 122; Christopher Greenwood, *Essays on War in International Law* (London: Cameron May, 2006), 206. The Soviet Union and its satellite states also wanted to prevent the rule from applying to resistance movements in Eastern Europe. Abi-Saab, "Wars of National Liberation," 387.

81. Statement by the President of the Islamic Republic of Mauritania, Mr. Ould Dada. *Official Records*, vol. 5, 12–14, 13.

82. Antonio Cassese, *International Law*, 2nd ed. (Oxford: Oxford University Press, 2005), 402.

83. Suter, *International Law of Guerrilla Warfare*, 13–17; Greenwood, *Essays on War in International Law*, 400.

84. Bothe, Partsch, and Solf, *New Rules for Victims*, 244–46; *Official Records*, vol. 14, 373.

85. Quoted in International Committee of the Red Cross, *Commentary of 1987: Combatants and Prisoners of War*, para. 1698 (emphasis added)., https://ihl-databases.icrc.org/applic/ihl/ihl.nsf/Comment.xsp?action=openDocument&documentId=D04A6A9CBBF8B28CC12563CD00433946.

86. Michael L. Gross, *Moral Dilemmas of Modern War* (Cambridge: Cambridge University Press, 2010), 38.

87. *Official Records*, vol. 15, 180.

88. Abi-Saab, "Wars of National Liberation," 383 (emphasis added).

89. Abi-Saab, 440.

90. Quoted in Kinsella, *Image before the Weapon*, 137.

91. *Official Records*, vol. 14, 477. See also statements made by delegates from Spain (vol. 14, 462) and the United Kingdom (vol. 5, 134).

92. Best, "Civilians in Contemporary Wars."

93. *Official Records*, vol. 5, 61 (Syria); vol. 15, 184 (PLO); and vol. 14, 466 (North Vietnam).

94. The representative of the Zimbabwe African National Union, an NLM, argued that the Western stance reflected a "total failure to understand the true nature of wars of national liberation. . . . The liberation movement is only a vanguard organization of the people [which] cannot be distinguishable from the masses of the people. A guerrilla fighter depends for his whole survival on his reliance on, and close cooperation with, the masses of the people." *Official Records*, vol. 14, 555. Similarly, the North Vietnamese delegate said of freedom fighters: "Their activities and their lives are inseparable from the civilian population. That is the new law of the people's war." *Official Records*, vol. 14, 466. See also the statement by Mexico, *Official Records*, vol. 15, 163.

95. See statements by delegates from Lesotho (*Official Records*, vol. 14, 500) and the Panafricanist Congress (vol. 14, 382).

96. See Greenwood, *Essays on War*, 403–5. The notion that even those who made this claim did not actually believe it is illustrated by the fact that non-Western states wanted to limit the guerrilla privilege to NLM fighters rather than adopt it as a general rule that would apply to all combatants. If the provision in fact made civilians safer, there was no reason to limit it to a certain small set of combatants who are fighting for a particular cause.

97. Gerald Draper, "Wars of National Liberation and War Criminality," in *Restraints on War: Studies in the Limitation of Armed Conflict*, ed. Michael Howard (Oxford: Oxford University Press, 1979), 160.

98. *Official Records*, vol. 8, 14.

99. *Official Records*, vol. 8, 13. See also the statements by the delegate from the Holy See (vol. 5, 123).

100. See in *Official Records* statements by the delegates of France (vol. 8, 14) and Norway (vol. 14, 482).

101. See in *Official Records* the statements by the delegates from Nigeria (vol. 15, 180) and the Soviet Union, the latter arguing that "the members of the Conference should make a concerted effort to find a solution which would improve the status of those combatants by giving them the means of attaining their objective" (vol. 14, 359).

102. Abi-Saab, "Wars of National Liberation," 416.

103. Abi-Saab, 420.

104. *Official Records*, vol. 5, 103.

105. *Official Records*, vol. 14, 465.

106. ICRC Commentaries, para. 1698, 529n40 (emphasis added). See also ICRC Commentaries, para. 1714.

107. ICRC Commentaries, para. 1688.

108. W. Hays Parks, "Conventional Aerial Bombing and the Law of War," *Proceedings of the U.S. Naval Institute* 108, no. 5 (May 1982): 106.

109. See in *Official Records* the statements by the delegates from Romania (vol. 5, 103), China (vol. 5, 120), Algeria (vol. 5, 148), North Korea (vol. 14, 128), and North Vietnam (vol. 14, 468).

110. The 1974 session of the Diplomatic Conference was attended by delegates from 126 countries, many of which had gained their independence since World War II. By comparison, the conference that produced the 1949 Geneva Conventions was attended by only 62 delegations, most of them from Western nations. Suter, *International Law of Guerrilla Warfare*, 130; Kinsella, *Image before the Weapon*, 133.

111. Howard S. Levie, "Review: *New Rules for Victims of Armed Conflicts*," *American Journal of International Law* 77, no. 2 (1983): 379.

112. Suter, *International Law of Guerrilla* Warfare, 150, 152.

113. Suter, 146.

114. Protocol I, article 44(3).

115. Kinsella, *Image before the Weapon*, 140.

116. B. C. Nirmal, "Wars of National Liberation and International Humanitarian Law," *Indian Journal of International Law* 28, no. 2 (1988): 210; Greenwood, *Essays on War*, 403.

117. Best, "Civilians in Contemporary Wars."

118. Kinsella, *Image before the Weapon*, 144.

119. Kinsella, 153.

120. Most commentators conclude that customary international law recognizes the right of such groups to use armed force, especially if their claims are being forcibly denied by the government. See W. Michael Reisman and Chris T. Antoniou, *The Laws of War* (New York: Vintage Books, 1994), 28–30; Malcolm N. Shaw, *International Law*, 5th ed.

(Cambridge: Cambridge University Press, 2005), 1037–38; Byers, *War Law*, 90–91; and Cassese, *International Law*, 374. Nevertheless, a sizable minority point to the persistent refusal of states such as the United States to formally endorse such a right as an impediment to the formation of the *opinio juris* required for customary law to form. See Gray, *International Law*, 52–56; Wilson, *International Law*, chap. 5; and Andreopoulos, "Age of National Liberation Movements," 211.

121. Gray, *International Law*, 57; Cassesse, *International Law*, 140.

122. Jackson, *Quasi-States*, 41–42.

123. In legal terms, the question of the status of territories occupied by Israel since 1967 is more often considered under the international law of belligerent occupation than as a matter of national liberation, though, as we shall see in chapter 4, it is often framed in the rhetoric of national liberation. Gray, *International Law*, 57–58.

124. Suter, *International Law of Guerrilla Warfare*, 142, 151; Bothe, Partsch, and Solf, *New Rules for Victims*, 52.

125. Wilson, *International Law*, 168.

126. W. Hays Parks, "National Security Law in Practice: The Department of Defense Law of War Manual," speech to the American Bar Association, 2010, http://www.ameri canbar.org/content/dam/aba/migrated/2011_build/law_national_security/hays_parks_ speech_2010.authcheckdam.pdf (emphasis in original). See also Suter, *International Law of Guerrilla Warfare*, chap. 6.

127. Claude, "Collective Legitimization," 377. See also Greenwood, *Essays on War*, 391.

128. Jackson, *Quasi-States*, 190.

129. Jackson says the distinction between legitimate and illegitimate self-determination movements hinges on "accidents of imperial history." Jackson, 41.

130. Gray, *International Law*, 58.

131. UN Security Council Resolution 1559, Middle East, S/RES/1559 (September 2, 2004), https://undocs.org/S/RES/1559(2004).

132. W. Michael Reisman, "The Resistance in Afghanistan Is Engaged in a War of National Liberation," *American Journal of International Law* 81, no. 4 (1987).

133. Matthew Luxmoore, "Putin's Ultranationalist Base Takes Aim at the West," Al Jazeera America, April 17, 2015, http://america.aljazeera.com/articles/2015/4/17/russian-ultranationalists-decry-fifth-column.html.

134. James Glanz and Alissa J. Rubin, "Iraqi Army Takes Last Basra Areas from Sadr Force," *New York Times*, April 20, 2008, http://www.nytimes.com/2008/04/20/world/middleeast/20iraq.html?th&emc=th; Neil MacFarquhar and Marlise Simons, "Bashir Defies War Crime Arrest Order," *New York Times*, March 5, 2009, https://www.nytimes.com/2009/03/06/world/africa/06sudan.html.

135. Kurdistan Workers Party, "Party Program of the Kurdistan Workers Party," 2005, http://www.kurdishlibrary.org/kurdish_library/SvenskaKB/Organisations_SWE/ PKK_Eng.html; Regnum News Agency, "Abkhazia's Parliament Convenes on Republic's Sovereignty," 2008, http://www.regnum.ru/english/1047988.html; State Committee on Information and Press of the Republic of South Ossetia (SCIPRSO), "Independence of the Republic of South Ossetia: A Guarantee of Safety and Reliable Future of the Ossetian People," October 9, 2008, http://cominf.org/node/1166478243; Ogaden National Liberation Front, "Political Objectives," accessed March 20, 2019, http://onlf.org/?page_id=14; All Parties Hurryat Conference, "Letter of the Chairman to the Secretary General of the Islamic Conference," May 13, 2007, accessed September 25, 2008, https://www.hurryat.net (site discontinued); Graeme Smith, "Talking to the Taliban," *Globe and Mail*, March 22, 2008, accessed March 15, 2019, http://v1.theglobeandmail.com/talkingtothetaliban/ (inactive link).

136. *Official Records*, vol. 14, 539.

137. *Official Records*, vol. 15, 73. See also statements by the delegates from Belgium (vol. 14, 490), Switzerland (vol. 14, 355), and Norway (vol. 14, 546).

138. Abi-Saab, "Wars of National Liberation," 397–98.

139. *Official Records*, vol. 15, 184.

140. Kinsella, *Image before the Weapon*, 130; W. Hays Parks, "The 1977 Protocols to the Geneva Conventions of 1949," in *Readings on International Law from the Naval War College Review, 1978–1994*, ed. John Norton Moore and Robert F. Turner (Newport, RI: Naval War College, 1995), 475; Ryan Nissim-Sabat, "Panthers Set Up Shop in Cleveland," in *Comrades: A Local History of the Black Panther Party*, ed. Judson L. Jeffries (Bloomington: Indiana University Press, 2007), 111.

141. Militias in Russia and to an extent Syria fit the "common cause" model, while nonstate groups in Brazil, India, and Colombia fit the latter description. See Luxmoore, "Putin's Ultranationalist Base"; Khaddour, "Syria's Troublesome Militias"; Williams, "Violent Non-State Actors," 4, 12; Podder, "Understanding the Legitimacy," 697.

142. Gian Gentile et al., *Reimagining the Character of Urban Operations for the U.S. Army: How the Past Can Inform the Present and Future* (Santa Monica, CA: RAND Corp., 2017); David E. Johnson, M. Wade Markel, and Brian Shannon, "The Battle of Sadr City." RAND Occasional Paper, 2011, https://www.rand.org/content/dam/rand/pubs/occasional_papers/2011/RAND_OP335.pdf; Raphael S. Cohen et al., *Lessons from Israel's Wars in Gaza* (Santa Monica, CA: RAND Corp., 2017); Gross, *Moral Dilemmas*, 36–39.

143. Benjamin Locks, "Bad Guys Know What Works: Asymmetric Warfare and the Third Offset," War on the Rocks, June 23, 2015, https://Warontherocks.Com/2015/06/Bad-Guys-Know-What-Works-Asymmetric-Warfare-And-The-Third-Offset/; Human Rights Watch, "Civilian Deaths in the NATO Air Campaign," 2000, https://www.hrw.org/reports/2000/nato; Barry R. Posen, "The War for Kosovo: Serbia's Political-Military Strategy," *International Security* 24, no. 4 (Spring 2000): 66–69. In what could be seen as a maritime version of these tactics, in the 2010s China sent fleets of fishing boats into disputed waters in the South and East China Seas to reinforce their claims there. Locks, "Bad Guys Know."

144. Locks, "Bad Guys Know"; Linda Robinson et al., *Improving Strategic Competence: Lessons from 13 Years of War* (Santa Monica, CA: RAND Corp., 2014), 24–29, 86–89; National Intelligence Council, *Global Trends 2030: Alternative Worlds*, December 2012, https://www.dni.gov/files/documents/GlobalTrends_2030.pdf.

145. Robinson et al., *Improving Strategic Competence*, 86. Paradoxically, even as major states increasingly adopt the tactics of nonstate actors, some nonstate actors are acquiring capabilities that allow them to fight like states when it serves their purposes. One RAND Corporation expert writes that ISIS had "significant military capabilities, mainly captured from the Syrians and Iraqis, including tanks, a variety of MANPADS and ATGMs [portable surface-to-air and antitank missiles], artillery, anti-aircraft guns, and multiple rocket launchers." David E. Johnson, "Ground Combat," RAND Commentary, December 23, 2015, RAND Corp., https://www.rand.org/blog/2015/12/ground-combat.html.

146. For an example of a Western appeal to "chivalry" and a non-Western response, see the exchange at the Diplomatic Conference between the delegates of Canada and Egypt found in *Official Records*, vol. 15, 97–98 and 104–105. On this issue see also Kinsella, *Image before the Weapon*, 154.

4. ONE MAN'S FREEDOM FIGHTER?

1. Polls show that "international terrorism" perennially tops Americans' list of "critical threat[s] to the vital interests of the United States." Poll results released in February

2016 show that 79 percent of the American public view international terrorism as a critical threat, a few points above the development of nuclear weapons by Iran and cyberterrorism. Justin McCarthy, "American Cite Cyberterrorism among Top Three Threats to U.S.," Gallup, February 10, 2016, https://news.gallup.com/poll/189161/americans-cite-cyberterrorism-among-top-three-threats.aspx.

2. Institute for Economics and Peace, *Global Terrorism Index 2018: Measuring the Impact of Terrorism* (Sydney: IEP, November 2018), 4, 31, https://www.visionofhumanity.org/wp-content/uploads/2020/10/GTI2018-A3-poster-wall-chart.pdf.

3. Gary LaFree and Laura Dugan, "Trends in Global Terrorism, 1970–2008," in *Peace and Conflict 2012*, ed. J. Joseph Hewitt, Jonathan Wilkenfeld, and Ted Robert Gurr (Boulder, CO: Paradigm, 2012), 41; Institute for Economics and Peace, *Global Terrorism Index 2018*, 42.

4. Shultz, Farah, and Lochard, "Armed Groups," 10.

5. Institute for Economics and Peace, *Global Terrorism Index 2018*, 15.

6. Hoffman, *Inside Terrorism*, 284.

7. Hoffman, 282.

8. Institute for Economics and Peace, *Global Terrorism Index 2018*, 50.

9. Audrey Kurth Cronin, "ISIS Is Not a Terrorist Group," *Foreign Affairs* 94, no. 1 (January/February 2015).

10. Institute for Economics and Peace, *Global Terrorism Index 2018*, 46.

11. Shlomo Bolts, "The Many Loopholes in 'ISIS Is Defeated,'" Defense One, March 6, 2019, https://www.defenseone.com/ideas/2019/03/many-loopholes-isis-defeated/155314/; Sarah Hunaidi, "ISIS Has Not Been Defeated. It's Alive and Well in Southern Syria," *Foreign Policy*, April 3, 2019, https://foreignpolicy.com/2019/04/03/isis-has-not-been-defeated-its-alive-and-well-in-southern-syria/.

12. Institute for Economics and Peace, *Global Terrorism Index 2018*, 62.

13. Steven Pinker, *The Better Angels of Our Nature: Why Violence Has Declined* (New York: Penguin, 2012), 344–45.

14. Quoted in Hoffman, *Inside Terrorism*, 23 (emphasis in original).

15. Hoffman, 21.

16. Crenshaw, "Thoughts on Relating Terrorism," 9.

17. See, e.g., Saul, *Defining Terrorism*.

18. Saul, 3.

19. In this chapter, as in the previous one, I usually use the word "civilian" rather than "noncombatant." Although the terms are often used interchangeably, they are not exactly the same; "noncombatant" can have a more technical and complicated meaning, sometimes, for example, referring to uniformed troops who are deemed to be improper objects of military attack because they are wounded, prisoners, located outside of a clear zone of combat operations, or for some other reason. While both terms have become less clear due to developments in the practice of warfare in the past 150 years, "civilian" is less prone to obscure or counterintuitive usage in an attempt to manipulate the scope of application of the term or of the definition of terrorism itself (as I mention later in regard to the US State Department's definition of terrorism). For these reasons, and to avoid possible confusion, I will also refer to the principle of "civilian immunity," although "noncombatant immunity" (a term of art in just war thinking) is more common.

20. Of course, micromotivational factors are real, potentially extremely powerful, and can translate into significant change when they are shared by an unusually large proportion of a given society. In such a case, however, we should ask what broader factors explain such an unusually high concentration.

21. Richardson, *What Terrorists Want*, 55–56; Walter Reich, "The Poverty Myth," *Wilson Quarterly* (Winter 2008), https://www.wilsonquarterly.com/quarterly/winter-2008-the-coming-revolution-in-africa/poverty-not-root-cause-islamist-terrorism/.

22. Walter Laqueur, *The Age of Terrorism* (Boston: Little, Brown, 1987), 157; Richardson, *What Terrorists Want*, 50–51.

23. Brynjar Lia and Katja H.-W. Skjølberg, "Why Terrorism Occurs: A Survey of Theories and Hypotheses on the Causes of Terrorism," FFI Research Report no. 02769 (Kjeller, NO: Forsvarets Forskningsinstitutt, 2000), 19–20, http://rapporter.ffi.no/rapporter/2000/02769.pdf.

24. Crenshaw, "Thoughts on Relating Terrorism," 17.

25. Richardson, *What Terrorists Want*, 57.

26. Michael J. Mazarr, "The Rise and Fall of the Failed-State Paradigm," *Foreign Affairs* 93, no. 1 (January/February 2013).

27. Laqueur, *Age of Terrorism*, 164–65.

28. Hoffman, *Inside Terrorism*, chap. 1; Alex P. Schmid and Albert J. Jongman, *Political Terrorism* (Amsterdam: North-Holland Publishing, 2005).

29. Laqueur, *Age of Terrorism*, 10.

30. See, e.g., Crenshaw, "Thoughts on Relating Terrorism," 4–12, and Hoffman, *Inside Terrorism*, 20–30.

31. Laqueur, *Age of Terrorism*, 142.

32. As we shall see, the UN General Assembly sessions after the 1972 Munich Olympics episode were especially pivotal.

33. See, e.g., Hoffman, *Inside Terrorism*, 25; Richardson, *What Terrorists Want*, 5; Audrey Kurth Cronin, "Behind the Curve: Globalization and International Terrorism," *International Security* 27, no. 3 (Winter 2002/3): 33.

34. See, e.g., Richardson, *What Terrorists Want*, 5; Laqueur, *Age of Terrorism*, 146.

35. Charles Tilly, "Terror, Terrorism, Terrorists," *Sociological Theory* 22, no. 1 (March 2004): 9.

36. Tilly, "Terror, Terrorism, Terrorists," 5. See also R. R. Baxter, "A Skeptical Look at the Concept of Terrorism," *Akron Law Review* 7, no. 3 (1974).

37. Martha Crenshaw, "The Logic of Terrorism: Terrorist Behavior as a Product of Strategic Choice," in *Origins of Terrorism*, ed. Walter Reich (Washington, DC: Woodrow Wilson Center Press, 1998), 7–8.

38. Hoffman, *Inside Terrorism*, 132.

39. Mervyn Frost, *Ethics in International Relations: A Constitutive Theory* (Cambridge: Cambridge University Press, 1996), 161.

40. Audrey Kurth Cronin, "Rethinking Sovereignty: American Strategy in the Age of Terrorism," *Survival* 44, no. 2 (Summer 2002): 125.

41. Hoffman, *Inside Terrorism*, 57.

42. Thomas, *Ethics of Destruction*, chap. 4.

43. Crenshaw, "Thoughts on Relating Terrorism," 5, 8.

44. Serge Stepniak, quoted in Tom Reiss, "The True Classic of Terrorism," *New York Times*, September 11, 2005, https://www.nytimes.com/2005/09/11/books/review/the-true-classic-of-terrorism.html. See also writings by Sergius Stepniak, Mikhail Bakunin, Nikolai Morozov, and Gerasim Tarnoski in *The Terrorism Reader*, ed. Walter Laqueur and Yonah Alexander (New York: NAL Penguin, 1987), 72–90.

45. Martin A. Miller, "The Intellectual Origins of Modern Terrorism in Europe," in *Terrorism in Context*, ed. Martha Crenshaw (University Park: Pennsylvania State University Press, 1994), 58.

46. Quoted in Miller, "Intellectual Origins," 47.

47. William Dodge Lewis, Henry Seidel Canby, and Thomas Kite Brown, eds., *The Winston Simplified Dictionary, Encyclopedic Edition* (Philadelphia: John C. Winston, 1931).

48. Quoted in Saul, *Defining Terrorism*, 272.

49. Saul, 284–87.

50. Saul, 285.

51. Saul, 273.

52. See Thomas, *Ethics of Destruction*, chap. 4.

53. Giulio Douhet, *The Command of the Air*, 2nd ed., ed. Joseph Patrick Harahan and Richard H. Kohn (Tuscaloosa: University of Alabama Press, 2009), 368.

54. Douhet, *Command of the Air*, 35.

55. Quoted in Phillip S. Meilinger, "Trenchard and 'Morale Bombing': The Evolution of Royal Air Force Doctrine before World War II," *Journal of Military History* 60, no. 2 (1996): 260.

56. Arie Perliger and Leonard Weinberg, "Jewish Self-Defence and Terrorist Groups prior to the Establishment of the State of Israel: Roots and Traditions," *Totalitarian Movements and Political Religions* 4, no. 3 (2003); Ian S. Lustick, "Terrorism in the Arab-Israeli Conflict: Targets and Audiences," in Crenshaw, *Terrorism in Context*, 517–33.

57. Quoted in Lustick, "Terrorism in Arab-Israeli Conflict," 527. See also Guela Cohen, *Woman of Violence: Memoirs of a Young Terrorist* (New York: Holt Rinehart, 1966).

58. Martha Crenshaw, "The Effectiveness of Terrorism in the Algerian War," in Crenshaw, *Terrorism in Context*.

59. Nelson Mandela, "'I Am Prepared to Die': Nelson Mandela's Statement from the Dock at the Opening of the Defence Case in the Rivonia Trial," April 20, 1964, http://db.nelsonmandela.org/speeches/pub_view.asp?pg=item&ItemID=NMS010&txtstr=prepared%20to%20die.

60. Quoted in Hoffman, *Inside Terrorism*, 21.

61. A telling example was a 1962 proposal by a US general for "paramilitary, sabotage, and/or terrorist activities against known communist proponents" in Colombia. It is hard to imagine an American general using the term in a similar setting today. Human Rights Watch, "Colombia's Killer Networks: The Military-Paramilitary Partnership and the United States," 1996, https://www.hrw.org/legacy/reports/1996/killer2.htm.

62. Che Guevara, *Guerrilla Warfare* (Lincoln: University of Nebraska Press, 1985), 61.

63. Harold E. Selesky, "Colonial America," in *The Laws of War: Constraints on Warfare in the Western World*, ed. Michael Howard, George J. Andreopoulos, and Mark R. Shulman (New Haven, CT: Yale University Press, 1994), 81; Martin van Creveld, *The Transformation of Warfare* (New York: Free Press, 1991), 206–7; Jay Winik, *April 1865: The Month That Saved America* (New York: Harper, 2001), 146–66.

64. Richard Shelly Hartigan, *Lieber's Code and the Law of War* (Chicago: Precedent, 1983), 24–25.

65. See, e.g., Kinsella, *Image before the Weapon*, chap. 7.

66. Walzer, *Just and Unjust Wars*, 144.

67. Ironically, in some of its other provisions, Protocol I shifted the balance away from military necessity, significantly limiting its scope in article 52(2)'s definition of "military objective" and article 57's formulation of the principle of proportionality.

68. Such tactics are often associated with Charles Dunlap's concept of "lawfare," which he defines as "the strategy of using—or misusing—law as a substitute for traditional military means to achieve an operational objective." Charles J. Dunlap, "Lawfare Today: A Perspective," *Yale Journal of International Affairs* 3, no. 1 (2008): 146. I have chosen a different term for two reasons. First, the tactics I am addressing constitute only a subset of practices that fall under "lawfare." Second, because civilian-centric tactics often involve practices that are clearly forbidden under international law, it is inaccurate and misleading to say that they rely on law for their effectiveness. They do, however, rely on international norms—and the disjuncture between law and norms is part of what interests me here.

69. Thomas, *Ethics of Destruction*, chap. 5.

70. On the violence in Congo, see Jeffrey Gettleman, "Report Cites Vast Civilian Killings in East Congo," *New York Times*, December 13, 2009, https://www.nytimes.com/2009/12/14/world/africa/14congo.html?_r=1.

71. Walzer, *Just and Unjust Wars*, xiv.

72. Hoffman, *Inside Terrorism*, 63.

73. Hoffman, 64.

74. Quoted in Hoffman, 64.

75. Hoffman, 64.

76. UN Security Council, Resolution 286, The Situation Created by Increasing Incidents Involving the Hijacking of Commercial Aircraft, S/RES/286 (September 9, 1970), https://undocs.org/S/RES/286(1970).

77. "Israeli Plane Hijacked and Flown to Algiers," *Irish Times*, July 24, 1968; "Arabs Hold 22 Israelis from Hijacked Airliner," *Boston Globe*, July 24, 1968.

78. Remi Brulin, "Defining 'Terrorism': The 1972 General Assembly Debates on 'International Terrorism' and Their Coverage in the *New York Times*," in *Societies under Siege: Media, Government, Politics and Citizens' Freedoms in an Age of Terrorism*, ed. Banu B. Hawks (Cambridge: Cambridge Scholar Press, 2012), https://www.nytexaminer.com/2013/09/defining-terrorism/.

79. Saul, *Defining Terrorism*, 199.

80. UN General Assembly Official Records (GAOR), 27th Sess., 2038th plen. mtg., UN Doc A/PV.2038, para. 87 (September 25, 1972).

81. See, e.g, the statement by Sudan's foreign minister, UN GAOR, 27th Sess., 2056th plen. mtg., UN Doc A/PV/.2056, para. 81 (October 6, 1972), and Brulin, "Defining 'Terrorism.'"

82. Saul, *Defining Terrorism*, 199–200.

83. See the statements by the representatives of People's Republic of the Congo, UN GAOR, 27th Sess., 2045th plen. mtg., UN Doc A/PV/.2045, paras. 258–62 (September 28, 1972); Nigeria, UN GAOR, 27th Sess., 2048th plen. mtg., UN Doc A/PV/.2048, paras. 179–80 (October 2, 1972); Yugoslavia, UN GAOR, 27th Sess., 2052nd plen. mtg., UN Doc A/PV/.2052, para. 10 (October 4, 1972); Iraq, UN GAOR, 27th Sess., 2055th plen. mtg., UN Doc A/PV/. 2055, para. 25 (October 4, 1972); Sudan, UN GAOR, 27th Sess., 2056th plen. mtg., UN Doc A/PV/.2056, para. 83 (October 6, 1972); Syria, UN GAOR, 27th Sess., 2058th plen. mtg., UN Doc A/PV/.2058, paras. 137–41 (October 9, 1972); and Yemen, UN GAOR, 27th Sess., 2059th plen. mtg., UN Doc A/PV/.2059, paras. 36–37 (October 9, 1972).

84. See the statement by Morocco, UN GAOR, 27th Sess., 2056th plen. mtg., UN Doc A/PV/.2056, para. 138 (October 6, 1972).

85. Quoted in John Dugard, "International Terrorism and the Just War," *Stanford Journal of International Studies* 12 (1977): 27–28. See also comments by representatives of Nigeria, UN GAOR, 27th Sess., 2048th plen. mtg., UN Doc A/PV/.2048, para. 122 (October 2, 1972); Chile, UN GAOR, 27th Sess., 2050th plen. mtg., UN Doc A/PV/.2050, para. 118 (October 3, 1972); Yugoslavia, UN GAOR, 27th Sess., 2052nd plen. mtg., UN Doc A/PV/.2052, para. 117 (October 4, 1972); Niger, UN GAOR, 27th Sess., 2057th plen. mtg., UN Doc A/PV/.2057, para. 22 (October 6, 1972); Ethiopia, UN GAOR, 27th Sess., 2063rd plen. mtg., UN Doc A/PV/.2063, para. 163 (October 11, 1972); and Somalia, UN GAOR, 27th Sess., 2063rd plen. mtg., UN Doc A/PV/.2063, para. 224 (October 11, 1972).

86. Quoted in Hoffman, *Inside Terrorism*, at 24.

87. See the statements by the United States, UN GAOR, 27th Sess., 2038th plen. mtg., UN Doc A/PV/.2038, para. 7 (September 25, 1972), and Israel, UN GAOR, 27th Sess., 2045th plen. mtg., UN Doc A/PV/.2045, para. 80 (September 28, 1972).

88. UN GAOR, 27th Sess., 2044th plen. mtg., UN Doc A/PV/.2044, para. 36 (September 28, 1972).

89. UN GAOR, 27th Sess., 2045th plen. mtg., UN Doc A/PV/.2045, para. 80 (September 28, 1972).

90. US Department of State memorandum, September 22, 1972, quoted in Brulin, "Defining 'Terrorism.'"

91. Brulin.

92. William Bennett, US delegate to the Sixth Committee of the General Assembly, November 13, 1972, quoted in Brulin.

93. "U.S. Draft Convention for Prevention and Punishment of Terrorism Acts," *International Legal Materials* 11 (1972): 1383.

94. William Bennett, quoted in Brulin, "Defining 'Terrorism.'"

95. Brulin.

96. UN GAOR, 27th Sess., 2050th plen. mtg., UN Doc A/PV/.2050, para. 127 (October 3, 1972); UN GAOR, 27th Sess., 2059th plen. mtg., UN Doc A/PV/.2059, para. 183 (October 9, 1972).

97. Quoted in Brulin, "Defining 'Terrorism.'"

98. Quoted in Brulin.

99. For a Western legal analysis that expresses perplexity at non-Western opposition to the draft convention, see John Dugard, "International Terrorism: Problems of Definition," *International Affairs* 50, no. 1 (January 1974): 81.

100. The significance of the use of the word "terrorism" itself can be seen by comparing the General Assembly debate to the work of the International Law Commission (ILC) earlier in 1972. In response to the growing number of militant attacks on diplomats (most frequently from Israel), the ILC produced a Convention on the Prevention and Punishment of Crimes against Internationally Protected Persons, Including Diplomatic Agents. The provisions in this document, including the steps states were required to take to prevent crimes and bring perpetrators to justice, were in many ways similar to those in the US draft convention on terrorism that would be pilloried in the General Assembly. Nevertheless, the ILC's convention contained no exceptions for those fighting for national liberation and in its commentary explicitly rejected the notion that even "the worthiest of motives" could justify criminal actions. One reason for the difference was that despite the fact that the non-Western bloc was well represented on the ILC, it was a much less overtly political body than the General Assembly. (Of the twenty-five members of the ILC in 1972, three were from Soviet-bloc states, and ten were from postcolonial states in Africa and Asia.) More important, however, was that although the ILC's convention did not necessarily define the crimes it addressed any more narrowly than the American draft convention did, the word "terrorism" did not appear anywhere in the ILC's document. Indeed, the document created little controversy until late in the year when it came before the General Assembly Sixth Committee—the locus of much of the brouhaha over "terrorism"—at which point non-Western states demanded that a provision be added making the convention inapplicable to anyone fighting for national liberation. Richard D. Kearney, "The Twenty-Fourth Session of the International Law Commission," *American Journal of International Law* 67 (1973): 89; Dugard, "International Terrorism and the Just War," 31.

101. Saul, *Defining Terrorism*, 207.

102. Saul, 202–3, 207.

103. Saul, 206.

104. Saul, 203.

105. Ricardo Méndez Silva, "United Nations General Assembly Resolutions on Terrorism," *Mexican Law Review* 7 (January 2007), http://info8.juridicas.unam.mx/cont/mlawr/7/arc/arc8.htm.

106. See UN General Assembly, Resolutions 32/147 (December 16, 1977), https://undocs.org/en/A/RES/32/147, 34/145 (December 17, 1979), https://undocs.org/en/A/RES/34/145, 36/109 (December 10, 1981), https://undocs.org/en/A/RES/36/109, 38/130 (December 19, 1983), https://undocs.org/en/A/RES/38/130, 40/61 (December 9, 1985), https://undocs.org/en/A/RES/40/61, 42/159 (December 7, 1987), https://undocs.org/en/A/RES/42/159, and 44/29 (December 4,1989), https://undocs.org/en/A/RES/44/29, all of which were titled "Measures to Prevent International Terrorism Which Endangers or Takes Innocent Human Lives or Jeopardizes Fundamental Freedoms, and Study of the Underlying Causes of Those Forms of Terrorism and Acts of Violence Which Lie in Misery, Frustration, Grievance and Despair and Which Cause Some People to Sacrifice Human Lives, including Their Own, in an Attempt to Effect Radical Changes."

107. Barry Rubin, *Revolution until Victory? The Politics and History of the PLO* (Cambridge, MA: Harvard University Press, 1994), 32.

108. Hezbollah, "An Open Letter: The Hizballah Program," 1985, https://www.ict.org.il/UserFiles/The%20Hizballah%20Program%20-%20An%20Open%20Letter.pdf.

109. Ibrahim Abu-Lughod, "Unconventional Violence and International Politics," *American Journal of International Law* 67, no. 5 (1973): 103.

110. Quoted in Hoffman, *Inside Terrorism*, 23.

111. Richardson, *What Terrorists Want*, 16.

112. Quoted in Hoffman, *Inside Terrorism*, 26.

113. M. Cherif Bassiouni, "Methodological Options for International Legal Control of Terrorism," *Akron Law Review* 7, no. 3 (Spring 1974): 392–93.

114. Quoted in Martin Kramer, "The Moral Logic of Hizballah," in Reich, *Origins of Terrorism*, 145.

115. Eqbal Ahmad, "Terrorism: Theirs and Ours," address at the University of Colorado, October 12, 1998, https://sangam.org/ANALYSIS/Ahmad.htm.

116. Baxter, "Skeptical Look," 386.

117. Quoted in Rubin, *Revolution until Victory?*, 24.

118. Quoted in Rubin, 151.

119. Miller, "Intellectual Origins," 42–44.

120. Richardson, *What Terrorists Want*, 6.

121. The phrase "collateral damage" is perhaps most notoriously associated with an act of US domestic terrorism; Timothy McVeigh used the phrase to describe the deaths of nineteen children in the bombing of a federal office building in Oklahoma City in 1995.

122. Quoted in Muhammad Munir, "Suicide Attacks and Islamic Law," *International Review of the Red Cross* 90, no. 869 (March 2008): 75.

123. Quoted in Geraghty, *Irish War*, 213.

124. Adrian Guelke, *The Age of Terrorism and the International Political System* (London: I. B. Tauris, 1995), 192–93.

125. UN GAOR, 27th Sess., 2057th plen. mtg., UN Doc A/PV/.2057, para. 143 (October 6, 1972).

126. UN GAOR, 27th Sess., 2045th plen. mtg., UN Doc A/PV/.2045, paras. 264–65 (September 28, 1972). See also statements by delegates from Guinea, UN GAOR, 27th Sess., 2049th plen. mtg., UN Doc A/PV/.2049, para. 209 (October 2, 1972), and Algeria, UN GAOR, 27th Sess., 2063rd plen. mtg., UN Doc A/PV/.2063, para. 282 (October 11, 1972).

127. Quoted in Geraghty, *Irish War*, 214.

128. Provisional IRA, "Freedom Struggle," in *Terrorism Reader*, ed. Laqueur and Alexander, 132.

129. Hoffman, *Inside Terrorism*, chap. 2; Guelke, *Age of Terrorism*, 80.

130. Hoffman, *Inside Terrorism*, 46.

131. Lustick, "Terrorism in the Arab-Israeli Conflict," 527–33.

132. UN GAOR, 27th Sess., 2057th plen. mtg., UN Doc A/PV/.2057, paras. 40–42 (October 6, 1972). Deir Yassin was a Palestinian village attacked by Israeli militias in 1948, resulting in about 120 deaths.

133. UN GAOR, 27th Sess., 2056th plen. mtg., UN Doc A/PV/.2056, para. 65 (October 6, 1972). See also statements by delegates from Syria, UN GAOR, 27th Sess., 2058th plen. mtg., UN Doc A/PV/.2058, paras. 141–44 (October 9, 1972); Saudi Arabia, UN GAOR, 27th Sess., 2045th plen. mtg., UN Doc A/PV/.2045, paras. 289–309 (September 28, 1972); and Kuwait, UN GAOR, 27th Sess., 2057th plen. mtg., UN Doc A/PV/.2057, paras. 177–81 (October 6, 1972).

134. Edward Said, *The Question of Palestine* (New York: Times Books, 1979), 44.

135. Abu-Lughod, "Unconventional Violence," 101.

136. Bassiouni, "Methodological Options," 393.

137. Quoted in Richardson, *What Terrorists Want*, 18.

138. Rubin, *Revolution until Victory?*, 25.

139. Hezbollah, "Open Letter." To add insult to injury, Israeli minister of defense Ariel Sharon, who an Israeli commission found to be at fault in the massacre, was elected prime minister in 2001.

140. Hamas, "The Covenant of the Islamic Resistance Movement," August 18, 1988, https://avalon.law.yale.edu/20th_century/hamas.asp.

141. "Seven Questions: The World According to Hamas," *Foreign Policy*, January 2008, https://foreignpolicy.com/2008/01/29/seven-questions-the-world-according-to-hamas/.

142. Said, *Question of Palestine*, xii, 172.

143. Yasser Arafat, "Address to the UN General Assembly in New York, 13 November 1974," https://al-bab.com/documents-section/speech-yasser-arafat-1974.

144. Frost, *Ethics in International Relations*, 161.

145. Robert K. Fullinwider, "Understanding Terrorism," in *Problems of International Justice*, ed. Steven Luper-Foy (Boulder, CO: Westview, 1988), 253.

146. Frost, *Ethics in International Relations*, 164.

147. Quoted in Hoffman, *Inside Terrorism*, 59.

148. Quoted in Hoffman, 90.

149. UN GAOR, 27th Sess., 2045th plen. mtg., UN Doc A/PV/.2045, para. 312 (September 28, 1972).

150. Baxter, "Skeptical Look," 380. Baxter, who was a legal consultant to the US State Department and US Defense Department and led the US delegation to the Diplomatic Conference in Geneva, wrote that actions could be considered terrorism "whether accomplished by members of regularly constituted armed forces or persons not recognized as belligerents."

151. Brulin, "Defining 'Terrorism.'"

152. Douglas J. Feith, "Protocol I: Moving Humanitarian Law Backwards," *Akron Law Review* 19, no. 4 (Spring 1986): 535.

153. Ronald Reagan, "Message to the Senate Transmitting a Protocol to the 1949 Geneva Conventions," January 29, 1987, Ronald Reagan Presidential Library and Museum, https://reaganlibrary.gov/archives/speech/message-senate-transmitting-protocol-1949-geneva-conventions.

154. Jack Goldsmith, *The Terror Presidency* (New York: Norton, 2007), 112–13.

155. One critic of the US stance explained: "The application of the law of international armed conflict to the national liberation movement in no way entails acceptance of terror tactics. In the President's message to the Senate, the aims and the practices of groups described as terrorist tend to be grouped together, as though acceptance of one necessarily implies acceptance of the other. Nothing could be further from the truth." Greenwood,

Essays on War, 398. See also Hans-Peter Gasser, "An Appeal for Ratification by the United States," *American Journal of International Law* 81, no. 4 (1987).

156. Quoted in Greenwood, *Essays on War*, 390.

157. Quoted in Schmid and Jongman, *Political Terrorism*, 33 (emphasis added).

158. Audrey Kurth-Cronin, The "FTO List" and Congress: Sanctioning Designated Foreign Terrorist Organizations (Washington, DC: Congressional Research Service, October 21, 2003), https://fas.org/irp/crs/RL32120.pdf; US Department of State, "State Sponsors of Terrorism," accessed December 11, 2020, https://www.state.gov/state-sponsors-of-terrorism/.

159. 22 United States Code § 2656f(d) (2). The phrase "usually intended to influence an audience" was dropped in 2004.

160. Quoted in Hoffman, *Inside Terrorism*, 31.

161. Quoted in Boaz Ganor, "Defining Terrorism: Is One Man's Terrorist Another Man's Freedom Fighter?," *International Institute for Counter-Terrorism*, January 1, 2010, https://www.ict.org.il/Article/1123/Defining-Terrorism-Is-One-Mans-Terrorist-Another-Mans-Freedom-Fighter#gsc.tab=0.

162. Ronald Reagan, "Remarks at the Annual Dinner of the Conservative Political Action Conference," March 1, 1985, https://www.reaganlibrary.gov/archives/speech/remarks-annual-dinner-conservative-political-action-conference. On methods employed by the Contras, see Guelke, *Age of Terrorism*, 137, and Schmid and Jongman, *Political Terrorism*, 17. On the mujahideen, see Schmid and Jongman, 15.

163. "Shultz Urges 'Active' Drive on Terrorism," *New York Times*, June 25, 1984, https://www.nytimes.com/1984/06/25/world/shultz-urges-active-drive-on-terrorism.html.

164. Daniel L. Byman, "The Changing Nature of State Sponsorship of Terrorism," Analysis Paper no. 16, Saban Center for Middle East Policy, Brookings Institution, May 2008, https://www.brookings.edu/wp-content/uploads/2016/06/05_terrorism_byman.pdf.; Lionel Beehner, "What Good Is a Terrorism List?," *Los Angeles Times*, October 20, 2008, https://www.latimes.com/archives/la-xpm-2008-oct-20-oe-beehner20-story.html.

165. Notably, almost all the dozens of Middle East–based organizations on the US FTO list are also on the UK list.

166. Brian Whitaker, "The Definition of Terrorism," *The Guardian*, May 7, 2001, https://www.theguardian.com/world/2001/may/07/terrorism.

167. Saul, *Defining Terrorism*, 76; Blair Shewchuck, "Terrorists and Freedom Fighters," CBC News Online, October 18, 2011, https:www.cbc.ca/news2/indepth/words/terrorists.html.

168. Charles David Freilich, "Israel's Counter-Terrorism Policy: How Effective?," *Terrorism and Political Violence* 29, no. 2 (2017): 365.

169. Freilich, "Israel's Counter-Terrorism Policy," 363.

170. Human Rights Watch, "Why They Died: Civilian Casualties in Lebanon during the 2006 War," September 5, 2007, https://hrw.org/en/node/10734; Human Rights Watch, "Country Summary: Israel / Occupied Palestinian Territories," January 2010, https://hrw.org/en/node/87711; United Nations Human Rights Council, *Human Rights Situation in Palestine and Other Occupied Arab Territories: Report of the Detailed Findings of the Independent Commission of Inquiry Established pursuant to Human Rights Council Resolution S-21/1*, June 23, 2015, http://www.ohchr.org/Documents/HRBodies/HRCouncil/CoIGaza/A_HRC_CRP_4.doc.

171. Freilich, "Israel's Counter-Terrorism Policy," 369.

172. US Department of Defense, "Military Commission Instruction No. 2," April 30, 2003, 13, https://biotech.law.lsu.edu/blaw/dodd/corres/mco/mci2.pdf. See also Saul, *Defining Terrorism*, 309–11.

173. Saul, *Defining Terrorism*, 225.

174. Saul, 225.

175. See UN Security Council, Resolutions 731, Libyan Arab Jamahiriya, S/RES/731 (January 21, 1992), https://undocs.org/S/RES/731(1992), and 748, Libyan Arab Jamahiriya, S/RES/748 (March 31, 1992), https://www.undocs.org/S/RES/748(1992).

176. Michael R. Pompeo, "Remarks to the Press," April 8, 2019, US Department of State, https://www.state.gov/secretary/remarks/2019/04/290966.htm.

177. Lustick, "Terrorism in the Arab-Israeli Conflict," 515.

178. Walzer, *Just and Unjust Wars*, 198.

179. UN General Assembly Resolution 43/160, Observer Status of National Liberation Movements Recognized by the Organization of African Unity and/or the League of Arab States, A/RES/43/160 (December 9, 1988), https://undocs.org/en/A/RES/43/160.

180. Hoffman, *Inside Terrorism*, 70.

181. Abraham Sofaer, "Terrorism and the Law," in *Terrorism Reader*, ed. Laqueur and Alexander, 372; Ganor, "Defining Terrorism."

182. Rubin, *Revolution until Victory?*, 213.

183. Daniel Byman, *Deadly Connections: States That Sponsor Terrorism* (Cambridge: Cambridge University Press, 2005), 1.

184. Rubin, *Revolution until Victory?*, 38–39.

185. Byman, *Deadly Connections*, 84–85; Hoffman, *Inside Terrorism*, 265.

186. Byman, *Deadly Connections*; Hoffman, *Inside Terrorism*, 259–63.

187. Hoffman, *Inside Terrorism*, 261; Richardson, *What Terrorists Want*, 54.

188. While the mujahideen are typically not classified as a terrorist organization in the West, as noted earlier, they sometimes employed tactics comparable to those usually cited when applying that moniker to groups such as Hezbollah and Hamas. Schmid and Jongman, *Political Terrorism*, 15; Philip Shenon, "U.S. Says It Might Consider Attacking Serbs," *New York Times*, March 1, 1999, https://www.nytimes.com/1998/03/13/world/us-says-it-might-consider-attacking-serbs.html.

189. Stuart Taylor Jr., "Lebanese Group Linked to C.I.A. Is Tied to Car Bombing Fatal to 80," *New York Times*, May 13, 1985, https://www.nytimes.com/1985/05/13/world/lebanese-group-linked-to-cia-is-tied-to-car-bombing-fatal-to-80.html. Whether the attack is properly considered an act of terrorism depends on whether Fadlallah is deemed a combatant. Even if not, it would remain extremely problematic in terms of proportionality and an example that actions that do not fit the definition of "terrorism" can be as morally troubling as those that do.

190. Richardson, *What Terrorists Want*, 52.

191. Richardson, 65–66. See also David C. Rapoport, "The Fourth Wave: September 11 in the History of Terrorism," *Current History* 100, no. 650 (December 2001): 422.

192. Hoffman, *Inside Terrorism*, chap. 4.

193. Hoffman, 267.

194. Crenshaw, "Why America?," 426; Byman, *Deadly Connections*, 10.

195. Byman, *Deadly Connections*, 244–54.

196. Price, *Chemical Weapons Taboo*; Thomas, *Ethics of Destruction*, chap. 3.

197. Byman, *Deadly Connections*, 108.

198. Hoffman, *Inside Terrorism*, 263; Gary Clyde Hufbauer, Jeffrey J. Schott, and Barbara Oegg, "Using Sanctions to Fight Terrorism," Peterson Institute for International Economics Policy Brief no. 01–11, November 2001, https://www.piie.com/publications/policy-briefs/using-sanctions-fight-terrorism.

199. Byman, *Deadly Connections*, 108.

200. Saul, *Defining Terrorism*, 159–61. The SCO comprised Russia, China, Kazakhstan, Kyrgzstan, Tajikistan, and Uzbekistan.

201. UN Security Council Resolution 1373, September 28, 2001.

202. See, e.g., Cronin, "Rethinking Sovereignty," 134, and Robert O. Keohane, "The Public Delegitimation of Terrorism and Coalition Politics," in *Worlds in Collision: Terror and the Future of Global Order*, ed. Ken Booth and Tim Dunne (New York: Palgrave Macmillan, 2002), 141–51.

203. Saul, *Defining Terrorism*, 247.

204. Saul, 182.

205. Shewchuck, "Terrorists and Freedom Fighters."

206. Saul, *Defining Terrorism*, 48.

207. Saul, 210–11; Nicholas Rostow, "Before and after: The Changed UN Response to Terrorism since September 11th," *Cornell International Law Journal* 35, no. 3 (2002): 488; Gholamali Khoshroo, "Statement by H. E. Mr. Gholamali Khoshroo, Ambassador and Permanent Representative of the Islamic Republic of Iran to the United Nations, on Behalf of the Non-Aligned Movement before the Sixth Committee of the 72nd Session of the United Nations General Assembly," October 2, 2017, Human Rights Voices, https://www.human rightsvoices.org/assets/attachments/documents/Iran_6th_terrorism_statement.pdf.

208. "Ad Hoc Committee Established by General Assembly Resolution 51/210 of 17 December 1996," United Nations, https://legal.un.org/committees/terrorism/; Joshua Muravchik, "Terrorism's Silent Partner at the UN," *Los Angeles Times*, October 21, 2004, https://www.latimes.com/news/printedition/opinion/la-oe-muravchik18oct19,1,207349. story.

209. Hoffman, *Inside Terrorism*, 69–71; Gross, *Moral Dilemmas*, 193–94.

210. Kramer, "Moral Logic of Hizballah," 141.

211. Hoffman, *Inside Terrorism*, 70; Seth G. Jones and Martin C. Libicki, *How Terrorist Groups End: Lessons for Countering al Qa'ida*, RAND Terrorism Incident Database, 2008, RAND Corp., https://www.rand.org/news/press/2008/07/29.html.

212. Hoffman argues that Palestinian groups were the first to make widespread use of networking among organizations and influential in spreading the model. *Inside Terrorism*, 78–79.

213. By 2015, ISIS reportedly included fighters from over eighty countries, and new recruits were coming in at a rate of about one thousand per month. Cronin, "ISIS Is Not a Terrorist Group," 89.

214. Ben Saul notes that while condemnation of terrorism is nearly universal, "the sheer diversity of regional definitions is sufficient to militate against the view that there is any embryonic customary definition of terrorism." *Defining Terrorism*, 144.

215. Gray, *International Law*, 57–58.

216. Adam Goldman and Ellen Nakashima, "CIA and Mossad Killed Senior Hezbollah Figure in Car Bombing," *Washington Post*, January 30, 2015; Anne Barnard, "Car Bombing Injures Dozens in Hezbollah Section of Beirut," *New York Times*, July 9, 2013, https://www.nytimes.com/2013/07/10/world/middleeast/syria.html.

217. See, e.g., Shultz, Farah, and Lochard, "Armed Groups," 21–23; Hoffman, *Inside Terrorism*, 25; and Laqueur, *Age of Terrorism*, 157. For thoughtful critiques of this proclivity, see Conor Gearty, "Terrorism and Morality: Understanding the Language of Terrorism," in *Essays on Human Rights and Terrorism: Comparative Approaches to Civil Liberties in Asia, the EU and North America*, ed. Conor Gearty (London: Cameron May, 2008), and Daniel Byman, "Beyond Counterterrorism," *Foreign Affairs* 94, no. 6 (November/December 2015). Byman also lists among the "logical fallacies" of US counterterrorism policy that "it assumes that because all terrorists are bad guys, all bad guys must be terrorists."

218. Council of the European Union, *Proposal for a Council Framework Decision on Combating Terrorism*, December 7, 2001, CEU, accessed March 11, 2016, https://www.europarl.europa.eu/.../CONS_CONS(2001)14845(REV1)_EN.doc (inactive link).

219. Saul, *Defining Terrorism*, 89.

220. The post-1945 contextualization of the right to use force clearly also contributed significantly to the developments related in this chapter, both in legitimizing nonstate groups' use of force in appropriate circumstances and delegitimizing state violence in circumstances seen as violating the rights of colonized or oppressed peoples. And the normative "revolt against the West" both suffused all efforts in the service of decolonization and framed many of the specific arguments in the contestation of "terrorism," as I have described.

5. FROM SOLDIERS OF FORTUNE TO FORTUNE 500

1. James Glanz and Alissa J. Rubin, "From Errand to Fatal Shot to Hail of Fire to 17 Deaths," *New York Times*, October 3, 2007, https://www.nytimes.com/2007/10/03/world/middleeast/03firefight.html?mtrref=www.google.com.

2. Michael S. Schmidt and Eric Schmitt, "Flexing Muscle, Baghdad Detains U.S. Contractors," *New York Times*, January 15, 2012.

3. Thomson, *Mercenaries, Pirates, and Sovereigns*, chaps. 3–5.

4. Singer, *Corporate Warriors*, 19. For overviews of the historical role of private force, see Singer, *Corporate Warriors*, chap. 2, and Thomson, *Mercenaries, Pirates, and Sovereigns*, chap. 2.

5. Singer, *Corporate Warriors*, 22–29.

6. Thomson, *Mercenaries, Pirates, and Sovereigns*, 32–41.

7. Singer, *Corporate Warriors*, 31.

8. Thomson, *Mercenaries, Pirates, and Sovereigns*, chap. 4.

9. Avant, "From Mercenary to Citizen Armies."

10. Avant; Eliot A. Cohen, *Citizens and Soldiers: The Dilemmas of Military Service* (Ithaca, NY: Cornell University Press, 1985).

11. Van Creveld, *Rise and Decline of the State*, 259; Thomson, *Mercenaries, Pirates, and Sovereigns*, 57.

12. Thomson, *Mercenaries, Pirates, and Sovereigns*, chap. 3.

13. Percy, *Mercenaries*, chap. 5. Percy takes issue with Thomson's explanation of the rise of the norm, claiming that Thomson ascribes too much significance to state interests and not enough to preexisting moral judgments. Points of emphasis aside, Thomson's argument is not altogether incompatible with Percy's; I have argued elsewhere that the strongest norms develop when abstract moral judgments align with the interests of influential actors in the system. Thomas, *Ethics of Destruction*, chap. 2. For another argument that the "observable decline of mercenary activity during the modern era" reflected both moral and political considerations, see Hin-Yan Liu and Christopher Kinsey, "Challenging the Strength of the Antimercenary Norm," *Journal of Global Strategic Studies* 3, no. 1 (2018): 94.

14. Percy, *Mercenaries*, 167.

15. Singer, *Corporate Warriors*, 37; Avant, *Market for Force*, 29.

16. The term "private military company" did not originally include the word "security," as noted in note 5 of chapter 1. Also, as we shall see, most authors date the beginning of the significant reemergence of private force to the end of the Cold War in 1990. I argue that the erosion of the norm had begun, albeit in subtle ways, some time before then.

17. Avant, *Market for Force*, 160; Robert Young Pelton, *Licensed to Kill: Hired Guns in the War on Terror* (New York: Crown, 2006), 265–72.

18. Avant, *Market for Force*, chaps. 3–4; Cullen, "Keeping the New Dog of War," 38.

19. Swati Srivastava, "Sovereignty under Contract: Tensions in American Security," paper presented at the 2018 Annual Meeting of the International Studies Association,

San Francisco, April 4–7, 2018, 3; Heidi M. Peters, Moshe Schwartz, and Lawrence Kapp, *Department of Defense Contractor and Troop Levels in Iraq and Afghanistan: 2007–2017* (Washington, DC: Congressional Research Service, April 28, 2017), https://fas.org/sgp/crs/natsec/R44116.pdf.

20. John M. Broder and James Risen, "Contractors Deaths in Iraq Soar to Record," *New York Times*, May 19, 2007, https:/www.nytimes.com/2007/05/19/world/middleeast/19contractors.html; Steve Fainaru, "Iraq Contractors Face Growing Parallel War," *Washington Post*, June 16, 2007, http://www.washingtonpost.com/wp-dyn/content/article/2007/06/15/AR2007061502602.html.

21. Jeremy Scahill, *Blackwater: The Rise of the World's Most Powerful Mercenary Army* (New York: Nation Books, 2007), 117–32.

22. Quoted in Scahill, *Blackwater*, 130.

23. Elke Krahmann, *Private Security Companies and the State Monopoly on Violence: A Case of Norm Change?*, PRIF Report no. 88, (Frankfurt am Main: Peace Research Institute Frankfurt, 2009), 14, https://www.hsfk.de/fileadmin/HSFK/hsfk_downloads/prif88_02.pdf.

24. US Department of the Army. *FM 3–24: Counterinsurgency* (Washington, DC: Headquarters, Department of the Army, 2006), secs. 2–6; Headquarters, International Security Assistance Force, "Tactical Directive," July 6, 2009, https://www.nato.int/isaf/docu/official_texts/Tactical_Directive_090706.pdf.

25. Tom Bowman, "As U.S. Military Exits Iraq, Contractors to Enter," National Public Radio, May 17, 2011.

26. Bowman, "As U.S. Military Exits Iraq"; Michael R. Gordon, "Civilians to Take U.S. Lead as Military Leaves Iraq," *New York Times*, August 18, 2010.

27. Micah Zenko, "The New Unknown Soldiers of Afghanistan and Iraq," *Foreign Policy*, May 29, 2015, http://foreignpolicy.com/2015/05/29/the-new-unknown-soldiers-of-afghanistan-and-iraq/.

28. Moshe Schwartz, *The Department of Defense's Use of Private Security Contractors in Afghanistan and Iraq: Background, Analysis, and Options for Congress* (Washington, DC: Congressional Research Service, May 13, 2011), 9, https://fas.org/sgp/crs/natsec/R40835.pdf.

29. T. Christian Miller, "This Year, Contractor Deaths Exceed Military Ones in Iraq and Afghanistan," ProPublica, September 23, 2010, https://www.propublica.org/article/this-year-contractor-deaths-exceed-military-ones-in-iraq-and-afgh-100923.

30. Molly Dunigan et al., *Out of the Shadows: The Health and Well-Being of Private Contractors Working in Conflict Environments* (Santa Monica, CA: RAND Corp., 2013), https://www.rand.org/content/dam/rand/pubs/research_reports/RR400/RR420/RAND_RR420.pdf.

31. Mark Mazzetti, "C.I.A. Sought Blackwater's Help to Kill Jihadists," *New York Times*, August 19, 2009, https://www.nytimes.com/2009/08/20/us/20intel.html.

32. James Risen and Mark Mazzetti, "Blackwater Guards Tied to Secret C.I.A. Raids," *New York Times*, December 11, 2009. Blackwater reportedly performed similar services under a contract with Pakistan, despite the Pakistani government's stated refusal to allow US or NATO forces into the country. Jeremy Scahill, "The Secret US War in Pakistan," *The Nation*, November 23, 2009, https://www.thenation.com/article/secret-us-war-pakistan/.

33. Quoted in Srivastava, "Sovereignty under Contract," 29. The close relationship between private security and US intelligence operations was strikingly highlighted by the case of American contractor Raymond Davis, who was arrested in January 2011 for the shooting deaths of two Pakistanis. At the time of his arrest Davis, a former Blackwater employee who had founded his own security firm, not only was on contract to the CIA but

was also reportedly the acting CIA station chief—in effect, the top-ranking US intelligence official in one of the most strategically sensitive countries in the world. *Mark Mazzetti et al.,* "American Held in Pakistan Worked with C.I.A.," *New York Times*, February 21, 2011, https://www.nytimes.com/2011/02/22/world/asia/22pakistan.html?%2334=&sq=&st=cse&%2359;=&scp=1&%2359;hyperion protective=&pagewanted=all; Jawad R. Awan, "Davis CIA's Acting Chief in Pakistan," *The Nation*, February 21, 2011, https://www.nation.com.pk/pakistan-news-newspaper-daily-english-online/Politics/21-Feb-2011/Davis-CIAs-acting-chief-in-Pakistan/1.

34. Singer, *Corporate Warriors*, 208.

35. Singer, 126–27; Avant, *Market for Force*, 101–5.

36. Sean McFate, "America's Addiction to Mercenaries," *The Atlantic*, August 12, 2016, https://www.theatlantic.com/international/archive/2016/08/iraq-afghanistan-contractor-pentagon-obama/495731/.

37. Sean McFate, "The 'Blackwater 2.0' Plan for Afghanistan," *The Atlantic*, July 17, 2017, https://www.theatlantic.com/international/archive/2017/07/afghanistan-erik-prince-trump-britain/533580/.

38. Mark Mazzetti and Emily B. Hager, "Secret Desert Force Set Up by Blackwater's Founder," *New York Times*, May 14, 2011, https://www.nytimes.com/2011/05/15/world/middleeast/15prince.html.

39. "UAE Sending Colombian Mercenaries to Yemen: Sources," *Daily Mail*, December 19, 2015, https://www.dailymail.co.uk/wires/afp/article-3366710/UAE-sending-Colombian-mercenaries-Yemen-sources.html.

40. Mark Mazzetti and Eric Schmitt, "Private Army Formed to Fight Somali Pirates Leaves Troubled Legacy," *New York Times*, October 4, 2012, https://www.nytimes.com/2012/10/05/world/africa/private-army-leaves-troubled-legacy-in-somalia.html.

41. Arnaud Delalande, "Erik Prince's Mercenaries Are Bombing Libya," War Is Boring, January 14, 2017, https://warisboring.com/erik-princes-mercenaries-are-bombing-libya/.

42. Arom Roston, "American Mercenaries: A Middle East Monarchy Hired American Ex-Soldiers to Kill Its Political Enemies. This Could Be the Future of War" Buzzfeed, October 16, 2018, https://www.buzzfeednews.com/article/aramroston/mercenaries-assassination-us-yemen-uae-spear-golan-dahlan.

43. Ostensen and Bukkvoll, *Russian Use of Private Military*; Pierre Vaux, "Fontanka Investigates Russian Mercenaries Dying for Putin in Syria and Ukraine," *The Interpreter*, March 29, 2016, http://www.interpretermag.com/fontanka-investigates-russian-mercenaries-dying-for-putin-in-syria-and-ukraine/.

44. Ostensen and Bukkvoll, *Russian Use of Private Military*, 26, 33; Maximilian Popp, Christoph Reuter, and Adam Asaad, "The Renewed Dependency on Mercenary Fighters," *Der Spiegel*, July 17, 2020, https://www.realclearworld.com/2020/07/17/why_mercenaries_are_on_the_rise_again_499290.html?utm_source=rcp-today&utm_medium=email&utm_campaign=mailchimp-newsletter&mc_cid=105863441a&mc_eid=60d94ea688.

45. Ostensen and Bukkvoll, *Russian Use of Private Military*, 26–27.

46. Ostensen and Bukkvoll, 26.

47. "Syria War: Who Are Russia's Shadowy Wagner Mercenaries?," BBC, February 23, 2018, https://www.bbc.com/news/world-europe-43167697; Neil Hauer, "Russia's Mercenary Debacle in Syria," *Foreign Affairs*, February 26, 2018, https://www.foreignaffairs.com/articles/syria/2018-02-26/russias-mercenary-debacle-syria.

48. In 2019, Wagner was reportedly operating not only in Syria and Ukraine but also in Libya, Sudan, the Central African Republic, Mozambique, and perhaps Venezuela. Mike Giglio, "Inside the Shadow War Fought by Russian Mercenaries," BuzzFeed, April 17,

2019, https://www.buzzfeednews.com/article/mikegiglio/inside-wagner-mercenaries-rus sia-ukraine-syria-prighozhin; Matthew Cole and Alex Emmons, "Erik Prince Offered Lethal Services to Sanctioned Russian Mercenary Firm Wagner," The Intercept, April 13, 2020, https:// theintercept.com/2020/04/13/erik-prince-russia-mercenary-wagner-libya-mozambique/

49. International Alert, "The Mercenary Issue at the UN Commission on Human Rights: The Need for a New Approach," 2001, 11, https://www.international-alert.org/ sites/default/files/MercenaryIssues_UNHCR_EN_2001.pdf.

50. A 2001 report by the NGO International Alert noted: "Levdan, for example, the largest Israeli company operating in the industry, is a subsidiary of Kardan Investment, an import-export company active in the diamond trade. International Defence and Security Ltd (IDAS) (a Belgian-Dutch security company with Israeli connections) also has a joint venture agreement with American Mineral Fields International on diamond concessions in the Lunda Norte province of Angola." International Alert, "Mercenary Issue," 11.

51. Elke Krahmann, "Private Security and Military Actors," in *The International Studies Encyclopedia*, ed. Robert A. Denemark (Hoboken, NJ: Blackwell, 2011); Avant, *Market for Force*, 7.

52. Krahmann, *Private Security Companies*, 11; Schwartz, "Department of Defense's Use," 3.

53. Pelton, *Licensed to Kill*, 4; Scahill, *Blackwater*, 368. Blackwater's website stated: "We are not simply a 'private security company.' We are a professional military, law enforcement, security, peacekeeping and stability operations firm who provides turnkey solutions." Blackwater USA, "About Us," accessed July 13, 2006, https://www.blackwaterusa. com/about/ (site discontinued). Similarly, Northbridge Services Group, a firm headed by a retired American officer and registered in the Dominican Republic with offices in the United Kingdom and Ukraine, offered services that included "Special Forces Units (including counter terrorist and counter narcotics), Air Assault Operations, Rapid Reaction Forces, Maritime Special Warfare Units, [and] Fire support co-ordination teams." Northbridge is apparently still operational, and its website listing this range of services has not changed since at least 2006. Northbridge Services Group, "Our Services," most recently accessed December 3, 2020, http://northbridgeservices.org/services_opsupport. htm. The firm did not respond to the author's request for more information.

54. Mark Landler, Eric Schmitt, and Michael R. Gordon, "Trump Aides Recruited Businessmen to Devise Options for Afghanistan," *New York Times*, July 10, 2017, https:// www.nytimes.com/2017/07/10/world/asia/trump-afghanistan-policy-erik-prince-ste phen-feinberg.html.

55. Tara Copp, "Here's the Blueprint for Erik Prince's $5 Billion Plan to Privatize the Afghanistan War," *Military Times*, September 5, 2018, https://www.militarytimes. com/news/your-military/2018/09/05/heres-the-blueprint-for-erik-princes-5-billion-plan-to-privatize-the-afghanistan-war/.

56. "A Private Air Force for Afghanistan?" *Military Times*, August 2, 2017, https:// www.militarytimes.com/news/2017/08/02/a-private-air-force-for-afghanistan/.

57. Aram Roston, "A Chinese Blackwater? Betsy DeVos's Brother, the Founder of Blackwater, Is Setting Up a Private Army for China, Sources Say," BuzzFeed, February 16, 2017, https://www.buzzfeed.com/aramroston/betsy-devoss-brother-is-setting-up-a-private-army-for-china?utm_term=.rj5mnVkWV#.ijeX7nZvn.

58. Krahmann, *Private Security Companies*, 15.

59. Krahmann, 10; Singer, *Corporate Warriors*, 49; Avant, *Market for Force*, 30–31.

60. Singer, *Corporate Warriors*, 49–60; Avant, *Market for Force*, 30–38. Interestingly, an article explaining the resurgence of private force in terms of supply and demand appeared in 1977, well before the trend is typically described as beginning. Pertti Joeniemmi,

"Two Models of Mercenarism: Historical and Contemporary," *Instant Research on Peace and Violence* 7, no. 3 (1977): 193.

61. PMSCs often have few full-time employees, instead drawing on a large database of individuals with specialized skills and training to meet the requirements of contracts as they arise. Avant, *Market for Force*, 16.

62. Avant, 30–31.

63. Singer, *Corporate Warriors*, 193–94. Singer writes that, not coincidentally, over 70 percent of the members of the old Soviet KGB reportedly worked for PMCs as of 2004. *Corporate Warriors*, 53.

64. Singer, 53–55; Herbert M. Howe, "The Privatization of International Affairs: Global Order and the Privatization of Security," *The Fletcher Forum of World Affairs Journal* 22, no. 1 (Summer/Fall 1998): 1; Jeffrey Herbst, "Responding to State Failure in Africa," *International Security* 21, no. 3 (Winter 1996/97): 123–24.

65. Avant, *Market for Force*, 36.

66. Avant, 31, 36; Coker, "Outsourcing War," 198–99.

67. Singer, *Corporate Warriors*, 15.

68. Singer, 61; Coker, "Outsourcing War," 200–201.

69. Singer, 49.

70. Singer, 66. See also Avant, *Market for Force*, 35, and Amy L. Eckert, *Outsourcing War: The Just War Tradition in the Age of Military Privatization* (Ithaca, NY: Cornell University Press, 2016), 56.

71. Coker, "Outsourcing War," 193–94, 202.

72. It is worth noting that the excess supply of trained soldiers after the end of the Cold War was by no means unprecedented. In fact, military demobilizations after most of the major wars from 1815 to 1990 produced much larger gluts of former soldiers, both in absolute numbers and as a percentage of predemobilization forces, than did the end of the Cold War. David J. Singer, Stuart Bremer, and John Stuckey, "Capability Distribution, Uncertainty, and Major Power War, 1820–1965," in *Peace, War, and Numbers*, ed. Bruce Russett (Beverly Hills, CA: SAGE, 1972), 19–48.

73. Singer, *Corporate Warriors*, 17–18.

74. Avant, *Market for Force*, 66.

75. Krahmann, *Private Security Companies*, 15–16.

76. This is consistent with the view of norms taken by neorealist theorists of international relations theorists. John J. Mearsheimer, "The False Promise of International Institutions," *International Security* 19, no. 3 (Winter 1995).

77. Gerry S. Thomas, *Mercenary Troops in Modern Africa* (Boulder, CO: Westview, 1984), 15–20.

78. UN Security Council, Resolutions 161, The Congo Question, S/RES/161 (February 21, 1961), https://undocs.org/S/RES/161(1961); 169, The Congo Question, S/RES/169 (November 24, 1961), https://undocs.org/S/RES/169(1961); 226, Question Concerning the Democratic Republic of the Congo, S/RES/226 (October 14, 1966), https://undocs.org/S/RES/226(1966); 239, Question Concerning the Democratic Republic of the Congo, S/RES/239 (July 10, 1967), https://undocs.org/S/RES/239(1967); 241, Question Concerning the Democratic Republic of the Congo, S/RES/241 (November 15, 1967), https://undocs.org/S/RES/241(1967); and 289, Complaint by Guinea, S/RES/289 (November 23, 1970), https://undocs.org/S/RES/289(1970).

79. UN General Assembly, Resolution 2465, Implementation of the Declaration on the Granting of Independence to Colonial Countries and Peoples, A/RES/2465 (December 20, 1968), https://undocs.org/en/A/RES/2465(XXIII).

80. UN General Assembly, Resolutions 2548, Implementation of the Declaration on the Granting of Independence to Colonial Countries and Peoples, A/RES/2548

(December 11, 1969), https://undocs.org/en/A/RES/2548(XXIV); 2708, Implementation of the Declaration on the Granting of Independence to Colonial Countries and Peoples, A/RES/2708 (December 14, 1970), https://undocs.org/en/A/RES/2708(XXV); and 3103, Basic Principles of the Legal Status of the Combatants Struggling against Colonial and Alien Domination and Racist Regimes, A/RES/3103 (December 12, 1973), https://undocs.org/en/A/RES/3103(XXVIII).

81. Antonio Cassese, "Mercenaries: Lawful Combatants or War Criminals?," *ZaoRV* 40 (1980): 8, http://www.zaoerv.de/40_1980/40_1980_1_a_1_30.pdf.

82. Cassese, "Mercenaries, 11.

83. Thomson, *Mercenaries, Pirates, and Sovereigns*, chaps. 2, 4; H.C. Burmester, "The Recruitment and Use of Mercenaries in Armed Conflicts," *American Journal of International Law* 72, no. 1 (January 1978).

84. Thomas, *Ethics of Destruction*, chap. 2.

85. The vote on Resolution 2465 was 53 for, 8 against, 43 abstaining; the vote on Resolution 3103 was 83 for, 13 against, 19 abstaining. Todd S. Milliard, "Overcoming Post-Colonial Myopia: A Call to Recognize and Regulate Private Military Companies," *Military Law Review* 176 (June 2003): 26, 28.

86. Organization of African Unity, "OAU Convention for the Elimination of Mercenarism in Africa," doc. CM/817 (XXIX), annex II, rev. I (1977), article 1, para. 2.

87. Decades after decolonization, this framing of the issue remains surprisingly common: South Africa's 2006 Prohibition of Mercenaries Act carved out an exception for participation in armed struggles "for national liberation, self-determination . . . or resistance against occupation, aggression or domination by foreign nationals or foreign forces." Scahill, *Blackwater*, 363.

88. Christopher Kinsey, *Corporate Soldiers and International Security: The Rise of Private Military Companies* (New York: Routledge, 2006), 47.

89. Quoted in Kinsey, *Corporate Soldiers*, 47.

90. Kinsey, 51.

91. Hannu Kyrolainen, "An Analysis of Trends in the U.S. Military Training and Technical Assistance in the Third World," *Instant Research on Peace and Violence* 7, no. 3/4 (1977): 183n1; Duncan Campbell, "Marketing the New 'Dogs of War,'" Center for Public Integrity, October 30, 2002, https://publicintegrity.org/national-security/making-a-killing/marketing-the-new-dogs-of-war/.

92. Shaw, *Post-Military Society*, 152.

93. *Report of the Committee of Privy Counsellors Appointed to Inquire into the Recruitment of Mercenaries* (hereafter Diplock Commission Report) (London: Her Majesty's Stationery Office, 1976), 1, http://psm.du.edu/media/documents/national_regulations/countries/europe/united_kingdom/united_kingdom_diplock_report_1976.pdf.

94. Diplock Commission Report, 2.

95. Diplock Commission Report, 4.

96. Thomson, *Mercenaries, Pirates, and Sovereigns*, 77–81.

97. Although the Gurkha regiments were of long standing, the decades after World War II saw an increase in the number of countries with foreigners serving in their national armies, reflecting another way in which decolonization created pressure on the norm against mercenaries. While in some cases this was a function of erstwhile colonial subjects serving in the armies of their former colonizers, as common was new states building their militaries by drawing on personnel from more established powers. In 1994, Thomson identified eighteen states using foreign troops; twelve had become independent since 1945. Of these, several employed officers from their former ruling powers, some of them officially seconded from those countries' militaries. A similar arrangement was used by Oman, which, although it had not formally been a British colony, had a long-standing

security relationship with Britain that was part and parcel of Britain's colonial-era military hegemony in the Persian Gulf. The only two examples of established powers employing foreign troops in meaningful numbers also were firmly rooted in the colonial experience: the Nepalese Gurkhas in the British Army and the French Foreign Legion. The presence of foreigners in standing armies was therefore largely a vestige of colonialism, in some cases exhibiting considerably continuity from the colonial era. After decolonization, however, these relationships had significantly different implications for state sovereignty and coexisted uneasily with a norm against mercenaries. Thomson, *Mercenaries, Pirates, and Sovereigns*, 90–93.

98. Avant, *Market for Force*, 35; Pelton, *Licensed to Kill*, 100–101.

99. Kyrolainen, "Analysis of New Trends."

100. Kyrolainen, 170, 172.

101. Kim Willenson, Nicholas C. Proffitt, and Lloyd Norman, "Persian Gulf: This Gun for Hire," *Newsweek*, February 24, 1975, 30.

102. "The Executive Mercenaries," *Time*, February 24, 1975, 20.

103. Associated Press, "Probe of Arab Arms Training Planned," *Wisconsin State Journal*, February 11, 1975, 6.

104. "Executive Mercenaries"; "Mideast Dilemma: Is U.S. Training a Future Foe?," *U.S. News and World Report*, February 24, 1975, 21.

105. "Executive Mercenaries."

106. Perhaps the closest either country came to such a reckoning was the British parliamentary investigation of the Sandline controversies of the late 1990s and the ensuing government green paper of 2002, which are discussed later in this chapter.

107. Protocol I, article 47.

108. Burmester, "Recruitment and Use," 38.

109. Henry W. Van Deventer, "Mercenaries at Geneva," *American Journal of International Law* 70, no. 4 (October 1976): 812–15.

110. UN General Assembly, Resolution 41/102, Use of Mercenaries as a Means to Violate Human Rights and to Impede the Exercise of the Right of Peoples to Self-Determination, A/RES/41/102 (December 4, 1986), https://undocs.org/en/A/RES/41/102 (emphasis added). The 1986 resolution passed with 123 votes in favor, 23 against, and 11 abstentions.

111. ICRC website, accessed January 2, 2019, https://ihl-databases.icrc.org/applic/ihl/ihl.nsf/States.xsp?xp_viewStates=XPages_NORMStatesParties&xp_treatySelected=530.

112. Mike Hoare, *Congo Mercenary* (London: Robert Hale, 1967), 68.

113. As of January 2019, ISOA had ninety-eight members, many of which were not PMSCs but logistics/support firms or law firms representing private companies. International Stability Operations Association, "Our Members," accessed January 2, 2019, https://stability-operations.org/page/Members. As of January 2019, SCEG had forty-seven members. Security in Complex Environments Group, "Members," accessed January 2, 2019, https://www.sceguk.org.uk/members/.

114. In early 2007, the *New York Times* reported that since 2000, the twenty largest contracting firms had spent almost $300 million on lobbying and donated $23 million to political campaigns. Scott Shane and Ron Nixon, "In Washington, Contractors Take On Biggest Role Ever," *New York Times*, February 4, 2007.

115. Anna Leander argues that most studies understate the influence of PMSCs because they fail to appreciate their "epistemic power" to shape the security agenda and influence preferences regarding options. They do this not only through lobbying and public affairs, Leander argues, but also in their roles as trainers, consultants, and intelligence providers. Anna Leander, "The Power to Construct International Security: On the Significance of Private Military Companies," *Millennium* 33, no. 3 (2005).

116. Pelton, *Licensed to Kill*, 3; Erik Prince, "Contractors, Not Troops, Will Save Afghanistan," *New York Times*, August 30, 2017, https://www.nytimes.com/2017/08/30/opinion/erik-prince-contractors-afghanistan.html?module=inline.

117. Gary Sturgess, "Tales of Wells Fargo," *Journal of International Peace Operations* 6, no. 1 (July/August 2010), accessed July 31, 2011, http://web.peaceops.com/archives/759#more-759 (site discontinued); Gary Sturgess, "Images of Contracting," *Journal of International Peace Operations* 5, no. 6 (May/June 2010); Gary Sturgess, "An Unlikely History of Contracting," *Journal of International Peace Operations* 4, no. 2 (September/October 2008), http://www.privatemilitary.org/ISOA/JIPO-2008-09%20IPOA-Humanitarian_Security_and_Support.pdf.

118. Doug Brooks, "How Many Is Too Many?," *Journal of International Peace Operations* 5, no. 4 (January/February 2010): 6.

119. J. J. Messner, "No Points for Trying," *Journal of International Peace Operations* 6, no. 1 (July/August 2010), accessed March 1, 2012, http://web.peaceops.com/archives/category/journal_content/columnists/messner (site discontinued).

120. "The Diamond Mercenaries of Africa," Radio National (Australia), August 4, 1996, http://www.abc.net.au/radionational/programs/backgroundbriefing/the-diamond-mercenaries-of-africa/3564008.

121. J. J. Messner, "What's in a Name?," *Journal of International Peace Operations* 2, no. 6 (May/June 2007): 24.

122. Quoted in Evan Thomas, "Profile: Blackwater's Erik Prince," *Newsweek*, October 13, 2007, http://www.newsweek.com/profile-blackwaters-erik-prince-103877; quoted in Srivastava, "Sovereignty under Contract," 28.

123. See, e.g., Sandline International, "An Open Letter," February 1999, accessed March 1, 2012, www.sandline.com (site discontinued).

124. Coker, "Outsourcing War," 189.

125. Pelton, *Licensed to Kill*, 4, 284–86.

126. Doug Brooks, interview by author, August 3, 2007, Washington, DC.

127. Brooks, interview by author.

128. "Code of Conduct—Version 13.1," ISOA website, accessed March 23, 2018, https://stability-operations.site-ym.com/?page=CodeofConduct_131&hhSearchTerms=%22Code+and+conduct%22; "Key Documents," BAPSC website, accessed March 23, 2018, https://www.bapsc.org.uk/key-documents.html; Sandline International, "Private Military Companies—Independent or Regulated?" (March 28, 1998), http://www.privatemilitary.org/publications/Sandline-PMCsIndependentorRegulated.pdf.

129. Pelton, *Licensed to Kill*, 265–72.

130. Tim Spicer, *An Unorthodox Soldier: Peace and War and the Sandline Affair* (Edinburgh: Mainstream Publishing, 1999), 38–40.

131. Spicer, *Unorthodox Soldier*, 40.

132. Spicer, 29, 35.

133. Spicer, 37.

134. Campbell, "Marketing the New 'Dogs of War.'"

135. Sandline, "Open Letter."

136. Sandline.

137. Quoted in Judith Woods, "'We Don't Operate in the Shadows,'" *Telegraph* (UK), December 3, 1999, https://www.telegraph.co.uk/htmlContent.jhtml=/archive/1999/12/03/tltim03.html (inactive link).

138. Sandline, "Private Military Companies," 2–3.

139. Sandline, "Open Letter."

140. Quoted in Woods, "We Don't Operate in the Shadows."

141. Thomas Legg and Robin Ibbs, *Report of the Sierra Leone Arms Investigation* (London: Stationery Office, 1998), 105–7.

142. Legg and Ibbs, *Sierra Leone Arms Investigation*, 115.

143. See, e.g., Mary Pat Flaherty and Dana Priest, "More Limits Sought for Private Security Teams," *Washington Post*, April 13, 2004, and Scahill, *Blackwater*, 356.

144. Jonathan Weisman, "House Acts in Wake of Blackwater Incident," *Washington Post*, October 5, 2007. For commentary and analysis critical of PMSCs, see Paul Krugman, "Hired Gun Fetish," *New York Times*, September 28, 2007; John F. Burns, "The Deadly Game of Private Security," *New York Times*, September 23, 2007; and Steve Fainaru, "Where Military Rules Don't Apply: Blackwater's Security Force in Iraq Give Wide Latitude by State Dept.," *Washington Post*, September 20, 2007.

145. John M. Broder, "U.S. Military to Supervise Iraq Security Convoys," *New York Times*, October 31, 2007; Suzanne Simons, *Master of War: Blackwater USA's Erik Prince and the Business of War* (New York: Harper 2009), 250.

146. Simons, *Master of War*, 254–55; J. J. Messner, "In or Out? And the Pursuit of a Definition of Inherently Governmental," *Journal of International Peace Operations* 5, no. 1 (July/August 2009). The reports emphasized the need to improve oversight of contractors but acknowledged their value and recommended no major changes in their use.

147. John M. Broder and James Risen, "Blackwater Mounts a Defense with Top Talent," *New York Times*, November 1, 2007, https://www.nytimes.com/2007/11/01/washington/01blackwater-sub.html?pagewanted=all; Erik D. Prince, "How Blackwater Serves America," *Wall Street Journal*, December 16, 2008, https://www.wsj.com/articles/SB122939188592109341.

148. Blackwater Worldwide, "A Request for Your Support," email to author, October 24, 2007.

149. Doug Brooks, "Shifting the Blame," *Journal of International Peace Operations* 5, no. 6 (May/June 2010), http://www.privatemilitary.org/ISOA/JIPO-2010-05-IPOA-Haiti.pdf.

150. Simons, *Master of War*, 247; Mike Baker, "Ex-Blackwater President, 4 Others Indicted on Conspiracy, Weapons Charges," *Huffington Post*, April 10, 2010, http://www.huffingtonpost.com/2010/04/16/gary-jackson-exblackwater_n_541046.html?view=screen (inactive link).

151. Simons, *Master of War*, 208–9.

152. Bruce Falconer, "IPOA Smackdown: DynCorp vs. Blackwater," *Mother Jones*, November 12, 2007, http://motherjones.com/print/6834.

153. Simons, *Master of War*, 263–64.

154. Robert Young Pelton, "Erik Prince: An American Commando in Exile," *Men's Journal*, November 2010.

155. Nathan Hodge, "Company Once Known as Blackwater Ditches Xe for Yet Another New Name," *Wall Street Journal*, December 21, 2011.

156. Katherine Fallah, "Corporate Actors: The Legal Status of Mercenaries in Armed Conflict," *International Review of the Red Cross* 88, no. 863 (September 2006): 604, https://www.icrc.org/en/doc/assets/files/other/irrc_863_fallah.pdf; Rajesh V. Fotedar, "Memorandum for the Office of the Prosecutor of the International Criminal Tribunal for Rwanda; Issue: The Legal Status, under International Humanitarian Law, of Captured Mercenaries in Internal Conflicts," Fall 2003, 21, accessed March 16, 2012, http://law.case.edu/war-crimes-research-portal/memoranda/Mercenaries.pdf (inactive link).

157. Lindsey Cameron, "Private Military Companies: Their Status under International Humanitarian Law and Its Impact on Their Regulation," *International Review of the Red Cross* 88, no. 863 (September 2006): 581, https://www.icrc.org/en/doc/assets/files/other/irrc_863_cameron.pdf; Fallah, "Corporate Actors," 603; Fotedar, "Memorandum for the Office," 26–27.

158. International Alert, "Mercenary Issue," 32.

159. Joana Abrisketa, "Blackwater: Mercenaries and International Law," *FRIDE Comment* (October 2007): 7.

160. International Code of Conduct Association. "Membership," accessed December 28, 2018, https://www.icoca.ch/en/membership. Experts disagree about how promising these MSIs are as a step toward effective governance. For sanguine assessments, see Deborah D. Avant, "Pragmatic Networks and Transnational Governance of Private Military and Security Companies," *International Studies Quarterly* (2016), and Deborah Avant and Virginia Haufler, "Public-Private Interactions and Practices of Security," in *The Oxford Handbook of International Security*, ed. Alexandra Gheciu and William C. Wohlforth (Oxford: Oxford University Press, 2015). For a critical assessment, see Berenike Prem, "Analyzing PMSC Power in Multi-Stakeholder Initiatives," paper presented at the 2018 Annual Meeting of the International Studies Association, San Francisco, April 4–7, 2018.

161. Foreign and Commonwealth Office, *Private Military Companies: Options for Regulation* (London: Stationery Office, 2002).

162. Foreign and Commonwealth Office, *Private Military Companies*, 4, 7–8.

163. Foreign and Commonwealth Office, 19.

164. Avant, *Market for Force*, 146–51.

165. Ulrich Petersohn, "Reframing the Anti-Mercenary Norm: Private Military and Security Companies and Mercenarism," *International Journal* 69, no. 4 (2014): 490.

166. Spicer, *Unorthodox Soldier*, 224.

167. See, e.g., Coker, "Outsourcing War"; Sebastian Mallaby, "Paid to Make Peace: Mercenaries Are No Altruists, but They Can Do Good," *Washington Post*, June 4, 2001; and Thomas Adams, "The New Mercenaries and the Privatization of Conflict," *Parameters* (Summer 1999). At a 1998 conference on "private armies and military intervention," the most commonly used terms were "mercenary armies," "private armies," "military companies," and "foreign soldiers." Campbell, "Marketing the New 'Dogs of War.'"

168. See, e.g., Avant, *Market for Force*, 9–23, and Singer, *Corporate Warriors*, 44–48.

169. Pelton, *Licensed to Kill*, 274–75.

170. Messner, "What's in a Name?"

171. Krahmann, "Private Security and Military Actors."

172. Percy, *Mercenaries*, 49.

173. Percy applies the term "mercenaries" only to individuals unaffiliated with a PMSC. Sarah Percy, "Morality and Regulation," in *From Mercenaries to Market: The Rise and Regulation of Private Military Companies*, ed. Simon Chesterman and Chia Lehnhardt (Oxford: Oxford University Press, 2007), 12–13.

174. "Secretary-General Reflects on 'Intervention' in Thirty-Fifth Annual Ditchley Foundation Lecture," press release SG/SM/6613, June 26, 1998, https://www.un.org/press/en/1998/19980626.sgsm6613.html.

175. "Transcript of Press Conference by Secretary-General Kofi Annan at United Nations Headquarters on 12 June," press release SG/SM/6255, June 12, 1997, http://www.un.org/News/Press/docs/1997/19970612.sgsm6255.html.

176. Petersohn, "Reframing the Anti-Mercenary Norm"; Petersohn, "Chequing Private Force?"

177. Petersohn, "Chequing Private Force?," 6.

178. Petersohn.

179. Petersohn, 14–20. Only the cases involving Russia's use of PMSCs in Ukraine and Syria attracted considerable international attention, Petersohn says, and even in these cases other governments focused their response on the PMSCs themselves rather than the Russian government.

180. Alec Klein, "U.S. Army Awards Iraq Security Work to British Firm," *Washington Post*, September 14, 2007, http://www.washingtonpost.com/wp-dyn/content/article/2007/09/13/AR2007091302237.html.

181. Quoted in Scahill, *Blackwater*, 161.

182. Theodoric Meyer, "Erik Prince Lobbies Up," *Politico*, October 24, 2018, https://www.politico.com/newsletters/politico-influence/2018/10/24/erik-prince-lobbies-up-387650.

183. Erik D. Prince, "The MacArthur Model for Afghanistan," *Wall Street Journal*, May 31, 2018, https://www.wsj.com/articles/the-macarthur-model-for-afghanistan-1496269058?mg=prod/accounts-wsj.

184. Karen DeYoung, Shane Harris, and Dan Lamothe, "Erik Prince, in Kabul, Pushes Privatization of the Aghan War," *Washington Post*, October 4, 2018, https://www.washingtonpost.com/world/national-security/erik-prince-in-kabul-pushes-privatization-of-the-afghan-war/2018/10/04/72a76d36-c7e5-11e8-b1ed-1d2d65b86d0c_story.html?noredirect=on&utm_term=.6a8a804bbe0e.

185. Prince, "MacArthur Model"; Carol E. Lee, Courtney Kube, and Josh Lederman, "Officials Worry Trump May Back Erik Prince Plan to Privatize War in Afghanistan," NBC News, August 17, 2018, https://www.nbcnews.com/news/military/officials-worry-trump-may-back-erik-prince-plan-privatize-war-n901401.

186. "Erik Prince and Tucker Carlson: Neocons and Corruption of Washington Keep Us in Afghanistan," Real Clear Politics, July 8, 2020, https://www.realclearpolitics.com/video/2020/07/08/erik_prince_and_tucker_carlson_neocons_and_corruption_of_washington_keep_us_in_afghanistan.html.

187. Enrique Bernales Ballesteros, "Use of Mercenaries as a Means of Violating Human Rights and Impeding the Exercise of the Right of Peoples to Self-Determination," UN doc. E/CN.4/1997/24, February 20, 1997, https://undocs.org/en/E/CN.4/1997/24, 28–34.

188. Ballesteros, "Use of Mercenaries," UN doc. E/CN.4/1997/24, 32.

189. Ballesteros, 30.

190. Ballesteros, 28–29.

191. Ballesteros, 33.

192. Ballesteros, 26.

193. Enrique Bernales Ballesteros, "Use of Mercenaries as a Means of Violating Human Rights and Impeding the Exercise of the Right of Peoples to Self-Determination," UN doc. E/CN.4/2004/15, December 24, 2003, https://undocs.org/en/E/CN.4/2004/15, 14.

194. Ballesteros, "Use of Mercenaries," UN doc. E/CN.4/2004/15 (emphasis added).

195. "Note by the Secretariat," August 31, 2005, UN doc. A/60/319.

196. Report of Shaista Shameen, "Use of Mercenaries as a Means of Violating Human Rights and Impeding the Exercise of the Right of Peoples to Self-Determination," UN doc. A/60/263, August 17, 2005, https://undocs.org/en/A/60/263, 15–16.

197. Shaimeen, "Use of Mercenaries," 13.

198. United Nations Working Group on the Use of Mercenaries as a Means of Violating Human Rights and Impeding the Exercise of the Right of Peoples to Self-Determination, "Guns for Hire," April 29, 2010, http://www.ohchr.org/EN/NewsEvents/Pages/Gunsforhire.aspx; "Report of the Working Group on the Use of Mercenaries as a Means of Violating Human Rights and Impeding the Exercise of the Right of Peoples to Self-Determination," UN doc. A/HRC/4/42, February 7, 2007, https://undocs.org/en/A/HRC/4/42, 20.

199. United Nations Office of the High Commissioner for Human Rights, "It's High Time to Close the Legal Gap for Private Military and Security Contractors—UN Expert Body on Mercenaries," 2010, http://newsarchive.ohchr.org/EN/NewsEvents/Pages/DisplayNews.aspx?NewsID=10000&LangID=E.

200. Messner, "No Points for Trying."

201. Shameen, "Use of Mercenaries," annex II, 21. See also Jeremy Scahill, "U.S. Mercenaries to UN: Stop Using the Word 'Mercenary' in Your Investigation into Mercenaries," Alternet, April 15, 2009, http://www.alternet.org/world/136861/u.s._mercenaries_to_un:_stop_using_the_word_'mercenary'_in_your_investigation_into_mercenaries/.

202. "Report of the Working Group on the Use of Mercenaries," UN doc. A/HRC/4/42, 20.

203. Thalif Deen, "UN Rejects Private Peacekeepers," Inter Press News, August 27, 2004, https://www.globalpolicy.org/security/peacekpg/training/0827rejects.htm; Percy, *Mercenaries*, 223.

204. Abby Stoddard, Adele Harmer, and Victoria DiDomenico, *Private Security Providers and Services in Humanitarian Operations* (London: Overseas Development Institute, 2008), https://www.odi.org/sites/odi.org.uk/files/odi-assets/publications-opinion-files/3703.pdf; Michael Meyer, "Dogs of Peace," *Newsweek*, August 24, 2003, http://www.newsweek.com/dogs-peace-135697

205. Avant, "From Mercenary to Citizen Armies"; Percy, *Mercenaries*, chap. 5.

206. For an account that highlights the role of changing views of military service as an obligation of citizenship in the rise of PMSCs, see Elke Krahmann, *States, Citizens and the Privatization of Security* (Cambridge: Cambridge University Press, 2010).

207. To be clear, my point here is not that PMSCs *are* actually "mercenaries." Indeed, this question has been made moot by the processes described in this chapter. To this extent, I agree with Avant that the term is not a useful description because there is no longer any consensus on what it means. Avant, *Market for Force*, 23. One premise of my argument, however, is that many PMSCs would have fallen under the meaning of the term as it was understood during the century and a half in which mercenaries were rarely seen.

6. WHAT'S AT STAKE?

1. Williams, "Violent Non-State Actors," 15; Vanessa Neumann, "The New Nexus of Narcoterrorism: Hezbollah and Venezuela," Foreign Policy Research Institute, December 3, 2011, https://www.fpri.org/article/2011/12/the-new-nexus-of-narcoterrorism-hezbollah-and-venezuela/; Shultz, Farah, and Lochard, "Armed Groups," 30; Lia and Skjølberg, *Why Terrorism Occurs*, 25.

2. Global Witness, *For a Few Dollars More: How Al-Qaeda Infiltrated the Diamond Business* (London: Global Witness, 2003), https://www.globalwitness.org/en/archive/few-dollar-more-how-al-qaeda-moved-diamond-trade/; Shultz, Farah, and Lochard, "Armed Groups," 30–31.

3. Williams, "Violent Non-State Actors," 18; Robert Windrem and Aram Roston, "Reputed Mobster: 'Usual Suspect' or Supporter of the Mumbai Attacks?," NBC News, December 3, 2008, http://deepbackground.msnbc.msn.com/archive/2008/12/03/1697231.aspx.

4. Williams, "Violent Non-State Actors," 15.

5. Lilian Bobea, "How Caribbean Organized Crime is Replacing the State," InSight Crime, July 23, 2013, https://www.insightcrime.org/news/analysis/the-benefits-of-organized-crime-in-the-caribbean/. Interestingly, John Picarelli argues that TOC, too, has benefited from changes in international norms as well as changes in the global economic system. Criminal endeavors, he writes, are bolstered by the rise of "enabling norms," which "allow, or greatly facilitate, actions that would otherwise by impossible or unlikely to occur." John T. Picarelli, "Enabling Norms and Human Trafficking," in *Crime and the Global Political Economy*, ed. H. Richard Friman (Boulder, CO: Lynne Rienner, 2009), 87.

6. Singer, *Corporate Warriors*, 10.

7. Singer, 14–15; UN Commission on Human Rights, "Report of the Third Meeting of Experts on Traditional and New Forms of Mercenary Activities as a Means of Violating Human Rights and Impeding the Exercise of the Right of Peoples to Self-Determination," UN doc. E/CN.4/2005/23, January 18, 2005, https://undocs.org/en/E/CN.4/2005/23, 12.

8. Mark Galeotti, "Moscow's Mercenaries Reveal the Privatization of Russian Geo-politics," Open Democracy, August 29, 2017, https://www.opendemocracy.net/en/odr/chvk-wagner-and-privatisation-of-russian-geopolitics/; Mark Galeotti, "Moscow's Mer-cenaries in Syria," War on the Rocks, April 5, 2016, https://warontherocks.com/2016/04/moscows-mercenaries-in-syria/.

9. US House of Representatives, Subcommittee on National Security and Foreign Affairs, Majority Staff, *Warlord, Inc.: Extortion and Corruption Along the U.S. Supply Chain in Afghanistan* (Washington: US House of Representatives Committee on Over-sight and Government Reform, June 2010), iii, http://www.cbsnews.com/htdocs/pdf/HNT_Report.pdf.

10. Popp, Reuter, and Asaad, "Renewed Dependency."

11. Stratfor, "The Use of Mercenaries in Syria's Crackdown," Stratfor, January 12, 2012, https://worldview.stratfor.com/article/use-mercenaries-syrias-crackdownt; Natasha Bertrand, "Syria 'Is Being Wwallowed Whole by Its Clients': Assad May Be Losing Control over His Own Militias," *Business Insider*, August 18, 2016, https://www.businessinsider.com/syrian-regime-militias-becoming-warlords-2016-8; Syrian Network for Human Rights, "On Human Rights Day, More than 75% of the Victims in Syria Are Civilians." December 10, 2014, http://sn4hr.org/wp-content/pdf/english/statement_on_the_Interna tional_Day_of_Human_Rights.pdf.

12. *Yassin al-Haj Saleh, "The* Syrian Shabiha and Their State—Statehood and Partici-pation," Heinrich Boell Foundation, March 3, 2014, https://lb.boell.org/en/2014/03/03/syrian-shabiha-and-their-state-statehood-participation.

13. Rao Komar, Christian Borys, and Eric Woods, "The Blackwater of Jihad," *Foreign Policy*, February 10, 2017, https://foreignpolicy.com/2017/02/10/the-world-first-jihadi-private-military-contractor-syria-russia-malhama-tactical/.

14. Komar, Borys, and Woods, "Blackwater of Jihad"; Uran Botobekov, "What Is the Future of Malhama Tactical?," *Eurasia Review*, December 30, 2018, https://www.eurasi areview.com/30122018-what-is-the-future-of-malhama-tactical-analysis/.

15. Hoffman, *Inside Terrorism*, 259.

16. Hoffman, 259.

17. See also Comfort Ero, "Vigilantes, Civil Defence Forces and Militia Groups: The Other Side of the Privatisation of Security in Africa," *Conflict Trends* (June 2000).

18. On the consequences of irresponsible policy choices generally, see Henkin, *How Nations Behave*, 50–60; Byers, *War Law*, 11; and Thomas, *Ethics of Destruction*, 35–37. For various views on the effectiveness of sanctions on Russia, see Andrew Chatzky, "Have Sanc-tions on Russia Changed Putin's Calculus?," Council on Foreign Relations, May 2, 2019, https://www.cfr.org/article/have-sanctions-russia-changed-putins-calculus; US Congres-sional Research Service, *U.S. Sanctions on Russia*, January 11, 2019, https://fas.org/sgp/crs/row/R45415.pdf; and Nigel Gould-Davies, "Economic Effects and Political impacts: Assess-ing Western Sanctions on Russia," BOFIT Policy Brief 2018, no. 8, August 9, 2018, https://helda.helsinki.fi/bof/bitstream/handle/123456789/15832/bpb0818.pdf?sequence=1.

19. Gray, *International Law*, 25.

20. Khalil Shikaki, "Can Hamas Moderate? Insights from Palestinian Politics dur-ing 2005–2011," Crown Center for Middle Eastern Studies, January 2015, https://www.brandeis.edu/crown/publications/meb/MEB88.pdf.

21. See Imad Alsoos and Nathan J. Brown, "Hamas: Constrained or Nimble?," Carnegie Endowment for International Peace, April 11, 2018, https://carnegieendowment.org/2018/04/11/hamas-constrained-or-nimble-pub-76047; Karin Brulliard, "In Gaza, Hamas Rule Has Not Turned Out as Many Expected," *Washington Post*, April 18, 2012, https://www.washingtonpost.com/world/asia_pacific/in-gaza-hamas-rule-has-not-turned-out-as-many-expected/2012/04/18/gIQAVWRxRT_story.html?utm_term=.cce937590781.

22. Renad Mansour, "More than Militias: Iraq's Popular Mobilization Forces Are Here to Stay," War on the Rocks, April 3, 2018, https://warontherocks.com/2018/04/more-than-militias-iraqs-popular-mobilization-forces-are-here-to-stay/; Abigail Hauslohner, "In Former Gaddafi Stronghold, a Sign of Libya's Deepening Divide," *Washington Post*, November 2, 2012, https://www.washingtonpost.com/world/middle_east/in-former-gaddafi-stronghold-a-sign-of-libyas-deepening-divide/2012/11/01/ef89990c-22ad-11e2-8448-81b1ce7d6978_story.html?utm_term=.69547dad58ef; Bertrand, "Syria 'Is Being Swallowed Whole.'"

23. Ryan E. Holroyd, "The Twilight of the Colombian Paramilitary," *Past Imperfect* 17 (2011): 69–70.

24. Sabrina Tavernese, "Cleric Is Said to Lose Reins of Parts of Iraqi Militia," *New York Times*, September 27, 2006.

25. J. J. Messner, interview by author, August 3, 2007, Washington, DC; Prince, "How Blackwater Serves America."

26. See Avant, *Market for Force*, chap. 6, and Laura A. Dickinson, "Accountability of Private Security Contractors under International and Domestic Law," *American Society of International Law* 11, no. 31 (2007), https://www.asil.org/insights/volume/11/issue/31/accountability-private-security-contractors-under-international-and. For an overview of this literature, see Krahmann, "Private Security and Military Actors."

27. P. W. Singer, "The Dark Truth about Blackwater," Brookings Institution, October 2, 2007, https://www.brookings.edu/articles/the-dark-truth-about-blackwater/.

28. McFate, "America's Addiction to Mercenaries."

29. Janine Roberts, *Glitter and Greed: The Secret World of the Diamond Cartel* (New York: Disinformation Books, 2007), 216.

30. Singer, *Corporate Warriors*, 158.

31. US House of Representatives, *Warlord, Inc.*, iii.

32. US House of Representatives, 34–40.

33. Kiril Avramov and Ruslan Trad, "An Experimental Playground: The Footprint of Russian Private Military Companies in Syria," *Defense Post*, February 17, 2018, https://thedefensepost.com/2018/02/17/russia-private-military-contractors-syria/.

34. Pierre Sautreuil, "Believe It or Not, Russia Dislikes Relying on Military Contractors," War Is Boring, May 8, 2016, https://medium.com/war-is-boring/believe-it-or-not-russia-dislikes-relying-on-military-contractors-8bad373f4793.

35. Quoted in Sautreuil, "Believe It or Not."

36. Tor Bukkvoll, comments at the Annual Meeting of the International Studies Association, San Francisco, April 5, 2018.

37. Mazzetti and Schmitt, "Private Army Formed to Fight Somali Pirates."

38. McFate, "America's Addiction to Mercenaries." See also Max Brooks, "Privatizing the United States Army Was a Mistake," *New York Times*, February 3, 2020.

39. Quoted in Srivastava, "Sovereignty under Contract," 27–28.

40. Srivastava, 6.

41. Scahill, *Blackwater*, 366–68.

42. Mazzetti and Hager, "Secret Desert Force."

43. Shawn Snow and Mackenzie Wolf, "Blackwater Founder Wants to Boost the Afghan Air War with His Private Air Force," *Military Times*, August 2, 2017, https://www.militarytimes.com/flashpoints/2017/08/02/blackwater-founder-wants-to-run-the-afghan-air-war-with-his-private-air-force/; Jeremy Scahill and Matthew Cole, "Echo Papa Exposed: Inside Erik Prince's Treacherous Drive to Build a Private Air Force," *The Intercept*, April 11, 2016, https://theintercept.com/2016/04/11/blackwater-founder-erik-prince-drive-to-build-private-air-force/; Mazzetti and Schmitt, "Private Army Formed."

44. Roston, "Chinese Blackwater?"

45. Allison Quinn, "Vladimir Putin Sent Russian Mercenaries to 'Fight in Syria and Ukraine'," *The Telegraph*, March 30, 2016, https://www.telegraph.co.uk/news/2016/03/30/vladimir-putin-sent-russian-mercenaries-to-fight-in-syria-and-uk/; Tim Lister, Mary Ilyushina, and Sebastian Shukla, "Several Russians Killed in US Airstrikes in Syria, Friends Say," CNN, February 13, 2018, https://www.cnn.com/2018/02/13/middleeast/russians-killed-us-airstrikes-syria-intl/index.html.

46. Cole and Emmons, "Erik Prince Offered Lethal Services."

47. Shane Harris, "Irony Alert: Pentagon Now Fears a Big Data National Security Threat," *Foreign Policy*, August 12, 2013, http://killerapps.foreignpolicy.com/posts/2013/08/12/irony_alert_pentagon_now_fears_a_big_data_national_security_threat.

48. Thomson, *Mercenaries, Pirates, and Sovereigns.*

49. Gibbons-Neff, "How a 4-Hour Battle." The *Times* article notes that private groups such as Wagner typically "earn of a share of the production proceeds from the oil fields they reclaim," creating a powerful incentive to launch attacks independently.

50. This is a problem even when nonstate actors collaborate with states; one concern about the increased use of PMSCs by the US government is that it lowers the threshold for using force and therefore effectively bypasses the democratic process for making such decisions. Allison Stanger, "Hired Guns: How Private Military Contractors Undermine World Order," *Foreign Affairs* 94, no. 4 (July/August 2015); Singer, *Corporate Warriors*, 213–15. Supporting other types of violent nonstate actors is likely to be more clandestine and thus even less subject to political debate.

51. Michael C. McGarrity, "Confronting the Rise of Domestic Terrorism in the Homeland," statement of Michael C. McGarrity (assistant director, FBI Counterterrorism Division) before the House Homeland Security Committee, May 8, 2019, https://www.fbi.gov/news/testimony/confronting-the-rise-of-domestic-terrorism-in-the-homeland; US Government Accountability Office, *Countering Violent Extremism Actions Needed to Define Strategy and Assess Progress of Federal Efforts* (Washington, DC: April 2017), 28–34, http://www.gao.gov/assets/690/683984.pdf.

52. Kurt Eichenwald, "Right Wing Extremists Are a Bigger Threat to America than ISIS," *Newsweek*, February 4, 2016, https://www.newsweek.com/2016/02/12/right-wing-extremists-militants-bigger-threat-america-isis-jihadists-422743.html; Casey Michel, "How Militias Became the Private Police for White Supremacists," *Politico*, August 17, 2017, https://www.politico.com/magazine/story/2017/08/17/white-supremacists-militias-private-police-215498; Simon Romero, "F.B.I. Arrests Leader of Right-Wing Militia That Detained Migrants in New Mexico," *New York Times*, April 20, 2019; Kate Sullivan, "Oregon GOP State Senators Again Fail to Show Up for Legislative Session amid Climate Bill Protest," CNN, June 23, 2019, https://www.cnn.com/2019/06/23/politics/oregon-gop-state-senators-legislative-session-climate/index.html.

53. Ostensen and Bukkvoll, *Russian Use of Private Military*, 7.

54. In March 2020 a UK-based law firm representing Yemeni victims of the operations presented evidence to the US Justice Department, requesting an investigation.

The Justice Department declined comment. Stoke White, "Press Release—Legal Proceedings on Behalf of Yemeni Clients," March 30, 2020, https://www.stokewhite.com/press-release-legal-proceedings-on-behalf-of-yemeni-clients/.

55. Deborah Avant, "Former U.S. Special Forces Were Reportedly Hired to Kill Yemen's Leaders. Did the Government Know?," *Washington Post*, October 19, 2018, https://www.washingtonpost.com/news/monkey-cage/wp/2018/10/19/former-u-s-special-forces-were-reportedly-hired-to-kill-yemens-leaders-did-the-government-know/?noredirect=on&utm_term=.faede85d9771.

56. On privateering, see Alexander Tabarrok and Alex Nowrasteh, "Privateers! Their History and Future," *Fletcher Security Review* 12, no. 1 (2015); David Isenberg, "PSCs: Privateer Security Contractors," *Huffington Post*, March 20, 2012 (updated May 20, 2012), https://m.huffpost.com/us/entry/1354991/amp; Ian C. Rice and Douglas A. Borer, "Bring Back the Privateers," *National Interest*, April 22, 2015, https://nationalinterest.org/feature/bring-back-the-privateers-12695. On collaboration with transnational criminal organizations, see Robert Mandel, "Fighting Fire with Fire: Privatizing Counterterrorism," paper presented at the Annual Meeting of the International Studies Association, Montreal, March 17–20, 2004.

57. W. Michael Reisman and Andrea Armstrong, "The Past and Future of the Claim of Preemptive Self-Defense," *American Journal of International Law* 100, no. 3 (July 2006); Matthew Light, "Roy Allison, Russia, the West, and Military Intervention," *Journal of Power Institutions in Post-Soviet Studies* 17 (2016), https://journals.openedition.org/pipss/4180; Alexander Velez-Green, "Russian Strategists Debate Preemption as Defense against NATO Surprise Attack," Russia Matters, March 14, 2018, https://www.russiamatters.org/analysis/russian-strategists-debate-preemption-defense-against-nato-surprise-attack; "Russian First Deputy Defense Minister Gerasimov: 'Our Response' Is Based on the 'Active Defense Strategy'; 'We Must Act Quickly' to 'Preempt the Enemy . . . Identify His Vulnerabilities, and Create Threats of Unacceptable Damage to It,'" *Middle East Media Research Institute*, March 14, 2019, https://www.memri.org/reports/russian-first-deputy-defense-minister-gerasimov-our-response-based-active-defense-strategy.

58. Donald Rumsfeld, "Defense Department Briefing, December 4," December 4, 2001, Global Security, http://www.globalsecurity.org/military/library/news/2001/12/mil-011204-usia01b.htm.

59. Adam Taylor, "Trump Said He Would 'Take Out' the Families of ISIS Fighters. Did an Airstrike in Syria Do Just That?," *Washington Post*, May 27, 2017.

60. See, e.g., Micah Zenko, "Obama's Embrace of Drone Strikes Will Be a Lasting Legacy," *New York Times*, January 20, 2016.

61. Edward Hallett Carr, *The Twenty Years' Crisis, 1919–1939* (New York: St. Martin's, 1939), 230–31.

62. Hedley Bull, *The Anarchical Society: A Study of Order in World Politics* (New York: Columbia University Press, 1977), 257–81.

63. Bull, *Anarchical Society*, 268.

64. James N. Rosenau, *Turbulence in World Politics: A Theory of Change and Continuity* (Princeton, NJ: Princeton University Press, 1990), 6. See also Mathews, "Power Shift."

65. Singer, *Corporate Warriors*, 212.

66. See, e.g., Keck and Sikkink, *Activists beyond Borders*; Price, "Reversing the Gun Sights"; Hurrell, *On Global Order*; and Ann M. Florini, ed., *The Third Force: The Rise of Transnational Civil Society* (Washington, DC: Carnegie Endowment for International Peace, 2000).

67. Van Creveld, *Rise and Decline of the State*, 408 (emphasis in original).

68. Stanger, "Hired Guns," 164, 166.

69. For a critique of the common condemnation of states as obstacles to progressive principles, see Mona Harrington, "What Exactly Is Wrong with the Liberal State as an Agent of Change?," in *Gendered States: Feminist (Re)Visions of International Relations Theory*, ed. V. Spike Peterson (Boulder: Lynne Rienner, 1992), 65–82.

70. For a critique of post–Cold War self-determination, see Amitai Etzioni, "The Evils of Self-Determination," *Foreign Policy* 89 (Winter 1992/93).

Bibliography

Abi-Saab, Georges. "Wars of National Liberation in the Geneva Conventions and Proto-cols." *Recueil des Cours* 165, no. 4 (1979): 353–445.

Abrisketa, Joana. "Blackwater: Mercenaries and International Law." *FRIDE Comment* (October 2007): 1–12.

Abu-Lughod, Ibrahim. "Unconventional Violence and International Politics." *American Journal of International Law* 67, no. 5 (1973): 100–104.

"Ad Hoc Committee Established by General Assembly Resolution 51/210 of 17 December 1996." United Nations. https://legal.un.org/committees/terrorism/.

Adams, Thomas. "The New Mercenaries and the Privatization of Conflict." *Parameters* (Summer 1999): 103–16.

"Affirmation of the Principles of International Law Recognized by the Charter of the Nurnberg Tribunal." Audiovisual Library of International Law. Accessed June 19, 2012. http://untreaty.un.org/cod/avl/ha/ga_95-I/ga_95-I.html.

Agence France-Presse. "ISIS Uses 2,000 Civilians from Northern Syria as 'Human Shields.'" The World, August 12, 2016. PRI. https://www.pri.org/stories/2016-08-12/isis-uses-2000-civilians-northern-syria-human-shields.

Ahmad, Eqbal. "Terrorism: Theirs and Ours." Address at the University of Colorado, October 12, 1998. https://sangam.org/ANALYSIS/Ahmad.htm.

Algerian Office. *White Paper on the Application of the Geneva Conventions of 1949 to the French-Algerian Conflict.* New York: Algerian Office, 1960.

All Parties Hurryat Conference. "Letter of the Chairman to the Secretary General of the Islamic Conference." May 13, 2007. Accessed September 25, 2008. www.hurryat.net (site discontinued).

Alsoos, Imad, and Nathan J. Brown. "Hamas: Constrained or Nimble?" Carnegie Endowment for International Peace, April 11, 2018. https://carnegieendowment.org/2018/04/11/hamas-constrained-or-nimble-pub-76047.

Amnesty International. "Syria: The Worst Humanitarian Crisis of Our Time." AI, April 7, 2015. https://www.amnesty.org.nz/syria-worst-humanitarian-crisis-our-time.

Andreopoulos, George J. "The Age of National Liberation Movements." In *The Laws of War: Constraints on Warfare in the Western World*, edited by Michael Howard, George J. Andreopoulos, and Mark R. Shulman, 191–213. New Haven, CT: Yale University Press, 1994.

"Arabs Hold 22 Israelis from Hijacked Airliner." *Boston Globe*, July 24, 1968.

Arafat, Yasser. "Address to the UN General Assembly in New York, 13 November 1974.'" https://al-bab.com/documents-section/speech-yasser-arafat-1974.

Arend, Anthony Clark, and Robert J. Beck. *International Law and the Use of Force: Beyond the UN Charter Paradigm.* London: Routledge, 1993.

"Armed Groups' Holdings of Guided Light Weapons." *Small Arms Survey* (December 2014). http://www.smallarmssurvey.org/fileadmin/docs/H-Research_Notes/SAS-Research-Note-47.pdf.

"Assad May Be Losing Control over His Own Militias." *Business Insider*, August 18, 2016. https://www.businessinsider.com/syrian-regime-militias-becoming-warlords-2016-8.

Associated Press. "Probe of Arab Arms Training Planned." *Wisconsin State Journal*, February 11, 1975.

Avant, Deborah. "Former U.S. Special Forces Were Reportedly Hired to Kill Yemen's Leaders. Did the Government Know?" *Washington Post*, October 19, 2018. https://www.washingtonpost.com/news/monkey-cage/wp/2018/10/19/former-u-s-special-forces-were-reportedly-hired-to-kill-yemens-leaders-did-the-gov ernment-know/?noredirect=on&utm_term=.faede85d9771.

——. "From Mercenary to Citizen Armies: Explaining Change in the Practice of War." *International Organization* 54, no. 1 (Winter 2000): 41–72.

——. "The Privatization of Security and Change in the Control of Force." *International Studies Perspectives* 5 (2004): 153–57.

Avant, Deborah D. *The Market for Force: The Consequences of Privatizing Security*. Cambridge: Cambridge University Press, 2005.

——. "The New Institutional Economics and Norms of Warfare." Paper presented at the Annual Meeting of the International Studies Association, Washington, DC, March 28–April 1, 1994.

——. "Pragmatic Networks and Transnational Governance of Private Military and Security Companies." *International Studies Quarterly* (2016): 330–42.

Avant, Deborah, and Virginia Haufler. "Public-Private Interactions and Practices of Security." In *The Oxford Handbook of International Security*, edited by Alexandra Gheciu and William C. Wohlforth, 350–64. Oxford: Oxford University Press, 2015.

Avant, Deborah D., Martha Finnemore, and Susan K. Sell, eds. *Who Governs the Globe?* Cambridge: Cambridge University Press, 2010.

Avramov, Kiril, and Ruslan Trad. "An Experimental Playground: The Footprint of Russian Private Military Companies in Syria." *Defense Post*, February 17, 2018. https://thedefensepost.com/2018/02/17/russia-private-military-contractors-syria/.

Awan, Jawad R. "Davis CIA's Acting Chief in Pakistan." *The Nation*, February 21, 2011. https://www.nation.com.pk/pakistan-news-newspaper-daily-english-online/ Politics/21-Feb-2011/Davis-CIAs-acting-chief-in-Pakistan/1.

Baker, Mike. "Ex-Blackwater President, 4 Others Indicted on Conspiracy, Weapons Charges." Huffington Post, April 10, 2010. http://www.huffingtonpost.com/2010/ 04/16/gary-jackson-exblackwater_n_541046.html?view=screen.

Ballesteros, Enrique Bernales. "Use of Mercenaries as a Means of Violating Human Rights and Impeding the Exercise of the Right of Peoples to Self-Determination." UN doc. E/CN.4/2004/15. December 24, 2003.

——. "Use of Mercenaries as a Means of Violating Human Rights and Impeding the Exercise of the Right of Peoples to Self-Determination." UN doc. E/CN.4/1997/24. February 20, 1997.

Barkin, J. Samuel, and Bruce Cronin. "The State and the Nation: Changing Norms and the Rules of Sovereignty in International Relations." *International Organization* 48, no. 1 (Winter 1994): 107–30.

Barnard, Anne. "Car Bombing Injures Dozens in Hezbollah Section of Beirut." *New York Times*, July 9, 2013. https://www.https://www.nytimes.com/2013/07/10/ world/middleeast/syria.html.

——. "Hezbollah's Role in Syria War Shakes the Lebanese." *New York Times*, May 20, 2013. https://www.nytimes.com/2013/05/21/world/middleeast/syria-develop ments.html?pagewanted=all&_r=0.

Barraclough, Geoffrey. *An Introduction to Contemporary History*. New York: Basic Books, 1964.

Bassiouni, M. Cherif. "Methodological Options for International Legal Control of Terrorism." *Akron Law Review* 7, no. 3 (Spring 1974): 388–96.

Baxter, Richard. "The Duty of Obedience to the Belligerent Occupant." *British Yearbook of International Law* 27 (1950): 235–59.

——. "A Skeptical Look at the Concept of Terrorism." *Akron Law Review* 7, no. 3 (1974): 380–87.

Beehner, Lionel. "What Good Is a Terrorism List?" *Los Angeles Times*, October 20, 2008. https://www.latimes.com/archives/la-xpm-2008-oct-20-oe-beehner20-story.html.

Bellal, Annyssa. *The War Report: Armed Conflict in 2018*. Geneva: Geneva Academy of International Humanitarian Law and Human Rights, 2019. https://www.geneva-academy.ch/joomlatools-files/docman-files/The%20War%20Report%20 2018.pdf.

Bellamy, Alex J. *The Responsibility to Protect: Towards a "Living Reality."* United Nations Association–UK, 2013. https://www.una.org.uk/sites/default/files/ The%20Responsibility%20to%20Protect%20Towards%20a%20Living%20Real ity%20-%20Professor%20Alex%20Bellamy.pdf.

Berger, Thomas U. *Cultures of Antimilitarism: National Security in Germany and Japan*. Baltimore: Johns Hopkins University Press, 2003.

Bergner, Daniel. "The Other Army." *New York Times*, August 15, 2005.

Bertrand, Natasha. "Syria 'Is Being Swallowed Whole by Its Clients': Assad May Be Losing Control over His Own Militias." *Business Insider*, August 18, 2016. https://www.businessinsider.com/syrian-regime-militias-becoming-warlords-2016-8.

Best, Geoffrey. "Civilians in Contemporary Wars." War studies lecture at King's College, University of London, 1983. Accessed April 23, 2006. www.airpower.max well.af.mil/airchronicles/aureview/1984/mar-apr/best.html (inactive link).

——. *War and Law since 1945*. Oxford: Clarendon Press, 1994.

Biersteker, Thomas, and Cynthia Weber, eds. *State Sovereignty as Social Construct*. Cambridge: Cambridge University Press, 1996.

Blackwater USA. "About Us." Accessed July 13, 2006. www.blackwaterusa.com/about/ (site discontinued).

Blackwater Worldwide. "A Request for Your Support." Email to author, October 24, 2007.

Bobea, Lilian. "How Caribbean Organized Crime Is Replacing the State." In *Insight Crime*, July 23, 2013. https://www.insightcrime.org/news/analysis/the-benefits-of-organized-crime-in-the-caribbean/.

Bolts, Shlomo. "The Many Loopholes in 'ISIS Is Defeated.'" Defense One, March 6, 2019. https:///www.defenseone.com/ideas/2019/03/many-loopholes-isis-defeated/ 155314/.

Bothe, Michael, Karl Josef Partsch, and Waldemar A. Solf. *New Rules for Victims of Armed Conflicts: Commentary on the Two 1977 Protocols Additional to the Geneva Conventions of 1949*. Boston: Martinus Nijhoff, 1982.

Botobekov, Uran. "What Is the Future of Malhama Tactical?" *Eurasia Review*, December 30, 2018. https://www.eurasiareview.com/30122018-what-is-the-future-of-malhama-tactical-analysis/.

Bowman, Tom. "As U.S. Military Exits Iraq, Contractors to Enter." National Public Radio, May 17, 2011.

Branigan, William. "Taliban's Human Shields." *Washington Post*, October 24, 2001.

Breslawski, Jori. "Terrorists, Militants and Criminal Gangs Join the Fight against the Coronavirus." The Conversation, April 10, 2020. https://theconversation.com/terrorists-militants-and-criminal-gangs-join-the-fight-against-the-coronavirus-135914.

Briggs, Herbert W., ed. *The Law of Nations*. New York: Appleton-Century-Crofts, 1952.

British Association of Private Security Contractors. "Key Documents." BAPSC. http://www.bapsc.org.uk/key-documents.html.

Broder, John M. "U.S. Military to Supervise Iraq Security Convoys." *New York Times*, October 31, 2007.

Broder, John M., and James Risen. "Blackwater Mounts a Defense with Top Talent." *New York Times*, November 1, 2007. https://www.nytimes.com/2007/11/01/washington/01blackwater-sub.html?pagewanted=all.

———. "Contractors Deaths in Iraq Soar to Record." *New York Times*, May 19, 2007. https://www.nytimes.com/2007/05/19/world/middleeast/19contractors.html.

Brooks, Doug. "How Many Is Too Many?" *Journal of International Peace Operations* 5, no. 4 (January/February 2010): 6.

———. Interview by author. Washington, DC, August 3, 2007.

———. "Shifting the Blame." *Journal of International Peace Operations* 5, no. 6 (May/June 2010): 4. http://www.privatemilitary.org/ISOA/JIPO-2010-05-IPOA-Haiti.pdf.

Brooks, Max. "Privatizing the United States Army Was a Mistake." *New York Times*, February 3, 2020.

Brulin, Remi. "Defining 'Terrorism': The 1972 General Assembly Debates on 'International Terrorism' and Their Coverage in the *New York Times*." In *Societies under Siege: Media, Government, Politics and Citizens' Freedoms in an Age of Terrorism*, ed. Banu B. Hawks (Cambridge: Cambridge Scholar Press, 2012). https://www.nytexaminer.com/2013/09/defining-terrorism/.

Brulliard, Karin. "In Gaza, Hamas Rule Has Not Turned Out as Many Expected." *Washington Post*, April 18, 2012. https://www.washingtonpost.com/world/asia_pacific/in-gaza-hamas-rule-has-not-turned-out-as-many-expected/2012/04/18/gIQAVWRxRT_story.html?utm_term=.cce937590781.

Buchanan, John. *Militias in Myanmar* (Yangon: Asia Foundation, 2016). https://asiafoundation.org/wp-content/uploads/2016/07/Militias-in-Myanmar.pdf.

Bukkvoll, Tor. Comments at the Annual Meeting of the International Studies Association, San Francisco, California, April 5, 2018.

Bull, Hedley. *The Anarchical Society: A Study of Order in World Politics*. New York: Columbia University Press, 1977.

———. "The Revolt against the West." In Hedley Bull and Adam Watson, eds., *The Expansion of International Society*. Oxford: Oxford University Press, 1985, 217–28.

Burmester, H. C. "The Recruitment and Use of Mercenaries in Armed Conflicts." *American Journal of International Law* 72, no. 1 (January 1978): 37–56.

Burns, John F. "The Deadly Game of Private Security." *New York Times*, September 23, 2007.

Buštíková, Lenka. "The Radical Right in Eastern Europe." *The Oxford Handbook of the Radical Right*. February 2018. http://www.oxfordhandbooks.com/view/10.1093/oxfordhb/9780190274559.001.0001/oxfordhb-9780190274559-e-28.

Byers, Michael. *War Law: Understanding International Law and Armed Conflict*. New York: Grove, 2005.

Byman, Daniel L. "Beyond Counterterrorism." *Foreign Affairs* 94, no. 6 (November/December 2015): 11–18.

———. "The Changing Nature of State Sponsorship of Terrorism." Analysis Paper no. 16, Saban Center for Middle East Policy, Brookings Institution, May 2008. https://www.brookings.edu/wp-content/uploads/2016/06/05_terrorism_byman.pdf.

———. *Deadly Connections: States That Sponsor Terrorism*. Cambridge: Cambridge University Press, 2005.

Cameron, Lindsey. "Private Military Companies: Their Status under International Humanitarian Law and Its Impact on Their Regulation." *International Review of the Red Cross* 88, no. 863 (September 2006): 573–98. https://www.icrc.org/en/doc/assets/files/other/irrc_863_cameron.pdf.

Campbell, Duncan. "Marketing the New 'Dogs of War.'" Center for Public Integrity. October 30, 2002. https://publicintegrity.org/national-security/making-a-killing/marketing-the-new-dogs-of-war/.

Carey, Sabine C., and Neil J. Mitchell. "Pro-Government Militias and Conflict." Oxford Research Encyclopedias: Politics. October 2016. http://oxfordre.com/politics/view/10.1093/acrefore/9780190228637.001.0001/acrefore-9780190228637-e-33.

Carr, Edward Hallett. *The Twenty Years' Crisis, 1919–1939.* New York: St. Martin's, 1939.

Carter, Jimmy. "Just War—or a Just War?" *New York Times*, February 9, 2003. https://www.nytimes.com/2003/03/09/opinion/just-war-or-a-just-war.html.

Cass, Loren. *The Failures of American and European Climate Policy: International Norms, Domestic Politics, and Unachievable Commitments.* Albany: State University of New York Press, 2006.

——. "Norm Entrapment and Preference Change: The Evolution of the European Union Position on International Emissions Trading." *Global Environmental Politics* 5, no. 2 (May 2005): 38–60.

Cassese, Antonio. *International Law.* 2nd ed. Oxford: Oxford University Press, 2005.

——. "Mercenaries: Lawful Combatants or War Criminals?" *ZaoRV* 40 (1980): 1–30. http://www.zaoerv.de/40_1980/40_1980_1_a_1_30.pdf.

Chatzky, Andrew. "Have Sanctions on Russia Changed Putin's Calculus?" Council on Foreign Relations, May 2, 2019. https://www.cfr.org/article/have-sanctions-russia-changed-putins-calculus.

Chughtai, Alia. "Syria's War: Who Controls What?" Al Jazeera, March 13, 2019. https://www.aljazeera.com/indepth/interactive/2015/05/syria-country-divided-150529144229467.html.

Claude, Inis L., Jr. "Collective Legitimization as a Political Function of the United Nations." *International Organization* 20, no. 3 (Summer 1966): 367–79.

Coady, Tony, and Michael O'Keefe, eds. *Terrorism and Justice: Moral Argument in a Threatened World.* Victoria: Melbourne University Press, 2002.

Cohen, Eliot A. *Citizens and Soldiers: The Dilemmas of Military Service.* Ithaca, NY: Cornell University Press, 1985.

Cohen, Guela. *Woman of Violence: Memoirs of a Young Terrorist.* New York: Holt Rinehart, 1966.

Cohen, Raphael S., David E. Johnson, David E. Thaler, Brenna Allen, Elizabeth M. Bartels, James Cahill, and Shira Efron. *Lessons from Israel's Wars in Gaza.* Santa Monica, CA: RAND Corp., 2017.

Coker, Christopher. "Outsourcing War." In *Non-State Actors in World Politics*, edited by Daphné Josselin and William Wallace, 189–202. Houndmills, UK: Palgrave, 2001.

Cole, Matthew, and Alex Emmons. "Erik Prince Offered Lethal Services to Sanctioned Russian Mercenary Firm Wagner." The Intercept, April 13, 2020. https://theintercept.com/2020/04/13/erik-prince-russia-mercenary-wagner-libya-mozambique/.

Copp, Tara. "Here's the Blueprint for Erik Prince's $5 Billion Plan to Privatize the Afghanistan War." *Military Times*, September 5, 2018. https://www.militarytimes.com/news/your-military/2018/09/05/heres-the-blueprint-for-erik-princes-5-billion-plan-to-privatize-the-afghanistan-war/.

Council of the European Union. *Proposal for a Council Framework Decision on Combating Terrorism.* December 7, 2001. CEU. Accessed March 11, 2016. https://www/europarl.europa.eu/.../CONS_CONS(2001)14845(REV1)_EN.doc (inactive link).

Crawford, Neta C. *Argument and Change in World Politics: Ethics, Decolonization, and Humanitarian Intervention.* Cambridge: Cambridge University Press, 2002.

——. "How Previous Ideas Affect Later Ideas." In *The Oxford Handbook of Contextual Political Analysis,* edited by Robert E. Goodin and Charles Tilly, 266–83. Oxford: Oxford University Press, 2006.

Crenshaw, Martha. "The Effectiveness of Terrorism in the Algerian War." In Crenshaw, *Terrorism in Context,* 473–513.

——. "The Logic of Terrorism: Terrorist Behavior as a Product of Strategic Choice." In Reich, *Origins of Terrorism,* 7–24.

——. "Thoughts on Relating Terrorism to Historical Contexts." In Crenshaw, *Terrorism in Context,* 4–23.

——. "Why America? The Globalization of Civil War." *Current History* 100, no. 650 (December 2001): 425–32.

Crenshaw, Martha, ed. *Terrorism in Context.* University Park: Pennsylvania State University Press, 1994.

Crenshaw Hutchinson, Martha. *Revolutionary Terrorism: The FLN in Algeria, 1954–1962.* Stanford, CA: Hoover Institution Press, 1978.

Cronin, Audrey Kurth. "Behind the Curve: Globalization and International Terrorism." *International Security* 27, no. 3 (Winter 2002/3): 30–58.

——. *The "FTO List" and Congress: Sanctioning Designated Foreign Terrorist Organizations.* Washington, DC: Congressional Research Service, October 21, 2003. https://fas.org/irp/crs/RL32120.pdf.

——. "ISIS Is Not a Terrorist Group." *Foreign Affairs* 94, no. 1 (January/February 2015): 87–98.

——. "Rethinking Sovereignty: American Strategy in the Age of Terrorism." *Survival* 44, no. 2 (Summer 2002): 119–39.

Cullen, Patrick. "Keeping the New Dog of War on a Tight Leash: Assessing Means of Accountability from Private Military Companies." *Conflict Trends* 2000, no. 1 (June 2000): 36–39.

Daoud, David. "Hezbollah's Latest Conquest: Lebanon's Cabinet." *Newsweek,* January 12, 2017. https://www.newsweek.com/hezbollahs-latest-conquest-lebanons-cabinet-541487.

Deen, Thalif. "UN Rejects Private Peacekeepers." Inter Press Service, August 27, 2004. https://www.globalpolicy.org/security/peacekpg/training/0827rejects.htm.

Delalande, Arnaud. "Erik Prince's Mercenaries Are Bombing Libya." War Is Boring, January 14, 2017. https://warisboring.com/erik-princes-mercenaries-are-bombing-libya/.

Desch, Michael C. "It's Kind to be Cruel: The Humanity of American Realism." *Review of International Studies* 29, no. 3 (2003): 415–26.

DeYoung, Karen, Shane Harris, and Dan Lamothe. "Erik Prince, in Kabul, Pushes Privatization of the Aghan War." *Washington Post,* October 4, 2018. https://www.washingtonpost.com/world/national-security/erik-prince-in-kabul-pushes-privatization-of-the-afghan-war/2018/10/04/72a76d36-c7e5-11e8-b1ed-1d2d65b86d0c_story.html?noredirect=on&utm_term=.6a8a804bbe0e.

"The Diamond Mercenaries of Africa." Radio National (Australia). August 4, 1996. http://www.abc.net.au/radionational/programs/backgroundbriefing/the-diamond-mercenaries-of-africa/3564008.

Dickinson, Laura A. "Accountability of Private Security Contractors under International and Domestic Law." *American Society of International Law* 11, no. 31 (2007). https://www.asil.org/insights/volume/11/issue/31/accountability-private-security-contractors-under-international-and.

Dinstein, Yoram. "Comments on Protocol I." *International Review of the Red Cross* 320 (1997): 515–19.

Douhet, Giulio. *The Command of the Air*. 2nd ed. Joseph Patrick Harahan and Richard H. Kohn, eds. Tuscaloosa: University of Alabama Press, 2009.

Draper, Gerald. "Wars of National Liberation and War Criminality." In *Restraints on War: Studies in the Limitation of Armed Conflict*, edited by Michael Howard, 135–62. Oxford: Oxford University Press, 1979.

Dugard, John. "International Terrorism: Problems of Definition." *International Affairs* 50, no. 1 (January 1974): 67–81.

——. "International Terrorism and the Just War." *Stanford Journal of International Studies* 12 (1977): 21–37.

Dunigan, Molly, Carrie M. Farmer, Rachel M. Burns, Alison Hawks, and Claude Messan Setodji. *Out of the Shadows: The Health and Well-Being of Private Contractors Working in Conflict Environments*. Santa Monica, CA: RAND Corp, 2013. https://www.rand.org/content/dam/rand/pubs/research_reports/RR400/RR420/RAND_RR420.pdf.

Dunlap, Charles J. "Lawfare Today: A Perspective." *Yale Journal of International Affairs* 3, no. 1 (2008): 146–54.

Eckert, Amy L. *Outsourcing War: The Just War Tradition in the Age of Military Privatization*. Ithaca, NY: Cornell University Press, 2016.

Eichenwald, Kurt. "Right Wing Extremists Are a Bigger Threat to America than ISIS." *Newsweek*, February 4, 2016. https://www.newsweek.com/2016/02/12/right-wing-extremists-militants-bigger-threat-america-isis-jihadists-422743.html.

Ellickson, Robert C. "The Evolution of Social Norms: A Perspective from the Legal Academy." In *Social Norms*, edited by Michael Hechter and Karl-Dieter Opp, 35–75. New York: Russell Sage Foundation, 2001.

Englehart, Neil A. "Non-State Armed Groups as a Threat to Global Security: What Threat, Whose Security?" *Journal of Global Security Studies* 1, no. 2 (May 2016): 171–83.

English, Richard. *Armed Struggle: The History of the IRA*. Oxford: Oxford University Press, 2003.

"Erik Prince and Tucker Carlson: Neocons and Corruption of Washington Keep Us in Afghanistan." Real Clear Politics, July 8, 2020. https://www.realclearpolitics.com/video/2020/07/08/erik_prince_and_tucker_carlson_neocons_and_corruption_of_washington_keep_us_in_afghanistan.html.

Ero, Comfort. "Vigilantes, Civil Defence Forces and Militia Groups: The Other Side of the Privatisation of Security in Africa." *Conflict Trends* (June 2000): 25–29.

Etzioni, Amitai. "The Evils of Self-Determination." *Foreign Policy* 89 (Winter 1992/93): 21–35.

"The Executive Mercenaries." *Time*, February 24, 1975, 20.

Fainaru, Steve. "Iraq Contractors Face Growing Parallel War." *Washington Post*, June 16, 2007. http://www.washingtonpost.com/wp-dyn/content/article/2007/06/15/AR2007061502602.html.

——. "Where Military Rules Don't Apply: Blackwater's Security Force in Iraq Give Wide Latitude by State Dept." *Washington Post*, September 20, 2007.

Falconer, Bruce. "IPOA Smackdown: DynCorp vs. Blackwater." *Mother Jones*, November 12, 2007. http://motherjones.com/print/6834.

Falk, Richard A. "On the Quasi-Legislative Competence of the General Assembly." *American Journal of International Law* 60, no. 4 (October 1966): 782–91.

Fallah, Katherine. "Corporate Actors: The Legal Status of Mercenaries in Armed Conflict." *International Review of the Red Cross* 88, no. 863 (September 2006): 599–611. https://www.icrc.org/en/doc/assets/files/other/irrc_863_fallah.pdf.

Feith, Douglas J. "Protocol I: Moving Humanitarian Law Backwards." *Akron Law Review* 19, no. 4 (Spring 1986): 531–35.

Finnemore, Martha. *National Interests in International Society*. Ithaca, NY: Cornell University Press, 1996.

Finnemore, Martha, and Kathryn Sikkink. "International Norms and Political Change." *International Organization* 52, no. 4 (1998): 887–917.

Flaherty, Mary Pat, and Dana Priest. "More Limits Sought for Private Security Teams." *Washington Post*, April 13, 2004.

Florini, Ann M. "The Evolution of International Norms." *International Studies Quarterly* (Fall 1996): 363–89.

——, ed. *The Third Force: The Rise of Transnational Civil Society*. Washington, DC: Carnegie Endowment for International Peace, 2000.

Foreign and Commonwealth Office. *Private Military Companies: Options for Regulation*. London: Stationery Office, 2002.

Fotedar, Rajesh V. "Memorandum for the Office of the Prosecutor of the International Criminal Tribunal for Rwanda; Issue: The Legal Status, under International Humanitarian Law, of Captured Mercenaries in Internal Conflicts." Fall 2003, 21. Accessed March 16, 2012. http://law.case.edu/war-crimes-research-portal/memoranda/Mercenaries.pdf (inactive link).

Freilich, Charles David. "Israel's Counter-Terrorism Policy: How Effective?" *Terrorism and Political Violence* 29, no. 2 (2017): 359–76.

Friedman, Thomas L. *The World Is Flat: A Brief History of the Twenty-First Century*. New York: Farrar, Straus and Giroux, 2005.

Frost, Mervyn. *Ethics in International Relations: A Constitutive Theory*. Cambridge: Cambridge University Press, 1996.

Fullinwider, Robert K. "Understanding Terrorism." In *Problems of International Justice*, edited by Steven Luper-Foy, 248–59. Boulder, CO: Westview, 1988.

Fussell, Paul. *The Great War and Modern Memory: 25th Anniversary Edition*. New York: Oxford University Press, 2000.

Galeotti, Mark. "Moscow's Mercenaries Reveal the Privatization of Russian Geopolitics." Open Democracy, August 29, 2017. https://www.opendemocracy.net/en/odr/chvk-wagner-and-privatisation-of-russian-geopolitics/.

——. "Moscow's Mercenaries in Syria." War on the Rocks, April 5, 2016. https://warontherocks.com/2016/04/moscows-mercenaries-in-syria/.

Ganor, Boaz. "Defining Terrorism: Is One Man's Terrorist Another Man's Freedom Fighter?" International Institute for Counter-Terrorism. January 1, 2010. https://www.ict.org.il/Article/1123/Defining-Terrorism-Is-One-Mans-Terrorist-Another-Mans-Freedom-Fighter#gsc.tab=0.

Gasser, Hans-Peter. "An Appeal for Ratification by the United States." *American Journal of International Law* 81, no. 4 (1987): 912–25.

Gearty, Conor. "Terrorism and Morality: Understanding the Language of Terrorism." In Gearty, *Essays on Human Rights and Terrorism: Comparative Approaches to Civil Liberties in Asia, the EU and North America*. London: Cameron May, 2008.

Geneva Convention Relative to the Treatment of Prisoners of War, 12 August 1949. Geneva Convention III. https://ihl-databases.icrc.org/applic/ihl/ihl.nsf/Treaty.xsp?documentId=77CB9983BE01D004C12563CD002D6B3E&action=openDocument.

Geneva International Center for Justice. *Syrian Civil War: Six Years into the Worst Humanitarian Tragedy since World War II*. Geneva: GICJ, 2017. http://www.gicj.org/images/2016/pdfs/Final-Report-Syria_June-2017.pdf.

Gentile, Gian, David E. Johnson, Lisa Saum-Manning, Raphael S. Cohen, Shara Williams, Carrie Lee, Michael Shurkin, Brenna Allen, Sarah Soliman, and James L. Doty III. *Reimagining the Character of Urban Operations for the U.S. Army: How the Past Can Inform the Present and Future*. Santa Monica, CA: RAND Corp., 2017.

Geraghty, Tony. *The Irish War*. London: HarperCollins, 1998.

Gettleman, Jeffrey. "Report Cites Vast Civilian Killings in East Congo." *New York Times*, December 13, 2009. https:///www.nytimes.com/2009/12/14/world/africa/14congo.html?_r=1.

Gibbons-Neff, Thomas. "How a 4-Hour Battle between Russian Mercenaries and U.S. Commandos Unfolded in Syria." *New York Times*, May 24, 2018. https://www.nytimes.com/2018/05/24/world/middleeast/american-commandos-russian-mercenaries-syria.html.

Giddens, Anthony A. *A Contemporary Critique of Historical Materialism, Vol. 2: The Nation-State and Violence*. Berkeley: University of California Press, 1985.

Giglio, Mike. "Inside the Shadow War Fought by Russian Mercenaries." BuzzFeed, April 17, 2019. https://www.buzzfeednews.com/article/mikegiglio/inside-wagner-mercenaries-russia-ukraine-syria-prighozhin.

Glanz, James, and Alissa J. Rubin. "From Errand to Fatal Shot to Hail of Fire to 17 Deaths." *New York Times*, October 3, 2007. https://www.nytimes.com/2007/10/03/world/middleeast/03firefight.html?mtrref=www.google.com.

———. "Iraqi Army Takes Last Basra Areas from Sadr Force." *New York Times*, April 20, 2008. https://www.nytimes.com/2008/04/20/world/middleeast/20iraq.html?th&emc=th.

Glennon, Michael J. *Limits of Law, Prerogatives of Power: Interventionism after Kosovo*. New York: Palgrave Macmillan, 2001.

Global Witness. *For a Few Dollars More: How Al-Qaeda Infiltrated the Diamond Business* (London: Global Witness, 2003). https://www.globalwitness.org/en/archive/few-dollar-more-how-al-qaeda-moved-diamond-trade/.

Goldman, Adam, and Ellen Nakashima. "CIA and Mossad Killed Senior Hezbollah Figure in Car Bombing." *Washington Post*, January 30, 2015.

Goldsmith, Jack. *The Terror Presidency*. New York: Norton, 2007.

Gordon, Michael R. "Civilians to Take U.S. Lead as Military Leaves Iraq." *New York Times*, August 18, 2010.

Gould-Davies, Nigel. "Economic Effects and Political Impacts: Assessing Western Sanctions on Russia." BOFIT Policy Brief 2018, no. 8. August 9, 2018. Bank of Finland. https://helda.helsinki.fi/bof/bitstream/handle/123456789/15832/bpb0818.pdf?sequence=1.

Gray, Christine. *International Law and the Use of Force*. Oxford: Oxford University Press, 2004.

Greenwood, Christopher. *Essays on War in International Law*. London: Cameron May, 2006.

Gross, Michael Joseph. "Gay Is the New Black?" *Advocate*, November 16, 2008. http://www.advocate.com/news/2008/11/16/gay-new-black?page=full.

Gross, Michael L. *Moral Dilemmas of Modern War*. Cambridge: Cambridge University Press, 2010.

Grovogui, Siba N. *Sovereigns, Quasi Sovereigns, and Africans: Race and Self-Determination in International Law*. Minneapolis: University of Minnesota Press, 1996.

Guelke, Adrian. *The Age of Terrorism and the International Political System*. London: I. B. Tauris, 1995.

Guevara, Che. *Guerrilla Warfare*. Lincoln: University of Nebraska Press, 1985.

"Guide to the Syrian Rebels." BBC News, December 13, 2013. https://www.bbc.com/news/world-middle-east-24403003.

Gwynn, Charles W. *Imperial Policing*. London: Macmillan 1934.

Haid, Haid. "Troublesome Allies: How the Syrian Regime Is Reintegrating Loyalist Militias." Middle East Eye, September 11, 2018. https://www.middleeasteye.net/opinion/troublesome-allies-how-syrian-regime-reintegrating-loyalist-militias.

Hamas. "The Covenant of the Islamic Resistance Movement." August 18, 1988. https://avalon.law.yale.edu/20th_century/hamas.asp.

Harrington, Mona. "What Exactly Is Wrong with the Liberal State as an Agent of Change?" In *Gendered States: Feminist (Re)Visions of International Relations Theory*, edited by V. Spike Peterson, 65–82. Boulder, CO: Lynne Rienner, 1992.

Harris, Shane. "Irony Alert: Pentagon Now Fears a Big Data National Security Threat." *Foreign Policy*, August 12, 2013. http://killerapps.foreignpolicy.com/posts/2013/08/12/irony_alert_pentagon_now_fears_a_big_data_national_security_threat.

Hartigan, Richard Shelly. *Lieber's Code and the Law of War*. Chicago: Precedent, 1983.

Hauer, Neil. "Russia's Mercenary Debacle in Syria." *Foreign Affairs*, February 26, 2018. https://www.foreignaffairs.com/articles/syria/2018-02-26/russias-mercenary-debacle-syria.

Hauslohner, Abigail. "In Former Gaddafi Stronghold, a Sign of Libya's Deepening Divide." *Washington Post*, November 2, 2012. https://www.washingtonpost.com/world/middle_east/in-former-gaddafi-stronghold-a-sign-of-libyas-deepening-divide/2012/11/01/ef89990c-22ad-11e2-8448-81b1ce7d6978_story.html?utm_term=.69547dad58ef.

Headquarters, International Security Assistance Force. "Tactical Directive." July 6, 2009. https://www.nato.int/isaf/docu/official_texts/Tactical_Directive_090706.pdf.

Henkin, Louis. *How Nations Behave: Law and Foreign Policy*. 2nd ed. New York: Columbia University Press, 1979.

Herbst, Jeffrey. "Responding to State Failure in Africa." *International Security* 21, no. 3 (Winter 1996/97): 120–44.

Hezbollah. "An Open Letter: The Hizballah Program." 1985. https://www.ict.org.il/UserFiles/The%20Hizballah%20Program%20-%20An%20Open%20Letter.pdf.

Higgins, Noelle. "The Application of International Law to Wars of National Liberation." *Journal of Humanitarian Assistance* (2004). http://sites.tufts.edu/jha/files/2011/04/a132.pdf.

Hoare, Mike. *Congo Mercenary*. London: Robert Hale, 1967.

Hodgdon, Barbara. *The First Part of King Henry the Fourth: Texts and Comments*. Boston: Bedford Books, 1997.

Hodge, Nathan. "Company Once Known as Blackwater Ditches Xe for Yet Another New Name." *Wall Street Journal*, December 21, 2011.

Hoffman, Bruce. *Inside Terrorism: Revised and Expanded Edition*. New York: Columbia University Press, 2006.

Holroyd, Ryan E. "The Twilight of the Colombian Paramilitary." *Past Imperfect* 17 (2011): 66–89.

Holsti, K. J. *Taming the Sovereigns: Institutional Change in International Politics*. Cambridge: Cambridge University Press, 2004.

Hopf, Ted. "The Promise of Constructivism in International Relations Theory." *International Security* 23, no. 1 (Summer 1998): 171–200.

Horne, Alistair. *A Savage War of Peace: Algeria 1954–1962*. New York: Viking, 1977.

Howard, Michael, George J. Andreopoulos, and Mark R. Shulman, eds. *The Laws of War: Constraints on Warfare in the Western World*. New Haven, CT: Yale University Press, 1994

Howe, Herbert M. "The Privatization of International Affairs: Global Order and the Privatization of Security." *Fletcher Forum of World Affairs Journal* 22, no. 1 (Summer/Fall 1998): 1–8.

Hufbauer, Gary Clyde, Jeffrey J. Schott, and Barbara Oegg. "Using Sanctions to Fight Terrorism." Peterson Institute for International Economics Policy Brief no. 01–11. November 2001. https://www.piie.com/publications/policy-briefs/using-sanctions-fight-terrorism.

Human Rights Watch. "Civilian Deaths in the NATO Air Campaign." 2000. https://www.hrw.org/reports/2000/nato.

——. "Colombia's Killer Networks: The Military-Paramilitary Partnership and the United States." 1996. https://www.hrw.org/legacy/reports/1996/killer2.htm.

——. "Country Summary: Israel / Occupied Palestinian Territories." January 2010. https://www.hrw.org/en/node/87711.

——. "Jenin: IDF Military Operations." May 2, 2002). https://www.hrw.org/en/reports/2002/05/02/jenin-0.

——. "Kosovo Human Rights Flash #33: Civilians at Risk by Yugoslav Use of Civilian Property for Military Purposes." April 30, 1999. https://www.hrw.org/campaigns/kosovo98/flash5.shtml.

——. *Off Target: The Conduct of the War and Civilian Casualties*. New York: Human Rights Watch, 2003.

——. "Pakistan: Taliban, Army Must Minimize Harm to Civilians." May 18, 2009. https://www.hrw.org/en/news/2009/05/18/pakistan-taliban-army-must-minimize-harm-civilians.

——. "Troops in Contact: Airstrikes and Civilian Deaths in Afghanistan." September 8, 2008. https://www.hrw.org/report/2008/09/25/troops-contact/airstrikes-and-civilian-deaths-afghanistan.

——. "War on the Displaced: Sri Lankan Army and LTTE Abuses against Civilians in the Vanni." February 19, 2009. https://www.hrw.org/report/2009/02/19/war-displaced/sri-lankan-army-and-ltte-abuses-against-civilians-vanni.

——. "Why They Died: Civilian Casualties in Lebanon during the 2006 War." September 5, 2007. https://www.hrw.org/en/node/10734.

Hunaidi, Sarah. "ISIS Has Not Been Defeated. It's Alive and Well in Southern Syria." *Foreign Policy*, April 3, 2019. https://foreignpolicy.com/2019/04/03/isis-has-not-been-defeated-its-alive-and-well-in-southern-syria/.

Hurrell, Andrew. *On Global Order*. Oxford: Oxford University Press, 2007.

Inglehart, Ronald F., and Pippa Norris. "Trump, Brexit, and the Rise of Populism: Economic Have-Nots and Cultural Backlash." HKS Working Paper no. RWP16–026. 2016. Kennedy School of Government, Harvard University.

Institute for Economics and Peace. *Global Terrorism Index 2018: Measuring the Impact of Terrorism*. Sydney: IEP, November 2018. https://www.visionofhumanity.org/wp-content/uploads/2020/10/GTI2018-A3-poster-wall-chart.pdf.

International Alert. "The Mercenary Issue at the UN Commission on Human Rights: The Need for a New Approach." 2001. https://www.international-alert.org/sites/default/files/MercenaryIssues_UNHCR_EN_2001.pdf.

International Code of Conduct Association. "Membership." Accessed December 28, 2018. https://www.icoca.ch/en/membership.

International Committee of the Red Cross. *Commentary of 1987: Combatants and Prisoners of War.* 1987. https://ihl-databases.icrc.org/applic/ihl/ihl.nsf/Comment.xsp?action=openDocument&documentId=D04A6A9CBBF8B28CC1256 3CD00433946.

——. *International Declaration Concerning the Laws and Customs of War.* 1874. https://ihl-databases.icrc.org/ihl/INTRO/135.

International Court of Justice. *Legality of the Threat or Use of Nuclear Weapons.* 1996. https://www.icj-cij.org/public/files/case-related/95/095-19960708-ADV-01-00-EN.pdf.

——. *Nicaragua v. United States.* 1986. http://www.icj-cij.org/docket/files/70/6503.pdf.

International Stability Operations Association. "Code of Conduct: Version 13.1." Accessed March 23, 2018. https://stability-operations.site-ym.com/?page=Code ofConduct_131&hhSearchTerms=%22Code+and+conduct%22.

——. "Our Members." Accessed January 2, 2019. https://stability-operations.org/page/Members.

Isenberg, David. "PSCs: Privateer Security Contractors." *Huffington Post,* May 20, 2012. https://m.huffpost.com/us/entry/1354991/amp.

"Israeli Plane Hijacked and Flown to Algiers." *Irish Times,* July 24, 1968.

Jackson, Robert H. *Quasi-States: Sovereignty, International Relations, and the Third World.* Cambridge: Cambridge University Press, 1990.

——. "The Weight of Ideas in Decolonization." In *Ideas and Foreign Policy,* edited by Judith Goldstein and Robert O. Keohane, 111–38. Ithaca, NY: Cornell University Press, 1993.

Jacobsen, Michael. "Terrorist Financing on the Internet." *CTC Sentinel* 2, no. 6 (June 2009). https://ctc.usma.edu/terrorist-financing-on-the-internet/.

Joeniemmi, Pertti. "Two Models of Mercenarism: Historical and Contemporary." *Instant Research on Peace and Violence* 7, no. 3 (1977): 184–96.

Jervis, Robert. *System Effects: Complexity in Political and Social Life.* Princeton, NJ: Princeton University Press, 1997.

Johnson, David E. "Ground Combat." RAND Commentary, December 23, 2015. RAND Corp. https://www.rand.org/blog/2015/12/ground-combat.html.

Johnson, David E., M. Wade Markel, and Brian Shannon. "The Battle of Sadr City." RAND Occasional Paper, 2011. RAND Corp. https://www.rand.org/content/dam/rand/pubs/occasional_papers/2011/RAND_OP335.pdf.

Jones, Seth G., and Martin C. Libicki. *How Terrorist Groups End: Lessons for Countering al Qa'ida.* RAND Terrorism Incident Database, 2008. RAND Corp. https://www.rand.org/news/press/2008/07/29.html.

Kaempf, Sebastian. *Saving Soldiers or Civilians? Casualty Aversion versus Civilian Protection in Asymmetric Conflicts.* Cambridge: Cambridge University Press, 2018.

Kagan, Robert. "Power and Weakness." *Policy Review* no. 113 (June 2002). https://www.hoover.org/research/power-and-weakness.

Kahl, Colin H. "In the Crossfire or the Crosshairs? Norms, Civilian Casualties, and U.S. Conduct in Iraq." *International Security* 32, no. 1 (2007): 7–46.

Keal, Paul. "'Just Backward Children': International Law and the Conquest of Non-European Peoples." *Australian Journal of International Affairs* 49, no. 2 (November 1995): 191–206.

Kearney, Richard D. "The Twenty-Fourth Session of the International Law Commission." *American Journal of International Law* 67 (1973): 84–101.

Keck, Margaret, and Kathryn Sikkink. *Activists beyond Borders.* Ithaca, NY: Cornell University Press, 1998.

Keegan, John. *A History of Warfare*. New York: Vintage Books, 1994.

Kennedy, John F. "Remarks of Senator John F. Kennedy in the Senate." Washington, DC, July 2, 1957. John F. Kennedy Presidential Library and Museum. https://www.jfklibrary.org/archives/other-resources/john-f-kennedy-speeches/united-states-senate-imperialism-19570702.

Keohane, Robert O. "The Public Delegitimation of Terrorism and Coalition Politics." In *Worlds in Collision: Terror and the Future of Global Order*, edited by Ken Booth and Tim Dunne, 141–51. New York: Palgrave Macmillan, 2002.

Khaddour, Kheder. "Syria's Troublesome Militias." Diwan, Carnegie Middle East Center, November 5, 2018. https://carnegie-mec.org/diwan/77635.

Khoshroo, Gholamali. "Statement by H. E. Mr. Gholamali Khoshroo, Ambassador and Permanent Representative of the Islamic Republic of Iran to the United Nations, on Behalf of the Non-Aligned Movement before the Sixth Committee of the 72nd Session of the United Nations General Assembly." October 2, 2017. Human Rights Voices. https://www.humanrightsvoices.org/assets/attachments/documents/Iran_6th_terrorism_statement.pdf.

Kinsella, Helen M. *The Image before the Weapon: A Critical History of the Distinction between Combatant and Civilian*. Ithaca, NY: Cornell University Press, 2011.

Kinsey, Christopher. *Corporate Soldiers and International Security: The Rise of Private Military Companies*. New York: Routledge, 2006.

Kirkpatrick, David D. "Libya Struggles to Curb Militias, the Only Police." *New York Times*, October 13, 2012. https://www.nytimes.com/2012/10/14/world/africa/libyan-government-struggles-to-rein-in-powerful-militias.html?nl=todaysheadlines&emc=edit_th_20121014&_r=0.

Klein, Alec. "U.S. Army Awards Iraq Security Work to British Firm." *Washington Post*, September 14, 2007. http://www.washingtonpost.com/wp-dyn/content/article/2007/09/13/AR2007091302237.html.

Komar, Rao, Christian Borys, and Eric Woods. "The Blackwater of Jihad." *Foreign Policy*, February 10, 2017. https://foreignpolicy.com/2017/02/10/the-world-first-jihadi-private-military-contractor-syria-russia-malhama-tactical/.

Kowert, Paul, and Jeffrey Legro. "Norms, Identities, and Their Limits: A Theoretical Reprise." In *The Culture of National Security*, edited by Peter Katzenstein, 488–90. Ithaca, NY: Cornell University Press, 1996.

Krahmann, Elke. "Private Security and Military Actors." In *The International Studies Encyclopedia*, edited by Robert A. Denemark. Hoboken, NJ: Blackwell, 2011.

——. *Private Security Companies and the State Monopoly on Violence: A Case of Norm Change?* PRIF Report No. 88. Frankfurt am Main: Peace Research Institute Frankfurt, 2009. https://www.hsfk.de/fileadmin/HSFK/hsfk_downloads/prif88_02.pdf.

——. *States, Citizens and the Privatization of Security*. Cambridge: Cambridge University Press, 2010.

Kramer, Martin. "The Moral Logic of Hizballah." In Reich, *Origins of Terrorism*, 131–57.

Krasner, Stephen D. *Sovereignty: Organized Hypocrisy*. Princeton, NJ: Princeton University Press, 1999.

Krause, Keith, and Jennifer Milliken. "Introduction: The Challenge of Non-State Armed Groups." *Contemporary Security Policy* 30, no. 2 (2009): 202–20.

Krugman, Paul. "Hired Gun Fetish." *New York Times*, September 28, 2007.

Kurdistan Workers Party. "Party Program of the Kurdistan Workers Party." 2005. http://www.kurdishlibrary.org/kurdish_library/SvenskaKB/Organisations_SWE/PKK_Eng.html.

Kyrolainen, Hannu. "An Analysis of Trends in the U.S. Military Training and Technical Assistance in the Third World." *Instant Research on Peace and Violence* 7, nos. 3/4 (1977): 167–83.

LaFree, Gary, and Laura Dugan. "Trends in Global Terrorism, 1970–2008." In *Peace and Conflict 2012*, edited by J. Joseph Hewitt, Jonathan Wilkenfeld, and Ted Robert Gurr, 39–52. Boulder, CO: Paradigm, 2012.

Landler, Mark, and Michael R. Gordon. "Air War in Kosovo Seen as Precedent in Possible Response to Syria Chemical Attack." *New York Times*, August 23, 2013. https://www.nytimes.com/2013/08/24/world/air-war-in-kosovo-seen-as-precedent-in-possible-response-to-syria-chemical-attack.html?pagewanted=all&_r=0.

Landler, Mark, Eric Schmitt, and Michael R. Gordon. "Trump Aides Recruited Businessmen to Devise Options for Afghanistan." *New York Times*, July 10, 2017. https://www.nytimes.com/2017/07/10/world/asia/trump-afghanistan-policy-erik-prince-stephen-feinberg.html.

Laqueur, Walter. *The Age of Terrorism*. Boston: Little, Brown, 1987.

Laqueur, Walter, and Yonah Alexander, eds. *The Terrorism Reader*. New York: NAL Penguin, 1987.

Leander, Anna. "The Power to Construct International Security: On the Significance of Private Military Companies." *Millennium* 33, no. 3 (2005): 803–26.

Lee, Bowen. "Safer in Danger: How War Treason Can Rescue the Principle of Noncombatant Immunity." Unpublished paper, December 2016.

Lee, Carol E., Courtney Kube, and Josh Lederman. "Officials Worry Trump May Back Erik Prince Plan to Privatize War in Afghanistan." NBC News, August 17, 2018. https://www.nbcnews.com/news/military/officials-worry-trump-may-back-erik-prince-plan-privatize-war-n901401.

Legg, Thomas, and Robin Ibbs. *Report of the Sierra Leone Arms Investigation*. London: Stationery Office, 1998.

Legro, Jeffrey W. "The Transformation of Policy Ideas." *American Journal of Political Science* 44, no. 3 (July 2000): 419–32.

——. "Which Norms Matter? Revisiting the 'Failure' of Internationalism in World War II." Paper presented at the Annual Conference of the American Political Science Association, Chicago, August 31–September 3, 1995.

Lema, Luis. "Torture in Algeria: The Report That Was to Change Everything." *Le Temps*, August 19, 2005. https://www.icrc.org/en/doc/resources/documents/article/other/algeria-history-190805.htm.

Levie, Howard S. "Review: *New Rules for Victims of Armed Conflicts*." *American Journal of International Law* 77, no. 2 (1983): 377–83.

Lewis, William Dodge, Henry Seidel Canby, and Thomas Kite Brown, eds. *The Winston Simplified Dictionary: Encyclopedic Edition*. Philadelphia: John C. Winston Company, 1931.

Lia, Brynjar, and Katja H.-W. Skjølberg. Why Terrorism Occurs: *A Survey of Theories and Hypotheses on the Causes of Terrorism*. FFI Research Report no. 02769. Kjeller, NO: Forsvarets Forskningsinstitutt, 2000). http://rapporter.ffi.no/rapporter/2000/02769.pdf.

Light, Matthew. "Roy Allison, Russia, the West, and Military Intervention." *Journal of Power Institutions in Post-Soviet Studies* 17 (2016). https://journals.openedition.org/pipss/4180.

Lister, Tim, Mary Ilyushina, and Sebastian Shukla. "Several Russians Killed in US Airstrikes in Syria, Friends Say." CNN, February 13, 2018. https://www.cnn.com/2018/02/13/middleeast/russians-killed-us-airstrikes-syria-intl/index.html.

Liu, Hin-Yan, and Christopher Kinsey. "Challenging the Strength of the Antimercenary Norm." *Journal of Global Strategic Studies* 3, no. 1 (2018): 93–110.

Locks, Benjamin. "Bad Guys Know What Works: Asymmetric Warfare and the Third Offset." War on the Rocks, June 23, 2015. https://Warontherocks.Com/2015/06/Bad-Guys-Know-What-Works-Asymmetric-Warfare-And-The-Third-Offset/.

Lustick, Ian S. "Terrorism in the Arab-Israeli Conflict: Targets and Audiences." In Crenshaw, *Terrorism in Context*, 514–52.

Luttwak, Edward N. "Where Are the Great Powers? At Home with the Kids." *Foreign Affairs* 73, no. 4 (July/August 1994): 23–28.

Luxmoore, Matthew. "Putin's Ultranationalist Base Takes Aim at the West." Al Jazeera America, April 17, 2015. http://america.aljazeera.com/articles/2015/4/17/russian-ultranationalists-decry-fifth-column.html.

MacFarquhar, Neil, and Marlise Simons. "Bashir Defies War Crime Arrest Order." *New York Times*, March 5, 2009. https://www.nytimes.com/2009/03/06/world/africa/06sudan.html.

Mahanta, Siddhartha. "These Baltic Militias Are Readying for War with Russia." *The Atlantic*, November 26, 2017. https://www.theatlantic.com/photo/2017/11/baltic-anti-russian-militia/545465/.

Malejacq, Romain. "Pro-Government Militias." Oxford Bibliographies, July 2017. http://www.oxfordbibliographies.com/view/document/obo-9780199743292/obo-9780199743292-0213.xml.

Mallaby, Sebastian. "Paid to Make Peace: Mercenaries Are No Altruists, but They Can Do Good." *Washington Post*, June 4, 2001.

Mandel, Robert. "Fighting Fire with Fire: Privatizing Counterterrorism." Paper presented at the Annual Meeting of the International Studies Association, Montreal, March 17–20, 2004.

Mandela, Nelson. "'I Am Prepared to Die': Nelson Mandela's Statement from the Dock at the Opening of the Defence Case in the Rivonia Trial." April 20, 1964. Nelson Mandela Foundation. http://db.nelsonmandela.org/speeches/pub_view.asp?pg=item&ItemID=NMS010&txtstr=prepared%20to%20die.

Mansour, Renad. "More than Militias: Iraq's Popular Mobilization Forces Are Here to Stay." War on the Rocks, April 3, 2018. https://warontherocks.com/2018/04/more-than-militias-iraqs-popular-mobilization-forces-are-here-to-stay/.

Maoz, Zeev, and Belgin San-Akca. "Rivalry and State Support for Non-State Armed Groups (NAGs), 1946–2001." *International Studies Quarterly* 56 (2012): 720–34.

March, James G., and Johan P. Olsen. *Rediscovering Institutions: The Organizational Basis of Politics*. New York: Free Press, 1989.

"'Marriage Equality' and the Civil Rights Movement." National Public Radio, August 26, 2011. https://www.npr.org/2011/04/26/135741226/marriage-equality-and-the-civil-rights-movement.

Mathews, Jessica T. "Power Shift." *Foreign Affairs* 76, no. 1 (January/February 1997): 50–66.

Mazarr, Michael J. "The Rise and Fall of the Failed-State Paradigm." *Foreign Affairs* 93, no. 1 (January/February 2013): 113–21.

Mazzetti, Mark. "C.I.A. Sought Blackwater's Help to Kill Jihadists." *New York Times*, August 19, 2009. https://www.nytimes.com/2009/08/20/us/20intel.html.

Mazzetti, Mark, and Emily B. Hager. "Secret Desert Force Set Up by Blackwater's Founder." *New York Times*, May 14, 2011. https://www.nytimes.com/2011/05/15/world/middleeast/15prince.html.

Mazzetti, Mark, Ashley Parker, Jane Perlez, and Eric Schmitt. "American Held in Pakistan Worked with C.I.A." *New York Times*, February 21, 2011. https://www.nytimes.com/2011/02/22/world/asia/22pakistan.html?%2334=&sq=&st=cse&%2359;=&scp=1&%2359;hyperion protective=&pagewanted=all.

Mazzetti, Mark, and Eric Schmitt. "Private Army Formed to Fight Somali Pirates Leaves Troubled Legacy." *New York Times*, October 4, 2012. https://www.nytimes.com/2012/10/05/world/africa/private-army-leaves-troubled-legacy-in-somalia.html.

McCarthy, Justin. "Americans Cite Cyberterrorism among Top Three Threats to U.S." Gallup, February 10, 2016. https://news.gallup.com/poll/189161/americans-cite-cyberterrorism-among-top-three-threats.aspx.

McFate, Sean. "America's Addiction to Mercenaries." *The Atlantic*, August 12, 2016. https://www.theatlantic.com/international/archive/2016/08/iraq-afghanistan-contractor-pentagon-obama/495731/.

———. "The 'Blackwater 2.0' Plan for Afghanistan." *The Atlantic*, July 17, 2017. https://www.theatlantic.com/international/archive/2017/07/afghanistan-erik-prince-trump-britain/533580/.

———. *The Modern Mercenary: Private Armies and What They Mean for World Order.* Oxford: Oxford University Press, 2015.

McGarrity, Michael C. "Confronting the Rise of Domestic Terrorism in the Homeland." Statement of Michael C. McGarrity (assistant director, FBI Counterterrorism Division) before the House Homeland Security Committee, May 8, 2019. Federal Bureau of Investigation. https://www.fbi.gov/news/testimony/confronting-the-rise-of-domestic-terrorism-in-the-homeland.

Mearsheimer, John J. "The False Promise of International Institutions." *International Security* 19, no. 3 (Winter 1995): 5–49.

Meilinger, Phillip S. "Trenchard and 'Morale Bombing': The Evolution of Royal Air Force Doctrine before World War II." *Journal of Military History* 60, no. 2 (1996): 243–70.

Merton, Robert K. "The Unanticipated Consequences of Purposive Social Action." *American Sociological Review* 1, no. 6 (December 1936): 894–904.

Messner, J. J. "In or Out? And the Pursuit of a Definition of Inherently Governmental." *Journal of International Peace Operations* 5, no. 1 (July/August 2009): 35–36.

———. Interview by author. Washington, DC, August 3, 2007.

———. "No Points for Trying." *Journal of International Peace Operations* 6, no. 1 (July/August 2010). Accessed March 1, 2012. http://web.peaceops.com/archives/category/journal_content/columnists/messner (site discontinued).

———. "What's in a Name?" *Journal of International Peace Operations* 2, no. 6 (May/June 2007): 24.

Meyer, Michael. "Dogs of Peace." *Newsweek*, August 24, 2003. http://www.newsweek.com/dogs-peace-135697.

Meyer, Theodoric. "Erik Prince Lobbies Up." *Politico*, October 24, 2018. https://www.politico.com/newsletters/politico-influence/2018/10/24/erik-prince-lobbies-up-387650.

Michel, Casey. "How Militias Became the Private Police for White Supremacists." *Politico*, August 17, 2017. https://www.politico.com/magazine/story/2017/08/17/white-supremacists-militias-private-police-215498.

"Mideast Dilemma: Is U.S. Training a Future Foe?" *U.S. News and World Report*, February 24, 1975, 21.

Miller, T. Christian. "This Year, Contractor Deaths Exceed Military Ones in Iraq and Afghanistan." ProPublica, September 23, 2010. https://www.propublica.org/article/this-year-contractor-deaths-exceed-military-ones-in-iraq-and-afgh-100923.

Miller, Martin A. "The Intellectual Origins of Modern Terrorism in Europe." In Crenshaw, *Terrorism in Context*, 27–62.

Milliard, Todd S. "Overcoming Post-Colonial Myopia: A Call to Recognize and Regulate Private Military Companies." *Military Law Review* 176 (June 2003): 1–86.

Minh, Ho Chi. "Declaration of Independence of the Democratic Republic of Vietnam." September 2, 1945. Liberté, Égalité, Fraternité: Exploring the French Revolution. http://chnm.gmu.edu/revolution/d/583/.

Moon, Ban-Ki. *Implementing the Responsibility to Protect: Report of the Secretary General*. United Nations General Assembly. Doc. A/63/677. January 12, 2009. http://responsibilitytoprotect.org/SGRtoPEng%20(4).pdf.

——, Ban-Ki. "Responsible Sovereignty: International Cooperation for a Changed World." July 15, 2008. http://www.globalpolicy.org/component/content/article/154/26074.html.

Mueller, John. *Retreat from Doomsday: The Obsolescence of Major War*. New York. Basic Books, 1989.

Müller, Harald. "Security Cooperation." In *Handbook of International Relations*, edited by Walter Carlsnaes, 477–506. London: SAGE.

Munir, Muhammad. "Suicide Attacks and Islamic Law." *International Review of the Red Cross* 90, no. 869 (March 2008): 71–89.

Muravchik, Joshua. "Terrorism's Silent Partner at the UN." *Los Angeles Times*, October 21, 2004. https://www.latimes.com/news/printedition/opinion/la-oe-muravchik18oct19,1,207349.story.

National Intelligence Council. *Global Trends 2030: Alternative Worlds*. December 2012. https://www.dni.gov/files/documents/GlobalTrends_2030.pdf.

"NATO: Gadhafi Using Mosques, Children's Parks as Shields." MSNBC, June 19, 2011. https://www.nbcnews.com/id/wbna43451301.

Neumann, Vanessa. "The New Nexus of Narcoterrorism: Hezbollah and Venezuela." Foreign Policy Research Institute. December 3, 2011. https://www.fpri.org/article/2011/12/the-new-nexus-of-narcoterrorism-hezbollah-and-venezuela/.

Nirmal, B. C. "Wars of National Liberation and International Humanitarian Law." *Indian Journal of International Law* 28, no. 2 (1988): 201–15.

Nissim-Sabat, Ryan. "Panthers Set Up Shop in Cleveland." In *Comrades: A Local History of the Black Panther Party*, edited by Judson L. Jeffries, 89–144. Bloomington: Indiana University Press, 2007.

Northbridge Services Group. "Our Services." NSG.http://northbridgeservices.org/services_opsupport.htm.

Nurick, Lester, and Roger W. Barrett. "Legality of Guerrilla Forces under the Laws of War." *American Journal of International Law* 40, no. 3 (July 1946): 563–83.

Oeter, Stefan. "Terrorism and 'Wars of National Liberation' from a Law of War Perspective." *Heidelberg Journal of International Law* 49, no. 3 (1989): 445–86.

Official Records of the Diplomatic Conference in Reaffirmation and Development of International Humanitarian Law Applicable to Armed Conflicts: Geneva 1974–1977. 17 vols. Bern, CH: Federal Political Department, 1978.

Ogaden National Liberation Front. "Political Objectives." OGNLF. Accessed March 20, 2019. http://onlf.org/?page_id=14.

Organization of African Unity. "OAU Convention for the Elimination of Mercenarism in Africa." Doc. CM/817 (XXIX), annex II, rev. I. 1977.

Ostensen, Ase Gilje, and Tor Bukkvoll. *Russian Use of Private Military and Security Companies: The Implications for European and Norwegian Security*. Norwegian Defence Research Establishment. September 11, 2018. https://www.ffi.no/no/Rapporter/18-01300.pdf.

Pape, Robert. "The New Standard for Humanitarian Intervention." *The Atlantic*, April 4, 2011. http://www.theatlantic.com/international/archive/2011/04/the-new-standard-for-humanitarian-intervention/73361/.

Parks, W. Hays. "Conventional Aerial Bombing and the Law of War." *Proceedings of the U.S. Naval Institute* 108, no. 5 (May 1982): 98–117.

——. "National Security Law in Practice: The Department of Defense Law of War Manual." Speech to the American Bar Association, 2010. http://www.americanbar. org/content/dam/aba/migrated/2011_build/law_national_security/hays_parks_ speech_2010.authcheckdam.pdf.

——. "The 1977 Protocols to the Geneva Conventions of 1949." In *Readings on International Law from the Naval War College Review, 1978–1994*, edited by John Norton Moore and Robert F. Turner, 467–78. Newport, RI: Naval War College, 1995.

Pelton, Robert Young. "Erik Prince: An American Commando in Exile." *Men's Journal*, November 2010.

——. *Licensed to Kill: Hired Guns in the War on Terror*. New York: Crown, 2006.

Percy, Sarah. *Mercenaries: The History of a Norm in International Relations*. Oxford: Oxford University Press, 2007.

——. "Morality and Regulation." In *From Mercenaries to Market: The Rise and Regulation of Private Military Companies*, edited by Simon Chesterman and Chia Lehnhardt, 11–28. Oxford: Oxford University Press, 2007.

Perliger, Arie, and Leonard Weinberg. "Jewish Self-Defence and Terrorist Groups prior to the Establishment of the State of Israel: Roots and Traditions." *Totalitarian Movements and Political Religions* 4, no. 3 (2003): 91–118.

Peters, Heidi M., Moshe Schwartz, and Lawrence Kapp. *Department of Defense Contractor and Troop Levels in Iraq and Afghanistan: 2007–2017*. Washington, DC: Congressional Research Service, April 28, 2017. https://fas.org/sgp/crs/natsec/ R44116.pdf.

Petersohn, Ulrich. "Chequing Private Force? The Re-Emergence of the Combat Market for Force." Unpublished manuscript, 2018.

——. "Reframing the Anti-Mercenary Norm: Private Military and Security Companies and Mercenarism." *International Journal* 69, no. 4 (2014): 475–93.

Philpott, Daniel. *Revolutions in Sovereignty: How Ideas Shaped Modern International Relations*. Princeton, NJ: Princeton University Press, 2001.

Picarelli, John T. "Enabling Norms and Human Trafficking." In H. Richard Friman, *Crime and the Global Political Economy*, 85–101. Boulder, CO: Lynne Rienner, 2009.

Pierce, Albert C. "Just War Principles and Economic Sanctions." *Ethics and International Affairs* 10 (1996): 99–113.

Pinker, Steven. *The Better Angels of Our Nature: Why Violence Has Declined*. New York: Penguin, 2012.

Podder, Sukanya. "Understanding the Legitimacy of Armed Groups: A Relational Perspective." *Small Wars and Insurgencies* 28, nos. 4/5 (2017): 686–708.

Pommier, Bruno. "The Use of Force to Protect Civilians and Humanitarian Action: The Case of Libya and Beyond." *International Review of the Red Cross* 93, no. 884 (December 2011): 1063–83.

Pompeo, Michael R. "Remarks to the Press." April 8, 2019. US Department of State. https://www.state.gov/secretary/remarks/2019/04/290966.htm.

Popp, Maximilian, Christoph Reuter, and Adam Asaad. "The Renewed Dependency on Mercenary Fighters." *Der Spiegel*, July 17, 2020. https://www.realclearworld. com/2020/07/17/why_mercenaries_are_on_the_rise_again_499290.html?utm_ source=rcp-today&utm_medium=email&utm_campaign=mailchimp- newsletter&mc_cid=105863441a&mc_eid=60d94ea688.

Posen, Barry R. "The War for Kosovo: Serbia's Political-Military Strategy." *International Security* 24, no. 4 (Spring 2000): 39–84.

Pregent, Michael, and Erica Hanichak. "Countering Iran Means Sanctioning Terrorist Militias." *The Hill*, September 27, 2018. https://thehill.com/opinion/international/408741-countering-iran-means-sanctioning-terrorist-militias.

Prem, Berenike. "Analyzing PMSC Power in Multi-Stakeholder Initiatives." Paper presented at the 2018 Annual Meeting of the International Studies Association, San Francisco, April 4–7, 2018.

Price, Richard. *The Chemical Weapons Taboo*. Ithaca, NY: Cornell University Press, 1997.

———. "Reversing the Gun Sights: Transnational Civil Society Targets Land Mines." *International Organization* 52, no. 3 (Summer, 1998): 613–44.

Prince, Erik D. "Contractors, Not Troops, Will Save Afghanistan." *New York Times*, August 30, 2017. https://www.nytimes.com/2017/08/30/opinion/erik-prince-contractors-afghanistan.html?module=inline.

———. "How Blackwater Serves America." *Wall Street Journal*, December 16, 2008. https://www.online.wsj.com/article/SB122939188592109341.html.

———. "The MacArthur Model for Afghanistan." *Wall Street Journal*, May 31, 2018. https://www.wsj.com/articles/the-macarthur-model-for-afghanistan-14962 69058?mg=prod/accounts-wsj.

"A Private Air Force for Afghanistan?" *Military Times*, August 2, 2017. https://www.militarytimes.com/news/2017/08/02/a-private-air-force-for-afghanistan/.

Program on Humanitarian Policy and Conflict Research. *Transnationality, War and the Law: A Report on a Roundtable on the Transformation of Warfare, International Law, and the Role of Transnational Armed Groups*. April 2006. Harvard Humanitarian Initiative, https://hhi.harvard.edu/publications/transnationality-war-and-law-roundtable-report.

Protocol Additional to the Geneva Conventions of 12 August 1949, and Relating to the Protection of Victims of International Armed Conflicts. 1977. https://ihl-data bases.icrc.org/applic/ihl/ihl.nsf/Treaty.xsp?documentId=D9E6B6264D7723C3C 12563CD002D6CE4&action=openDocument.

Provisional IRA. "Freedom Struggle." In Laqueur and Alexander, *Terrorism Reader*, 132–34.

Quinn, Allison. "Vladimir Putin Sent Russian Mercenaries to 'Fight in Syria and Ukraine.'" *Telegraph*, March 30, 2016. https://www.telegraph.co.uk/news/2016/03/30/vladimir-putin-sent-russian-mercenaries-to-fight-in-syria-and-uk/.

Raghavan, Sudarsan. "Surge in Fighting among Libya's 'Super Militias' Imperils Western Peace Efforts." *Washington Post*, October 2, 2018. https://www.washingtonpost.com/world/surge-in-fighting-among-libyas-super-militias-imperils-western-peace-efforts/2018/10/01/54969c5c-c0d0-11e8-9f4f-a1b7af255aa5_story.html?utm_term=.98e1bf94d206.

Rapoport, David C. "The Fourth Wave: September 11 in the History of Terrorism," *Current History* 100, no. 650 (December 2001): 419–24.

Reagan, Ronald. "Message to the Senate Transmitting a Protocol to the 1949 Geneva Conventions." January 29, 1987. Ronald Reagan Presidential Library and Museum. https://reaganlibrary.gov/archives/speech/message-senate-trans mitting-protocol-1949-geneva-conventions.

———. "Remarks at the Annual Dinner of the Conservative Political Action Conference." March 1, 1985. https://www.reaganlibrary.gov/archives/speech/remarks-annual-dinner-conservative-political-action-conference.

Regnum News Agency. "Abkhazia's Parliament Convenes on Republic's Sovereignty." 2008. Regnum. http://www.regnum.ru/english/1047988.html.

Reich, Walter, ed. *Origins of Terrorism*. Washington, DC: Woodrow Wilson Center Press, 1990.

——. "The Poverty Myth." *Wilson Quarterly* (Winter 2008). https://www.wilsonquar
terly.com/quarterly/winter-2008-the-coming-revolution-in-africa/poverty-
not-root-cause-islamist-terrorism/.

Reisman, W. Michael. "The Resistance in Afghanistan Is Engaged in a War of National
Liberation." *American Journal of International Law* 81, no. 4 (1987): 906–9.

Reisman, W. Michael, and Chris T. Antoniou. *The Laws of War*. New York: Vintage
Books, 1994.

Reisman, W. Michael, and Andrea Armstrong. "The Past and Future of the Claim of
Preemptive Self-Defense." *American Journal of International Law* 100, no. 3 (July
2006): 525–50.

Reiss, Tom. "The True Classic of Terrorism." *New York Times*, September 11, 2005.
https://www.nytimes.com/2005/09/11/books/review/the-true-classic-of-terror
ism.html.

Renfrew, Barry. "Chechnya." In *Crimes of War 2.0: What the Public Should Know*.
2007. Accessed February 8, 2010. crimesofwar.org/thebook/chechnya.html (site
discontinued).

*Report of the Committee of Privy Counsellors Appointed to Inquire into the Recruitment
of Mercenaries* (Diplock Commission Report). London: Her Majesty's Stationery Office, 1976. http://psm.du.edu/media/documents/national_regulations/
countries/europe/united_kingdom/united_kingdom_diplock_report_1976.pdf.

"Report: Gadhafi Forces Perched Children on Tanks to Deter NATO Attacks." MSNBC,
August 30, 2011. https://www.nbcnews.com/id/wbna44323971.

Rice, Ian C., and Douglas A. Borer. "Bring Back the Privateers." *National Interest*, April
22, 2015. https://nationalinterest.org/feature/bring-back-the-privateers-12695.

Richardson, Louise. *What Terrorists Want: Understanding the Enemy, Containing the
Threat*. New York: Random House, 2006.

Risen, James, and Mark Mazzetti. "Blackwater Guards Tied to Secret C.I.A. Raids."
New York Times, December 11, 2009.

Risse, Thomas. "Let's Argue! Communicative Action in World Politics." *International
Organization* 54, no. 1 (Winter 2000): 1–39.

Risse, Thomas, Stephen C. Ropp, and Kathryn Sikkink, eds. *The Power of Human
Rights: International Norms and Domestic Change*. Cambridge: Cambridge
University Press, 1999.

Risse-Kappen, Thomas. "Ideas Do Not Float Freely: Transnational Coalitions, Domestic
Structures, and the End of the Cold War." *International Organization* 48, no. 2
(March 1994): 185–214.

Roberts, Adam, and Richard Guelff. *Documents on the Laws of War*. 2nd ed. Oxford:
Clarendon Press, 1989.

Roberts, Janine. *Glitter and Greed: The Secret World of the Diamond Cartel*. New York:
Disinformation Books, 2007.

Robinson, Linda, Paul D. Miller, John Gordon IV, Jeffrey Decker, Michael Schwille, and
Raphael S. Cohen. *Improving Strategic Competence: Lessons from 13 Years of War*.
Santa Monica, CA: RAND Corp., 2014.

Romero, Simon. "F.B.I. Arrests Leader of Right-Wing Militia That Detained Migrants
in New Mexico." *New York Times*, April 20, 2019.

Rosen, Stephen Peter. "Military Effectiveness: Why Society Matters." *International
Security* 19, no. 4 (Spring 1995): 5–31.

Rosenau, James N. *Turbulence in World Politics: A Theory of Change and Continuity*.
Princeton, NJ: Princeton University Press, 1990.

Roston, Arom. "American Mercenaries: A Middle East Monarchy Hired American Ex-Soldiers to Kill Its Political Enemies; This Could Be the Future of

War." BuzzFeed, October 16, 2018. https://www.buzzfeednews.com/article/
aramroston/mercenaries-assassination-us-yemen-uae-spear-golan-dahlan.

——. "A Chinese Blackwater? Betsy DeVos's Brother, the Founder of Blackwater, Is
Setting Up a Private Army for China, Sources Say." BuzzFeed, February 16, 2017.
https://www.buzzfeed.com/aramroston/betsy-devoss-brother-is-setting-up-a-
private-army-for-china?utm_term=.rj5mnVkWV#.ijeX7nZvn.

Rostow, Nicholas. "Before and After: The Changed UN Response to Terrorism since
September 11th." Cornell International Law Journal 35, no. 3 (2002): 475–90.

Rubin, Barry. Revolution until Victory? The Politics and History of the PLO. Cambridge,
MA: Harvard University Press, 1994.

Rumsfeld, Donald. "Defense Department Briefing, December 4." December 4, 2001.
Global Security. http://www.globalsecurity.org/military/library/news/2001/12/
mil-011204-usia01b.htm

"Russian First Deputy Defense Minister Gerasimov: 'Our Response' Is Based on the
'Active Defense Strategy'; 'We Must Act Quickly' to 'Preempt the Enemy . . .
Identify His Vulnerabilities, and Create Threats of Unacceptable Damage to It.'"
Middle East Media Research Institute, March 14, 2019. https://www.memri.org/
reports/russian-first-deputy-defense-minister-gerasimov-our-response-based-
active-defense-strategy.

Said, Edward. The Question of Palestine. New York: Times Books, 1979.

Saleh, Yassin al-Haj. "The Syrian Shabiha and Their State: Statehood and Participation."
Heinrich Boell Foundation, March 3, 2014. https://lb.boell.org/en/2014/03/03/
syrian-shabiha-and-their-state-statehood-participation.

Sandholtz, Wayne. Prohibiting Plunder: How Norms Change. New York: Oxford University Press, 2007.

Sandline International. "An Open Letter." February 1999. Accessed July 12, 2006. www.
sandline.com (site discontinued).

Sandline International, "Private Military Companies—Independent or Regulated?"
March 28, 1998. http://www.privatemilitary.org/publications/Sandline-PMCs
IndependentorRegulated.pdf.

Sarkees, Meredith Reid, and Frank Wayman. Resort to War: 1816–2007. Washington DC:
CQ Press, 2010.

Sassen, Saskia. A Sociology of Globalization. New York: W.W. Norton, 2006.

Saul, Ben. Defining Terrorism in International Law. Oxford: Oxford University Press, 2008.

Sautreuil, Pierre. "Believe It or Not, Russia Dislikes Relying on Military Contractors."
War Is Boring, May 8, 2016. https://medium.com/war-is-boring/believe-it-or-
not-russia-dislikes-relying-on-military-contractors-8bad373f4793.

Scahill, Jeremy. Blackwater: The Rise of the World's Most Powerful Mercenary Army.
New York: Nation Books, 2007.

——. "The Secret US War in Pakistan." The Nation, November 23, 2009. https://www.
thenation.com/article/secret-us-war-pakistan/.

——. "U.S. Mercenaries to UN: Stop Using the Word 'Mercenary' in Your Investigation into Mercenaries." Alternet, April 15, 2009. http://www.alternet.org/
world/136861/u.s._mercenaries_to_un:_stop_using_the_word_'mercenary'_in_
your_investigation_into_mercenaries/.

Scahill, Jeremy, and Matthew Cole. "Echo Papa Exposed: Inside Erik Prince's Treacherous
Drive to Build a Private Air Force." The Intercept, April 11, 2016. https://theinter
cept.com/2016/04/11/blackwater-founder-erik-prince-drive-to-build-private-air-
force/.

Schmid, Alex P., and Albert J. Jongman. Political Terrorism. Amsterdam: North-Holland
Publishing, 2005.

Schmidt, Michael S., and Eric Schmitt. "Flexing Muscle, Baghdad Detains U.S. Contractors." *New York Times*, January 15, 2012.

Schmitt, Eric, David D. Kirkpatrick, and Suliman Ali Zway. "U.S. May Have Put Mistaken Faith in Libya Site's Security." *New York Times*, September 30, 2012. https://www.nytimes.com/2012/10/01/world/africa/mistaken-sense-of-security-cited-before-envoy-to-libya-died.html?pagewanted=3&ref=world.

Schwartz, Moshe. *The Department of Defense's Use of Private Security Contractors in Afghanistan and Iraq: Background, Analysis, and Options for Congress*. Washington, DC: Congressional Research Service, May 13, 2011. https://fas.org/sgp/crs/natsec/R40835.pdf.

Seal, Lizzie. "A Brief History of Capital Punishment in Britain." History Extra, March 2018. https://www.historyextra.com/period/modern/a-brief-history-of-capital-punishment-in-britain/.

"Secretary-General Reflects on 'Intervention' in Thirty-Fifth Annual Ditchley Foundation Lecture." press release SG/SM/6613, June 26, 1998. https://www.un.org/press/en/1998/19980626.sgsm6613.html.

Security in Complex Environments Group. "Members." Accessed January 2, 2019. https://www.sceguk.org.uk/members/.

Selesky, Harold E. "Colonial America." In *The Laws of War: Constraints on Warfare in the Western World*, edited by Michael Howard, George J. Andreopoulos, and Mark R. Shulman, 59–85. New Haven, CT: Yale University Press, 1994.

"Seven Questions: The World According to Hamas." *Foreign Policy*, January 2008. https://foreignpolicy.com/2008/01/29/seven-questions-the-world-according-to-hamas/.

Sewall, Sarah B. *Chasing Success: Air Force Efforts to Reduce Civilian Harm*. Maxwell AFB, AL: Air University Press, 2016.

Shameen, Shaista. "Use of Mercenaries as a Means of Violating Human Rights and Impeding the Exercise of the Right of Peoples to Self-Determination." UN doc. A/60/263. August 17, 2005.

Shane, Scott, and Ron Nixon. "In Washington, Contractors Take On Biggest Role Ever." *New York Times*, February 4, 2007.

Shaw, Malcolm N. *International Law*. 5th ed. Cambridge: Cambridge University Press, 2005.

Shaw, Martin. *Post-Military Society: Militarism, Demilitarization and War at the End of the Twentieth Century*. Philadelphia: Temple University Press, 1991.

Shenon, Philip. "U.S. Says It Might Consider Attacking Serbs." *New York Times*, March 1, 1999. https://www.nytimes.com/1998/03/13/world/us-says-it-might-consider-attacking-serbs.html.

Shewchuck, Blair. "Terrorists and Freedom Fighters." CBC News Online, October 18, 2011. https://www.cbc.ca/news2/indepth/words/terrorists.html.

Shikaki, Khalil. "Can Hamas Moderate? Insights from Palestinian Politics during 2005–2011." Crown Center for Middle Eastern Studies, January 2015. https://www.brandeis.edu/crown/publications/meb/MEB88.pdf.

Shultz, Richard H., Douglas Farah, and Itamara V. Lochard. "Armed Groups: A Tier-One Security Priority." INSS Occasional Paper no. 57. USAF Institute for National Security Studies, September 2004.

"Shultz Urges 'Active' Drive on Terrorism." *New York Times*, June 25, 1984. https://www.nytimes.com/1984/06/25/world/shultz-urges-active-drive-on-terrorism.html.

Sieradzka, Monika. "Paramilitary Groups Ready to Defend Poland." Real Clear World, June 13, 2016. http://www.realclearworld.com/articles/2016/06/13/paramilitary_groups_ready_to_defend_poland_111906.html.

Silva, Ricardo Méndez. "United Nations General Assembly Resolutions on Terrorism." *Mexican Law Review* 7 (January 2007). http://info8.juridicas.unam.mx/cont/mlawr/7/arc/arc8.htm.

Simons, Suzanne. *Master of War: Blackwater USA's Erik Prince and the Business of War.* New York: Harper 2009.

Singer, David J., Stuart Bremer, and John Stuckey. "Capability Distribution, Uncertainty, and Major Power War, 1820–1965." In *Peace, War, and Numbers*, edited by Bruce Russett, 19–48. Beverly Hills, CA: SAGE, 1972.

Singer, P. W. *Corporate Warriors: The Rise of the Privatized Military Industry.* Cornell Studies in Security Affairs. Ithaca, NY: Cornell University Press, 2004.

———. "Corporate Warriors: The Rise of the Privatized Military Industry and Its Ramifications for International Security." *International Security* 26, no. 3 (Winter 2001–2002): 193–97.

———. "The Dark Truth about Blackwater." Brookings Institution, October 2, 2007. https://www.brookings.edu/articles/the-dark-truth-about-blackwater/.

———. Remarks at the Carnegie Council on Ethics and International Affairs, December 5, 2005. https://www.carnegiecouncil.org/studio/multimedia/20051201-corporate-warriors-the-privatized-military-and-iraq.

Smith, Graeme. "Talking to the Taliban." *Globe and Mail*, March 22, 2008. Accessed March 15, 2019. http://v1.theglobeandmail.com/talkingtothetaliban/ (inactive link).

Snow, Shawn, and Mackenzie Wolf. "Blackwater Founder Wants to Boost the Afghan Air War with His Private Air Force." *Military Times*, August 2, 2017. https://www.militarytimes.com/flashpoints/2017/08/02/blackwater-founder-wants-to-run-the-afghan-air-war-with-his-private-air-force/.

Sofaer, Abraham. "The Rationale for the United States Decision." *American Journal of International Law* 82 (1988): 784–87.

———. "Terrorism and the Law." In Laqueur and Alexander, *Terrorism Reader*, 369–78.

Spicer, Tim. *An Unorthodox Soldier: Peace and War and the Sandline Affair.* Edinburgh: Mainstream Publishing, 1999.

Spyer, Jonathan. "Syria's Civil War Is Now 3 Civil Wars." *Foreign Policy*, March 18, 2019. https://foreignpolicy.com/2019/03/18/syrias-civil-war-is-now-3-civil-wars/.

Srivastava, Swati. "Sovereignty under Contract: Tensions in American Security." Paper presented at the 2018 Annual Meeting of the International Studies Association, San Francisco, April 4–7, 2018.

Stanger, Allison. "Hired Guns: How Private Military Contractors Undermine World Order." *Foreign Affairs* 94, no. 4 (July/August 2015): 163–69.

State Committee on Information and Press of the Republic of South Ossetia (SCIPRSO). "Independence of the Republic of South Ossetia: A Guarantee of Safety and Reliable F of the Ossetian People." October 9, 2008. http://cominf.org/node/1166478243.

Stoddard, Abby, Adele Harmer, and Victoria DiDomenico. *Private Security Providers and Services in Humanitarian Operations.* London: Overseas Development Institute, 2008. https://www.odi.org/sites/odi.org.uk/files/odi-assets/publications-opinion-files/3703.pdf.

Stoke White. "Press Release: Legal Proceedings on Behalf of Yemeni Clients." March 30, 2020. https://www.stokewhite.com/press-release-legal-proceedings-on-behalf-of-yemeni-clients/.

Stratfor. "The Use of Mercenaries in Syria's Crackdown." Stratfor, January 12, 2012. https://worldview.stratfor.com/article/use-mercenaries-syrias-crackdown.

Sturgess, Gary. "Images of Contracting." *Journal of International Peace Operations* 5, no. 6 (May/June 2010): 39–40.

———. "Tales of Wells Fargo." *Journal of International Peace Operations* 6, no. 1 (July/August 2010). Accessed July 31, 2011. http://web.peaceops.com/archives/759#more-759 (site discontinued).

———. "An Unlikely History of Contracting." *Journal of International Peace Operations* 4, no. 2 (September/October 2008), 27–28. http://www.privatemilitary.org/ ISOA/JIPO-2008-09%20IPOA-Humanitarian_Security_and_Support.pdf.

Sullivan, Kate. "Oregon GOP State Senators Again Fail to Show Up for Legislative Session amid Climate Bill Protest." CNN, June 23, 2019. https://www.cnn.com/ 2019/06/23/politics/oregon-gop-state-senators-legislative-session-climate/ index.html.

Suter, Keith. *An International Law of Guerrilla Warfare: The Global Politics of Law-Making.* New York: St. Martin's, 1984.

"Syria War: Who Are Russia's Shadowy Wagner Mercenaries?" BBC, February 23, 2018. http://www.bbc.com/news/world-europe-43167697.

"Syrian Children Used as Human Shields, Says UN Report." BBC, June 12, 2012. https://www.bbc.com/news/world-middle-east-18405800.

"Syrian Rebels Using Caged Civilian Captives as 'Human sShields." *Telegraph*, November 2, 2015. https://www.telegraph.co.uk/news/worldnews/middleeast/syria/11971269/ Syrian-rebels-using-caged-pro-Assad-captives-as-human-shields.html.

Syrian Network for Human Rights. "On Human Rights Day, More than 75% of the Victims in Syria Are Civilians." SNHR, December 10, 2014. http://sn4hr.org/ wp-content/pdf/english/statement_on_the_International_Day_of_Human_ Rights.pdf.

Tabarrok, Alexander, and Alex Nowrasteh. "Privateers! Their History and Future." *Fletcher Security Review* 12, no. 1 (2015): 55–62.

Tavernese, Sabrina. "Cleric Is Said to Lose Reins of Parts of Iraqi Militia." *New York Times*, September 27, 2006.

Taylor, Adam. "Trump Said He Would 'Take Out' the Families of ISIS Fighters. Did an Airstrike in Syria Do Just That?" *Washington Post*, May 27, 2017.

Taylor, Stuart, Jr. "Lebanese Group Linked to C.I.A. Is Tied to Car Bombing Fatal to 80." *New York Times*, May 13, 1985. https://www.nytimes.com/1985/05/13/ world/lebanese-group-linked-to-cia-is-tied-to-car-bombing-fatal-to-80.html.

Thakur, Ramesh Chandra. *The United Nations, Peace and Security.* Cambridge: Cambridge University Press, 2006.

Thomas, Evan. "Profile: Blackwater's Erik Prince." *Newsweek*, October 13, 2007. http:// www.newsweek.com/profile-blackwaters-erik-prince-103877.

Thomas, Gerry S. *Mercenary Troops in Modern Africa.* Boulder, CO: Westview, 1984.

Thomas, Ward. *The Ethics of Destruction: Norms and Force in International Relations.* Ithaca, NY: Cornell University Press, 2001.

Thomson, Janice E. *Mercenaries, Pirates, and Sovereigns: State-Building and Extraterritorial Violence in Early Modern Europe.* Princeton, NJ: Princeton University Press, 1994.

Tilly, Charles. "Reflections on the History of European State-Making." In *The Formation of National States in Western Europe*, edited by Charles Tilly, 3–83. Princeton, NJ: Princeton University Press, 1975.

———. "Terror, Terrorism, Terrorists." *Sociological Theory* 22, no. 1 (March 2004): 5–13.

———. "War Making and State Making as Organized Crime." In *Bringing the State Back In*, edited by Peter B. Evans, Dietrich Rueschemeyer, and Theda Skocpol, 169–91. Cambridge: Cambridge University Press, 1975.

"Transcript of Press Conference by Secretary-General Kofi Annan at United Nations Headquarters on 12 June." Press Release SG/SM/6255. June 12, 1997. http://www.un.org/News/Press/docs/1997/19970612.sgsm6255.html.

Tucker, Robert W., and David C. Hendrickson. "The Sources of American Legitimacy." *Foreign Affairs* 83, no. 6 (November/December 2004): 18–32.

"UAE Sending Colombian Mercenaries to Yemen: Sources." *Daily Mail*, December 19, 2015. https://www.dailymail.co.uk/wires/afp/article-3366710/UAE-sending-Colombian-mercenaries-Yemen-sources.html.

United Nations Commission on Human Rights. "Report of the Third Meeting of Experts on Traditional and New Forms of Mercenary Activities as a Means of Violating Human Rights and Impeding the Exercise of the Right of Peoples to Self-Determination," UN doc. E/CN.4/2005/23. January 18, 2005. https://undocs.org/en/E/CN.4/2005/23.

United Nations General Assembly. Resolution 1573, Question of Algeria, A/RES/1573. December 19, 1960. https://undocs.org/en/A/RES/1573(XV).

———. Resolution 2465, Implementation of the Declaration on the Granting of Independence to Colonial Countries and Peoples, A/RES/2465. December 20, 1968. https://undocs.org/en/A/RES/2465(XXIII).

———. Resolution 2548, Implementation of the Declaration on the Granting of Independence to Colonial Countries and Peoples, A/RES/2548. December 11, 1969. https://undocs.org/en/A/RES/2458(XXIV).

———. Resolution 2708, Implementation of the Declaration on the Granting of Independence to Colonial Countries and Peoples, A/RES/2708. December 14, 1970. https://undocs.org/en/A/RES/2708(XXV).

———. Resolution 3103, Basic Principles of the Legal Status of the Combatants Struggling against Colonial and Alien Domination and Racist Regimes, A/RES/3103. December 12, 1973. https://undocs.org/en/A/RES/3103(XXVIII).

———. Resolution 32/147, Measures to Prevent International Terrorism Which Endangers or Takes Innocent Human Lives or Jeopardizes Fundamental Freedoms, and Study of the Underlying Causes of Those Forms of Terrorism and Acts of Violence Which Lie in Misery, Frustration, Grievance and Despair and Which Cause Some People to Sacrifice Human Lives, including Their Own, in an Attempt to Effect Radical Changes, A/RES/32/147. December 16, 1977. https://undocs.org/en/A/RES/32/147.

———. Resolution 34/115, Measures to Prevent International Terrorism Which Endangers or Takes Innocent Human Lives or Jeopardizes Fundamental Freedoms, and Study of the Underlying Causes of Those Forms of Terrorism and Acts of Violence Which Lie in Misery, Frustration, Grievance and Despair and Which Cause Some People to Sacrifice Human Lives, including Their Own, in an Attempt to Effect Radical Changes, A/RES/34/115. December 17, 1979. https://undocs.org/en/A/RES/34/115.

———. Resolution 36/109, Measures to Prevent International Terrorism Which Endangers or Takes Innocent Human Lives or Jeopardizes Fundamental Freedoms, and Study of the Underlying Causes of Those Forms of Terrorism and Acts of Violence Which Lie in Misery, Frustration, Grievance and Despair and Which Cause Some People to Sacrifice Human Lives, including Their Own, in an Attempt to Effect Radical Changes, A/RES/36/109. December 10, 1981. https://undocs.org/en/A/RES/36/109.

———. Resolution 38/130, Measures to Prevent International Terrorism Which Endangers or Takes Innocent Human Lives or Jeopardizes Fundamental Freedoms, and Study of the Underlying Causes of Those Forms of Terrorism and Acts of

Violence Which Lie in Misery, Frustration, Grievance and Despair and Which Cause Some People to Sacrifice Human Lives, including Their Own, in an Attempt to Effect Radical Changes, A/RES/38/130. December 19, 1983. https://undocs.org/en/A/RES/38/130.

——. Resolution 40/61, Measures to Prevent International Terrorism Which Endangers or Takes Innocent Human Lives or Jeopardizes Fundamental Freedoms, and Study of the Underlying Causes of Those Forms of Terrorism and Acts of Violence Which Lie in Misery, Frustration, Grievance and Despair and Which Cause Some People to Sacrifice Human Lives, including Their Own, in an Attempt to Effect Radical Changes, A/RES/40/61. December 9, 1985. https://undocs.org/en/A/RES/40/61.

——. Resolution 42/159, Measures to Prevent International Terrorism Which Endangers or Takes Innocent Human Lives or Jeopardizes Fundamental Freedoms, and Study of the Underlying Causes of Those Forms of Terrorism and Acts of Violence Which Lie in Misery, Frustration, Grievance and Despair and Which Cause Some People to Sacrifice Human Lives, including Their Own, in an Attempt to Effect Radical Changes, A/RES/42/159. December 7, 1987. https://undocs.org/en/A/RES/42/159.

——. Resolution 43/160, Observer Status of National Liberation Movements Recognized by the Organization of African Unity and/or the League of Arab States, A/RES/43/160. December 9, 1988. https://undocs.org/en/A/RES/43/160.

——. Resolution 44/29, Measures to Prevent International Terrorism Which Endangers or Takes Innocent Human Lives or Jeopardizes Fundamental Freedoms, and Study of the Underlying Causes of Those Forms of Terrorism and Acts of Violence Which Lie in Misery, Frustration, Grievance and Despair and Which Cause Some People to Sacrifice Human Lives, including Their Own, in an Attempt to Effect Radical Changes, A/RES/44/29. December 4, 1989. https://undocs.org/en/A/RES/44/29.

United Nations Human Rights Council. *Human Rights Situation in Palestine and Other Occupied Arab Territories: Report of the Detailed Findings of the Independent Commission of Inquiry Established pursuant to Human Rights Council Resolution S-21/1.* June 23, 2015. https://ohchr.org/Documents/HRBodies/HRCouncil/CoIGaza/A_HRC_CRP_4.doc.

United Nations Office of the High Commissioner for Human Rights. "Battle for Mosul: ISIL Forces Thousands of Civilians from Their Homes and Executes Hundreds." October 28, 2016. https://ohchr.org/EN/NewsEvents/Pages/DisplayNews.aspx?NewsID=20783&LangID=E.

——. "It's High Time to Close the Legal Gap for Private Military and Security Contractors—UN Expert Body on Mercenaries." 2010. http://newsarchive.ohchr.org/EN/NewsEvents/Pages/DisplayNews.aspx?NewsID=10000&LangID=E.

United Nations Office on Drugs and Crime. *The Use of the Internet for Terrorist Purposes.* New York: United Nations, 2012. https://www.unodc.org/documents/frontpage/Use_of_Internet_for_Terrorist_Purposes.pdf.

United Nations Working Group on the Use of Mercenaries as a Means of Violating Human Rights and Impeding the Exercise of the Right of Peoples to Self-Determination. "Guns for Hire." April 29, 2010. http://www.ohchr.org/EN/NewsEvents/Pages/Gunsforhire.aspx.

——. "Report of the Working Group on the Use of Mercenaries as a Means of Violating Human Rights and Impeding the Exercise of the Right of Peoples to Self-Determination." UN doc. A/HRC/4/42, February 7, 2007. https://undocs.org/en/A/HRC/4/42.

United Nations Security Council. Resolution 161, The Congo Question, S/RES/161. February 21, 1961. https://undocs.org/S/RES/161(1961).

——. Resolution 169, The Congo Question, S/RES/169. November 24, 1961. https://undocs.org/S/RES/169(1961).

——. Resolution 226, Question Concerning the Democratic Republic of the Congo, S/RES/226. October 14, 1966. https://undocs.org/S/RES/226(1966).

——. Resolution 232, Southern Rhodesia, S/RES/232. December 16, 1966. https://undocs.org/S/RES/232(1966).

——. Resolution 239, Question Concerning the Democratic Republic of the Congo, S/RES/239. July 10, 1967. https://undocs.org/S/RES/239(1967).

——. Resolution 241, Question Concerning the Democratic Republic of the Congo, S/RES/241. November 15, 1967. https://undocs.org/S/RES/241(1967).

——. Resolution 286, The Situation Created by Increasing Incidents Involving the Hijacking of Commercial Aircraft, S/RES/286 (September 9, 1970), https://undocs.org/S/RES/286(1970).

——. Resolution 289, Complaint by Guinea, S/RES/289. November 23, 1970). https://undocs.org/S/RES/289(1970).

——. Resolution 312, Territories under Portuguese Administration, S/RES/312. February 4, 1972. https://undocs.org/S/RES/312(1972).

——. Resolution 731, Libyan Arab Jamahiriya, S/RES/731. January 21, 1992. https://undocs.org/S/RES/731(1992).

——. Resolution 748, Libyan Arab Jamahiriya, S/RES/748. March 31, 1992. https://www.undocs.org/S/RES/748(1992).

——. Resolution 1559, Middle East, S/RES/1559. September 2, 2004. https://undocs.org/S/RES/1559(2004).

United States Conference of Catholic Bishops. *The Challenge of Peace: God's Promise and Our Response*. 1983. http://old.usccb.org/sdwp/international/TheChallengeofPeace.pdf.

US Congressional Research Service. *U.S. Sanctions on Russia*. January 11, 2019. https://fas.org/sgp/crs/row/R45415.pdf.

"U.S. Draft Convention for Prevention and Punishment of Terrorism Acts." *International Legal Materials* 11 (1972): 1382–87.

US Department of the Army. *FM 3–24: Counterinsurgency*. Washington, DC: Department of the Army, 2006.

US Department of Defense. "Military Commission Instruction No. 2." April 30, 2003. https://biotech.law.lsu.edu/blaw/dodd/corres/mco/mci2.pdf.

US Department of State. "Foreign Terrorist Organizations." Accessed January 25, 2019. https://www.state.gov/j/ct/rls/other/des/123085.htm.

——. "State Sponsors of Terrorism." Accessed December 11, 2020. https://www.state.gov/state-sponsors-of-terrorism/.

US Government Accountability Office. *Countering Violent Extremism Actions Needed to Define Strategy and Assess Progress of Federal Efforts*. April 2017. https://www.gao.gov/assets/690/683984.pdf.

US House of Representatives, Subcommittee on National Security and Foreign Affairs, Majority Staff. *Warlord, Inc.: Extortion and Corruption along the U.S. Supply Chain in Afghanistan*. Washington, DC: US House of Representatives Committee on Oversight and Government Reform, June 2010. http://www.cbsnews.com/htdocs/pdf/HNT_Report.pdf.

van Creveld, Martin. *The Rise and Decline of the State*. Cambridge: Cambridge University Press, 1999.

——. *The Transformation of Warfare*. New York: Free Press, 1991.

Van Deventer, Henry W. "Mercenaries at Geneva." *American Journal of International Law* 70, no. 4 (October 1976): 811–16.

Vaux, Pierre. "Fontanka Investigates Russian Mercenaries Dying for Putin in Syria and Ukraine." *The Interpreter*, March 29, 2016. http://www.interpretermag.com/fontanka-investigates-russian-mercenaries-dying-for-putin-in-syria-and-ukraine/.

Velez-Green, Alexander. "Russian Strategists Debate Preemption as Defense against NATO Surprise Attack." Russia Matters, March 14, 2018. https://www.russia matters.org/analysis/russian-strategists-debate-preemption-defense-against-nato-surprise-attack.

Waltz, Kenneth. *Theory of International Politics.* Reading, MA: Addison-Wesley, 1979.

Walzer, Michael. *Just and Unjust Wars.* 5th ed. New York: Basic Books, 2015.

Weber, Max. "Politics as a Vocation." Accessed February 14, 2017. http://anthropos-lab.net/wp/wp-content/uploads/2011/12/Weber-Politics-as-a-Vocation.pdf.

Weisman, Jonathan. "House Acts in Wake of Blackwater Incident." *Washington Post*, October 5, 2007.

Wendt, Alexander. *Social Theory of International Politics.* Cambridge: Cambridge University Press, 1999.

Whitaker, Brian. "The Definition of Terrorism." *Guardian*, May 7, 2001. https://www.theguardian.com/world/2001/may/07/terrorism.

Willenson, Kim, Nicholas C. Proffitt, and Lloyd Norman. "Persian Gulf: This Gun for Hire." *Newsweek*, February 24, 1975, 30.

Williams, Phil. "Violent Non-State Actors and National and International Security." International Relations and Security Network, 2008. https://www.files.ethz.ch/isn/93880/vnsas.pdf.

Wilson, Heather A. *International Law and the Use of Force by National Liberation Movements.* Oxford: Clarendon Press, 1988.

Windrem, Robert, and Aram Roston. "Reputed Mobster: 'Usual Suspect' or Supporter of the Mumbai Attacks?" NBC News, December 3, 2008. http://deepbackground.msnbc.msn.com/archive/2008/12/03/1697231.aspx.

Winik, Jay. *April 1865: The Month That Saved America.* New York: Harper, 2001.

Woods, Judith. "'We Don't Operate in the Shadows.'" *Telegraph* (UK), December 3, 1999. Accessed July 31, 2011. www.telegraph.co.uk/htmlContent.jhtml=/archive/1999/12/03/tltim03.html (inactive link).

Zenko, Micah. "Obama's Embrace of Drone Strikes Will Be a Lasting Legacy." *New York Times*, January 20, 2016.

——. "The New Unknown Soldiers of Afghanistan and Iraq." *Foreign Policy*, May 29, 2015. http://foreignpolicy.com/2015/05/29/the-new-unknown-soldiers-of-afghanistan-and-iraq/.

Index

CPSIA information can be obtained
at www.ICGtesting.com
Printed in the USA
LVHW031119151221
706182LV00014B/767/J